Increase Your Web Traffic

In a Weekend

WILLIAM R. STANEK

PRIMA PUBLISHING

P

PRIMA is a registered trademark of Prima Publishing, a division of Prima Communications, Inc. Prima Publishing is a registered trademark of Prima Communications, Inc. In a Weekend is a trademark of Prima Publishing, a division of Prima Communications, Inc.

Prima Publishing, Rocklin, California 95677.

Publisher: Matthew H. Carleson

Managing Editor: Dan J. Foster

Acquisitions Editor: Deborah Abshier

Project Editor: Susan Christophersen

Development Editor: Chris Katsaropoulos

Technical Reviewer: Emily B. Kim

Indexer: Emily Glossbrenner

Interior Layout: Jimmie Young

Cover Design: Prima Design Team

ISBN: 0-7615-1194-6

Library of Congress Catalog Card Number: 97-67396

Printed in the United States of America

98 99 BB 10 9 8 7 6 5 4 3

*Special thanks to my wife and family, who
continue to put up with the tappety-tap of my keyboard
at all hours of the day and night.
Without your support, Increase Your Web Traffic In a Weekend
wouldn't have been possible. Yes, Junior, daddy is finally finished. :-)*

CONTENTS

ACKNOWLEDGMENTS

Wow! Writing this book was really a lot of fun. I love the *In a Weekend* series and the fact that the books are designed to be fun, fast, and easy to use. I would really like to thank everyone at Prima Publishing who worked so hard to make this book a reality.

During the writing of this book, Prima moved its computer book operations from Indianapolis, Indiana to its main offices in Rocklin, California. Thanks to everyone who kept in close touch with this overworked author during the transition. Personal thanks to Matt Carleson, Dan Foster, and Debbie Abshier.

I would also like to personally thank Chris Katsaropoulos for doing such a great job developing the book, and Susan Christophersen for meticulously editing the book.

ABOUT THE AUTHOR

As a publisher and writer with a Master of Science in Information Systems degree and more than a decade of hands-on experience with advanced programming and development, William Stanek (director@tvpress.com) brings a solid voice of experience on the Internet and Web development to his many projects. He is a leading Internet technology expert, an award-winning author, a top Web site designer, and the author of numerous books. Over the years, his practical and thorough advice has helped Web publishers, programmers, and developers all over the world. Whereas many Internet books provide partial examples and perhaps a few working programs, William prefers to work with a balanced load of teaching examples as well as real-world examples that help you develop practical and usable skills.

William is also a regular columnist and feature writer for magazines. He is a contributing editor and columnist for the *Web Database Developer* column in Dr. Dobb's Sourcebook and a regular contributor to *PC Magazine*.

William served in the Persian Gulf War as a combat crew member on an Electronic Warfare aircraft. During the war, he flew on numerous combat missions into Iraq and was awarded nine medals for his wartime service, including one of the United States' highest flying honors, the Air Force Distinguished Flying Cross.

INTRODUCTION

These days, everyone seems to have a home page or a Web site. Just because you create and publish a Web page doesn't mean that anyone will visit it, though. The reality is that of the millions of Web pages, only a relative handful actually attract a steady readership; and these same Web pages are the ones that attract advertisers.

What can you do when you build a home page that no one visits? What can you do to earn money instead of lose money on your Web site? Is there an easy way to attract readers and advertisers without spending a fortune? Fortunately, there are ways to attract readers and advertisers to your home page or Web site without spending a dime, and *Increase Your Web Traffic In a Weekend* shows you how.

What's This Book About?

With 50 million Web users from dozens of countries around the world, the Web has an extremely diverse audience. Trying to tap into the tremendous potential of the Web can be a daunting task. Enter *Increase Your Web Traffic In a Weekend.* The goal of this book is to lay out a comprehensive plan that anyone from beginner to expert can use to build an audience for a home page or Web site without spending a dime.

The cost-free Web promotion and advertising techniques that I explore in this book have been gathered from years of practical experience. These are secrets that I haven't shared with anyone. Secrets that have helped me attract millions of readers to my Web sites and the Web sites of my customers. Secrets that could save you thousands of dollars. Now, that's something to think about!

The plan that I lay out isn't for the faint of heart. You will need to roll back your sleeves and really dive into the project at hand, which is to promote the heck out of your Web site using the techniques revealed here. Although this will require some effort on your part, the plan *is* designed to be implemented in a weekend. Do you already see the light at the end of the tunnel? You should.

How Is This Book Organized?

Making this book easy to follow and understand was my number one goal! I really want anyone, skill level or work schedule aside, to be able to learn the secrets of successful Web promotion and advertising.

To make the book easy to use, I've divided it into five sections. The book begins with a Friday evening preview of what is ahead for the weekend. Saturday is broken down into a morning and an afternoon session. These sessions are designed to help you understand the following:

Who is currently visiting your home page

How to track and analyze visitor statistics

How to put those statistics to work

How to direct visitors to popular areas of your Web site

How to gain readers who otherwise would have been lost because they used the wrong URL

Sunday is also divided into morning and afternoon sessions. These sessions are designed to help you understand:

Where to publicize your home pages for free

How to register with search engines

How to get your home page listed as the Cool Site of the Day

Techniques that you can use to attract the masses

The right way to sell your site through e-mail

How to create, track, and manage banner advertising

How to place ads on other sites without spending a dime

Who Should Read This Book?

Anyone who wants to learn how to attract visitors to a home page or Web site should read this book. Specifically, if you can answer yes to any one of these questions, you'll know that this book is for you:

Are you disappointed with the results that you've achieved through Web publishing?

Have you created wonderful Web pages, yet receive only a few visitors?

Do you think that the lack of visitors means that your ideas, interests or products aren't interesting?

Do you want to reach a larger audience?

Do you want to learn how to attract a steady readership at your Web site?

Do you want to learn the secrets of Web promotion and marketing?

Do you want to attract advertisers to your Web site?

Do you want to learn how to tap into the tremendous potential of the Web?

Do you want to learn the secrets of marketing without spending a dime?

Again, if you can answer yes to any one of the previous questions, this book is definitely for you.

What Do You Need to Use This Book?

The most important ingredients for using this book are a connection to the Internet and a home page or Web site that you want to promote. For some of the concepts discussed in this book, you will need access to the server log files for your Web site. Late on Saturday morning, I present ways that you can obtain statistics without server logs. Depending on the alternative that you decide to use, you may need to install a CGI script. If you have no idea what server logs or scripts are used for, don't worry—all these elements are explained in the book. All you need to do before you get started though is to ask your Internet Service Provider where log files and CGI scripts are stored on the server.

What Do You Need to Know to Use This Book?

Increase Your Web Traffic In a Weekend is designed as a guide to everything you need to successfully promote your Web site or home page. To get the most useful information into your hands without the clutter of a ton of background material, I had to assume several things. If you are reading this book, I hope that you already have a home page or Web site and, although you certainly don't need to be an HTML wizard, you should know at least the basics of HTML. Finally, you should also know the basics of Web browsing. If this is all true, we're on the right track.

Conventions Used in This Book

I've used a variety of elements to help keep the text clear and easy to follow. You'll find code terms and listings in `monospace` type, except when I tell you to actually type a command. In that case, the command appears in **bold** type. When I introduce and define a new term, I put it in *italics*.

Other conventions include:

Notes enhance a discussion in the text by drawing your attention to a particular point that needs emphasis.

Tips offer helpful hints or additional information.

You'll find this icon next to paragraphs that contain an online address. URLs appear in `monospace` type.

I truly hope you find that *Increase Your Web Traffic In a Weekend* provides everything you need to attract the masses to your home page or Web site.

William R. Stanek

(director@tvpress.com)

FRIDAY EVENING

Getting Started

Thousands of Web publishers have created home pages to sell products and services, or simply to share ideas. Often, they have been disappointed with the results they've achieved through Web publishing. They have created wonderful pages, yet received only a few visitors. These publishers may think that their ideas, interests, and products aren't interesting, but nothing could be further from the truth. Capitalizing on available resources and knowing how to promote your site are the keys to increasing your Web traffic. By the end of this weekend, you'll know a great deal more about how to do that.

So go ahead—get started. It's Friday evening (at least if you're following the schedule). The Friday evening schedule, which is divided into two parts, provides an overview of what you need to get started and what you'll be doing throughout the weekend. The second part gets you acquainted with crucial issues and resources on which you'll be focusing to get your Web site noticed by the masses.

Warming Up

With 50 million Web users from dozens of countries around the world, the Web has an extremely diverse audience. Still, trying to tap into the tremendous potential of the Web can be a daunting task. Enter *Increase Your Web Traffic in a Weekend*—your guide to everything you need to promote the heck out of your Web site without spending a dime.

You Built It, But Will They Come?

As incredible as it may seem, cyberspace contains more than 200 million Web pages. As if the virtually limitless possibilities that these millions of pages provide weren't bad enough, there are no road maps and relatively few sign posts to guide readers anywhere. So, how can anyone find your Web site? Unfortunately, no easy answer to this question exists.

After spending hours of your time and possibly hundreds or thousands of dollars creating a home page, it is certainly disheartening when no one visits your site, or the traffic is so minimal that it might as well be nonexistent. Take a look at Figure 1-1. Early in 1994, this was one of the first Web sites I created. When I created the Writer's Gallery, I added a counter that

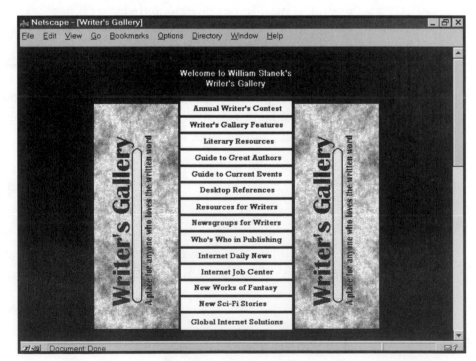

Figure 1-1

A cool Web site can't be found unless it is promoted properly.

told me every time the page was accessed. I really thought the counter was quite wonderful. Not only could I see how many times my pages were accessed, but I could show the world these numbers as well. Though I dreamed of a great flood of visitors, the numbers told me otherwise.

All right, I thought, perhaps not that many people are interested in literature. What else do I know about that might interest people? At the time, I was using the Web daily to search for a new career. I had a ton of information covering online job hunting and job resources on the Internet, so I put together the site shown in Figure 1-2. I waited, but again, the great flood of visitors didn't come.

Usually, the next step for many Web publishers is to try to launch their own promotion campaign. They register with all the search engines they can find, blanket the newsgroups and mailing lists with information about their home page, tell everyone they know to visit their home page—in other words, they explore all the promotion avenues that they've heard and

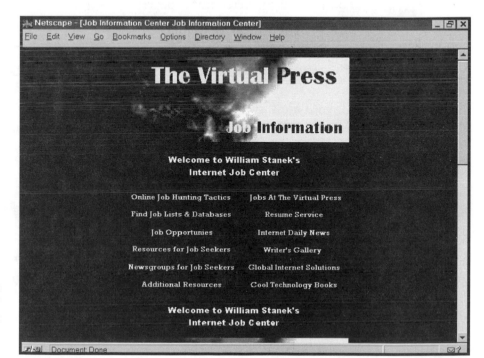

Figure 1-2

Another snazzy home page, but how come no one was visiting?

read about. Unfortunately, unless you truly understand Web marketing and promotion, these types of blanket efforts are like throwing good money after bad.

You could register with search engines till your fingers won't type any more. But unless you truly understand how search engines work and how to use their indexing features, you are wasting your time.

You could send out tons of e-mail through mailing lists and newsgroups. But unless you know what you are doing, you will get so much hate mail that you will truly wish you had never published a home page in the first place.

In the end, when the euphoria over getting a new Web page noticed wears off, many Web publishers wake up to the cruel reality that creating a Web page doesn't automatically create visitors to it. Now you may be thinking, "All right, if none of this works, why not sit back and hope that people stumble into my home page?" In truth, you have better odds of winning the New York State lottery than having someone wander into your unannounced, unregistered home page.

Fortunately, there are reliable ways to get your Web site noticed as well as to substantially increase traffic to your Web site, and in this book I show you every single one. By the end of this book, you will have everything you need to successfully attract a following to your Web site, gain an audience for your ideas, and promote your Web site to the world. As a case in point, millions of people now visit my Web sites every year, and the Internet Job Center and the Writer's Gallery are two of my most popular attractions. But it is a long way from zero to hero.

Can You Really Promote Your Web Site without Spending a Dime?

Invariably, the first question people ask when I tell them about my proven Web promotion and marketing techniques is, "How much will it cost?" If you've been publishing on the Web for a while or have done some considerable browsing, you have probably come across sales pitches like the following:

❂ Get 325 E-mail addresses for the top magazines, newspapers and e-zines—only $325

❂ We'll submit your site everywhere for $275

❂ Send e-mail promotions to millions for pennies apiece

Unfortunately, whether these types of pitches sell you on a pennies-apiece concept or a flat-fee-per-use concept, they are usually nothing more than cleverly designed ways to get you to open your pocketbook. For example, out of the list of 325 top magazines, newspapers, and e-zines, usually only a handful are really interested in the topic that your site covers, and you could get these e-mail addresses simply by visiting the related Web site yourself. So, why pay $325 for a few e-mail addresses that you could get yourself in less than an hour? I certainly don't have that kind of money to throw away and you probably don't either, which is why I sought out every possible avenue for effective and cost-free promotion.

When I say cost-free promotion, I mean it. None of the techniques or concepts I explore in this book requires you to pay anyone for anything. That said, the Web is constantly changing and what may be free today may not be free tomorrow. For this reason, I try to present more than one cost-free alternative for each specific technique or concept that I explore. With that approach, if you can't use option A, you will have options B, C, and D.

Gearing Up for the Ride

Increase Your Web Traffic in a Weekend is designed as a guide to everything that you need to successfully promote your Web site or home page. To get the most useful information into your hands without the clutter of a ton of background material, I had to assume several things. If you are reading this book, I hope that you already have a home page or Web site and, although you certainly don't need to be an HTML wizard, you should know at least the basics of HTML. Finally, you should also know the basics of Web browsing. If this is all true, we're on the right track, but before we can gear up for the ride, there are several things that you may want to take along.

Later, under "Boosting Visibility in 48 Hours: The Master Plan," I lay out the master plan for increasing traffic to your Web site. The key ingredient for making this plan work is a promise to dedicate your time and follow the techniques that I outline.

Later in this section, under "Promoting Your Web Site to the World," I examine the Web Promoter's Log Book, which is a log that you can use to keep track of your promotion efforts. Next, for some of the concepts discussed in the Saturday morning section of this book, you will need access to the server log files for your Web site. If you've never accessed these log files or don't know what they look like, don't worry—it's all covered in the Saturday morning section. Make a note to yourself to ask your service provider where these logs files are stored or, better yet, send your service provider an e-mail message now.

Although most service providers make logs available to Web publishers, a few service providers restrict access to these files. Often, all you need to do is ask permission. On the off chance that logs aren't available, I provide alternative ways to obtain visitor statistic without server logs. At the book's Web site (www.tvpress.com/promote/), you will also find sample log files that you can use. With these resources, you can master the techniques that I examine regardless of your situation.

● ●

NOTE Saturday morning's section has a part called "Simple Ways to Obtain Stats without Server Logs," which presents ways that you can obtain stats without server logs. Depending on the alternative that you decide to use, you may need to install a CGI script. Thus, while you are talking to your Internet service provider, you may want to ask someone there whether you can use CGI scripts and, if so, what the file path to the directory that you can use to store scripts is.

● ●

Finally, to get the most out of this book, you really need a connection to the Internet. Whether this connection is a dial-up account with an Internet service provider or a dedicated T1 doesn't matter as long as you can use the connection. During the next two days, you will use this connection to put to use the hundreds of Web promotion techniques that I examine in this book.

Putting the Motion in Promotion

After you create a wonderful home page, you need to tell the world about it, and the way you do this is through *promotion*. Promotion is many different things to many different people. In this book, promotion encompasses publicizing, marketing, advertising, and all other techniques that help build traffic to a Web site. Although promotion is 35 percent inspiration and 65 percent perspiration, promoting your Web site can be an awful lot of fun.

Before you get started, you really need to understand who is visiting your Web site right now, and what areas of your Web site these visitors find appealing. You do this by tracking visitor and page usage statistics, as shown in the section from Saturday morning called "Using Web Stats to Understand Your Site's Visitors." After you have a clear idea of who is visiting and why, as well as what about your Web site interests them, you can use this information to make your current Web site a better place to visit (see the part of Saturday afternoon's section called "Transforming the Numbers into Meaningful Data").

After you've taken a close look at your Web site and understand its appeal, you are ready to put the motion in promotion. The place to start is with search engines. Search engines provide the main sign posts in cyberspace, and millions of people use search engines every day. Yet, as I have mentioned, simply registering with a search engine isn't enough. You need to learn how search engines work and how you can take advantage of their indexing mechanisms. Fortunately, you'll learn all about this on Saturday afternoon in the section called "Capitalizing on Search Engine Fundamentals."

The Web has thousands of search engines, and registering with them all would be a waste of your time, which is why you'll also spend some time on Saturday afternoon learning about registering your Web site with what I call the top search engines on the planet. You'll also learn about the top lists, guides, and directories on the Web, and how to go about getting your site listed with these important promotional services. Sunday morning will continue the exploration of various types of search engines and directories that will prove invaluable to your goal of increasing your Web site's traffic. Sunday afternoon, you'll finish working with search engines for the time being, and then begin to focus your promotion campaign on mailing lists, newsgroups, and targeted e-mail. Finally, on Sunday evening, you'll see how to capitalize on the use of sweepstakes and other types of giveaways that can draw many visitors by offering challenge, entertainment, and fun. Then you'll move into more traditional Web advertising areas, such as banner advertising—but why pay for banner advertising when you can advertise for free? You'll see how to tap into free advertising opportunities in the section called "Cost-Free Banner Advertising: No Joke."

Wrapping Up and Looking Ahead

With luck, you now have a clear understanding of what this book covers and what you need to get started. In the next part of this section, I cover the basics of promoting your Web site to the world. As you will discover, making the Web work for you isn't an easy task, but it can be a lot of fun.

Promoting Your Web Site to the World

You created a wonderful home page or Web site but it doesn't seem to be catching on the way you thought it would. Well, don't fret, because in a few hours that will all change. The simple truth is that anyone can use the proven strategies and tasks that I present to bring the masses to his or her Web site.

Getting Your Web Site Noticed

Increasing your Web site traffic starts with you taking a closer look at your Web site to understand the big picture, which focuses on who is visiting your Web site and why. Trying to promote your Web site without understanding the big picture is like trying to play baseball without a ball—you just can't do it.

Although I would like to tell you that there is a magic button to press to give you the big picture for your Web site, there is no such button. The only way to get from A to Z is to roll back your sleeves and dive in. Diving in involves slogging through the server log files, examining your Web site with an honest eye, and taking a look at problem areas at your Web site.

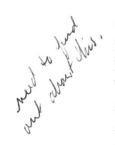

By examining the server log files, you will see firsthand the pages at your Web site that are getting the most visitors, and the pages at your Web site that aren't getting any visitors. When you dig through the server log files, you are gathering statistics—stats—that will tell you many things about your Web site's current traffic.

When you examine your site's traffic, you will move beyond tracking file accesses and zero in on the things that matter, such as page views and the actual number of visitors. When you look at page views and visitor counts, some of the questions that you can answer about your Web site include:

What are the busiest days of the week?

What are the busiest hours of the day?

What are the most requested pages?

Where do visitors live and work?

What is the average number of page views per day?

What is the average number of visitors per day?

What is the average number of page views per visitor?

What is the length of the average visit?

What is the total number of visitors?

You will use stats not only to understand who is visiting your Web site right now and why, but also to put together a promotion campaign for your Web site. By digging deeper through the server logs, you can find out whether people like what they see or are just racing through. You also can discover problem areas at your Web site that may be causing you to lose visitors who otherwise may have come back to your Web site repeatedly. You'll find more information on finding trouble spots at your Web site on Saturday morning, under "Gaining Lost Readers from the Error Logs."

■ ■

TIP If you find out that you can't access your server log files for whatever reason, don't worry. Later, on Saturday morning, you'll discover ways that you can gather stats without server log files.

■ ■

To make tracking stats easier, I put together the Web Promoter's Log Book, which you will find on the book's Web site at `www.tvpress.com/promote/log`. You can use this log book to help track your Web site's stats. The log book also has pages for keeping records on the key information that you need to maintain your Web site, such as a record for where files are kept and a page revision history.

After I help you develop a clear understanding of your Web site, I take you through the steps necessary to put your Web site's stats to work. The first step is to summarize the stats and transform them into meaningful data. Then you will use the stats to make your Web site a better place to visit by taking care of the following:

✪ Cleaning up unused pages

✪ Clearing out dead-ends

✿   Fixing errors

You can also use the stats to build cross-traffic and to attract users to popular areas of your Web site. Learning how to put the stats to work is the subject of the section within Saturday afternoon's coverage called "Putting the Stats to Work."

Making the Web Work for You

Making the Web work for you is where you conduct your Web promotion campaign. As with any campaign, your promotion efforts start with careful planning and a firm understanding of the subjects that you plan to tackle—such as Web site promotion through search engines. Although everyone has used search engines to find Web resources, few people truly understand how search engines do what they do. Now it is time to make those search engines work for you. Rather than visit InfoSeek's Web site, shown in Figure 1-3, you will use InfoSeek to bring visitors to your Web site.

You start by learning to take advantage of the way search engines find and

Figure 1-3

InfoSeek: One of the top search engines.

retrieve information. Although the inner workings of search engines aren't exactly state secrets, each individual search engine does things differently, which is why you will use many different techniques to make your Web pages more friendly to search engines. Web pages that are optimized for search engines using the techniques covered Saturday afternoon under "Capitalizing on Search Engine Fundamentals" will help put your Web site on the map. These techniques make obtaining references to your Web pages easier.

After you have gained a firm understanding of how search engines work, you should register your Web site with the search engines that are used by the majority of Web users. Although your promotion efforts begin with search engines, you don't stop there. Afterward, you move on to Web guides, lists, and directories, such as Yahoo!, shown in Figure 1-4.

Just as few people understand how search engines work, few people have ever taken the time to plot out how to get the most out of Web guides, lists and directories, which is exactly what you will find toward the end of the Saturday afternoon, in the section called "Submitting Your Site to the Top

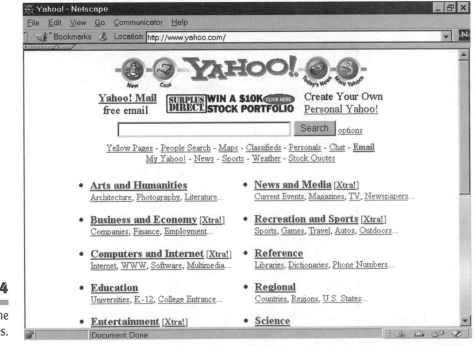

Figure 1-4

Yahoo!: One of the top Web directories.

Guides, Lists, and Directories." Again, the focus is on the top guides rather than all guides. The reason for this is to encourage you to use your time and resources wisely. Why waste your time registering with every single search engine and directory on the planet when 90 percent of Web users find what they are looking for through the top 10 percent of the Web search and directory sites?

In the top search and directory sites, you will find many search and directory sites that focus on specific types of information. These search and directory sites include Yellow Pages directories, White Pages directories, category-specific directories, and specialty directories. Although these search and directory sites have narrow focuses, they are popular and frequently used to find information. For example, anyone looking for a business listing can use a Yellow Pages directory, such as ComFind shown in Figure 1-5. Anyone looking for a long-lost friend or associate can use a White Pages directory, such as Four11, which is shown in Figure 1-6.

NOTE •

You will learn how to promote your Web site using Yellow Pages directories on Sunday morning, under "The Best Business Search Engines and Yellow Pages Directories." Web promotion in White Pages directories is covered that morning under "Promoting Your Web Site in Specialty Directories."

• •

Promoting Your Web Site to Joe Web Surfer

Joe Web surfer is your average person browsing the Web. He's been there and done that. Now he's out looking for a bit of excitement or trying to find something—gasp!—useful. He's looking for a site like yours. He just doesn't know it yet. Well, to help Joe on his way, you have to give him a bit of prodding and grab his attention.

In the real world, you could grab Joe's attention by putting up a flashing neon sign that says, "Hey, Joe, over here!" In cyberspace, you grab Joe's attention using the tools of the Web promotion trade.

If Joe is looking for something cool, you grab Joe's attention by getting

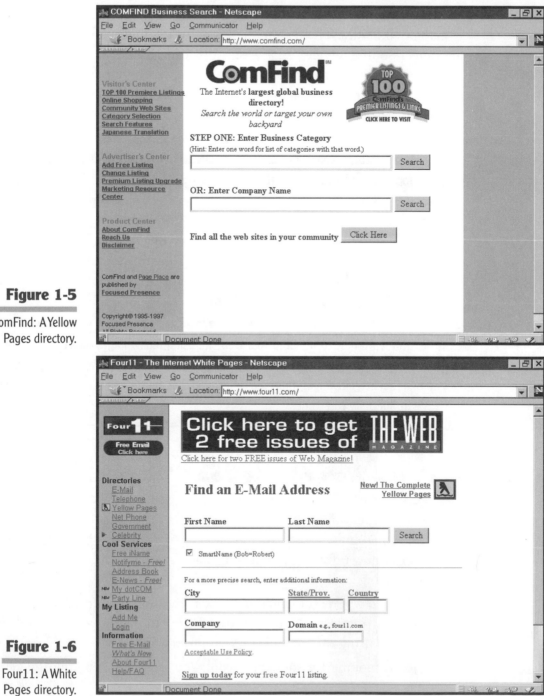

Figure 1-5

ComFind: A Yellow
Pages directory.

Figure 1-6

Four11: A White
Pages directory.

your site listed as the Cool Site of the Day. Although Cool Site of the Day is one of the key awards that will get your Web site noticed, many other awards exist that will get Joe Web Surfer to notice your site as well. Joe may be looking for something crazy, or wild. In this case, he may be looking for sites like those featured as the Craziest site of the Day by Very Crazy Productions (see Figure 1-7).

NOTE

• •

You'll find more information on these and other awards on Sunday morning, under "Getting Your Site Listed as the Cool Site of the Day."

• •

If Joe is looking to get something for nothing, you grab Joe's attention with freebies, such as a giveaway. Then again, Joe may be interested in some other type of freebie, such as a contest, sweepstakes, or treasure hunt. Catching Joe's eye when he's looking for freebies is covered Sunday afternoon under "Attracting the Masses with Giveaways, Contests, Sweepstakes, and More."

Other ways to grab Joe's attention include getting him where he lives and

Figure 1-7

Four11: A White Pages directory.

using straight-forward Web advertising. Most Web users have a newsgroup or mailing list they like to follow, and Joe is no exception. So, to get Joe where he lives, you have to visit the discussion groups and forums where he hangs out. If Joe is interested in topics similar to those covered at your Web site, chances are good that you will find him hanging out in a like-minded newsgroup or mailing list. Web site promotion through newsgroups and mailing lists is featured Sunday afternoon under "Selling Your Web Site through E-Mail."

Sometimes, the best way to get Joe's attention is to use good old-fashioned advertising. On the Web, this means using a banner advertisement. Although we all love to hate banner ads, you have to admit that sometimes you do click on them, and so does Joe. If something grabs his eye, he's going to click on it, and when he does, you want it to be your site that he visits. To help Joe on his way, you can use the cost-free advertising techniques that you'll explore Sunday afternoon under "Cost-Free Banner Advertising: No Joke."

Using The Web Promoter's Log Book

You will find the Web Promoter's Log Book in Appendix D online at www.primapublishing.com/cpd/corrections/index.html or www.tvpress.com/promote/notes.htm. You can use the Web Promoter's Log Book to keep track of just about everything you do in this book. The purpose of the log book is to make maintaining and promoting your Web site easier, as well as to help you develop a record that you can use to gauge the long-term performance of your Web site. The log book is divided into three sections: Stat Tracking Logs, Web Site Maintenance Logs, and Site Registration Logs.

I have designed the stat tracking logs to help you keep track of statistics for individual pages and areas at your Web site. You should use the stat tracking logs whenever you examine the stats for your Web site. Individual logs that you can find in this section of the log book include:

> **Weekly Hit Summary:** Used as a weekly record of hits for an entire Web site or area of a Web site by date and hit total

Monthly Hit Summary: Used to record monthly hit summaries for an entire Web site or area of a Web site by month and hit total

Page Views: Used to record page views for specific pages at your Web site; also includes a column for tracking average page views per day

Area Summaries: Used to summarize all the hits and page views for a specific area within your Web site. An area is a collection of Web pages with a similar theme

You can use the Web site maintenance logs to help you track Web site maintenance, schedule updates, and find your files. You should use the Web site maintenance logs whenever you work with Web pages, images, or banners. Logs that you can find in this section of the log book include:

Directories for Web Files: Helps you track where you store Web-related files on your hard disk and the corresponding directory for the files on your Web server

Web Page Change Log: Helps you track the revision history of your Web pages and whether you need to update the directory listings for these Web pages

Image Change Log: Helps you track the revision history of your Web-related images

Banner Change Log: Helps you track banner advertisements and banner exchange advertising

You can use the site registration logs to help you track when and where you've registered your Web site, and to record essential information that will make updating your information at a later date, such as your account name and password, easy. The site registration logs come in handy to track the details of your promotion campaign. The logs that you can find in this section of the log book include:

Search Engine Registration Log: Helps you track the Web sites that you've registered in search engines

Directory Registration Log: Helps you track the pages that you've registered in Web directories

Yellow Pages Registration Log: Helps you track the pages that you've registered in Yellow Pages directories as well as related account information

White Pages Registration Log: Helps you track the pages and e-mail addresses that you've registered in White Pages directories, as well as related account information

Web Guide and Awards Registration Log: Helps you track the pages that you've submitted for awards and recognition, as well as when you may want to submit your site again

Specialty Directory Registration Log: Helps you track the pages that you've registered in specialty directories

Freebies and Contest Registration Log: Helps you track freebies and contests

Banner Exchange Registration Log: Helps you track your accounts with banner exchanges

As you explore the promotion techniques that I outline in this book, be sure to record your efforts in the log book. Although some of the information you will be asked to record may not make sense right now, I wanted you to know about the log book before you started using any of the promotion techniques that I outline. In this way, you will be able to see your progress and record all the information that will make maintaining and promoting your Web site easier over the long term.

Wrapping Up and Looking Ahead

Spending a few hours promoting a Web site that you spent days creating and weeks perfecting makes sense. Promoting your Web site to the world starts with you taking a closer look at your Web site, and then moves on into a carefully planned promotion campaign. Now that the preview of what's ahead is over, it is time to roll back your sleeves and get ready to dive in. In the next section, I show you how you can use Web statistics to understand who is visiting your Web site and why.

Working with Statistics and Logs

- ⚙ Using Web Stats to Understand Your Site's Visitors
- ⚙ Understanding Visits and Page Views
- ⚙ Gaining Lost Readers from the Error Logs
- ⚙ Simple Ways to Obtain Stats without Server Logs

Before you launch a promotion campaign that'll bring the masses to your Web site, you really need to understand what is happening at your Web site right now. The way to do this is to examine the current traffic at your Web site. Your site's stats are the single most important means for discovering what people really think about your Web site, and you will probably be surprised when you discover which of your resources are bringing in readers, and which resources aren't.

If you're tempted to pay only cursory attention to this section, ask yourself this: what do I really know about the flow of traffic to my site? How do I know which pages are drawing visitors and which ones are being skipped? If you're making assumptions about your readers that the stats wouldn't support, then your lack of awareness could be costing you dearly.

So settle in with a good cup of coffee or some juice to get you alert— it's Saturday morning and time to roll.

By the end of the morning, you'll know how to find out who is visiting your site, and why. You'll also know how to make use of the stats to begin increasing your Web traffic right away.

Using Web Stats to Understand Your Site's Visitors

Web site stats tell you much more than which Web pages at your site interest readers. By tracking stats, you also learn many things about those who visit your Web site, such as how long they visit, whether they really read the pages that you present or just skip on by, what days of the week are the most popular, what time of day is the best time to make updates, and a whole lot of other things as well.

You need to know what kind of people are drawn to your site so that you can keep them coming back for more and attract others like them. You need to know about errors and other circumstances that couldbe making your site an obstacle course that's preventing visitors from coming or staying. You need to know how to use logs effectively so that you can intrepet the data and make informed decisions. This effort is what will remove your site from the ranks of hit-or-miss Web sites and give it the stamp of professionalism.

Web Site Stats Are a Necessary Evil

Yes, Web site stats truly are a necessary evil. We all hate the thought of statistics, which is why I present this topic early in the book. If you don't track the stats at your Web site, however, you never truly understand who is visiting your Web site and, more important, why.

Before you start having flashbacks of high school algebra class, you should know that tracking and analyzing Web site stats isn't rocket science. As a matter of fact, tracking and analyzing stats is fairly easy as long as you follow the practical advice I give you in the next couple of days. In this section, I show you how to obtain stats for your Web site using server logs. Next, I show you how to use those stats to get the big picture for your Web site.

●●●

NOTE Although my server log files are located in the directory `/www/logs/`, the location of server log files is defined when a server is installed, which means that the server log files you need are probably located somewhere else. The best way to find the server log files is to ask your service provider or the Webmaster for your server where these files are located.

Keep in mind that if you have your own domain, such as `www.yourname.com`, you should have separate log files regardless of whether you actually have your own server or you use someone else's. If multiple domains are served by the same server, the logs probably have a prefix that indicates the domain. Otherwise, you, like anyone using a service provider, will share server logs with everyone else using the server.

●●●

Here are a few reasons that you may have to track stats:

- ✿   To discover popular resources
- ✿   To learn more about the people who visit your site
- ✿   To find out when people visit

Discover Popular Resources

By tracking and analyzing stats, you can discover which of the pages at your Web site are the most visited. Although you may think that your top-level home page is the most popular, this isn't always the case. In fact, your analysis may reveal that most people are visiting some other page at your Web site. The reason for this is that the Web allows anyone to visit any page at your Web site, and visitors don't have to start at your home page.

An example of tracking page accesses is shown in Figure 2-1. By examining the figure, you can see how Web site stats can be analyzed using a software application. When I first started using tracking software, I was pleasantly surprised to discover that my Internet Job Center was just as popular as my daily news service, called Internet Daily News. At that time, most visitors to the Web site weren't starting on the site's home page. The majority of visitors were, in fact, starting at the site's resource pages.

Using the techniques detailed in this book, I was able to draw those same visitors to the site's home page, and now the home page is the most popular resource at the site. The main idea was to give visitors the chance to learn about everything the site has to offer. It worked wonderfully.

Learn More about the People Who Visit Your Site

By tracking your site's stats, you also can learn more about the people who are visiting, such as where they live, where they work, and how they access your Web site. One of the best ways to learn more about your site's visitors is to examine the domain that the visitor uses.

Figure 2-2 shows an example of how you can track domain classes. Each domain class can tell you something about the person who uses it. For

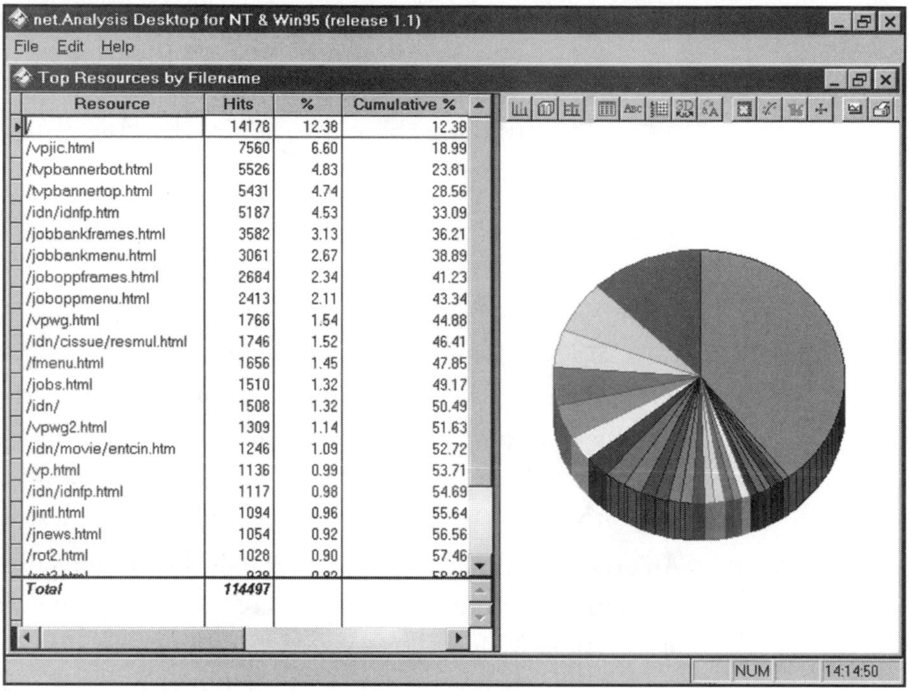

Figure 2-1

Tracking page accesses can help you learn many things about who's visiting your site and why.

example, users from the education domain—domains ending in .edu—are usually college students or faculty members. For more information on domain classes, see the part of this morning's section called "The Host Field."

Find Out When People Visit

Finding out when people visit your Web site is extremely useful, especially if you use this information to plan updates for your Web pages. As Figure 2-3 shows, you can use stats to determine the activity level at your Web site throughout the week. In this example, Monday is the busiest day of the week and the weekend is the slowest time of the week.

My discovery that most people visited this site on a Monday and that weekends were the slowest time of the week opened a whole new world of possibilities. Before this discovery, I made weekly updates to this Web site on Wednesdays because I assumed that the busiest times were Fridays and weekends.

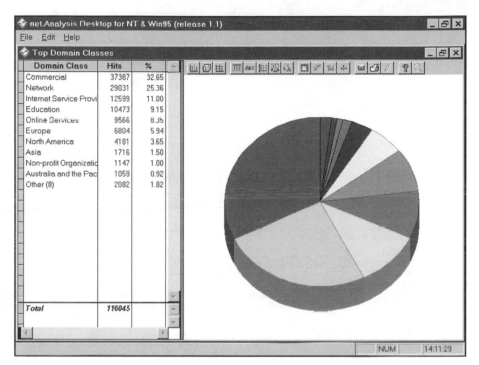

Figure 2-2

Getting an idea of who the reader is by tracking domain classes.

As it turned out, this wasn't the case at all, and the news tidbits that I posted on Wednesday weren't read by the vast majority of visitors until five days later. By moving the updates to Sunday evenings, I was able to give the Monday crowd information that was truly fresh. As a result, the site as a whole gained more readers over time.

Tracking Stats: The Basics

When you analyze your site's stats, you may be in for a big surprise. Often, people track Web site stats by counting file accesses rather than actual visitors. Unfortunately, the number of file accesses alone isn't an accurate way to measure the popularity of a Web site.

Understanding Hits

File accesses are also referred to as *hits*. When you browse a Web page, every file that is accessed to display the page in your browser is considered

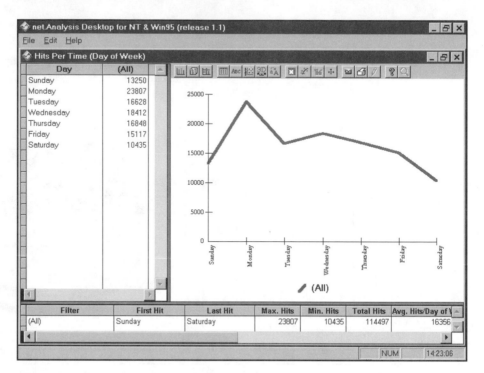

Figure 2-3

The busiest days of the week may reveal important trends.

to be a hit. If you access a Web page with five graphics, up to six hits could be generated. One of these hits would be for the page itself. The other five hits would be for each of the images displayed with the page.

FIND IT ▶ ONLINE

To put this in perspective, take a jaunt over to the home page of Internet Daily News on the Web at `http://www.netdaily.com/`. The home page for this site is shown in Figure 2-4. When you type the URL for the home page, the following files are loaded into your browser:

index.html - The HTML source for the page

glnet.gif - The first image

glmail.gif - The second image

site2.gif - The third image

site1.gif - The fourth image

cal.gif - The fifth image

wpupr.gif - The sixth image

fpu97.gif - The seventh image

Thus, every time that the home page for Internet Daily News is accessed in a graphics-capable browser, eight hits are generated. If you follow a link to an article in the newspaper, up to six more hits are generated. When you put both page accesses together, you get a total of 14 hits. As you can see, 14 hits definitely does not equal 14 visitors, and it is rather unfortunate that the hit is sometimes used to advertise the popularity of a Web site.

Recording Hits

Hits are logged in a special file on the server called an *access log*. When a resource at a Web site is requested by a browser, the server retrieves the file and then writes an entry in the access log for the request. Entries in the server access log indicate many things about the file transfer, including the success or failure of the transfer. You'll learn more about the access log in

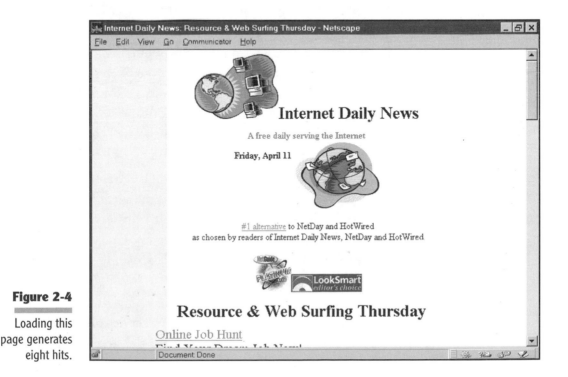

Figure 2-4

Loading this page generates eight hits.

the section of this morning's coverage titled "Unlocking the Secrets of the Access Logs."

The access log is not the only server log file. If the server can't find the file or if an error occurs, the server usually makes an entry in the access log and in an *error log*. The purpose of the error log is to provide more detail about each specific error. Although the error log is useful, many service providers configure the Web server so that error logs aren't used at all. Saving space on the file system is the primary reason for this.

TIP

Errors can tell you many things about your Web site. By examining errors, you can find links or references that are broken in your Web site. Fixing these errors can help you build a steady readership at your Web site.

You'll learn more about errors later this morning under the section called "Gaining Lost Readers from the Error Logs." If your service provider doesn't use error logs, don't worry. Errors are still recorded in the access logs.

Other server log files include the referrer log and the agent log. The *referrer log* is used to record the URL from which a request comes, which can help you learn exactly how visitors are accessing your Web site. The *agent log* is used to record the type of browser that requests a resource at your Web site, which can tell you whether someone used Netscape Navigator 3.0, Internet Explorer 4.0, or Mosaic 2.0 to access your Web site. I cover more about the referrer and agent logs a little later under "Using Other Server Logs."

Although knowing the user's URL and browser is certainly important, many service providers do not use the referrer log or the agent log. Again, this is to save space on the file system. Before you fault your service provider for not using the extra log files, imagine having to log every request for a file in four different logs. Not only does this eat up file space, it also uses up system resources, such as CPU time.

To reduce the drain on system resources yet retain the valuable information that agent and referrer logs provide, some service providers use what is called a *combined log*. In the combined log, the access, user, and agent entries are all logged in a single file. As Web servers continue to evolve, the combined log may increase in popularity.

The wonderful thing about server log files is that they are ordinary text files, which means that they contain no special formatting characters or codes other than those used for standard ASCII text. Generally, entries in the server logs are entered chronologically, with new entries appended to the end of the log.

Unlocking the Secrets of the Access Logs

The access log is the key to discovering who is visiting your Web site and why. Every time someone requests a file from your Web site, an entry goes into the access log, making the access log a running history of every successful and unsuccessful attempt to retrieve information from your Web site. Because each entry has its own line, entries in the access log can be extracted easily when you want to compile stats for your Web site. Compiling stats from access log entries is covered later this morning under "Understanding Visits and Page Views."

The most prevalent format for server access logs is the *Common Log Format*. In the Common Log Format, entries in the log file have seven fields. These fields are as follows:

Host

Identification

User Authentication

Time Stamp

HTTP Request Type

Status Code

Transfer Volume

Although just about every Web server available has been standardized on the Common Log Format, some servers use a *combined* or *extended* log format. Fortunately for us, the first seven fields in these additional formats are generally the same as those used in the Common Log Format. In the combined log format, two additional fields are added to the original seven fields. These fields are Referrer and Agent. In the extended log format, one or more additional fields are added to the original seven fields. These extended fields are generally specific to the server that uses them.

Listing 2-1 shows entries in a sample access log. As you can see from the sample, log fields are separated with spaces. In the sections that follow, I examine each of these fields and explain what they mean.

Listing 2-1   Sample Entries from a Server Access Log

```
pc4.att.net - - [02/Mar/1997:12:37:20 -0800] "GET / HTTP/1.0"
   304 -
pc4.att.net - - [02/Mar/1997:12:37:22 -0800] "GET /lightn.jpg
   HTTP/1.0" 304 -
pc4.att.net - - [02/Mar/1997:12:37:23 -0800] "GET /ns.gif
   HTTP/1.0" 304 -
pc4.att.net - - [02/Mar/1997:12:37:28 -0800] "GET /writ.htm
   HTTP/1.0" 304 -
pc4.att.net - - [02/Mar/1997:12:37:28 -0800] "GET /wpupr.gif
   HTTP/1.0" 304 -
pc4.att.net - - [02/Mar/1997:12:37:28 -0800] "GET /wpd.gif
   HTTP/1.0" 304 -
pc4.att.net - - [02/Mar/1997:12:37:28 -0800] "GET /fp97.gif
   HTTP/1.0" 304 -
pc4.att.net - - [02/Mar/1997:12:37:28 -0800] "GET /dice.gif
   HTTP/1.0" 304 -
pc4.att.net - - [02/Mar/1997:12:37:29 -0800] "GET /ticket.gif
   HTTP/1.0" 304 -
pc4.att.net - - [02/Mar/1997:12:37:29 -0800] "GET /keyb.gif
   HTTP/1.0" 304 -
pc4.att.net - - [02/Mar/1997:12:37:42 -0800] "GET /wdream.htm
   HTTP/1.0" 304 -
195.173.163.34 - - [02/Mar/1997:13:22:04 -0800] "GET / HTTP/
   1.0" 200 1970
ds.ucla.edu - - [02/Mar/1997:13:37:57 -0800] "GET / HTTP/1.0"
   200 1970
```

```
ds.ucla.edu - - [02/Mar/1997:13:38:06 -0800] "GET /ns.gif
   HTTP/1.0" 200 1052
ds.ucla.edu - - [02/Mar/1997:13:38:28 -0800] "GET /writ.htm
   HTTP/1.0" 200 5835
ds.ucla.edu - - [02/Mar/1997:13:38:31 -0800] "GET /dice.gif
   HTTP/1.0" 200 1714
ds.ucla.edu - - [02/Mar/1997:13:38:31 -0800] "GET /wpupr.gif
   HTTP/1.0" 200 6376
ds.ucla.edu - - [02/Mar/1997:13:38:31 -0800] "GET /wpd.gif
   HTTP/1.0" 200 10423
ds.ucla.edu - - [02/Mar/1997:13:38:31 -0800] "GET /tp97.gif
   HTTP/1.0" 200 5306
ds.ucla.edu - - [02/Mar/1997:13:38:38 -0800] "GET /keyb.gif
   HTTP/1.0" 200 1934
ds.ucla.edu - - [02/Mar/1997:13:38:41 -0800] "GET /ticket.gif
   HTTP/1.0" 200 2015
195.173.163.34 - - [02/Mar/1997:13:22:04 -0800] "GET /ns.gif
   HTTP/1.0" 200 1970
```

The Host Field

The first field in the access log identifies the host computer requesting a file from your Web server. The value in this field is either the fully qualified domain name of the remote host, such as:

```
pc4.att.net - - [02/Mar/1997:12:37:20 -0800] "GET / HTTP/1.0" 304 -
```

or the value is the IP address of the remote host, such as:

```
195.173.163.34 - - [02/Mar/1997:13:22:04 -0800] "GET / HTTP/1.0"
   200 1970
```

Examining Domain Names

When an entry has the fully qualified domain name of the remote host, you can examine that domain name to learn a great deal about the user accessing your server. Divisions within the domain are separated by periods, such as:

```
pc4.att.net - - [02/Mar/1997:12:37:20 -0800] "GET / HTTP/1.0"
   304 -
```

In this example, the domain name is broken down into three divisions:

> pc4 - Identifies the remote host as a terminal

> att - The organization associated with the remote host, AT&T

> net - The domain class for the host

The first piece of the puzzle, the identity of the remote host, isn't as important as the organization and the domain class with which the host is associated. With most service providers, remote host names are allocated dynamically when you dial up and connect, which is why you may see identifiers in the first field, such as PC4, AT1, or CLIENT99.

The second piece of the puzzle tells you about the organization with which the remote host is associated. Often, several fields may be here, which identify divisions within the organization, such as the human resources department at IBM.

The final piece of the puzzle is the domain class, which can tell you where the user lives and works. Table 2-1 describes the six basic domain classes.

TABLE 2-1 BASIC DOMAIN CLASSES	
Domain Name	**Description**
COM	Commercial; users from commercial Internet services and Web sites
EDU	Education; users from colleges and universities
GOV	All U.S. government agencies, except military
MIL	U.S. Military; users who work at a military installation
NET	Network sites, includes service providers and true network developers
ORG	Nonprofit organizations; users who work for nonprofit organizations

Domain classes are also organized geographically. These domain classes end in a two- or three-letter designator that tells you the state or country the user lives in. Because there are hundreds of state and country designators, I won't outline them here and I don't recommend memorizing them, either. Just make a note that if you see a domain class you don't recognize, it is probably a designator for a specific state or country.

Examining IP Addresses

IP addresses are the numeric equivalent of fully qualified domain names. Here's an example:

```
195.173.163.34      [02/Mar/1997:13:22:04 -0800] "GET / HTTP/
   1.0" 200 1970
```

Although the bunch of numbers that you see in the host field doesn't tell you much, there are ways to equate the IP address with a specific host name, and your server can even be configured to do this job for you. Keep in mind, though, that resolving an IP address to a host name requires server resources and usually isn't worth the effort in the end. Suffice it to say that if you see an IP address in the host field, moving on to the next entry or simply working with the remaining fields in the current entry is easier.

The Identification Field

The second field in the access log is the identification field. Although this field is meant to identify users by their username, this field is rarely used. Because of this, you will generally see a hyphen (-) in this field, as in the following:

```
ds.ucla.edu - - [02/Mar/1997:13:37:57 -0800] "GET / HTTP/1.0"
   200 1970
```

The problem with the identification field is that even if only by chance you do see something in this field, the username cannot be trusted. The username is not validated, so it could be made up.

The User Authentication Field

The third field in the access log comes into play whenever you have protected areas at your Web site. Unless you have a password-protected area at your Web site, you will usually see a hyphen (-) in this field, such as:

```
ds.ucla.edu - - [02/Mar/1997:13:37:57 -0800] "GET / HTTP/1.0"
  200 1970
```

If you have a password-protected area at your Web site, users must authenticate themselves with a username and password that is registered for this area. After users validate themselves with their username and password, their username is entered in the user authentication field. Keep in mind that the entry in this field is not the actual username but rather the username for your Web site.

The Time Stamp Field

Beyond what generally equates to two dashes is the time stamp field. This field tells you exactly when someone accessed a file on the server. Because the format of the time field is very specific, the time field can be extracted to perform many different calculations. The format for the time stamp field is as follows:

```
DD/MMM/YYYY:HH:MM:SS OFFSET
```

Right now you are probably thinking, wow, rocket science again. But if you examine the time field a bit at a time, you can begin to get a clear picture of how the time stamp is used. Look again at a sample of the time stamp in an actual entry:

```
pc4.att.net - - [02/Mar/1997:12:37:20 -0800] "GET / HTTP/1.0" 304 -
```

After looking at the time stamp, you may understand the following:

DD - Refers to a two-digit day designator, such as 02 for the second day of the month

MMM - Refers to a three-letter month, such as Mar for March

YYYY - Refers to a four-digit year designator, such 1997

HH - Refers to a two-digit hour designator, such as 12 for 12 p.m.

MM - Refers to a two-digit minute designator, such as 37 for 37 minutes after the hour

SS - Refers to a two-digit second designator, such as 20

The only designator that probably doesn't make sense is the OFFSET designator, which indicates the server's offset from GMT (Greenwich Mean Time) standard time. Here, the offset is minus eight hours, meaning that the server time is eight hours behind GMT. Although this offset is the same unless the server time changes according to daylight savings time, the server nevertheless logs it with every entry.

As you will discover later this morning, you can use the time stamp to learn many things about the users visiting your Web site, such as how long they stay on a particular page. If you are really determined, you can even extrapolate the throughput between your server and the remote host, which can ultimately tell you the modem transfer rate that was used.

NOTE

Throughput refers to the transfer rate between the server and the client. By examining throughput, you can gauge the average transfer speed used by visitors to your Web site, which can tell you a great deal about the core visitors to your Web site. Are they coming from the corporate world? Are they dialing up from home? Generally, visitors from the corporate sector have very fast transfer speeds—imagine a T-1 transferring megabytes in seconds—and visitors from the private sector have relatively slow dial-up modem speeds. You will find more on computing transfer speeds and what transfer speeds can tell you a little later this morning.

The HTTP Request Field

The HTTP request field is the fifth field in the access log. You will use this field to determine three things:

- ✿ The method that the remote client used to request the information
- ✿ The file that the remote client requested
- ✿ The HTTP version that the client used to retrieve the file

The most important item in the HTTP request field is the relative URL of the file being requested. By *relative URL*, I mean an URL that is relative only to your Web server. Relative URLs are interpreted by the server. For example, if you request the file:

```
http://www.tvpress.com/writing/writing2.htm
```

The server will use the relative URL, `/writing/writing2.htm`, to log where the file is found. Similarly, if you use the URL:

```
http://www.tvpress.com/
```

the server will use the relative URL of `/` and create an entry in the access log similar to the following:

```
pc4.att.net - - [02/Mar/1997:12:37:20 -0800] "GET / HTTP/1.0"
  200 -
```

TIP

When you see an entry that ends in a slash, keep in mind that this refers to the default document for a directory, which is typically called index.html or default.html.

Only the most hard-core techies in the group will want to know exactly what the first and last items in the HTTP request field tell us. If this is you, jump to Appendix C online (`www.primapublishing.com/cpd/corrections/index.html` or `www.tvpress.com/promote/notes.htm`) to learn more about these items. To sum it all up, though, the method identifies a specific request type used by the client and is always either GET, POST, or HEAD. The HTTP version item identifies the specific HTTP version used to transfer the file—usually, HTTP/0.9, HTTP/1.0, or HTTP/1.1.

The Status Code Field

The status code field is the sixth field in the access log. Status codes are diamonds in the rough. From this single code, you can learn whether files were transferred correctly, weren't found, were loaded from cache, and more. The key to status codes is that they are defined in the HTTP specification, making them universal to all Web servers. This means that the status codes used in your server access log are the same as the status codes used in anyone else's server access log.

Status Code Classes

All status codes are three-digit numbers. Because the first digit of the status code indicates the class of the code, you can often tell at a glance what has happened. Table 2-2 shows the general classes for status codes.

Following Table 2-2, you can see that status codes fall into five general categories. Because the first category is used rarely and only with HTTP version 1.1, you really need to remember only the other four categories. If you have a status code that begins with 2, the associated file transferred successfully. A status code that begins with 3 indicates that the server performed a redirect. A status code that begins with 4 indicates some type of client error or failure. Finally, a status code that begins with 5 tells you that a server error occurred.

TABLE 2-2	GENERAL CLASSES OF STATUS CODES
Code Class	**Description**
1XX	Continue/Protocol Change
2XX	Success
3XX	Redirection
4XX	Client error/failure
5XX	Server error

To put this in perspective, look at two entries in the access log:

```
ds.ucla.edu - - [02/Mar/1997:13:38:06 -0800] "GET /ns.gif
  HTTP/1.0" 200 1052

pc4.att.net - - [02/Mar/1997:12:37:20 -0800] "GET / HTTP/1.0"
  304 -
```

The first entry in the access log has a status code of 200, and the 2, as you now know, indicates a successful transfer. The second entry in the access log has a status code of 304 and the 3 indicates a server redirect. Although servers sometimes redirect users to files that have been moved, the redirect usually means that the file has not been modified since it was last requested, and therefore the browser can use a cached version of the file instead of having the server retransfer the file.

Individual Status Codes

To really understand what is happening on the server, you will sometimes want to know exactly what a status code means. For this reason, I've taken the most important status codes from the HTTP specification and compiled them in the tables in this section.

Appendix C online (`www.primapublishing.com/cpd/corrections/index.html` or `www.tvpress.com/promote/notes.htm`) provides a complete list of all the status codes defined in the HTTP 1.1 specification.

The two most common status codes for successful file transfers are shown in Table 2-3. If you see status code 200, you know that the file transferred successfully and no errors occurred. On the other hand, the status code of 204 indicates that the file was found and transferred but it had no content. This usually tells you that one your CGI scripts created a bad header, which may be the result of a form being submitted with improper content.

The two most common redirection codes are shown in Table 2-4. A status code of 302 usually means that the user typed an URL without the trailing

TABLE 2-3 COMMON STATUS CODES FOR SUCCESS	
Code	**Description**
200	Successful file transfer; file transfer OK
204	Successful file transfer but file had no content

slash and the server redirected them to the proper URL. Thus, if you enter the URL `http://www.tvpress.com`, your server may issue a redirect to `http://www.tvpress.com/`. A status code of 304 tells you that the file was

TABLE 2-4	COMMON STATUS CODES FOR REDIRECTION
Code	**Description**
302	Redirected client to new file; file moved temporarily
304	File not modified; client loaded from cache

not modified since it was last requested by the client, which allowed the client to load it from cache.

Status codes to which you should pay particular attention are those that indicate client error or failure to transfer the file. These status codes are shown in Table 2-5.

A status code of 400 indicates that the user made an invalid request, which can usually be interpreted as the server couldn't determine what the heck the client was trying to request. The status codes of 401 and 403 indicate similar problems and usually mean that the file or directory requested couldn't be accessed due to an access restriction on the server.

Finally, the status code of 404 indicates that the file was not found. If you've browsed the Web, you've probably seen the dreaded 404 many times.

TABLE 2-5	COMMON STATUS CODES FOR CLIENT ERROR/FAILURE
Code	**Description**
400	Invalid request
401	Client not authorized to access file
403	Client forbidden from accessing file or directory
404	File not found

Later this morning, under "Gaining Lost Readers from the Error Log," you'll see how to eliminate the 404-File Not Found error.

You should also pay particular attention to status codes that indicate server errors (see Table 2-6). Suffice it to say that server errors are bad news. Depending on the type of server you use, you may see server errors occasionally. In this case, don't get alarmed. But if you start to see server errors routinely, notify your Webmaster.

TABLE 2-6	COMMON STATUS CODES FOR SERVER ERROR
Code	**Description**
500	Internal server error
502	Bad gateway
503	Service unavailable

The Transfer Volume Field

In the Common Log Format, the last field in the access log is the transfer volume. This field indicates the number of bytes transferred to the client as a result of the request. If a status code other than a success code is used in field six, this field will contain a hyphen (-) or a zero to indicate that no data was transferred.

In this example, 256 bytes were transferred:

```
ps4.att.net - - [02/Mar/1997:14:00:00 -0800] "GET /cool.gif
  HTTP/1.0" 200 256
```

Sometimes, entries that have a status code of 200 will also have a hyphen or zero in the transfer volume field. This usually indicates that the client requested only a HTTP header for the file and not the actual file itself. *HTTP headers* tell your browser about the data being transferred. Intelligent agents, such as those that verify links in Web pages, often request only a file header and then use the status code returned to determine whether the file exists.

Using Other Server Logs

The access log isn't the only log available. On some servers, you will also find a referrer log and an agent log. Keep in mind that these are optional logs that may or may not be available.

TIP

In place of the referrer log and the agent log, some servers use a combined log format (described previously) that appends the referrer and agent information to entries in the access log. Generally, a referrer field becomes the eighth field and an agent field becomes the ninth field in the access log.

The Referrer Log

The referrer log tells you exactly where a client was before coming to your Web site, which is certainly useful information if you want to see firsthand how people get to your Web site. Entries in the referrer log look like this:

```
http://www.netdaily.com/ -> /ci/w2.htm
```

The URL in the first field of the referrer log indicates the referrer—the site from which the user came. The hyphen and the greater than symbol in the second field are used simply to separate the first and last fields. The last field in the referrer log is the relative URL on the server that the client requested.

In the Common Log Format, no way exists to correlate the entry in the referrer log with entries in the access log. A matching access log entry for the example referrer entry would look something like this, however:

```
pc4.att.net - - [02/Mar/1997:12:37:28  0800] "GET /ci/w2.htm
   HTTP/1.0" 200 7892
```

The Agent Log

The agent log tells you the name and version of the browser that requested a file on your server. The values placed in the agent log are taken from the User_Agent field that all browsers supply in the HTTP header accompanying a file request. Although entries in the agent log don't follow a strict format, a general format for entries is as follows:

```
browser name/version (supplemental information)
```

Entries in an actual agent log look like this:

```
Mozilla/4.0 (Windows 95)
aolbrowser/1.1 InterCon-Web-Library 1.2 (Macintosh, 68K)
Lynx/2-4-2 libwww/unknown
```

By examining the agent log, you can determine the browser name, version, and operating system most used by those visiting your Web site. The most common entry is a reference to Mozilla, which is the code name for Netscape Navigator. Watch out, though: If the Mozilla entry also references compatible or MSIE, the entry is for Microsoft Internet Explorer. The reason for this is that Microsoft Internet Explorer emulates Netscape Navigator under certain circumstances. An agent log entry for Microsoft Internet Explorer may look like this:

```
Mozilla/3.0 (compatible; MSIE 4.0; Macintosh)
```

Together, Netscape Navigator and Microsoft Internet Explorer have about 90 percent of the browser market, which means that most entries in the agent log will pertain to one of these browsers. Beyond Navigator and Internet Explorer is a myriad of other browsers that are used by a small percentage of those browsing the Web. Other entries that you might see in the agent log may refer to America Online's Web browser, the `aolbrowser`, or Lynx, a text-only browser.

You may also see entries for search engines that are indexing your Web site. These entries will reference the search engine wandering your site by name, such as Infoseek, MetaCrawler, or WebCrawler.

Wrapping Up and Looking Ahead

Understanding how logs are used on your server is the first step to getting a bird's eye view of the big picture for your Web site. The most important log is the access log. The entries in the access log provide just about everything you need to determine who is visiting your site and why. Now you'll move on to learn how to use the entries in the access log.

Understanding Visits and Page Views

Now that you know what the access log looks like, you can use this knowledge to put together the big picture for your Web site. The big picture will tell you how many people are visiting, what pages they are reading, how long they stay at the Web site, and more. You will use the big picture to help you improve and promote your Web site.

Wandering through the Log Files

The access log was meant to be wandered through. After all, it is an ASCII text file. For a Web site that is just getting started, you may find that wandering through the entries looking at the domain name of visitors and the files that they access a lot of fun. Before your Web site attracts a following, you can often get a very clear picture of who is visiting and what files they view simply by reading the access log every day.

Finding the Access Log

Because the location of the access log is determined when the server is installed, your access log may be in a totally different location than my access log or anyone else's. The best way to find the access log is to ask your service provider or the Webmaster where this file is located.

When you start to wander the access log, the advantage of having your own domain becomes clear. For anyone with his or her own domain, the access log will be in a separate file that is easy to search and use. This is true regardless of whether you have your own server or you use someone else's. When multiple domains are served by the same Web server, the log usually has a prefix that indicates the domain, such as `tvpress-access-log` for the access log of `www.tvpress.com`. Otherwise, the access log is usually named `access log`.

Lots of people publishing on the Web don't have their own domain. If you have an account with a service provider and do not have your own domain, you will share the access log with everyone else using the Web server. For the access log to be meaningful, you will need to extract entries that pertain to your home pages. The part of this section titled "Extracting Information from the Access Log" explains how to do this.

Reading the Access Log

To read the access log, you can use any standard text editor or word processor. Although viewing the file on the Web server is often the easiest option, you can transfer the file from the Web server to your file system and view it locally. To do this, you use FTP (File Transfer Protocol). If you need help with transferring files, be sure to ask your service provider.

Viewing the access log in a text editor can be useful, especially when you are getting started. Keep in mind, however, that the access log can grow rather quickly. Every entry in the access log eats up about 90 bytes of disk space. This means that if a visitor requests a Web page with eight images, the access log will grow by about 810 bytes. Multiply this by a few page requests and a few visitors every day and you will see that even a Web site with minimal traffic can have a fairly large access log.

Extracting Information from the Access Log

UNIX is the most widely used Web server platform, and most service providers use a UNIX-based Web server. If your service provider uses a UNIX server, you can extract information from the access log using the `grep` command. The basic syntax for this command is as follows:

```
grep what from_where
```

TIP

Mac users, don't despair. The `grep` command is universally popular—so much so that it has been ported to the Mac. You can retrieve a copy of `grep` using one of the following URLs:

`ftp://ftp.ucs.ubc.ca/pub/mac/info-mac/text/egrep.hqx`
`ftp://ftp.hawaii.edu/mirrors/info-mac/text/egrep.hqx`
`ftp://mrcnext.cso.uiuc.edu/pub/info-mac/text/egrep.hqx`

NOTE

As you will see later this morning, egrep is a more powerful version of grep that allows you to match multiple parameters. After you install egrep, you can perform any of the searches described in this section. Be sure to substitute the keyword egrep for grep wherever necessary.

Following the basic syntax for grep, you could search the access log for all entries that reference the page `writing.htm` using this command:

```
grep writing.htm access-log
```

Anyone who uses Windows 3.1, Windows 95, or Windows NT can use the DOS `find` command to extract information from files as well. The syntax for `find` is nearly identical to the syntax for `grep`. The key difference is that double quotation marks must surround the search parameter. The basic syntax for the find command is as follows:

```
find "what" from_where
```

Following the basic syntax for `find`, you can search the access log for all entries that reference the page `writing.htm` using this command:

```
find "writing.htm" access-log
```

To search for multiple items simultaneously, you can use the `egrep` command. When you use `egrep`, you use quotation marks to surround the entire query, and the pipe symbol (|) to separate each item that you are looking for, such as:

```
egrep "writing.htm|writing2.htm" access-log
```

In this example, you are searching the access log for all entries related to `writing.htm` and `writing2.htm`. Be sure that you don't put unnecessary spaces around the pipe symbol, because the server may interpret the spaces literally and search only for occurrences that include the spacing that you specify.

NOTE

● ●

Although you can search for multiple parameters with `egrep` for the Mac, no equivalent exists for the DOS `find` command. A workaround would be to perform consecutive searches of the access log.

● ●

Although `grep` and `egrep` usually print their output to the screen, you can redirect the output to a file using the UNIX redirect command (>).

To redirect a search to a file called save.txt, you could use the following command:

```
grep writing.htm access-log > save.txt
```

DOS understands the redirect command as well. Here is an example that uses the DOS `find` command and then redirects the results of search into a text file:

```
find "writing.htm" access-log > save.txt
```

Often, you may simply want to count the number of times a file has been accessed. You do this by directing the output of the `grep` command through the word count program. The word count program is called `wc`. You use the pipe symbol to connect the `grep` command and the `wc` command, as in the following:

```
grep writing.htm access-log | wc
```

The results that you see will look something like this:

```
7       91      612
```

Forget about the last two numbers and focus on the first number, which is the number of times that the file was accessed.

To count the number of times that a file has been accessed in DOS, you use the `/C` option for the `find` command. The `/C` option tells the `find` command to count the lines in the search result, which gives you the number of entries pertaining to a specific file. You can use the `/C` option as follows:

```
find /C "writing.htm" access-log
```

Hits, Hits, and More Hits

Every time a client requests a file from the Web server, an entry goes into the access log. Each file request is considered to be a hit. As you learned earlier this morning under "Using Web Stats to Understand Your Site's Visitors," the hit is not a very accurate measurement of how many people are visiting your site. This is because recorded hits can be very misleading, especially when you consider that one hit rarely equals one visitor.

Getting Entries from the Log

Listing 2-2 shows a 15-minute slice of entries for an actual access log from the Web site at `www.tvpress.com`. To make the entries easier to follow, I extracted the entries for an entire day and then cut out the entries from 00:00 to about 00:15. The commands that I used to obtain the entries for an entire day and put them in a file are shown in the following example:

```
grep "11/Apr/1997" access-log > $HOME/temp.txt
```

Here, the `grep` command is used to extract all entries containing the string "11/Apr/1997" from a file called `access-log`. Next, I redirected the output of the `grep` command to a file in my home directory called `temp.txt`. To a UNIX computer, the keyword `$HOME` is generally the same as the full path to your directory on the server.

You could perform a similar operation in DOS with the `find` command, as follows:

```
find "11/Apr/1997" access-log > C:/your_directory/temp.txt
```

You will find this sample access log and other examples online at `http://www.tvpress.com/promote/examples/`. The filename is access-log.txt.

As you examine the entries in the access log, note that most of the entries are for files ending in the .gif extension, which designates an image file in GIF format. Note also that all of these entries pertain to three specific domains:

 pc8.att.net

 at1.vl.com

○ 198.23.25.3

Although you could assume that all these entries pertain to three distinct visitors, this isn't always the case. Consider for a moment that any of these fully qualified domain names could belong to a multiuser computer with lots of users online at any given time. In multiuser environments, it is not uncommon for 25, 50, or even 100 users to be using the same host. That said, determining whether the hits belong to more than three specific visitors is very difficult. For now, I assume that the hits belong to three visitors. Rest assured that I discuss visitors in more detail later this morning. Look for the section titled "Zeroing in on the Visit."

Listing 2-2 Entries from an Access Log

```
pc8.att.net - - [11/Apr/1997:00:01:18 -0700] "GET / HTTP/1.0"
   200 8355
pc8.att.net - - [11/Apr/1997:00:01:25 -0700] "GET /ban2.gif
   HTTP/1.0" 200 1373
pc8.att.net - - [11/Apr/1997:00:01:25 -0700] "GET /
   tvpgis2.gif HTTP/1.0" 200 2809
pc8.att.net - - [11/Apr/1997:00:01:25 -0700] "GET /tvpgis.gif
   HTTP/1.0" 200 7923
pc8.att.net - - [11/Apr/1997:00:01:25 -0700] "GET /bu_off.gif
   HTTP/1.0" 200 926
pc8.att.net - - [11/Apr/1997:00:01:29 -0700] "GET /ban1.gif
   HTTP/1.0" 200 1436
pc8.att.net - - [11/Apr/1997:00:01:25 -0700] "GET /bu_on.gif
   HTTP/1.0" 200 933
pc8.att.net - - [11/Apr/1997:00:01:37 -0700] "GET /tvpgis.gif
   HTTP/1.0" 200 7923
pc8.att.net - - [11/Apr/1997:00:01:37 -0700] "GET /ban5.gif
   HTTP/1.0" 200 1407
pc8.att.net - - [11/Apr/1997:00:01:38 -0700] "GET /ban6.gif
   HTTP/1.0" 200 1452
pc8.att.net - - [11/Apr/1997:00:01:39 -0700] "GET /ban7.gif
   HTTP/1.0" 200 1461
pc8.att.net - - [11/Apr/1997:00:01:40 -0700] "GET /ban8.gif
   HTTP/1.0" 200 1400
pc8.att.net - - [11/Apr/1997:00:01:40 -0700] "GET /ban9.gif
   HTTP/1.0" 200 1265
pc8.att.net - - [11/Apr/1997:00:01:42 -0700] "GET /cbox.gif
   HTTP/1.0" 200 662
pc8.att.net - - [11/Apr/1997:00:01:43 -0700] "GET /bu_on.gif
   HTTP/1.0" 200 926
pc8.att.net - - [11/Apr/1997:00:01:44 -0700] "GET /main5b.gif
   HTTP/1.0" 200 1118
```

```
pc8.att.net - - [11/Apr/1997:00:01:45 -0700] "GET /main6b.gif
   HTTP/1.0" 200 1081

pc8.att.net - - [11/Apr/1997:00:01:46 -0700] "GET /main8b.gif
   HTTP/1.0" 200 1088

pc8.att.net - - [11/Apr/1997:00:01:46 -0700] "GET /main7b.gif
   HTTP/1.0" 200 1101

pc8.att.net - - [11/Apr/1997:00:01:46 -0700] "GET /ban10.gif
   HTTP/1.0" 200 1377

pc8.att.net - - [11/Apr/1997:00:01:47 -0700] "GET /fp97.gif
   HTTP/1.0" 200 5306

pc8.att.net - - [11/Apr/1997:00:01:48 -0700] "GET /banner.gif
   HTTP/1.0" 200 1421

pc8.att.net - - [11/Apr/1997:00:01:49 -0700] "GET /main4b.gif
   HTTP/1.0" 200 1053

pc8.att.net - - [11/Apr/1997:00:01:50 -0700] "GET /
   main10b.gif HTTP/1.0" 200 1027

pc8.att.net - - [11/Apr/1997:00:01:53 -0700] "GET /main9b.gif
   HTTP/1.0" 200 1089

pc8.att.net - - [11/Apr/1997:00:01:55 -0700] "GET /ban4.gif
   HTTP/1.0" 200 1356

pc8.att.net - - [11/Apr/1997:00:01:56 -0700] "GET /main2b.gif
   HTTP/1.0" 200 1113

pc8.att.net - - [11/Apr/1997:00:01:57 -0700] "GET /main3b.gif
   HTTP/1.0" 200 1059

pc8.att.net - - [11/Apr/1997:00:01:58 -0700] "GET /ban3.gif
   HTTP/1.0" 200 1372

pc8.att.net - - [11/Apr/1997:00:01:59 -0700] "GET /mainb.gif
   HTTP/1.0" 200 1081

pc8.att.net - - [11/Apr/1997:00:02:00 -0700] "GET /wpupr.gif
   HTTP/1.0" 200 6376

pc8.att.net - - [11/Apr/1997:00:02:07 -0700] "GET /wpd.gif
   HTTP/1.0" 200 10423

pc8.att.net - - [11/Apr/1997:00:03:28 -0700] "GET /vpjic.html
   HTTP/1.0" 200 7256

pc8.att.net - - [11/Apr/1997:00:03:35 -0700] "GET /jban6.gif
   HTTP/1.0" 200 1508

pc8.att.net - - [11/Apr/1997:00:03:35 -0700] "GET /jban5.gif
   HTTP/1.0" 200 1844
```

```
pc8.att.net - - [11/Apr/1997:00:03:35 -0700] "GET /jban3.gif
    HTTP/1.0" 200 1505
pc8.att.net - - [11/Apr/1997:00:03:35 -0700] "GET /jban1.gif
    HTTP/1.0" 200 2134
pc8.att.net - - [11/Apr/1997:00:03:35 -0700] "GET /jban2.gif
    HTTP/1.0" 200 1978
pc8.att.net - - [11/Apr/1997:00:03:35 -0700] "GET /jban4.gif
    HTTP/1.0" 200 1975
pc8.att.net - - [11/Apr/1997:00:03:40 -0700] "GET /jban8.gif
    HTTP/1.0" 200 2228
pc8.att.net - - [11/Apr/1997:00:03:44 -0700] "GET /jban10.gif
    HTTP/1.0" 200 1701
pc8.att.net - - [11/Apr/1997:00:03:44 -0700] "GET /jban12.gif
    HTTP/1.0" 200 2188
pc8.att.net - - [11/Apr/1997:00:03:48 -0700] "GET /
    jbanner.gif HTTP/1.0" 200 1643
pc8.att.net - - [11/Apr/1997:00:03:48 -0700] "GET /job7.gif
    HTTP/1.0" 200 1139
pc8.att.net - - [11/Apr/1997:00:03:49 -0700] "GET /job8.gif
    HTTP/1.0" 200 1047
pc8.att.net - - [11/Apr/1997:00:03:52 -0700] "GET /job9.gif
    HTTP/1.0" 200 1099
pc8.att.net - - [11/Apr/1997:00:03:53 -0700] "GET /job11.gif
    HTTP/1.0" 200 1124
pc8.att.net - - [11/Apr/1997:00:03:54 -0700] "GET /jban7.gif
    HTTP/1.0" 200 1733
pc8.att.net - - [11/Apr/1997:00:03:56 -0700] "GET /jban11.gif
    HTTP/1.0" 200 1643
pc8.att.net - - [11/Apr/1997:00:03:56 -0700] "GET /job10.gif
    HTTP/1.0" 200 1073
pc8.att.net - - [11/Apr/1997:00:03:56 -0700] "GET /job12.gif
    HTTP/1.0" 200 1119
pc8.att.net - - [11/Apr/1997:00:03:57 -0700] "GET /job3.gif
    HTTP/1.0" 200 1075
pc8.att.net - - [11/Apr/1997:00:04:00 -0700] "GET /job5.gif
    HTTP/1.0" 200 1164
pc8.att.net - - [11/Apr/1997:00:04:01 -0700] "GET /mstats.gif
    HTTP/1.0" 200 6958
```

```
pc8.att.net - - [11/Apr/1997:00:04:06 -0700] "GET /job4.gif
   HTTP/1.0" 200 1132

pc8.att.net - - [11/Apr/1997:00:04:08 -0700] "GET /job1.gif
   HTTP/1.0" 200 1154

pc8.att.net - - [11/Apr/1997:00:04:08 -0700] "GET /jicttl.gif
   HTTP/1.0" 200 20288

pc8.att.net - - [11/Apr/1997:00:04:09 -0700] "GET /job2.gif
   HTTP/1.0" 200 1152

pc8.att.net - - [11/Apr/1997:00:04:16 -0700] "GET /job6.gif
   HTTP/1.0" 200 1095

pc8.att.net - - [11/Apr/1997:00:04:19 -0700] "GET /jban9.gif
   HTTP/1.0" 200 1997

at1.vl.com - - [11/Apr/1997:00:04:57 -0700] "GET /idn/cissue/
   resmul.htm HTTP/1.0" 200 396

pc8.att.nct - - [11/Apr/1997:00:05:04 -0700] "GET /vpepc.html
   HTTP/1.0" 200 2741

at1.vl.com - - [11/Apr/1997:00:05:04 -0700] "GET /idn/
   idnttl3.gif HTTP/1.0" 200 4612

pc8.att.net - - [11/Apr/1997:00:05:10 -0700] "GET /epc.html
   HTTP/1.0" 200 501

pc8.att.net - - [11/Apr/1997:00:05:10 -0700] "GET /
   vpepc2.html HTTP/1.0" 200 544

pc8.att.net - - [11/Apr/1997:00:05:10 -0700] "GET /
   ziptour.html HTTP/1.0" 200 526

pc8.att.net - - [11/Apr/1997:00:05:13 -0700] "GET /
   crights.gif HTTP/1.0" 200 5173

pc8.att.net - - [11/Apr/1997:00:05:13 -0700] "GET /
   epubunl2.gif HTTP/1.0" 200 2406

pc8.att.net - - [11/Apr/1997:00:05:19 -0700] "GET /mail.gif
   HTTP/1.0" 200 962

pc8.att.net - - [11/Apr/1997:00:05:29 -0700] "GET /zip2.html
   HTTP/1.0" 200 470

pc8.att.net - - [11/Apr/1997:00:05:34 -0700] "GET /
   vpepc3.html HTTP/1.0" 200 728

at1.vl.com - - [11/Apr/1997:00:05:34 -0700] "GET /idn/
   idnfp.htm HTTP/1.0" 200 7610

pc8.att.net - - [11/Apr/1997:00:05:37 -0700] "GET /
   epubunl2.gif HTTP/1.0" 200 2406
```

```
pc8.att.net - - [11/Apr/1997:00:05:43 -0700] "GET /rote.html
   HTTP/1.0" 200 333
pc8.att.net - - [11/Apr/1997:00:05:46 -0700] "GET /
   vpsttl1.gif HTTP/1.0" 200 14361
at1.vl.com - - [11/Apr/1997:00:05:49 -0700] "GET /idn/bg1.gif
   HTTP/1.0" 200 612
at1.vl.com - - [11/Apr/1997:00:05:49 -0700] "GET /idn/
   glnet.gif HTTP/1.0" 200 7425
at1.vl.com - - [11/Apr/1997:00:05:49 -0700] "GET /idn/
   glmail.gif HTTP/1.0" 200 7501
pc8.att.net - - [11/Apr/1997:00:05:53 -0700] "GET /zip3.html
   HTTP/1.0" 200 281
at1.vl.com - - [11/Apr/1997:00:05:56 -0700] "GET /idn/
   site2.gif HTTP/1.0" 200 3097
at1.vl.com - - [11/Apr/1997:00:05:57 -0700] "GET /idn/
   site1.gif HTTP/1.0" 200 1487
pc8.att.net - - [11/Apr/1997:00:06:00 -0700] "GET /wgttl.jpg
   HTTP/1.0" 200 20594
pc8.att.net - - [11/Apr/1997:00:06:02 -0700] "GET /
   vpepc4.html HTTP/1.0" 200 679
at1.vl.com - - [11/Apr/1997:00:06:07 -0700] "GET /idn/cal.gif
   HTTP/1.0" 200 6713
at1.vl.com - - [11/Apr/1997:00:06:15 -0700] "GET /idn/wpd.gif
   HTTP/1.0" 200 10423
pc8.att.net - - [11/Apr/1997:00:06:18 -0700] "GET /
   epubunl2.gif HTTP/1.0" 304 -
at1.vl.com - - [11/Apr/1997:00:06:18 -0700] "GET /idn/
   wpupr.gif HTTP/1.0" 200 6376
pc8.att.net - - [11/Apr/1997:00:06:35 -0700] "GET /
   vpepc5.html HTTP/1.0" 200 582
at1.vl.com - - [11/Apr/1997:00:06:51 -0700] "GET /idn/
   fp97.gif HTTP/1.0" 200 5306
pc8.att.net - - [11/Apr/1997:00:06:58 -0700] "GET /
   vpepc6.html HTTP/1.0" 200 668
pc8.att.net - - [11/Apr/1997:00:07:31 -0700] "GET /rotc2.html
   HTTP/1.0" 200 331
pc8.att.net - - [11/Apr/1997:00:07:34 -0700] "GET /
   vpsttl2.gif HTTP/1.0" 200 14108
```

```
pc8.att.net - - [11/Apr/1997:00:07:47 -0700] "GET /
  vpepc5.html HTTP/1.0" 304 -
pc8.att.net - - [11/Apr/1997:00:08:18 -0700] "GET /
  vpepc6.html HTTP/1.0" 304 -
198.23.25.3 - - [11/Apr/1997:00:09:14 -0700] "GET /idn/
  cissue/resmul.htm HTTP/1.0" 200 4516
198.23.25.3 - - [11/Apr/1997:00:09:20 -0700] "GET /idn/
  bg2.gif HTTP/1.0" 200 18079
198.23.25.3 - - [11/Apr/1997:00:09:23 -0700] "GET /idn/
  colttl3.gif HTTP/1.0" 200 1127
pc8.att.net - - [11/Apr/1997:00:09:27 -0700] "GET /zip2.html
  HTTP/1.0" 304 -
198.23.25.3 - - [11/Apr/1997:00:09:29 -0700] "GET /idn/
  resttl2.gif HTTP/1.0" 200 3730
pc8.att.net - - [11/Apr/1997:00:09:32 -0700] "GET /
  vpepc3.html HTTP/1.0" 304 -
pc8.att.net - - [11/Apr/1997:00:09:40 -0700] "GET /rote.html
  HTTP/1.0" 304 -
pc8.att.net - - [11/Apr/1997:00:09:57 -0700] "GET /
  vpsttl1.gif HTTP/1.0" 304 -
pc8.att.net - - [11/Apr/1997:00:10:13 -0700] "GET /rote2.html
  HTTP/1.0" 304 -
pc8.att.net - - [11/Apr/1997:00:10:32 -0700] "GET /
  joboppmenu.html HTTP/1.0" 200 1297
pc8.att.net - - [11/Apr/1997:00:10:32 -0700] "GET /
  tvpbannertop.html HTTP/1.0" 200 132
pc8.att.net - - [11/Apr/1997:00:10:32 -0700] "GET /
  tvpbannerbot.html HTTP/1.0" 200 607
pc8.att.net - - [11/Apr/1997:00:10:27 -0700] "GET /
  joboppframes.html HTTP/1.0" 200 1592
pc8.att.net - - [11/Apr/1997:00:10:34 -0700] "GET /tvp64.gif
  HTTP/1.0" 200 3231
pc8.att.net - - [11/Apr/1997:00:10:34 -0700] "GET /tvp192.gif
  HTTP/1.0" 200 16648
at1.vl.com - - [11/Apr/1997:00:10:37 -0700] "GET /idn/bio/
  bioerev.html HTTP/1.0" 200 6027
pc8.att.net - - [11/Apr/1997:00:11:04 -0700] "GET /
  jscience.html HTTP/1.0" 200 2508
```

```
pc8.att.net - - [11/Apr/1997:00:11:22 -0700] "GET /jintl.html
   HTTP/1.0" 200 2122

pc8.att.net - - [11/Apr/1997:00:12:53 -0700] "GET /
   jdisab.html HTTP/1.0" 200 1197

pc8.att.net - - [11/Apr/1997:00:13:21 -0700] "GET /tvpgis.gif
   HTTP/1.0" 200 7923

pc8.att.net - - [11/Apr/1997:00:13:22 -0700] "GET /tvpgis.gif
   HTTP/1.0" 304 -

198.23.25.3 - - [11/Apr/1997:00:14:39 -0700] "GET /idn/
   idnfp.htm HTTP/1.0" 304 -
```

Examining Log Entries

By looking at individual hits in the log, you can get a better understanding of what is happening on the server. This section follows one of the users through the log. For easy reference, I call this user Joe, as in Joe Web Surfer. Joe's first hit is a request for the top-level home page:

```
pc8.att.net - - [11/Apr/1997:00:01:18 -0700] "GET / HTTP/1.0"
   200 8355
```

You know this because of the request for the file called /, which is the default document in the main directory at the Web site. In examining this hit, Joe entered the URL http://www.tvpress.com/ into his browser and the server logged the file request in the access log at 00:01:18. From the status code 200, you know that the document was transferred successfully. You also know that 8,355 bytes were transferred.

If you examine the source for the Web page at http://www.tvpress.com/, you will see that it contains many images. Some of these images are displayed when the page is loaded. Other images are hidden and are displayed only when the user performs a specific action, such as moving the mouse pointer over an image linked to another Web page. In all, 31 entries in the access log pertain to this page, as follows:

```
pc8.att.net - - [11/Apr/1997:00:01:25 -0700] "GET /ban2.gif
   HTTP/1.0" 200 1373

pc8.att.net - - [11/Apr/1997:00:01:25 -0700] "GET /
   tvpgis2.gif HTTP/1.0" 200 2809
```

```
pc8.att.net    - - [11/Apr/1997:00:01:25 -0700] "GET /tvpgis.gif
  HTTP/1.0" 200 7923
pc8.att.net - - [11/Apr/1997:00:01:25 -0700] "GET /bu_off.gif
  HTTP/1.0" 200 926
pc8.att.net - - [11/Apr/1997:00:01:29 -0700] "GET /ban1.gif
  HTTP/1.0" 200 1436
pc8.att.net - - [11/Apr/1997:00:01:25 -0700] "GET /bu_on.gif
  HTTP/1.0" 200 933
pc8.att.net - - [11/Apr/1997:00:01:37 -0700] "GET /tvpgis.gif
  HTTP/1.0" 200 7923
pc8.att.net - - [11/Apr/1997:00:01:37 -0700] "GET /ban5.gif
  HTTP/1.0" 200 1407
pc8.att.net - - [11/Apr/1997:00:01:38 -0700] "GET /ban6.gif
  HTTP/1.0" 200 1452
pc8.att.net - - [11/Apr/1997:00:01:39 -0700] "GET /ban7.gif
  HTTP/1.0" 200 1461
pc8.att.net    - [11/Apr/1997:00:01:40 -0700] "GET /ban8.gif
  HTTP/1.0" 200 1400
pc8.att.net - - [11/Apr/1997:00:01:40 -0700] "GET /ban9.gif
  HTTP/1.0" 200 1265
pc8.att.net - - [11/Apr/1997:00:01:42 -0700] "GET /cbox.gif
  HTTP/1.0" 200 662
pc8.att.net - - [11/Apr/1997:00:01:43 -0700] "GET /bu_on.gif
  HTTP/1.0" 200 926
pc8.att.net - - [11/Apr/1997:00:01:44 -0700] "GET /main5b.gif
  HTTP/1.0" 200 1118
pc8.att.net - - [11/Apr/1997:00:01:45 -0700] "GET /main6b.gif
  HTTP/1.0" 200 1081
pc8.att.net - - [11/Apr/1997:00:01:46 -0700] "GET /main8b.gif
  HTTP/1.0" 200 1088
pc8.att.net - - [11/Apr/1997:00:01:46 -0700] "GET /main7b.gif
  HTTP/1.0" 200 1101
pc8.att.net - - [11/Apr/1997:00:01:46 -0700] "GET /ban10.gif
  HTTP/1.0" 200 1377
pc8.att.net - - [11/Apr/1997:00:01:47 -0700] "GET /fp97.gif
  HTTP/1.0" 200 5306
pc8.att.net - - [11/Apr/1997:00:01:48 -0700] "GET /banner.gif
  HTTP/1.0" 200 1421
```

```
pc8.att.net - - [11/Apr/1997:00:01:49 -0700] "GET /main4b.gif
   HTTP/1.0" 200 1053
pc8.att.net - - [11/Apr/1997:00:01:50 -0700] "GET /
   main10b.gif HTTP/1.0" 200 1027
pc8.att.net - - [11/Apr/1997:00:01:53 -0700] "GET /main9b.gif
   HTTP/1.0" 200 1089
pc8.att.net - - [11/Apr/1997:00:01:55 -0700] "GET /ban4.gif
   HTTP/1.0" 200 1356
pc8.att.net - - [11/Apr/1997:00:01:56 -0700] "GET /main2b.gif
   HTTP/1.0" 200 1113
pc8.att.net - - [11/Apr/1997:00:01:57 -0700] "GET /main3b.gif
   HTTP/1.0" 200 1059
pc8.att.net - - [11/Apr/1997:00:01:58 -0700] "GET /ban3.gif
   HTTP/1.0" 200 1372
pc8.att.net - - [11/Apr/1997:00:01:59 -0700] "GET /mainb.gif
   HTTP/1.0" 200 1081
pc8.att.net - - [11/Apr/1997:00:02:00 -0700] "GET /wpupr.gif
   HTTP/1.0" 200 6376
pc8.att.net - - [11/Apr/1997:00:02:07 -0700] "GET /wpd.gif
   HTTP/1.0" 200 10423
```

By putting the image hits together with the page hit, you can see how long Joe's browser took to finish loading the page. The first request had a time stamp of

```
[11/Apr/1997:00:01:18 -0700]
```

The last request for this page had a time stamp of

```
[11/Apr/1997:00:02:07 -0700]
```

By calculating the difference between the time stamps, you can see that 49 seconds elapsed between the first file request and the last file request. To see how long the page actually took to load completely, you need to figure out how long the final image took to load. Based on previous entries in the log, say that the final image took nine seconds to load, which puts the total load time for the page at 58 seconds.

On the Web, 59 seconds is a lifetime. Fortunately for this visitor, the page has a lot of text and most of the graphics are at the bottom of the page.

TIP

For the hard-core techies in the crowd, you can tell the exact throughput that this user got by totaling the number of bytes transferred and then dividing by the number of seconds that the total transfer took. For this example, the formula is as follows:

70337 / 58 = 1213 bytes per second

Using the rate of 1213 bytes per second, you can also figure out the modem speed of the transfer, which in turn can be used to approximate what type of modem Joe has. Knowing that a byte has 8 bits, you can figure the modem rate as follows:

1213 x 8 = 9704 bps (9.7 kbps)

Wow, Joe is probably using a 9600-bps modem!

Next, Joe selected the link to the Internet Job Center at `http://www.tvpress.com/vpjic.html`. The entry in the log for this hit is the following:

```
pc8.att.net - - [11/Apr/1997:00:03:28 -0700] "GET /vpjic.html
  HTTP/1.0" 200 7256
```

Here, Joe selected a hypertext link that brought him to the page called `vpjic.html`. Although Joe didn't enter the actual URL, you know that the URL to the page is `http://www.tvpress.com/vpjic.html`. The server logged the file request in the access log at `00:03:28`. The status code `200` tells you that the document was transferred successfully. You also know that `7,256` bytes were transferred.

By examining the time difference between the previous page request and this page request, you can learn how long Joe stayed on the top-level home page. The top-level home page was requested at

`[11/Apr/1997:00:01:18 -0700]`

The page for the Internet Job Center was requested at

`[11/Apr/1997:00:03:28 -0700]`

This information shows that Joe spent 2 minutes and 10 seconds on the home page. Granted, part of this time was probably spent waiting for graphics to load, but the total page viewing time is still meaningful, especially if the page has a lot of text.

The top-level page for the Internet Job Center is a graphics-intensive page with very little text that isn't part of a graphic image. The next 27 entries in the access log pertain to graphics in this page:

```
pc8.att.net - - [11/Apr/1997:00:03:35 -0700] "GET /jban6.gif
   HTTP/1.0" 200 1508
pc8.att.net - - [11/Apr/1997:00:03:35 -0700] "GET /jban5.gif
   HTTP/1.0" 200 1844
pc8.att.net - - [11/Apr/1997:00:03:35 -0700] "GET /jban3.gif
   HTTP/1.0" 200 1505
pc8.att.net - - [11/Apr/1997:00:03:35 -0700] "GET /jban1.gif
   HTTP/1.0" 200 2134
pc8.att.net - - [11/Apr/1997:00:03:35 -0700] "GET /jban2.gif
   HTTP/1.0" 200 1978
pc8.att.net - - [11/Apr/1997:00:03:35 -0700] "GET /jban4.gif
   HTTP/1.0" 200 1975
pc8.att.net - - [11/Apr/1997:00:03:40 -0700] "GET /jban8.gif
   HTTP/1.0" 200 2228
pc8.att.net - - [11/Apr/1997:00:03:44 -0700] "GET /jban10.gif
   HTTP/1.0" 200 1701
pc8.att.net - - [11/Apr/1997:00:03:44 -0700] "GET /jban12.gif
   HTTP/1.0" 200 2188
pc8.att.net - - [11/Apr/1997:00:03:48 -0700] "GET /
   jbanner.gif HTTP/1.0" 200 1643
pc8.att.net - - [11/Apr/1997:00:03:48 -0700] "GET /job7.gif
   HTTP/1.0" 200 1139
pc8.att.net - - [11/Apr/1997:00:03:49 -0700] "GET /job8.gif
   HTTP/1.0" 200 1047
pc8.att.net - - [11/Apr/1997:00:03:52 -0700] "GET /job9.gif
   HTTP/1.0" 200 1099
pc8.att.net - - [11/Apr/1997:00:03:53 -0700] "GET /job11.gif
   HTTP/1.0" 200 1124
pc8.att.net - - [11/Apr/1997:00:03:54 -0700] "GET /jban7.gif
   HTTP/1.0" 200 1733
pc8.att.net - - [11/Apr/1997:00:03:56 -0700] "GET /jban11.gif
   HTTP/1.0" 200 1643
pc8.att.net - - [11/Apr/1997:00:03:56 -0700] "GET /job10.gif
   HTTP/1.0" 200 1073
```

```
pc8.att.net    [11/Apr/1997:00:03:56 -0700] "GET /job12.gif
   HTTP/1.0" 200 1119

pc8.att.net - - [11/Apr/1997:00:03:57 -0700] "GET /job3.gif
   HTTP/1.0" 200 1075

pc8.att.net - - [11/Apr/1997:00:04:00 -0700] "GET /job5.gif
   HTTP/1.0" 200 1164

pc8.att.net - - [11/Apr/1997:00:04:01 -0700] "GET /mstats.gif
   HIIP/1.0" 200 6958

pc8.att.net - - [11/Apr/1997:00:04:06 -0700] "GET /job4.gif
   HIIP/1.0" 200 1132

pc8.att.net - - [11/Apr/1997:00:04:08 -0700] "GET /job1.gif
   HTTP/1.0" 200 1154

pc8.att.net - - [11/Apr/1997:00:04:08 -0700] "GET /jicttl.gif
   HTTP/1.0" 200 20288

pc8.att.net - - [11/Apr/1997:00:04:09 -0700] "GET /job2.gif
   HTTP/1.0" 200 1152

pc8.att.net    [11/Apr/1997:00:04:16 -0700] "GET /job6.gif
   HTTP/1.0" 200 1095

pc8.att.net - - [11/Apr/1997:00:04:19 -0700] "GET /jban9.gif
   HTTP/1.0" 200 1997
```

By reviewing the entries for the Internet Job Center page, you can see that the total loading time is about 54 seconds. The next page request comes at 00:05:04, when Joe requests the page shown in this log entry:

```
pc8.att.net - - [11/Apr/1997:00:05:04 -0700] "GET /vpepc.html
   HTTP/1.0" 200 2741
```

When you determine the time difference between the page requests, you see that Joe spent one minute and 36 seconds at the Internet Job Center page. Although this may not seem like a long time, the top-level page for the Internet Job Center is really just a graphical doorway to the job center's resources, such as the page at vpepc.html.

As you continue to follow Joe through the Web site, you see lots of page hits in rapid succession. The primary reason for this is that vpepc.html is a frame-enhanced page with three frames. The loading of the frames is logged with these entries:

```
pc8.att.net - - [11/Apr/1997:00:05:10 -0700] "GET /epc.html
   HTTP/1.0" 200 501
```

```
pc8.att.net - - [11/Apr/1997:00:05:10 -0700] "GET /
   vpepc2.html HTTP/1.0" 200 544

pc8.att.net - - [11/Apr/1997:00:05:10 -0700] "GET /
   ziptour.html HTTP/1.0" 200 526
```

Graphic images in those three frames are logged with these entries:

```
pc8.att.net - - [11/Apr/1997:00:05:13 -0700] "GET /
   crights.gif HTTP/1.0" 200 5173

pc8.att.net - - [11/Apr/1997:00:05:13 -0700] "GET /
   epubun12.gif HTTP/1.0" 200 2406

pc8.att.net - - [11/Apr/1997:00:05:19 -0700] "GET /mail.gif
   HTTP/1.0" 200 962
```

The page at vpepc.html also uses client pull to create a rolling slide show. *Client pull* is a technology that allows you to tell a browser to load a specific file at a specific time. All these entries in the log are for slides—pages and their images—in the slide show:

```
pc8.att.net - - [11/Apr/1997:00:05:29 -0700] "GET /zip2.html
   HTTP/1.0" 200 470

pc8.att.net - - [11/Apr/1997:00:05:34 -0700] "GET /
   vpepc3.html HTTP/1.0" 200 728

pc8.att.net - - [11/Apr/1997:00:05:37 -0700] "GET /
   epubun12.gif HTTP/1.0" 200 2406

pc8.att.net - - [11/Apr/1997:00:05:43 -0700] "GET /rote.html
   HTTP/1.0" 200 333

pc8.att.net - - [11/Apr/1997:00:05:46 -0700] "GET /
   vpsttl1.gif HTTP/1.0" 200 14361

pc8.att.net - - [11/Apr/1997:00:05:53 -0700] "GET /zip3.html
   HTTP/1.0" 200 281

pc8.att.net - - [11/Apr/1997:00:06:00 -0700] "GET /wgttl.jpg
   HTTP/1.0" 200 20594

pc8.att.net - - [11/Apr/1997:00:06:02 -0700] "GET /
   vpepc4.html HTTP/1.0" 200 679

pc8.att.net - - [11/Apr/1997:00:06:18 -0700] "GET /
   epubun12.gif HTTP/1.0" 304 -

pc8.att.net - - [11/Apr/1997:00:06:35 -0700] "GET /
   vpepc5.html HTTP/1.0" 200 582

pc8.att.net - - [11/Apr/1997:00:06:58 -0700] "GET /
   vpepc6.html HTTP/1.0" 200 668
```

```
pc8.att.net - - [11/Apr/1997:00:07:31 -0700] "GET /rote2.html
  HTTP/1.0" 200 331

pc8.att.net - - [11/Apr/1997:00:07:34 -0700] "GET /
  vpsttl2.gif HTTP/1.0" 200 14108

pc8.att.net - - [11/Apr/1997:00:07:47 -0700] "GET /
  vpepc5.html HTTP/1.0" 304 -

pc8.att.net - - [11/Apr/1997:00:08:18 -0700] "GET /
  vpepc6.html HTTP/1.0" 304 -

pc8.att.net - - [11/Apr/1997:00:09:27 -0700] "GET /zip2.html
  HTTP/1.0" 304 -

pc8.att.net - - [11/Apr/1997:00:09:32 -0700] "GET /
  vpepc3.html HTTP/1.0" 304 -

pc8.att.net - - [11/Apr/1997:00:09:40 -0700] "GET /rote.html
  HTTP/1.0" 304 -

pc8.att.net - - [11/Apr/1997:00:09:57 -0700] "GET /
  vpsttl1.gif HTTP/1.0" 304 -

pc8.att.net - - [11/Apr/1997:00:10:13 -0700] "GET /rote2.html
  HTTP/1.0" 304 -
```

When you examine the hits for the slide show, note the status code 304 that appears in later entries. Here, Joe's browser is requesting a file, but because the file hasn't been modified since it was last viewed, the browser loads the file from its file or memory cache.

Joe spends quite a bit of time viewing the slide show before moving on. Joe accessed the slide show at 00:05:04 when he followed the link to vpepc.html; not until 00:10:27 did he move on to a new area of the Web site. Thus, the total time spent viewing the slide show was 5 minutes, 23 seconds.

The next page request is logged with this entry:

```
pc8.att.net - - [11/Apr/1997:00:10:27 -0700] "GET /
  joboppframes.html HTTP/1.0" 200 1592
```

If you view the entry without understanding how the site is organized, you miss the fact that there is no way to get from the slide show to the job opportunities page at the Internet Job Center. So, what happened?

Well, Joe probably pressed the Back button in his browser's menu (older browsers don't move back through frames) and jumped back to the top-level page of the Internet Job Center. Because this page was completely loaded from cache, no log entry occurred. The job opportunities page is another frame-enhanced page, so the next three requests for HTML documents pertain to this single page:

```
pc8.att.net - - [11/Apr/1997:00:10:32 -0700] "GET /
  tvpbannertop.html HTTP/1.0" 200 132
pc8.att.net - - [11/Apr/1997:00:10:32 -0700] "GET /
  tvpbannerbot.html HTTP/1.0" 200 607
pc8.att.net - - [11/Apr/1997:00:10:32 -0700] "GET /
  joboppmenu.html HTTP/1.0" 200 1297
```

These pages contain only two graphics:

```
pc8.att.net - - [11/Apr/1997:00:10:34 -0700] "GET /tvp64.gif
  HTTP/1.0" 200 3231
pc8.att.net - - [11/Apr/1997:00:10:34 -0700] "GET /tvp192.gif
  HTTP/1.0" 200 16648
```

● ●

NOTE If you examine the original log entries, you will see that the request for the `joboppframes.html` page is logged after the requests for the frames that are a part of the page. The reason for this is that Joe's browser got ahead of itself and started loading the pages before it finished with the main page.

● ●

The left side frame in the job opportunities page acts as a menu. When you click on links in the side frame, pages are loaded into the main frame to the right. The log entries show that Joe selected three of the menu options and that two images were associated with the last option:

```
pc8.att.net - - [11/Apr/1997:00:11:04 -0700] "GET /
  jscience.html HTTP/1.0" 200 2508
pc8.att.net - - [11/Apr/1997:00:11:22 -0700] "GET /jintl.html
  HTTP/1.0" 200 2122
pc8.att.net - - [11/Apr/1997:00:12:53 -0700] "GET /
  jdisab.html HTTP/1.0" 200 1197
pc8.att.net - - [11/Apr/1997:00:13:21 -0700] "GET /tvpgis.gif
  HTTP/1.0" 200 7923
pc8.att.net - - [11/Apr/1997:00:13:22 -0700] "GET /tvpgis.gif
  HTTP/1.0" 304 -
```

Because the menu pages contain links to job-related Web sites and the log shows no more entries for this user, it is safe to assume that Joe followed one of the links and wandered off into cyberspace. Looking back, you can see that this user really put the Web site to the test. The log shows about 100 hits for this particular user. By figuring the time difference between the first hit at 00:01:18 and the last hit at 00:13:22, you can see that Joe spent more than 12 minutes browsing the Web site.

Although individual hits aren't good indicators of a site's popularity, groups of hits do provide insight into what is happening at your Web site. The first few times that you read the access log, you may want to take the time to really understand what you see. To do this, you can use the techniques I've used in this section. After you gain a clearer picture of what is happening at your Web site, you probably won't want to spend much time reviewing individual entries in the log, which is why later parts of this section focus less on individual entries and more on the bigger picture.

Assessing Page Views

Another statistic that Web publishers often track is the page view. A *page view* is an entry in the access log that belongs to a document file, such as a Web page. When you search the log for page views, you get a more accurate picture of the popularity of your Web site and the resources that people find interesting. You can use this information to help you determine how to market and promote your Web site. Tracking page views can also be an enlightening experience, especially when you discover that the most visited pages aren't the pages that you expected to be the most popular.

Obtaining Page Views

Most page views at a Web site pertain to requests for HTML documents. You can extract page views for Web pages from the access log using commands similar to the following:

```
grep .htm access-log
```

or

```
find ".htm" access-log
```

Here, I searched for document files ending in the .htm extension. Because `grep` and `find` use pattern matching, these commands also return entries for filenames that end in the .html extension.

Unfortunately, a search for document files ending in the .htm and .html extensions misses page accesses for default documents in directories. As you may remember, default documents are logged as / or `directory_name/`. Because / is used to designate directories within the file system, however, you need to find a way to search exclusively for default documents. To do this, you follow the / with a space, such as:

```
grep "/ " access.log
```

To put the search for HTML documents and default documents together, you need to use the `egrep` command in UNIX, such as:

```
egrep ".htm|/ " access-log > save2.txt
```

NOTE The space between the slash and the quotation mark is important. If you do not use the space, you will get matches every time an entry has a directory path.

In DOS, you can perform a similar search using a clever workaround. The first step is to perform the search for files ending in the .htm extension and then put the results in a file:

```
find ".htm" access-log > save2.txt
```

Then, you search the access log for default documents and append the results to the end of the same file:

```
find "/ " access-log >> save2.txt
```

TIP The append command (>>) works in both DOS and UNIX.

If you perform the `egrep` or `find` search against the `access-log.txt` file, your results will be similar to those shown in Listing 2-3.

Listing 2-3   Page Views in the Access Log

```
pc8.att.net - - [11/Apr/1997:00:01:18  0700] "GET / HTTP/1.0"
   200 8355

pc8.att.net - - [11/Apr/1997:00:03:28 -0700] "GET /vpjic.html
   HTTP/1.0" 200 7256

at1.vl.com - - [11/Apr/1997:00:04:57 -0700] "GET /idn/cissue/
   resmul.htm HTTP/1.0" 200 396

pc8.att.net - - [11/Apr/1997:00:05:04 -0700] "GET /vpepc.html
   HTTP/1.0" 200 2741

pc8.att.net - - [11/Apr/1997:00:05:10 -0700] "GET /epc.html
   HTTP/1.0" 200 501

pc8.att.net - - [11/Apr/1997:00:05:10 -0700] "GET /
   vpepc2.html HTTP/1.0" 200 544

pc8.att.net - - [11/Apr/1997:00:05:10 -0700] "GET /
   ziptour.html HTTP/1.0" 200 526

pc8.att.net - - [11/Apr/1997:00:05:29 -0700] "GET /zip2.html
   HTTP/1.0" 200 470

pc8.att.net - - [11/Apr/1997:00:05:34 -0700] "GET /
   vpepc3.html HTTP/1.0" 200 728

at1.vl.com - - [11/Apr/1997:00:05:34 -0700] "GET /idn/
   idnfp.htm HTTP/1.0" 200 7610

pc8.att.net - - [11/Apr/1997:00:05:43 -0700] "GET /rote.html
   HTTP/1.0" 200 333

pc8.att.net - - [11/Apr/1997:00:05:53 -0700] "GET /zip3.html
   HTTP/1.0" 200 281

pc8.att.net - - [11/Apr/1997:00:06:02 -0700] "GET /
   vpepc4.html HTTP/1.0" 200 679

pc8.att.net - - [11/Apr/1997:00:06:35 -0700] "GET /
   vpepc5.html HTTP/1.0" 200 582

pc8.att.net - - [11/Apr/1997:00:06:58 -0700] "GET /
   vpepc6.html HTTP/1.0" 200 668

pc8.att.net - - [11/Apr/1997:00:07:31 -0700] "GET /rote2.html
   HTTP/1.0" 200 331

pc8.att.net - - [11/Apr/1997:00:07:47 -0700] "GET /
   vpepc5.html HTTP/1.0" 304 -

pc8.att.net - - [11/Apr/1997:00:08:18 -0700] "GET /
   vpepc6.html HTTP/1.0" 304 -
```

```
198.23.25.3 - - [11/Apr/1997:00:09:14 -0700] "GET /idn/
   cissue/resmul.htm HTTP/1.0" 200 4516
pc8.att.net - - [11/Apr/1997:00:09:27 -0700] "GET /zip2.html
   HTTP/1.0" 304 -
pc8.att.net - - [11/Apr/1997:00:09:32 -0700] "GET /
   vpepc3.html HTTP/1.0" 304 -
pc8.att.net - - [11/Apr/1997:00:09:40 -0700] "GET /rote.html
   HTTP/1.0" 304 -
pc8.att.net - - [11/Apr/1997:00:10:13 -0700] "GET /rote2.html
   HTTP/1.0" 304 -
pc8.att.net - - [11/Apr/1997:00:10:32 -0700] "GET /
   joboppmenu.html HTTP/1.0" 200 1297
pc8.att.net - - [11/Apr/1997:00:10:32 -0700] "GET /
   tvpbannertop.html HTTP/1.0" 200 132
pc8.att.net - - [11/Apr/1997:00:10:32 -0700] "GET /
   tvpbannerbot.html HTTP/1.0" 200 607
pc8.att.net - - [11/Apr/1997:00:10:27 -0700] "GET /
   joboppframes.html HTTP/1.0" 200 1592
at1.vl.com - - [11/Apr/1997:00:10:37 -0700] "GET /idn/bio/
   bioerev.html HTTP/1.0" 200 6027
pc8.att.net - - [11/Apr/1997:00:11:04 -0700] "GET /
   jscience.html HTTP/1.0" 200 2508
pc8.att.net - - [11/Apr/1997:00:11:22 -0700] "GET /jintl.html
   HTTP/1.0" 200 2122
pc8.att.net - - [11/Apr/1997:00:12:53 -0700] "GET /
   jdisab.html HTTP/1.0" 200 1197
198.23.25.3 - - [11/Apr/1997:00:14:39 -0700] "GET /idn/
   idnfp.htm HTTP/1.0" 304 -
```

Understanding Page Views

Like the hit, the page view can be a misleading statistic, especially if you interpret page views literally. For example, if you access a frame-enhanced page with three frames, four page views are generated. These entries from the access log are an example of a single page request generating multiple page views:

```
pc8.att.net - - [11/Apr/1997:00:05:04 -0700] "GET /vpepc.html
   HTTP/1.0" 200 2741
```

```
pc8.att.net    [11/Apr/1997:00:05:10 -0700] "GET /epc.html
  HTTP/1.0" 200 501
pc8.att.net - - [11/Apr/1997:00:05:10 -0700] "GET /
  vpepc2.html HIIP/1.0" 200 544
pc8.att.net - - [11/Apr/1997:00:05:10 -0700] "GET /
  ziptour.html HTTP/1.0" 200 526
```

Still, when you want to determine the popularity of a Web site, the page view is definitely a more accurate statistic than the hit. Tracking page views can help you learn which areas of your Web site are the most popular, and after you determine the most popular pages, you can direct your energies to those pages. Although this certainly doesn't mean that you should abandon areas of your site that don't generate steady traffic, you will want to rethink your Web publishing strategy.

If you think about it, focusing your time and resources on the most popular areas of your Web site makes sense. After all, there are only so many hours in a week. Determining the most popular pages at your Web site can also help you promote your Web site to the world (more on this on Saturday afternoon under "Transforming the Numbers into Meaningful Data").

Tracking page views requires time and patience but the rewards are well worth the effort, especially when you discover whether people truly enjoy your Web site or are just racing through in their quest to find the best of the Web. Earlier in this section, I tracked Joe Web Surfer through the access log. Joe's visit lasted about 12 minutes and took him to many different pages at the Web site. In each of the areas Joe visited, he stayed a reasonable length of time, so you can assume that he not only browsed but read. Based on this assumption, it is fairly safe also to assume that Joe liked what he saw.

When you examine page views at your Web site, look for indicators that can tell you whether people liked what they saw. As you examine page views, some of the questions that you can ask yourself include:

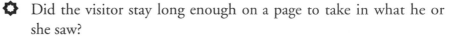

- ✪ How long did the average visitor stay?

- ✪ How many pages did the visitor access at the site?

- ✪ Did the visitor stay long enough on a page to take in what he or she saw?

Tips for Tracking Page Views

Savvy Web advertisers will ask you how many page views your site gets rather than zeroing in on hits. Tracking page views for a Web site with a single focus is easy; all you need to do is perform daily, weekly, or monthly searches against the access log for page requests. Then, you total the requests to come up with the magic number that you can display at your Web site or give to a would-be advertiser.

One way to total page views is to send the output of grep or egrep to the word count program, wc. After running this command, the result that you see on your screen is the total number of page accesses for the period covered by the log:

```
egrep ".htm|/ " access-log | wc
```

NOTE   As stated previously, the result that you see will have three different numbers. Forget about the last two numbers and focus on the first number, which is the number of times that the file was accessed.

In DOS, you can perform a similar search using two different find commands and then adding the results:

```
find /C ".htm" access-log

find /C "/ " access-log
```

Although the previous examples total the page views for the entire Web site, you won't know the specific areas of the Web site that are generating the bulk of the traffic. One way to make tracking page views in different areas of a Web site easier is to create subdirectories for document files that belong to the various resources, such as /job/, for your site's job-related area, and /writing/, for your site's writing-related area. You should also place image files in a directory called images.

If you use subdirectories, you can count page views for each area at your Web site, using commands such as the following:

```
grep /job/ access-log | wc
```

or

```
find /C "/writing/" access-log
```

If you don't use subdirectories, you can use egrep or multiple finds to search for all the document files of a particular area. For a small Web site with a few pages, this type of search is not that difficult, but as your site grows, you will really wish that you had created subdirectories. An example of searching for multiple pages in the access log and then totaling the result follows.

```
egrep "job1.html|jobintl.html|jobres.html|topjob.html" ac-
  cess-log | wc
```

Here, I searched for four specific Web pages in the access log and then counted the results to determine the total number of page views.

Zeroing in on the Visit

The most meaningful Web site statistic is the visit. A *visit* is a collection of hits and page views that pertain to a specific person who requested files from your Web site. Thus, when you count visits, you are counting the number of people who stopped by your Web site.

Putting Visits Together

Although visits are the most important Web site statistic, tracking visits isn't easy without defining exactly what is and isn't a visit. One way to count visits is to tally every distinct domain name in the access log. Although the number that you came up with certainly would be a summary of all the domains in the log, it wouldn't necessarily be an accurate picture of all the visits to your Web site.

As I stated earlier, a domain name could pertain to a multiuser host with 25, 50, or even 100 users. Yet, even if you could eliminate the possibility of the multiuser host, is it fair to count all accesses by the same user as a single visit? What if the user accessed the Web site 50 different times over a period of 30 days? Is this 50 visits or 1 visit?

Well, there's a big difference between someone shopping at your store 1 time and 50 times, so there is certainly a big difference between someone visiting a Web site 1 time and 50 times. In all fairness, you need to limit the scope of visits to a specific time period, such as all consecutive file requests that are separated by no more than 30 minutes. Following this, you would say that if a person browsed your site for 5 minutes one day and 15 minutes the next day, you have two different visits. On the other hand, if a person browsed your site for 10 minutes, went away, and then came back 15 minutes later, you have a single visit.

Tracking Visits

The best way to track visits in the access log is with tracking software. You'll learn all about tracking software this afternoon. Tracking software also counts visits by limiting the scope of visits to specific time frames. For now, though, I show you how to put together visits on your own.

When I examined Joe's visit, I showed you that you can track individual visits in the log quite easily. As long as the domain pertains to a single-user host, all you need to do is find the domain name that you want to track, and then extract all the hits for that domain. When you track individual visits, you are mostly interested in the summary information, such as:

- How long did the person visit?
- What page did the person start on?
- What areas did the person visit?
- How long did the person stay in each area?
- What was the total number of hits for this visitor?
- What was the total number of page views for this visitor?

A summary of Joe's visit would look something like this:

Minimum length of visit:

　　　12 minutes, 4 seconds

Start page:

/

Main pages visited and duration:

/ - 2 minutes 10 seconds

`vpjic.html` - 1 minute, 36 seconds

`vpepc.html` - 5 minutes, 28 seconds

`joboppframes.html` - 2 minutes, 50 seconds

Total hits:

97

Total page views:

27

If you wanted to search for all the hits for `at1.v1.com`, you could use the following command:

```
grep at1.v1.com access-log > save.txt
```

This command would create a file called save.txt containing all the hits for `at1.v1.com`. Using a text editor, you could open the file for viewing and examine the hits. Keep in mind that you would want to look at the hits only for the specific date that you are analyzing.

Using the techniques discussed previously in the section titled "Examining Log Entries," you could put together a picture of the visit for `at1.v1.com`. The summary for this visit looks something like this:

Minimum length of visit:

5 minutes, 40 seconds

Start page:

`/idn/cissue/resmul.htm`

Main pages visited and duration:

`/idn/cissue/resmul.htm` - 37 seconds

`idnfp.htm` - 5 minutes 3 seconds

`/idn/bio/biorev.html` - unknown

Total hits:

13

Total page views:

3

The last visit in the access log is for the host at IP address 198.23.25.3. The summary for this visit looks something like this:

Minimum length of visit:

5 minutes, 25 seconds

Start page:

`/idn/cissue/resmul.htm`

Main pages visited and duration:

`/idn/cissue/resmul.htm` - 5 minutes 25 seconds

`idnfp.htm` - unknown

Total hits:

5

Total page views:

2

Getting the Big Picture

Although the three sample visits in the access log may not seem like much, you can use the statistics gathered to gain a clearer understanding of the big picture for this Web site. The big picture takes into account all visits to the Web site during a specific period of time, such as the 15-minute time slice used in this section.

When you put together the big picture, you must ask yourself many important questions. The answers to these questions will help you understand who is visiting your Web site and why. The main questions that you will want to ask include:

> What was the total number of visitors for this time period?
>
> What was the length of the average visit?
>
> What was the average duration of a page view?
>
> What was the average number of page views per visitor?
>
> What was the average number of hits per visitor?
>
> What domain classes and geographic areas are represented (percentages)?

When you examine the logs over a periods of days or weeks, you will want to ask these additional questions:

> What are the busiest hours of the day?
>
> What are the busiest days of the week?
>
> What are the most requested pages?
>
> What are the most common last pages requested?

Right about now, you may be wondering why you would want some of these statistics. Before I answer that question, go back to the three visits in the access log and put together the big picture for these visits. When you answer the main questions, you come up with stats that look like this:

Visitor count:

> 3

Duration of analysis:

> 15 minutes

Length of the average visit:

> 7 minutes, 3 seconds

Average duration of page view:

2 minutes 54 seconds

Average number of page views per visitor:

10.67

Average number of hits per visitor:

38.3

Domain classes and geographic areas:

50% Net

50% Com

NOTE Throwing out the IP address helps to make the domain class statistic more concrete and meaningful. Because correlating IP addresses to actual domains is difficult, most tracking software will do the same thing.

With these stats in hand, you can now answer the all-important questions concerning who is visiting and why. The list that follows provides descriptions that can help you make sense out of the stats you've gathered so far. Keep in mind that these are generalities meant to get you started thinking about how you can use these stats to promote your Web site and to make your Web site a better place to visit.

Visitor count: Tells you how many people are visiting. You can use this to gauge the true popularity of your Web site. Whereas a new or low-traffic Web site may get 5 to 100 visitors a day, a popular Web site may get 5,000 to 10,000 visitors a day.

Length of the average visit: This is an indicator of whether people are really reading pages at your Web site or just browsing. It can also be an indicator of whether people like what they see. The longer the average visit, the more information the visitor is finding and reading.

Average duration of page view: This can be an indicator of whether people are reading or just browsing. When you examine this statistic, you also need to keep in mind the length and style of pages that you have at your Web site. Are they highly textual, highly graphical, or both?

Average number of page views per visitor: Generally, the more pages people view, the happier they are, and if people are viewing many pages at your Web site, they are finding information that interests them. When you count page views, you need to keep in mind the setup of your pages. Do you use frame sets that result in multiple page views? Do you use client pull to create slide shows?

Average number of hits per visitor: Over time, this information could be used to estimate the number of visitors without having to wander through the logs.

Domain classes and geographic areas: This can tell you where people visiting your Web site live and work. Great information to have if you want to attract advertisers.

Busiest hours of the day: Tells you the time of day when most people are visiting your Web site. This statistic can help you plan daily updates, promotion campaigns, and advertising.

Busiest days of the week: Tells you the day of the week when most people are visiting your Web site. This statistic can help you plan weekly updates, promotion campaigns, and advertising.

Most requested pages: Tells you the pages that visitors find the most interesting and/or useful. Can be used to tailor your Web site to visitors' needs and to help you determine which pages should receive most of your attention.

Most commonly requested last pages: Can help you spot trends and bad pages. If the last page requested has lots of links to external Web sites, this statistic tells you that this is the point from which most visitors are leaving. If the last page requested doesn't have links to external Web sites, you may want to examine the page in question.

Wrapping Up and Looking Ahead

Hits, page views, and visits are the statistics that you will use to promote your Web site to the world and to make your Web site more effective. Hits are generated whenever files are requested, meaning that a single page request can generate many hits in the access log. Because hits can be a misleading statistic, you can look to page views to give you a more accurate picture of the areas of your Web site that are attracting an audience. When you want to determine how many people are stopping by your Web site, the visit is the statistic that you will use. Finally, hits, page views, and visits come together to help you create the big picture for your Web site.

After pouring your time and resources into a Web site, do you really want to risk losing people who visit your Web site but don't get to where they expected? Not really, especially when every visitor is someone who could help spread the news about your terrific Web site. The next part of this section covers how to gain readers who otherwise would have been lost because of bad links at your site or bad references from other sites.

Gaining Lost Readers from the Error Logs

Don't lose visitors once they've found a doorway into your slice of cyberspace. Nothing stops would-be visitors dead in their tracks like an error. They see errors as brick walls and often race off as quickly as they can click the mouse. How many times have you seen the dreaded `404 - File Not Found?` Did you hang around the Web site that you were trying to access or did you just click your browser's Back button and head off in some other direction?

Errors are often the result of bad links in your Web pages or bad references to your pages from other Web sites. When it comes to finding and fixing bad links in your pages, you have total control and can easily track down the problems—if you know how. When it comes to bad references to your pages at your Web site, you may think that finding and fixing these problems is beyond your control. Nothing could be further from the truth, however. You can fix errors regardless of their source, and you're about to find out how.

Errors: We All Hate Them

We all hate errors, yet we've grown so accustomed to them that they seem like an everyday part of the quest to browse the Web. Stop and think for a moment about your reaction when you encounter an error like the one shown in Figure 2-5. Your reaction, be it restrained contempt or outright indignation, is mirrored thousands of times around the world every day.

After the initial outrage at hitting a dead end in cyberspace passes, what is your next reaction? Most of the time, you probably click on your browser's Back button to return to the site that sent you to the wrong address. Or perhaps you enter a new URL into the browser and head off into another direction. The person who is persistent enough to puzzle through the error, trying to figure out another way to get at the information using the bad URL, is rare. As a result, just about every time that your server displays an error, you lose a visitor—and maybe forever.

When you are trying to increase traffic at your Web site, the last thing you want to do is lose visitors. Thus, one of the keys to increasing and maintaining traffic to your Web site is to reduce errors and help readers find their way, which is exactly what you're about to learn.

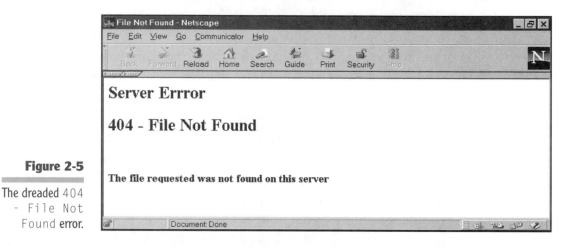

Figure 2-5

The dreaded 404 - File Not Found error.

Understanding Web Server Errors

Web servers record errors in two different log files. File requests that result in errors are recorded in the access log. A more detailed description of the error is also recorded in the error log.

Access Log Errors

Anytime that an error is related to an entry in the access log, you will find a status code that describes the error. As you learned this morning under "Using Web Stats to Understand Your Site's Visitors," status codes indicate the general type of the error and fall into one of these categories: success, redirection, client error, and server error.

In error tracking for your Web site, the client error status codes are the most helpful. A typical error recorded in the access log looks like this:

```
pc8.att.net - - [11/Apr/1997:00:01:00 -0700] "GET /home.htm
   HTTP/1.0" 404 -
```

Here, the status code 404 indicates that the file was not found. Other status codes for client errors are shown in Table 2-7. Note that the status codes 405[nd]415 are defined in the HTTP 1.1 specification and are not part of the older HTTP specifications.

TABLE 2-7 STATUS CODES FOR CLIENT ERROR	
Code	Description
400	Invalid request
401	Not authorized
402	Payment required
403	Forbidden
404	File not found
405	Method not allowed
406	Not acceptable
407	Proxy authentication required
408	Request time-out
409	Conflict
415	Unsupported media type

The Error Log

The error log provides a running record of just about everything that happens on the server. Entries in the error log are placed on a single line with a time stamp and a short descriptive statement that explains what actually occurred. Unfortunately, the Common Log Format for time stamps does not apply to the error log, which means that some servers may use a different format for the time stamp in the error log.

The File Not Found error is the most common error that you will find in the error log. Other types of errors recorded in the error log include lost connections and time outs.

Error: File Not Found

The File Not Found error is a very common occurrence in the error log. A typical error log entry for this error looks like this:

```
[11/Apr/1997:00:01:02 -0700] access to /usr/www/docs/tvpress/
  home.htm failed
for pc8.att.net, reason: File does not exist
```

Here, the server records that the host `pc8.att.net` requested the file `home.htm` but the file was not found. The server maps the requested URL, `http://www.tvpress.com/home.htm`, to the actual directory on the server containing the file, which in this case is `/usr/www/docs/tvpress/`. Note also that the entry was placed on two lines so that it would fit on the page.

● ●

NOTE The best way to see the format of time stamps for your error log is to examine some of the entries. Keep in mind that the error log is an optional log, which means that your server may or may not be configured to use one.

● ●

Error: Lost Connection

Whenever the connection from the server to the client is broken, the server records a Lost Connection message in the error log. Although a lost connection may sound like a bad thing, more often than not the user is to blame for this type of error. Anytime that you click on the Stop button in middle of a transfer, you cause the server to lose the connection and, in turn, the server records the lost connection in the error log. Similarly, if you click on the Back button or exit your browser during the loading of a page, the server loses the connection to your browser and records the lost connection in the error log.

A server loses connection at one of two key times, as follows:

⚙ Just after the request has come in and before the server has processed the request

⚙ After the request has been processed and during the file transfer

When the server loses the connection just after the request has come in, the server records a Request Connection Lost message. When the server loses the connection during the file transfer, the server records a Send Connection Lost message. A Lost Connection error looks like this:

```
[11/Apr/1997:05:05:05 -0700] request lost connection to cli
    ent pc0.att.net
```

Error: Time Out

A less common error for the server to record is a time out. If the server has to wait too long for a client to respond, the server will break the open connection and log a time-out. The length of time that the server waits before timing out is the time-out rate. Typically, this rate is set high so that the server doesn't issue a time out inadvertently. A time out error looks like this:

```
[11/Apr/1997:05:05:35 -0700] time out to client pc8.att.net
```

Here, the connection time-out rate has elapsed. The server breaks the open connection to the client and logs the time out in the error log.

Administrative Messages

Servers use the error log to record much more than errors. In the error log, you will also find administrative messages. These messages record server startup, server shutdown, and other server status changes. Here's an example of an administrative message:

```
[11/Apr/1997:00:01:02 -0700] HTTPd: starting as httpd -d /
    usr/www/
```

In this example, the administrative message records the start of the main Web server process, HTTPd—the process that handles Web server transactions.

Finding Trouble Spots in the Logs

Errors are frustrating for everyone. Wouldn't it be great to have a way to fix errors? Well, there are ways to fix errors and you start with the logs to find trouble spots. The three major trouble spots that can cause you to lose potential visitors forever have to do with the following:

- Missing files
- Lost connections
- Server time outs

Because the server records a time stamp and the domain information for client-related requests and errors, tracking trouble spots in the logs is fairly straightforward. You can use `grep` or `find` to extract errors from the access log based on the status code that you are looking for, such as 404. Then, if you want to get a better description of the error, look for the matching entry in the error log.

 NOTE Keep in mind that the server doesn't necessarily record access log and error log entries simultaneously. For this reason, there may be a few seconds difference between the access log time stamp and the error log time stamp.

Missing Files

The most common errors are those that relate to files that the server can't find. Contrary to what you might think, the Web publisher is to blame for this error more often than the user is, and I'll readily admit that I am guilty of causing the dreaded 404-File Not Found error.

What Causes the File Not Found Error?

Bad links are a key reason for the File Not Found error. When you create a Web page, you add hypertext links that relate to pages at your Web site as well as other Web sites. Although all your links may work perfectly when you first create your Web site, things change over time. You update pages.

You move pages to different locations. You combine some pages. You delete other pages.

Unfortunately, every time that you move or delete Web pages, you may unwittingly start an avalanche of errors. Joe, who bookmarked one of the pages that you moved or deleted, can't get to the page anymore. Mary, who created a page showing links to her favorite Web sites, now has several invalid links that point to your Web site. Worse, the search engines with which you registered indexed your Web site; and now, hundreds of people who are looking for resources like yours can't find your pages anymore.

How Are Missing Files Logged?

In the access log, files that the server can't find are recorded with entries that look like this:

```
at1.vl.com - - [11/Apr/1997:23:59:00 -0800] "GET /samp.htm
   HTTP/1.1" 404 -
```

The corresponding entry in the error log will look something like this:

```
[11/Apr/1997:23:59:00 -0800] access to /usr/www/docs/tvpress/
   samp.htm failed
for at1.vl.com, reason: File does not exist
```

In this example, the server could not find the file called samp.htm. The server recorded the failed request in the access log and then recorded a description of the error in the error log.

How Can You Find File Problems?

You can search for the File Not Found error in the access log using `grep` or `find`. Because the status code may not be a unique element in the access log, you may want to surround the search string in quotation marks and include spacing, as in the following examples:

```
grep " 404 " access-log > save.txt
```

or

```
find " 404 " access-log > save.txt
```

• •

NOTE As discussed earlier, `grep` is a UNIX command and `find` is a DOS command. Mac users may be able to search using the `egrep` command, which must be installed on your system.

• •

I recommend searching for problem files in the logs weekly for large sites or sites that change frequently, and at least monthly for other sites. If you've never checked for problem files, now is a good time.

How Can You Fix File Problems?

After you have compiled a list of files that the server couldn't find, use the list to help you find trouble spots at your Web site. Start by printing the list. Next, compare the filenames on the list to the actual files on your server. If you find a file that is on the list and available on your server, use your browser to try to retrieve the file from the server. Be sure to use the same URL that the user entered. If the file loads without problems, cross the file off the list and move on to the next file on the list. Here, there was probably an intermittent problem with the user's Internet connection, which doesn't necessarily mean that anything is wrong on your server.

If the file doesn't load in your browser, check the filename. Does the filename on the server exactly match the URL that you entered? Most servers are case sensitive, meaning that the mixture of uppercase and lowercase letters must match exactly. When you find a naming problem, you have a bad reference in one of your Web pages that you need to fix. The easiest way to find the problem page—and possibly other pages that contain the bad reference—is to search your Web directories using the `grep` or `egrep` command for the bad reference.

A bad reference to a Web page called `welcome.htm` that should have been referenced as `welcome.html` could be fixed as follows:

 Change to the directory containing your Web pages. If you have multiple document directories, examine each in turn.

 Use `grep` or `egrep` to search for references to the filename `welcome.htm`, such as `grep welcome.htm *`

- Record the list of filenames containing the bad reference.
- Edit the files and correct the bad references.

Additionally, you can find the specific file that contains the bad reference, by looking for the previous Web page accessed by the user. To do this, find the error in the access log and then move back through earlier entries in the log. Usually, the first page access that you find prior to the error is the page containing the error. I say *usually*, because with framed documents, a group of Web pages may have been loaded simultaneously. In such a case, you would need to examine each of the documents that are a part of the frame-enhanced page.

If you don't have a naming problem, you may have a permission problem. On UNIX Web servers, the directory and the file must have specific permissions before readers can access your files. Generally, the directory needs to be executable and the file needs to have read access. If you don't know how to check or set file permissions, ask your Internet Service Provider.

Next, highlight all the files that don't relate to Web pages or other document files, such as references to image files. Most likely, the highlighted list of files points to broken references in your Web pages. Fix these references by either updating the related page or by moving the file to where it is supposed to be.

Now that you've narrowed the list a bit, look for URLs that belong to files that you've moved or deleted. When you find a reference to a file that you moved, jot down the new name of the file. When you find a reference to a file that you deleted, make a note to yourself that the file was deleted.

Because users are looking for these files and you want to build rather than lose readership, you will want to redirect these lost visitors to the new location of the resource. Alternatively, you can create a placeholder document with the old URL, telling visitors that the resource is no longer available and then redirecting them to another area of your Web site. For details on how to redirect users to new locations, see the section titled "Redirecting Lost Readers."

Although the remaining files on your list should pertain to true errors on the part of the user or someone else, you don't want to discard the list just yet. Take a look at the list one more time and ask yourself whether any patterns exist. For example, one of my resource pages is located at `http://www.tvpress.com/idn/`. I found that some users were requesting the page `http://www.tvpress.com/idn.htm`. I don't know why they were looking for this page, but they did it often enough that it seemed worthwhile to create a placeholder page. The job of the placeholder page was to direct lost visitors to the resource for which they were looking.

Lost Connections

Lost connections are often the result of impatient users not wanting to wait for your page, its graphics, and other multimedia files to finish loading. Consequently, if you find a page that has lots of lost connections related to it, you may want to examine the page and change it so that it either loads quicker or follows sound design techniques that allow the visitor to use or peruse the page before it finishes loading.

Interestingly enough, lost connections are recorded in the access log with a status code of 200. As you may recall, this status code means that the document was successfully retrieved. Well, here's what happens and why lost connections are recorded with a success code: The server finds the referenced file and correlates the success with the status code of 200. When the connection is lost, the server completes the entry in the access log and then records the lost connection in the error log.

If you have pages with lots of text, graphics, or multimedia, you may want to periodically check for lost connections. To do this, search the error log for entries containing the keywords `lost connection`. When you find entries for lost connections, try to match those entries to specific entries in the access log.

Use the time stamp to help you find candidate entries—those with matching or similar time stamps. Next, examine the actual bytes transferred for those entries. If the number of bytes transferred for an entry is less than the byte size of the file, you can be sure that you've found the corresponding entry in the access log. For example, although the byte size of the file home.htm is 9672 bytes, the server recorded that 956 bytes were transferred in this entry:

```
pc8.att.net - - [11/Apr/1997:00:01:00 -0700] "GET /home.htm
    HTTP/1.0" 200 956
```

The corresponding entry in the error log is as follows:

```
[11/Apr/1997:00:01:00 -0700] send lost connection to client
    pc8.att.net
```

TIP If you don't have access to the error log, you can still look for lost connections. To do this, look for file accesses logged with the incorrect file size just as outlined previously.

Unfortunately, sometimes the connection is lost after the server completely transfers the file but before the client completely processes the data. When the server loses the connection after completing the transfer, the bytes transferred will match the byte size of the file. In this case, you may not be able to determine the cause of the error and should just move on to the next item on the list.

Time Outs

Although time outs are rather rare on Web servers, this coverage would be incomplete without at least mentioning how to spot them. A time out is sort of like the server getting impatient with the client and wanting to move on. You probably won't see time outs unless you have large multimedia or compressed files that are retrieved using the standard Web file transfer protocol, HTTP.

Unfortunately, if your server uses an older version of the transfer protocol, you can find time outs only if you have access to the error log. Further, matching access and error log entries for time outs is not practical if the access log has no corresponding entry. For this reason, you won't be able to determine the specific files that are causing the time out.

With the newest version of the transfer protocol, determining the cause of a time out is much easier. In the access log, you look for entries with the status code 408, such as:

```
at1.v1.com - - [11/Apr/1997:23:59:00 -0800] "GET /samp.mpeg
   HTTP/1.1" 408 -
```

If you see time outs frequently for the same file, you may want to tell your Internet Service provider about the problem. Although the service provider should be able to set the time out ratio higher, the service provider may also tell you that the byte size for the offending file is unreasonably large. In the latter case, you may want to break the large file into several parts.

Redirecting Lost Readers

As you learned earlier in this section, every time that you move or delete a Web page, you can start an avalanche of errors. Anyone who has bookmarked the page that you changed will get an error. Anyone who has created a link to the page from his or her own Web site will be unwittingly directing people to dead ends. Anyone who uses a search engine to find resources may also get a retrieval containing references to the pages that you've changed.

The result is that lots of people who otherwise would have been visitors to your wonderful niche of cyberspace are now lost. They've hit the proverbial brick wall and are about to run off in some other direction. And they may never return. When a user gets all the way to your Web site through the maze of cyberspace, do you really want to risk losing that user because of something that you can fix?

To remedy this situation, you should create a placeholder document. The key to the placeholder document is that it takes the place of a Web page or other document file that you moved or deleted, and then redirects the user to a different location at your Web site. If you have a list of documents that you've moved or deleted, why not create a few placeholder documents right now? Every visitor counts.

TIP The way to avoid brick walls and placeholder documents altogether is to plan out your Web site before you build it. The simplest planning rule is to give each area of your Web site its own directory to start with, and to make the default document for this directory the home page for the area. Unfortunately, in the real world, most Web publishers (myself included) don't like to plan things out before we dive in, which means that we should use placeholder documents to help direct traffic whenever necessary.

Redirection Basics

The technique that you use to redirect visitors can be as simple as the one shown in Figure 2-6. Here, you tell visitors that the resource has been moved or deleted. Next, you provide them with the URL of the new resource or an escape route to another location at your Web site.

The source for the redirection page is shown as Listing 2-4. In the examples area of the book's Web site (www.tvpress.com/examples), you will find the source code in the file stanek.htm.

Listing 2-4   Redirecting the User

```
<HTML>
<HEAD>
<TITLE>William's Bio and FAQ Pages Have Moved</TITLE>
</HEAD>

<BODY BGCOLOR="#ffffff">

<DIV ALIGN=CENTER>

<H1>Thanks for visiting!</H1>
<H2>The resource you are looking for has moved to a new
   home.</H2>

<H2>You will find William's Bio and FAQ Pages at
```

```
<A HREF="http://www.tvpress.com/writing/">
http://www.tvpress.com/writing/
</A>
</H2>

</DIV>
</BODY>
</HTML>
```

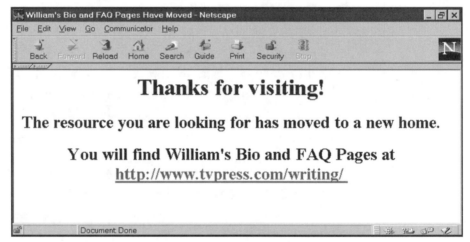

Figure 2-6

Helping lost readers find their way makes sense.

More Redirection Techniques

Another technique for redirecting visitors is to automate the redirection with client pull technology. With client pull, you insert an instruction in the Web page that tells the visitor's browser to retrieve a new document after a specified amount of time has elapsed. Thus, the visitor can get to the new location of a resource or be redirected to any location on your Web site without having to do anything. Most browsers are capable of using client pull.

The HTML tag that you will use to redirect the visitor's browser is the <META> tag, which can be used only in the HEAD element of your Web page. You will use the HTTP-EQUIV attribute of the <META> tag to tell the browser that you want to refresh the browser window. You will use the CONTENT attribute of the `<META>` tag to tell the browser two things: how long to wait and what document to load.

An example of the `<META>` tag follows:

```
<META HTTP-EQUIV="Refresh" CONTENT="5; URL=http://
  www.tvpress.com/">
```

Here, the `HTTP-EQUIV` attribute is assigned the keyword `Refresh`, which tells the browser that you want to prepare to refresh the current window. The `CONTENT` attribute has two parts separated by a semicolon and a space. The `5` tells the browser to wait five seconds before refreshing the browser window. The next part of the `CONTENT` attribute tells the browser the URL of the page that you want to load into the refreshed window. The URL must have the full path specified, including the `http://`.

Figure 2-7 shows an example page that redirects the visitor to a new location at a Web site. As you see, the page still has an informative and helpful explanation of what has happened. Just in case the user has a browser that doesn't support the technology, the appropriate links are placed on the page as well.

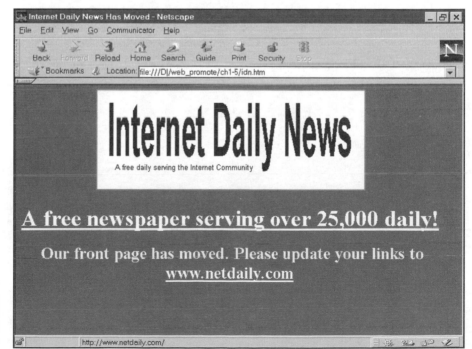

Figure 2-7

Why not use client pull to redirect the user?

FIND IT ▶
ONLINE The markup for the sample page is shown as Listing 2-5. Online, you will find the source code in the file idn.htm.

Listing 2-5   Automating the Redirection

```html
<HTML>
<HEAD>
<TITLE>Internet Daily News Has Moved</TITLE>
<META HTTP-EQUIV="Refresh" CONTENT="2; URL=http://
  www.netdaily.com/">
</HEAD>

<BODY BGCOLOR="#0000ff" text="#ffff00" link="#fffbf0"
vlink="#808000" alink="#ff0000">

<DIV ALIGN=CENTER>

<P>
   <A HREF="http://www.netdaily.com/">
   <IMG SRC="idnttl3.gif" ALT="Internet Daily News Logo">
   </A>
</P>
<H1>
   <A HREF="www.netdaily.com">A free newspaper serving over
  25,000 daily!</A>
</H1>

<H2>Our front page has moved. Please update your links to
<A HREF="http://www.netdaily.com">http://www.netdaily.com</A>
</H2>

</DIV>
</BODY>
</HTML>
```

No More 404 - File Not Found

The typical errors servers report are meaningless to most people, and even the people who know what the status codes mean probably would much rather have a helpful pointer than an error that says 404 - File Not Found. Fortunately, ways to fix it are available so that the nondescriptive and meaningless errors reported by servers go the way of the dinosaur. This section shows you how to eliminate this error message for good.

Earlier, you learned that status codes are recorded with entries in the access log. Status codes are also used by the server to determine which error documents to display.

When the Web server software was installed, the technician who set up the server defined specific parameters that told the server how to report errors and which error documents to display. Because the default error documents are rarely replaced, chances are good that visitors to your Web site see errors like the one shown previously in Figure 5-1. You can confirm this by entering an invalid URL that refers to your Web site, such as:

```
http://www.your_server.com/nothingatall.html
```

If your server reports a vague error message, don't worry; this can be changed by defining new error documents. On most servers, regardless of operating system, you define the documents to retrieve when an error occurs with the ErrorDocument directive. Using the ErrorDocument directive, you can define the document that the server should retrieve when an error occurs. The syntax for the ErrorDocument directive is as follows:

```
ErrorDocument status_code document_URL
```

Following this syntax, you could specify documents to retrieve for the common client and server errors shown in the table on the following page.

Keep in mind that this directive applies only to document files, such as Web pages, and not to images or other multimedia files. After receiving the status code specified in the directive, the server retrieves the corresponding error document using the relative URL specified. Because the server expects a relative URL, the server will start in the directory for Web documents.

ErrorDocument 400	/badreq.html
ErrorDocument 401	/unauth.html
ErrorDocument 403	/deny_access.html
ErrorDocument 404	/not_found.html
ErrorDocument 500	/server_error.html
ErrorDocument 502	/bad_gateway.html
ErrorDocument 503	/unavailable.html

For example, if the domain is `www..tvpress.com`, the server will look for the badreq.html document using the following URL:

```
http://www.tvpress.com/badreq.html
```

For most servers, the `ErrorDocument` directive is defined in a server configuration file, which means that only someone with top-level access to the server can make the necessary changes. With the thought of eliminating the dreaded 404 - File Not Found error forever, take a chance and talk to the head technician or Webmaster who works for your Internet service provider. The question to ask is, "Can you help me set up unique error documents for my domain or, at the very least, is it possible to create some informative error messages for everyone who uses the Web server?"

Wrapping Up and Looking Ahead

Errors are show stoppers. Don't let people who want to visit your site think that what they are looking for is gone. Every visitor counts, especially when you are trying to increase traffic to your Web site. But the reason for fixing trouble spots goes well beyond preventing the loss of someone trying to find your Web site. You need to do everything within your power to build a steady readership. To attract and maintain an audience over the long haul, you need to maintain your site and provide readers with lifelines when you move or delete files.

Although all this talk about the access log and the error log is certainly useful, you may sometimes want to gather stats without having to dig through the server log files. Also, sometimes server logs simply aren't available. For this reason, the next part of this section looks at ways for you to obtain stats without using server logs.

Simple Ways to Obtain Stats without Server Logs

The whole idea behind gathering stats is to put together the big picture for your Web site. When you want to get a clear idea of exactly who is visiting and why, nothing beats the detailed records that you can gather from the access log. But log files aren't the only way to gather stats for your Web site. In this chapter, I examine ways to gather stats that don't require server logs.

Tracking Stats without Logs

Server logs files are invaluable when it comes to tracking stats and understanding the traffic to your Web site. Anytime you track stats without the server log files, you risk missing the big picture completely. For this reason, the techniques that I discuss in this chapter may be best used to supplement the stats you are tracking in the log file rather than completely replace gathering stats from the logs. Supplementing the stats that you track using server log files with the techniques discussed in this chapter gives you additional avenues for obtaining stats and getting feedback from visitors. If you have access to server log files, however, I recommend skipping this chapter altogether.

Still, sometimes you may prefer to forget about the logs and look at alternative ways to track stats. Although alternatives are your only option to gather stats if you are truly locked out of the log files, you may also want to consider using alternatives to log files when you have a very small Web site or a limited collection of home pages. Specifically, if you publish fewer than five Web pages, such as a home page with links to three other related pages, you should strongly consider tracking stats without the server logs.

Although many techniques to track stats without server logs are available, this chapter focuses on the ones that you can implement right now, such as:

✪ Counters to track hits or page views

✪ Guest books to learn more about visitors and to get feedback from visitors

When you deal with counters and guest books, you usually have to work with CGI scripts. A script is a program that runs on the server. You can use scripts to process information submitted by users. The *Common Gateway Interface* (CGI) is a standard that allows scripts to act as gateways—that is, interfaces—between a browser and the server. On most Web servers, CGI scripts can be executed only if they are in a specific directory. Usually, this directory is called cgi-bin.

If you do not have your own domain, the cgi-bin directory that you will use is often located at /usr/cgi-bin. If you have your own domain, the cgi-bin directory that you will use is usually located within your public directory for Web documents, such as:

```
your home dir/public_html/cgi-bin
```

or

```
your_home_dir/www/cgi-bin
```

NOTE   To confirm the directory that you need to use for CGI scripts, ask your Internet Service Provider or read the FAQ pages at the service provider's Web site.

Scripts are executed in one of two ways: automatically, when a page containing a reference to the script is loaded; or, only at a specific time, such as when a user submits a form containing a reference to the script. Although counters and guest books that use CGI are great, not everyone can use CGI. Your service provider may restrict the use of scripts or the Web server software may not be configured to use scripts. Because of these possibilities, I provide alternatives to CGI-based counters and guest books that anyone can use.

Introducing Counters

A counter is a script that you place in a Web page to tell you and other visitors how many times the page or files related to a page have been accessed. Counters can be configured to track hits, page views, and other statistics. The exact behavior of a counter depends on the programming in the script. Some counters are fairly advanced and tell you many different things about the hits and page views. Other counters are very basic and simply tally the number of hits or page views.

Although having a fancy counter that gives you lots of stats may seem great, a basic counter that will tally page views is usually just what the doctor ordered. Whether the counter displays text values or a graphical representation of the value is a matter of personal preference. Keep in mind that the primary reason you are using the counter is so that you can gather stats for your Web site.

All over the Web, you will find counter scripts that people have written and made available for others to use for free. With so many great choices, selecting a counter script for your Web site can be difficult. To narrow the field to a manageable number that you can implement right now, I chose two specific counters for this chapter.

In the next section, you will find step-by-step instructions for installing a counter script written in Perl, a scripting language commonly used for CGI scripts. If your Web server is UNIX-based and you can use CGI scripts at your Web site, give this script a try. On the other hand, if your Web server isn't UNIX-based or you can't use scripts, jump forward to the section titled "A Counter That Anyone Can Use." In this section, you will find a counter that you can use no matter what.

Installing a Counter Step by Step

The script that I chose for this section is called TextCounter. TextCounter is a CGI script written in Perl that will run on any Web server running UNIX or Linux. Before you can use this script, you need to know the following:

 Whether the server allows CGI scripts

 Whether the server is configured to use server-side includes

NOTE Don't worry about the terminology. Simply ask your Internet Service Provider whether the server is configured to use CGI and server-side includes.

Provided that the answer to both of these questions is yes, you will be able to install and use the script. The other information that you need to know before you get started is as follows:

🟆 The file path to the directory that you can use for CGI scripts

🟆 The URL path to the directory for CGI scripts

NOTE After seeing how much work it is to install, configure, and test a counter script, you may be ready to throw in the towel. Don't. Try installing the script; if you have problems, just skip ahead to the section titled "A Counter That Anyone Can Use."

Downloading and Unarchiving the Script

FIND IT ▶
ONLINE
After you have all the information you need to get started, you are ready to download the script. You will find the source for the script at:

`http://worldwidemart.com/scripts/textcounter.shtml`

Fire up your browser and jaunt over to Matt Wright's Script Archive using the URL provided. This page has links to several different compressed versions of the TextCounter script. Select the script archive labeled

`textcounter.zip`

Next, click on the form button labeled Download to start the file transfer to your PC. On your PC, use an unzip utility such as PKUNZIP to extract the archive. If you don't have an unzip utility, visit the utilities area of the Web site for this book so that you can find a site to download an unzip utility. You will find the utilities area at `http://www.tvpress.com/promote/utilities/`.

TIP If you use a DOS unzip utility, the 8 + 3 naming convention for filenames will apply, meaning that the filename will look something like textco~1.zip. On my PC, PKUNZIP complained that it couldn't extract the archive, yet the files came out just fine. I also noted that the filename had changed to Counter.pl, so I moved the file to counter.pl (all lowercase).

After you unzip the archive, you will find two files in the current directory:

○ README: A file containing the installation instructions

○ counter.pl: The Perl script for the counter

Obtaining Information from the Server

Use Telnet, Windows HyperTerminal, or some other terminal emulator to access the Web server. On the Web server, type the following:

whereis perl

or

which perl

The server will return the directory path to the Perl scripting language. The TextCounter script expects Perl to be located at:

`/usr/local/bin/perl`

If your server returns a different directory path, write down the directory path. You will need to change the directory path in the first line of the TextCounter script.

Next, change to the directory for your Web documents and type the following command:

pwd

This command tells the server to print the present work directory. Write down the directory path; you will need this for the script. Keep the terminal session open because I take you back to it in a moment.

Editing the Script

Now that you've unarchived the TextCounter script, you need to edit the script in your text editor or word processor. Start by changing the directory path information if necessary. If your server's Perl directory is not at the following address:

```
/usr/local/bin/perl
```

you need to change the directory path referenced in the first line of the program. For example, if Perl is located at /usr/bin/perl, you would change the first line of the program to read:

```
#!/usr/bin/perl
```

Each Web page that uses the counter will use a separate data file to store and retrieve the current tally of page views. The following variable in the script tells the server where to look for these data files:

```
$data_dir
```

You make the variable assignment at the very top of the script. Start by appending the directory path /data/ to the Web directory path that you obtained earlier, and set the value of the $data_dir variable to this value. My Web directory path is /home/william/www, so I set the $data_dir variable to the following:

```
$data_dir = "/home/william/www/data/";
```

Save the file. You're done with the modification. Although you can configure lots of optional variables, the default settings work just fine.

Installing the Script on the Server

You are now ready to transfer the file to the server. Use whatever tool you normally use for file transfers, such as FTP. Then, in your Telnet or terminal window, type the following command:

chmod 755 counter.pl

This command tells the server that anyone can read and execute the counter.pl script. Next, move the script to the directory designated for CGI

scripts, which is typically /usr/cgi-bin. If /usr/cgi-bin is the correct directory on your server, the command to move the file is as follows:

```
mv counter.pl /usr/cgi-bin/
```

Now that you've installed the script, you can create the data directory. To
create this directory and set the permissions properly, ensure that you are
in your Web directory and then type the following commands:

mkdir data

chmod 777 data

Here, you've created a directory called `data` and changed the permissions
so that the directory is readable and writable.

Testing and Using the Script

The final step is to update one of your Web pages to call the script and
display the page view count. Although updating all of your pages to use the
counter immediately may be tempting, you should test the installation
first. If you have any problems, retrace the steps discussed earlier.

Most counters are displayed as one of the last elements on a Web page. For
this reason, you probably want to add the counter to the latter portion of
your Web page. The line to call the script looks like this:

```
<!-#exec cgi="/URL/path/to/scripts/counter.pl"->
```

Be sure to substitute the relative URL path to CGI scripts on your server,
such as:

```
<!-#exec cgi="/cgi-bin/counter.pl"->
```

or

```
<!-#exec cgi="../cgi-bin/counter.pl"->
```

If the script is installed correctly, the counter displays a message similar to
the following in your Web page:

```
00001 hits since July 4, 1997
```

If you have problems, the primary culprits are the following: the location
of the `data` directory and the permissions on the `data` directory. Ensure
that the `data` directory is located within your Web directory. Further, you

should ensure that the permissions on the data directory are set exactly as specified previously.

Figure 2-8 shows an example of a Web page that uses the TextCounter script. The source for this Web page is available as Listing 2-6. Online, you will find this file saved as count_samp.htm. Look for this file at http://www.tvpress.com/promote/examples/.

Listing 2-6   A Sample Page with a Counter

```
<HTML>
<HEAD>
<TITLE>Working With Counters</TITLE>
</HEAD>

<BODY BGCOLOR="#FFFFFF">

<DIV ALIGN=CENTER>

<H1>William R. Stanek's <BR>Home On the Web</H1>

<H2><A HREF="http://www.tvpress.com/writing/
  writing.htm">FAQ</A>
- Frequently Asked Questions</H2>
<H2><A HREF="http://www.tvpress.com/writing/
  writing2.htm">Books</A>
- Web publishing & Design</H2>
<H2><A HREF="http://www.tvpress.com/writing/
  writing3.htm">Interview</A>
- An Interview With William</H2>

<!-#exec cgi="/cgi-tvpress/counter.pl"->
</DIV>
</BODY>
</HTML>
```

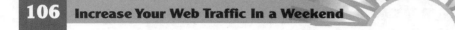

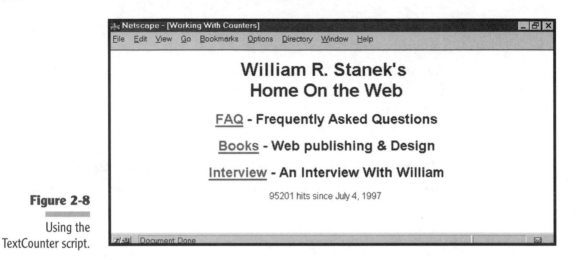

Figure 2-8

Using the
TextCounter script.

A Counter That Anyone Can Use

If you tried your hand at installing and configuring the text counter in the previous section, you saw just how much work it is to work with scripts. If you are technically inclined and have the right server software, you probably got the script up and running in a few minutes. On the other hand, if you aren't technically inclined, trying to install the script was probably a frustrating process.

Thanks to a wonderful script created by Heini Withagen from the Netherlands, I have set up a counter script at my Web site that anyone can use—regardless of the type of server he or she has. Every time a page containing this script is accessed, the counter is increased. Because the counter is completely graphics based, it uses small GIF images to represent the total number of page views. Figure 2-9 shows a Web page that uses the universal counter.

Working with the Universal Counter

Beyond the fact that anyone can use this script, the really wonderful news is that you don't have to install or configure the script at all. The script runs entirely on my Web site at www.netdaily.com. To use the script, just place a directive to my server in your Web page.

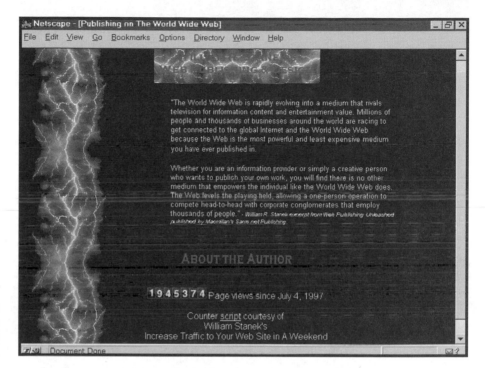

Figure 2-9

The universal counter.

The two primary parameters that you can pass to the script are the following:

- `width` - The number of digits that you want the counter to have
- `link` - The absolute URL to the page that uses the counter

If you want your counter to have seven digits, you can set the `width` parameter as follows:

```
width=7
```

If your Web page that uses the counter is at the following address:

```
http://www.your_isp.com/~you/index.html
```

you can set the link parameter as follows:

```
link=http://www.your_isp.com/~you/index.html
```

After you determine how you want the counter to look and the page URL, you can add the counter directive to your Web page. The counter directive is always assigned to the SRC attribute of an image tag that calls the counter script. The call to the counter script looks like this:

```
http://www.netdaily.com/cgi-netdaily/nph-count?
```

In your Web page, all this comes together as follows:

```
<IMG SRC="http://www.netdaily.com/cgi-netdaily/nph-count?
width=7&link=http://www.your_isp.com/~you/index.html">
```

Increasing the Counter

You can manually set the counter to a specific value using the final parameter that the script accepts, called `increase`. Whenever you use the `increase` parameter, you must also use the `link` parameter to tell the counter script the specific counter you want to `increase`. As the parameter name implies, whenever you increase the counter value, the script adds the current value to the number that you reference.

When you increase the counter, you must type the complete URL into your browser's URL field—just as you would if you were visiting the URL. The next time you access the corresponding page, you see the counter increase. The URL that you use to change a page at the following address:

```
http://www.your_isp.com/~you/index.html
```

looks like this:

```
http://www.netdaily.com/cgi-netdaily/nph-count?
link=http://www.your_isp.com/~you/index.html&increase=value
```

where `value` is the numeric value by which you want the counter to increase, such as 500.

Using the Universal Counter in a Web Page

Now that you know the parameters that the counter script expects, you can use the counter in any of your Web pages. As I stated earlier in the chapter, counters are normally one of the last elements in a Web page, but there's no reason that you can't prominently display your counter at the top of your Web page.

Potentially thousands of people will use this script, which in turn means that at any given time, thousands of people will be running the script remotely on my server. Although I set aside a few days to install, modify, and configure the counter script, I do not have time to troubleshoot problems that may periodically occur if you use the script. I may also need to occasionally clear out the counter log, which effectively resets all counters. Don't worry—I will not clear out the counter log unless it is absolutely necessary. That said, you should track your page views on a regular basis, such as weekly, and record the statistics. Online, you can find the current status of the counter script by visiting http://www.tvpress.com/promote/counter/.

In exchange for using the script on my server, all I ask is the following:

- Please don't abuse the script.

- Please be patient with the server; all the activity may bog it down during peak usage periods.

- Please add a note to pages that use the script telling people that you learned about the script in this book.

To ensure that visitors know that the counter tracks page views, you should add some descriptive information about the counter to your page as well, such as:

```
<P>
<IMG SRC="http://www.netdaily.com/cgi-netdaily/nph-count?
width=7&link=http://www.tvpress.com/writing/index.html">
 Page views since July 4, 1997.
</P>
<P>Counter <A HREF="http://www.tvpress.com/promote/">
script</A> courtesy of William Stanek's Increase
Your Web Traffic in a Weekend</P>
```

Introducing Guest Books

Guest books give publishers a way to obtain information about visitors as well as vital feedback about the site. You can think of guest books as cyberspace versions of the traditional guest books that were popular in the quaint inns of yesteryear. Guest books used by inns were popular because anyone visiting the inn could see who had visited previously. Guest books used on the Web are popular for much the same reason.

Most guest books on the Web ask visitors for personal information, such as full name, e-mail address, and country or state of residence. Guest books also invite visitor comments, and it is this vital feedback that gives publishers insight into exactly what people think about the Web site.

An example guest book is shown in Figure 2-10. This guest book from the Internet Daily News Web site allows visitors to create an entry in the guest book and also allows them to join a mailing list for readers of the newspaper.

Like counters, guest books are quite popular, so many guest book scripts are available. In the next section, you will find step-by-step instructions for installing a guest book script written in Perl. If your Web server is UNIX-based and you can use CGI scripts at your Web site, give this script a try. On the other hand, if your Web server isn't UNIX-based or you can't use

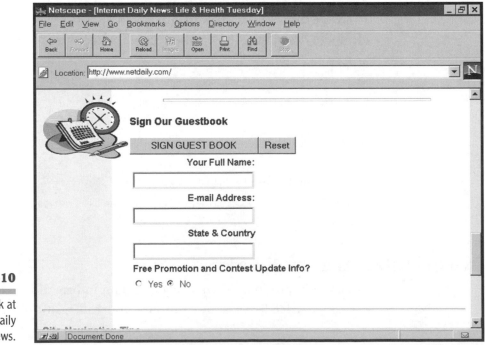

Figure 2-10

A guest book at Internet Daily News.

scripts, jump forward to the section titled "A Guest Book That Anyone Can Use." There you will find a guest book that you can use no matter what.

Installing a Guest book Step by Step

The script that I have chosen for this section is called Guestbook. Guestbook is a CGI script written in Perl that will work on any Web server that runs UNIX or Linux. The author of this script is Matt Wright. Before you can use this script, you need to know the following:

✿ Whether the server allows CGI scripts

✿ Whether the server is configured to use server-side includes

NOTE As stated previously, don't worry about the terminology. Simply ask your Internet Service Provider whether the server is configured to use CGI and server-side includes.

Provided that the answer to both of these questions is yes, you will be able to install and use the script. The other information that you need before you get started is as follows:

✿ The directory that you can use for CGI scripts

✿ The URL path to the directory for CGI scripts

Downloading and Unarchiving the Script

FIND IT ▶ ONLINE

After you have all the information that you need to get started, you are ready to download the script. You will find the source for the script at:

http://www.worldwidemart.com/scripts/guestbook.shtml

The referenced page contains links to several different compressed versions of the Guestbook script. Select the script archive labeled:

guestbook.zip

Next, click on the form button labeled Download to start the file transfer to your PC. On your PC, use an unzip utility such as PKUNZIP to extract the archive.

NOTE If you use a DOS unzip utility, the 8+3 naming convention for filenames will apply, meaning that the filenames will look something like guestbo~1.zip. On my PC, PKUNZIP complained that it couldn't extract the archive, yet the files came out just fine. I also noted that the file names had changed to GUESTBOO.PL, GUESTLOG.HTM, ADDGUEST.HTM, and GUESTLOG.HTM.

After you unzip the archive, you will find five files in the current directory:

- README: A file containing the installation instructions

- guestbook.pl: The Perl script for the guest book

- addguest.html: The guest book form that visitors can use to add an entry

- guestbook.html: The actual page that displays the guest book entries

- guestlog.html: A page for displaying entries without comments

Getting Information from the Server

Use Telnet, Windows HyperTerminal, or some other terminal emulator to access the Web server. On the Web server, type the following:

whereis perl

or

which perl

The server will return the directory path to the Perl scripting language. The Guestbook script expects Perl to be located at:

`/usr/local/bin/perl`

If your server returns a different directory path, write down the directory path. You will need to change the directory path in the first line of the Guestbook script.

Next, type one of the following:

whereis date

or

which date

The server will return the directory path to the `date` program. The Guestbook script expects `date` to be located at:

```
/usr/bin/date
```

Now, type the following command:

cd; pwd

This command tells the server to go to your home directory and then print the current work directory. Write down the directory path. You will need this for the script. Keep the terminal session open, because I take you back to it in a moment.

Updating the HTML Pages for the Guest Book

Because the original guest book pages were rather generic, I've created new pages for you to use. These pages are ready to go with minimal modification, and you will find them in the folder for this chapter on the Web site for this book.

The addguest.htm Page

The main page for adding entries to the guest book is called addguest.htm (see Figure 2-11). The source for this page is shown in Listing 2-7. The add guest form that you see in this page is designed so that it can be put into any page at your Web site. You just need to copy the markup from the line that reads "Begin Copy" to the line that reads "End Copy"; then, paste the markup in your Web page.

Hypertext links at the bottom of the addguest.htm page are meant to link to your home page and the guest book. Check these links to ensure that they are valid for your Web site. If they are, the only modification that you need to make is in the line that calls the script. Currently, this line reads as follows:

```
<FORM METHOD=POST ACTION="http://www.your_isp.com/cgi-bin/
  guestbook.pl">
```

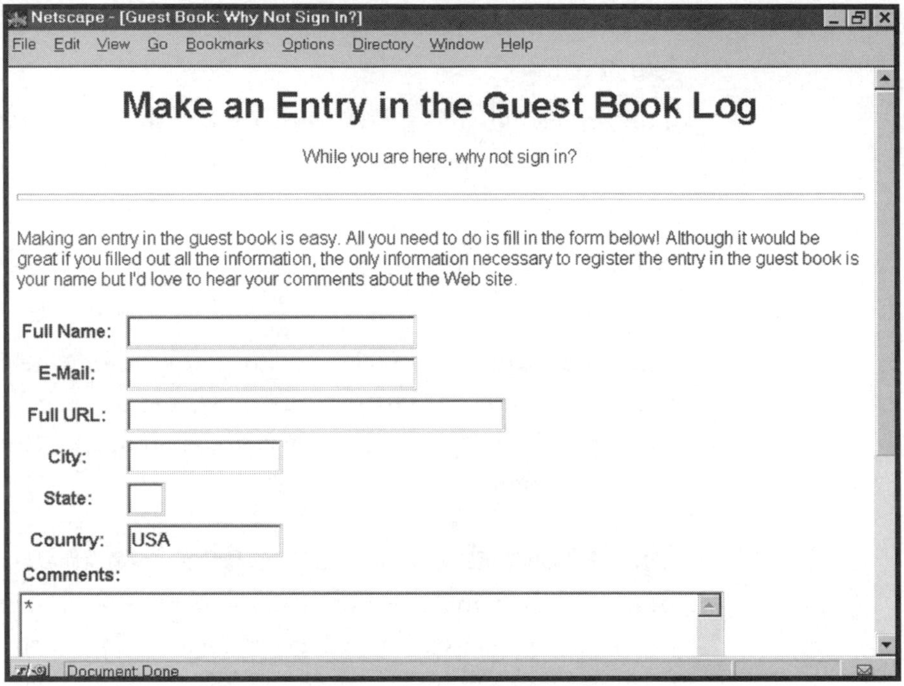

Figure 2-11

A Web page for adding entries in the guest book.

Update the ACTION attribute so that it points to the correct location of the Guestbook script on your server. Save the page after you make the changes.

Listing 2-7   The addguest.htm Page

```
<HTML>
<HEAD>
<TITLE>Guest Book: Why Not Sign In?</TITLE>
</HEAD>
<BODY BGCOLOR="#FFFFFF" LINK="#FF0000" VLINK="#FF0000">

<!- Begin Copy ->
<H1 ALIGN=CENTER>Make an Entry in the Guest Book Log</H1>
<P ALIGN=CENTER>While you are here, why not sign in?</P>
<HR SIZE=5>
<P>Making an entry in the guest book is easy.
All you need to do is fill in the form below!
```

Although it would be great if you filled out all
the information, the only information necessary to
register the entry in the guest book is your name
but I'd love to hear your comments about the Web site.</P>

```
<FORM METHOD=POST ACTION="http://www.your_isp.com/cgi-bin/
  guestbook.pl">
<TABLE CELLPADDING=1 CELLSPACING=1>
<TR><TH>Full Name:
<TD><INPUT TYPE=TEXT NAME=realname SIZE=30>
<TR><TH>E-Mail:
<TD><INPUT TYPE=TEXT NAME=username SIZE=30>
<TR><TH>Full URL:
<TD><INPUT TYPE=TEXT NAME=url SIZE=40>
<TR><TH>City:
<TD><INPUT TYPE=TEXT NAME=city SIZE=15>
<TR><TH>State:
<TD><INPUT TYPE=TEXT NAME=state SIZE=2>
<TR><TH>Country:
<TD><INPUT TYPE=TEXT VALUE=USA NAME=country SIZE=15>
<TR><TH>Comments:<TD> 
</TABLE>
<TEXTAREA NAME=comments COLS=60 ROWS=4>*</TEXTAREA>
<P><INPUT TYPE=SUBMIT VALUE="Sign the Guest Book">
<INPUT TYPE=RESET>
</FORM>

<!- End Copy ->

<HR>
<P><A HREF="/">Home Page</A> || <a href-"gbook.htm">
Guest Book </a></P>
<P>Guest book script created by Matt Wright.</P>

</BODY>
</HTML>
```

The gbook.htm Page

The page for displaying entries in the guest book is called gbook.htm (see Figure 2-12). The source for this page is shown in Listing 2-8. You shouldn't need to make any changes to this page.

Figure 2-12

The main guest book page.

Listing 2-8   The gbook.htm Page

```
<HTML>
<HEAD>
<TITLE>Guest Book: Who's Been Visiting?</TITLE>
</HEAD>
<BODY BGCOLOR="#FFFFFF" LINK="#FF0000" VLINK="#FF0000">

<DIV ALIGN=CENTER>
<H1>Welcome to the Guest Book Log</H1>
<H2>See Who's Been Visiting </H2>
<P>While you are here, <a href="addguest.htm">fill out</A>
 the guest book and stay awhile.</P>
</DIV>

<HR SIZE=5>
```

```
<!-begin->
<HR>
<P><A HREF="../">Back to My Home Page</A></P>
<P>Guest book script created by Matt Wright.</P>
</BODY>
</HTML>
```

The glog.htm Page

The page for displaying guest book summaries and errors is called glog.htm (see Figure 2-13). The source for this page is shown in Listing 2-9. You shouldn't need to make any changes to this page.

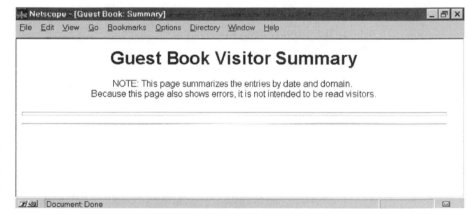

Figure 2-13

The summary and error page for the guest book.

Listing 2-9   The glog.htm Page

```
<HTML>
<HEAD>
<TITLE>Guest Book: Summary</TITLE>
</HEAD>
<BODY BGCOLOR="#FFFFFF" LINK="#FF0000" VLINK="#FF0000">

<DIV ALIGN=CENTER>
<H1>Guest Book Visitor Summary</H1>
```

```
<P>NOTE: This page summarizes  the entries by date and do-
    main.
<BR>Because this page also shows errors,
it is not intended to be read visitors.</P>
</DIV>

<HR SIZE=5>

<!-begin->
<HR>
```

Editing the Script

Now that you've unarchived the GuestBook script, you need to edit the script in your text editor or word processor. Start by changing the directory path for Perl information if necessary. If your server's Perl directory is not at the following URL:

```
/usr/local/bin/perl
```

you need to change the directory path referenced in the first line of the program. For example, if Perl is located at `/usr/bin/perl`, you would change the first line of the program to read as follows:

```
#!/usr/bin/perl
```

On your the Web server, you will store the script in the directory for CGI scripts and the guest book pages in the directory for Web pages. Before you do this, you need to set the following variables in the script:

`$guestbookurl`	The absolute URL to the guest book log page at your Web site
`$guestbookreal`	The actual file path to the page that displays the guest book entries
`$guestlog`	The actual file path to the summary version of the guest book
`$cgiurl`	The URL path to the guestbook.pl script
`$date_command`	The path to the date command

You will find the variable assignments at the very top of the script. Start by assigning a value to the $guestbookurl variable. The value that you assign to the $guestbookurl variable is the absolute URL to the guest book log page at your Web site, such as:

```
$guestbookurl = "http://www.your_isp/~you/gbook.htm";
```

Next, assign a value to the $guestbookreal variable. This variable tells the Guestbook script the actual file path to the guest book log page. Append the directory path for your Web documents to the home directory path that you obtained earlier; then, set the value of the $guestbookreal variable to this value. My home path is /home/william and my Web documents are in the directory www, so I set the $guestbookreal variable to the following:

```
$guestbookreal = "/home/william/www/";
```

Now set the $guestlog variable. The value for this variable is the actual file path to the summary version of the guest book, such as:

```
$guestlog = "/home/william/public_html/glog.htm";
```

The next variable is the URL to guestbook.pl. Enter the full URL path to this script, such as:

```
$cgiurl = "http://www.tvpress.com/cgi-bin/guestbook.pl";
```

Finally, if the path to the date program on your Web server isn't /usr/bin/date, you need to set the $date_command variable. For example, if the date program on your server is at /usr/date, you would set the $date_command variable as follows:

```
$date_command = "/usr/date";
```

Save the file. You're done with the modification. Although you can configure many optional variables, the default settings work just fine.

NOTE Keep in mind that if you use the forms that I created rather than use the default forms, the filenames are different. I changed `guestlog.html` to `glog.htm` and `guestbook.html` to `gbook.htm`.

Installing the Script and Pages on the Server

You are now ready to transfer the Guestbook script and the associated Web pages to the server. Use whatever tool you normally use for file transfers, such as FTP. Then, in your telnet or terminal window, type the following command:

chmod 755 guestbook.pl

This command tells the server that anyone can read and execute the guestbook.pl script. Next, move the script to the directory designated for CGI scripts, which is typically /usr/cgi-bin. If /usr/cgi-bin is the correct directory on your server, type the following command to move the file:

mv guestbook.pl /usr/cgi-bin/

Now that you've installed the script, you can move the Web pages for the guest book to your directory for Web pages. Next, set the gbook.htm and glog.htm files so that they can be read and written with the following:

```
chmod 777 gbook.htm
```

and

```
chmod 777 glog.htm
```

Last, change the access to addguest.htm page using the following command:

```
chmod 744 addguest.htm
```

Testing and Using the Guest Book

The final step is to test the guest book. Enter the full URL to the add guest.htm page at your Web site and try to make an entry. If you have any problems, retrace the steps discussed earlier. Otherwise, you now have a terrific means of finding out who is visiting and of getting feedback.

A Guest Book That Anyone Can Use

After seeing how much work installing a guest book entails, you may be wondering whether there is a quick and easy way to put up a guest book without the hassles of CGI. Yes, you can have a guest book that is virtually hassle free, but best of all, you can use this guest book no matter what type of server you are on. As you will learn in a moment, however, there is a catch to using the universal guest book.

Working with the Universal Guest Book

The universal guest book takes advantage of the mailto: action that you can assign to HTML forms. When you use the mailto: action, the contents of the form are mailed directly to you. The guest book at Internet Daily News shown earlier in Figure 2-10 uses this very technique to send e-mail to my server, where it is logged and processed.

Although the mailto: action is a great way to obtain data without needing CGI, it does have a slight drawback. The data that comes to you will be URL-encoded, meaning that spaces and formatting marks will be encoded with special characters, such as %20 for the space character. Most of the time, you will be able to read the messages posted to you without doing anything. For quick reference, a summary of URL-encoded values is shown in Table 2-8.

Online, I've also set up a Web page that you can use to decode your messages (see Figure 2-14, which appears on page 123). You will find this page at http://www.tvpress.com/promote/decode/. To decode your messages using this page, just paste the message or a group of messages into the text window provided and click on the Reveal Message button. You can then copy the results and paste them into a word processing document so that you can save the results for future reference.

Implementing the Universal Guest Book

You can implement the universal guest book by adding a form to any of your Web pages that references the mailto: action. The value that you assign to the mailto: action is your e-mail address, such as director@tvpress.com.

When you use the universal guest book, try to keep it simple, especially if you don't want to have to decipher URL-encoded values. Listing 2-10 shows an example guest book that asks users to fill in their full name, city, state, and country. You will find this listing online saved as guest.htm. Look in

TABLE 2-8	COMMON URL-ENCODED VALUES
Character Description	**URL-encoded Value**
Tab	%09
Space	%20
Number sign (#)	%23
Percent sign (%)	%25
Ampersand (&)	%26
Apostrophe (')	%27
Question mark (?)	%3f
At symbol (@)	%40
Caret symbol (^)	%5f

the examples area at http://www.tvpress.com/promote/examples/.

If you want to use this example, just modify the e-mail address and paste the markup into a Web page. When the form is submitted, the visitor's entry will be mailed directly to you.

Listing 2-10   A Universal Guest Book

```
<HTML>
<HEAD>
<TITLE>The Universal Guest Book</TITLE>
</HEAD>
<BODY BGCOLOR="#FFFFFF">
```

```
<H3>Sign the Guestbook</H3>
<FORM method="POST" ACTION="mailto:you@your_domain.com">

<TABLE>
<TR><TH>Your Name:<TR><TD><INPUT NAME="YourName" SIZE="25">
<TR><TH>City:<TR><TD><INPUT NAME="email" SIZE="25">
<TR><TH>State &amp; Country<TR><TD><INPUT NAME="Address"
   SIZE="25">
<TR><INPUT TYPE="SUBMIT" VALUE="SIGN GUEST BOOK"><INPUT
   TYPE="RESET">
</TABLE>

</FORM>

</BODY>
</HTML>
```

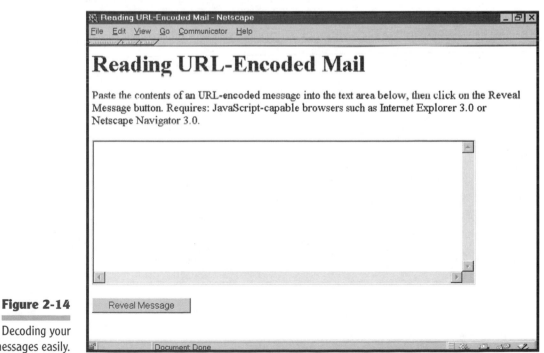

Figure 2-14

Decoding your messages easily.

Wrapping Up and Looking Ahead

Using the techniques described in this section, you can gather vital stats that can tell you who is visiting your Web site and why. Using a page view counter, you can track the all-important page view stats. Using a guest book, you can track domain information and get feedback from visitors. In the next part of the book (Saturday afternoon), you learn how to use your site's stats to attract visitors and to make your Web site a better place to visit.

Putting the Motion in Promotion

- ✿ Transforming the Numbers into Meaningful Data
- ✿ Capitalizing on Search Engine Fundamentals
- ✿ Registering with the Top Search Engines on the Planet
- ✿ Submitting Your Site to the Top Guides, Lists, and Directories

Saturday morning covered how to unlock the secrets of the server log files and how to use the logs to obtain key Web site stats such as number of hits, page views, and visits. Together, these stats help you unravel the big picture for your Web site. You also saw how to use the error logs to clear up the trouble spots at your Web site and gain readers you otherwise would have lost. Finally, you learned about gathering stats without using server logs.

This afternoon, you learn how to put the stats to work. You start by summarizing the stats and transforming them into meaningful data. Then, you use the stats to make your Web site a better place to visit and to find your niche in the wonderful world of cyberspace. Enhancing your Web site based on what the stats tell you, and using your Web site's niche to your advantage, are key ingredients that will help you attract the masses.

This afternoon, you'll also begin delving into the rich array of resources available on the Web to help you get your site noticed. The array is almost *too* rich, though. Rather than present you with a hodgepodge of hit-or-miss choices, I put my countless hours of research and experience into these pages to bring you what I consider the best. This way, you can maximize your time without spending a dime.

Transforming the Numbers into Meaningful Data

All the data that you've gathered so far is great, but to make it useful, you need to transform the raw statistics into meaningful data. You can create meaningful data either by rolling up your sleeves and digging in, or using tracking software that does the job for you.

When you track stats by hand, you get to see all data first-hand, which gives you a keener sense of exactly what is happening at your Web site. Tracking stats by hand isn't difficult, but it is somewhat time consuming because you have to slog through the server logs.

When you track stats using tracking software, the software compiles the stats for you. You have to choose the type and format of reports that are compiled from the stats, however. For tracking software that runs on your PC, each different type of report is generally compiled separately, and you have to wait while your computer slowly plods through the data before you can view a report. For tracking software that runs on a server, you generally have to pre-select the types of reports that you want to see when you install the tracking software, meaning that you cannot easily generate new types of reports.

Tracking Day-to-Day Traffic By Hand

When you track day-to-day traffic by hand, the stats on which you want to focus are hits and page views. Your primary means of gathering stats is the access log. If the server logs aren't available, you can also use counters to gather stats. The best types of counters are those that count page views.

In this section, I show you additional techniques that you can use to summarize Web site stats. Use these techniques in addition to those discussed in the Saturday morning section under "Understanding Visits and Page Views." The reason to summarize stats is to help you gain a better understanding of your Web site's big picture. As stated earlier in the book, the big-picture questions that you can answer when you track hits and page views are the following:

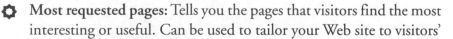 **Most requested pages:** Tells you the pages that visitors find the most interesting or useful. Can be used to tailor your Web site to visitors'

needs and to help you determine which pages get most of your attention.

✿ **Average duration of page view**: Can be an indicator of whether people are reading or just browsing. When you examine this statistic, you also need to keep in mind the length and style of pages that you have at your Web site. Are they highly textual, highly graphical, or both?

✿ **Domain classes and geographic areas:** Can tell you where people visiting your Web site live and work. Great information to have if you want to attract advertisers.

✿ **Busiest hours of the day:** Tells you the time of day most people are visiting your Web site. This statistic can help you plan daily updates, promotion campaigns, and advertising.

✿ **Busiest days of the week:** Tells you the day of the week that most people are visiting your Web site. This statistic can help you plan weekly updates, promotion campaigns, and advertising.

✿ **Most commonly requested last pages:** Can help you spot trends and bad pages. If the last page requested contains lots of links to external Web sites, this statistic tells you that this is the point of departure for most visitors. If the last page requested doesn't have links to external Web sites, you may want to examine the page in question.

Summarizing Hits

Each entry in the access log represents a hit. Usually, when you look at hits, you will want only summary data, such as how many hits are in the access log right now. Summary data provides you with an overview of the activity at your Web site.

Searching the Logs

As covered under "Understanding Visits and Page Views," you can track day-to-day stats using the `find` or `grep` command. The `find` command is available at the DOS prompt on all Windows-based systems. You can use the `find` command to search through the server log files and to count hits and page views, such as:

```
find "overview.html" access-log > save.txt
```

Here, the `find` command is used to search for all entries that reference the page overview.html. The results of the `find` search are put into a file called save.txt. Entries in the save.txt file are complete lines and look exactly like those in the access log:

```
pc8.att.net - - [11/Apr/1997:00:01:18 -0700] "GET / HTTP/1.0"
  200 8355
pc8.att.net - - [11/Apr/1997:00:01:25 -0700] "GET /ban2.gif
  HTTP/1.0" 200 1373
```

As discussed earlier, you can use the `grep` command to search the server logs files on UNIX systems. Although the `grep` command originated on UNIX platforms, an extended version of `grep`, called `egrep`, is available for the Macintosh. In this example, the `grep` command is used to search for all page views for the file overview.html:

```
grep overview.html access-log
```

Getting the Stats

Regardless of whether you use `find` or `grep`, these commands match the keyword for which you are looking to entries in a named file, such as access-log or tvpress-access-log. The results of the search are printed to the screen by default but are preferably directed to a file that you can read or search later.

To count the number of hits in the access log at any given time, search for a string that is common to all entries in the access log. Because all log entries have the bracket character ([), you can summarize hits as follows:

```
find /C "[" access-log
```

or

```
grep "[" access-log | wc
```

The result of either of these searches is the total number of entries in the file called access-log. To make this result meaningful, you need to determine the number of days that the access log covers so that you can come up with a figure that represents the average number of daily hits.

Making Sense of the Numbers

The entries in your access log could cover a few days or a few months. Most access logs are archived monthly. This means that last month's log is usually moved to an archive directory or compressed using ZIP, GZIP, or some other compression utility that saves space on the file system. Although you would expect the log to be archived on a specific day of the month, this isn't always the case. Often, the log is archived when it grows to a specific size, such as 10 megabytes.

If the old log files are available in the same directory, you can look at the date on last month's log file to determine when it was archived. The time difference between the most recently archived log and the current date tells you the number of days that the current log represents.

Another way to determine the number of days that the log covers is to examine the access-log file directly. Trying to load the file into a text editor usually isn't practical, however, because the file size may be several megabytes. On a UNIX system, you can use the `head` or `pg` commands to look at the beginning of the file:

```
head access-log
```

or

```
pg access-log
```

On a Windows system, you can use the `more` command to ensure that you see entries one page at a time. At the DOS prompt, enter the usual search information and then redirect the output through the `more` command with the pipe symbol (|). After you record the time stamp on the first entry, press Ctrl+C to end the search. An example of using the `more` command is as follows:

```
find "[" access-log | more
```

To determine the average daily hits to your Web site, divide the hit count by the number of days the log covers, such as:

```
3502 / 30
```

The average number of hits can help you estimate how much traffic your Web site is generating without your having to wade through the logs or using Web site tracking software. If you look for hits related to specific days, you also can tell busy days from slow days without digging deeper into the logs. You'll learn more about summarizing hits for specific days in the next section.

Tallying Page Views by Hand

A page view is an important statistic because it tells you how many times a particular Web page has been accessed. You can use this statistic to determine the popularity of each individual page at your Web site.

Adopting a Schedule

Whenever you track page views by hand, you should do so on a regular basis, such as daily, weekly, or monthly. I recommend gathering stats daily at first, and then moving to a weekly or monthly schedule when you get into a solid routine that makes tracking stats seem like second nature. Next, make a list of the Web pages you want to track. Although you may want to track all pages at your Web site, tracking page views for individual Web pages isn't always practical. For this reason, you may want to select only the top-level pages at your site, such as your home page or the main page for a uniquely focused area at your Web site.

When you want to track stats on a regular basis, you can use to your advantage the time stamp that all access log entries have. To track stats daily, you search for all references to a specific date, such as:

```
grep "11/Apr/1997" access-log > $HOME/temp.txt
```

To track stats weekly, you repeat the daily search for each day of the week, such as:

```
grep "14/Apr/1997" access-log > $HOME/temp.txt

grep "15/Apr/1997" access-log >> $HOME/temp.txt

grep "16/Apr/1997" access-log >> $HOME/temp.txt

grep "17/Apr/1997" access-log >> $HOME/temp.txt

grep "18/Apr/1997" access-log >> $HOME/temp.txt
```

```
grep "19/Apr/1997" access-log >> $HOME/temp.txt

grep "20/Apr/1997" access-log >> $HOME/temp.txt
```

NOTE The append command (>>) tells grep and find to add the results to a specified file. Keep in mind that grep is a UNIX command and find is a DOS command. Mac users can use a command called egrep but must install this on their system. For more details on these commands, look in the Saturday morning section under "Understandng Visits and Page Views."

To track stats monthly, you search for the month string, such as:

```
find "Apr/199/" access-log >> save.txt
```

Checking Individual Page Views

After you extract page views for a particular time period, you can summarize the stats relating to each page. To do this, search the file that you just created for each page individually; then, count the number of entries. The /C option of the find command lets you count the number of entries for each page:

```
find /C "overview.html" save.txt
```

On UNIX systems, you will use the wc command to count the number of entries for each page:

```
grep overview.html save.txt | wc
```

Because typing the commands repeatedly can be tedious, you can create a batch file to help automate the tracking process. The batch file can contain the initial search through the access log as well as searches for each page that you want to track.

Say that you want to track stats for the following pages on a daily basis:

> / - Your home page
>
> vpbg.htm - Your background page
>
> /writing/ - A top-level page

You need to create a file containing the appropriate commands to check the stats for these pages. The most important thing to remember is to update the search parameters, such as the date you are looking for, before you run the batch file. After you edit and save the batch file, you can run it to check the stats.

On a UNIX platform, your batch file contains the following commands:

```
grep "11/Apr/1997" /www/logs/access-log > $HOME/temp.txt
echo "Home Page Count: "
grep " / " temp.txt | wc
echo "Background Page Count: "
grep "vpbg.htm" temp.txt | wc
echo "Writing Area Count: "
grep "/writing/ " temp.txt | wc
```

NOTE When you examine the example, note the reference to the directory /www/logs. If your access log is not in this directory, you need to enter the actual directory path for your system. Note also the use of the `echo` command to display descriptive text during the search. Don't let all these commands confuse you; just practice using the commands and change the examples to meet your needs.

After you create and save the file, change the mode of the file so that you can execute it. If the filename is stat_track, you can change the mode as follows:

```
chmod 755 stat_track
```

As long as you are in your home directory, you run the batch file from the command prompt by typing:

stat_track

The output from this batch file looks like this:

```
Home Page Count:
152
```

```
Background Page Count:
43
Writing Area Count:
28
```

Here, the page views for /, vpbg.htm, and /writing/ are 152, 43, and 28, respectively. Although the name of the batch file on a UNIX system isn't restricted, your batch file on a Windows-based computer should end with the .bat extension, such as track.bat. Based on the previous example, the batch file for a Windows-based system looks like this:

```
find "11/Apr/1997" access-log > save.txt
find /C " / " save.txt
find /C "vpbg.htm" save.txt
find /C "/writing/ " save.txt
```

NOTE If your access log is not in the same directory as the batch file, you need to enter the actual directory path for your system. Again, please don't allow these commands to confuse you. Practice using the commands and work through the examples.

If you save the file as track.bat, you run it from the DOS prompt by typing:

track

The output from this batch file looks like this:

```
D:\>find "11/Apr/1997" access-log > save.txt
D:\>find /C " / " save.txt
——— save.txt: 29
D:\>find /C "vpbg.htm" save.txt
——— save.txt: 13
D:\>find /C "/writing/ " save.txt
——— save.txt: 2
```

Here, the page views for /, vpbg.htm, and /writing/ are 29, 13, and 2, respectively.

Don't Waste Your Money on Commercial Tracking Software

Although tracking stats by hand definitely gives you a sense that you have hands-on control over your Web site and its destiny, you can find software that will handle the task of tracking stats for you. As you would expect with any type of software, commercial tracking software is available as well as freeware and shareware tracking software. You will find that most of the commercial tracking software comes with all the bells and whistles that you would expect, along with a price tag likely to leave you wide-eyed with sticker shock. Fortunately, the freeware and shareware tracking solutions available are really quite good and ideally suited to the needs of the average Web publisher. For this reason, I say don't waste your money on commercial tracking software, especially when you can find free software that will meet your needs.

Why Use Tracking Software?

Tracking software is great for tracking hits, page views, and the nebulous visit. Because tracking software makes it possible to track visits, you can use tracking software to obtain all the pieces of the big picture for your Web site. From Saturday morning's work, you know that the big picture helps you answer these questions related to your site's traffic:

What was the total number of visitors for this time period?

What was the length of the average visit?

What was the average duration of a page view?

What was the average number of page views per visitor?

What was the average number of hits per visitor?

What domain classes and geographic areas were represented (percentages)?

What were the busiest hours of the day?

What were the busiest days of the week?

What were the most requested pages?

What were the most common last pages requested?

Helping you answer these questions with limited fuss is what tracking software is all about. Still, working with tracking software requires a trade-off. Everything that tracking software does is based on your server log files. You need to configure the software to access your Web server and retrieve the log files. You also need to be patient with the software while it searches through the logs and extracts the information for which you are looking. The larger your log's files, the longer and harder the tracking software has to work to get the stats.

At first glance, tracking software may seem to potentially save you a lot of time, but that isn't always the case. I spent an entire day to obtain, install, configure, and test tracking software for my Web server. The result of that initial eight-hour investment is that the software runs automatically and the reports are generated weekly. Every week, I spend 45 to 60 minutes reviewing and analyzing the reports. Making configuration changes to the software takes about an hour, and afterward, I can retrieve different types of reports.

For desktop tracking software, you have to transfer the server logs to your PC. On a weekly basis, I download the server's log files for a moderately active Web site. The download time using a 28.8 Kbps modem takes just over two hours. After the logs are on my PC, the tracking software usually optimizes the data—a process that takes me anywhere from 15 to 30 minutes. Next, I have to generate individually each of the reports that I want to see—a process that takes 5 to 15 minutes per report on my PC. Then, I spend 15 to 20 minutes reviewing and recording the data.

To see how tracking stats by hand compares to tracking software, I also examined the amount of time that I spend tracking stats by hand. On a daily basis, I look at hits and page views for each of four major areas at my Web site as well as total hits and page views for the entire Web site. It takes me about five minutes to obtain the necessary stats when I type the commands by hand, but only a few seconds to update and run a batch file with the same commands. Afterward, I spend 20 to 25 minutes summarizing, analyzing, and recording the stats.

As you can see, the main reason to use tracking software isn't always to save time. Rather, the main reason to use tracking software is that the software does most of the work for you.

■ ■

Because this book is designed to be used in a weekend—a mere 48 hours—the ins and outs of installing and using the various tracking software is beyond the scope of this book. As you will see when you start to use tracking software, you can spend an entire day just to get a good feel for the software. That said, this book would not be complete without a fairly comprehensive discussion on tracking software, which you will find in the sections that follow. Supplementing this discussion is a list of tracking software programs and their locations on the Web. That list is on the Web site for this book, at:

http://www.tvpress.com/promote/utilities/

■ ■

An Overview of Tracking Software

Most tracking software creates graphical representations of the traffic at your Web site. Graphs and charts are great for helping you understand the activity at your site without having to dig through the numbers. A summary of visits using a graph is shown in Figure 3-1. The software that I used to create the graph is called net.Analysis Desktop.

● ●

net.Analysis Desktop is commercial software from net.Genesis Corporation; the software runs on Windows 95, Windows NT, and Solaris platforms. You can obtain a free trial version of net.Analysis Desktop by visiting www.netgen.com.

● ●

Other tracking software summarizes your site's traffic using completely text-based means, which doesn't necessarily mean that the results lack graphs and charts. Graphs can be created using text characters, such as the dash or plus sign.

As a matter of fact, Analog 2.0 from the University of Cambridge Statistical Laboratory generates a daily report graph using only text. The daily

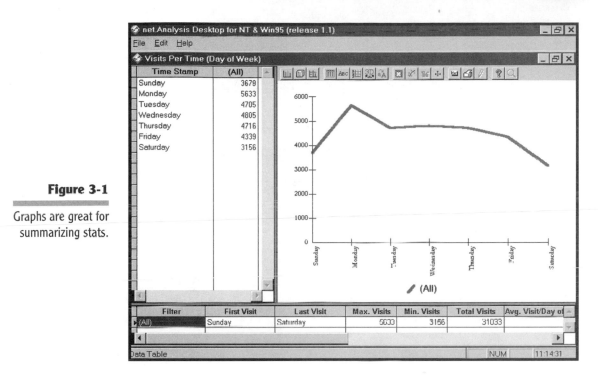

Figure 3-1

Graphs are great for summarizing stats.

report graph summarizes page views by representing a set amount of pages with a plus sign. An example of this daily report is shown in Listing 3-1.

TIP

FIND IT ◆ ONLINE

Analog 2.0 is created by Steve Turner from the University of Cambridge Statistical Laboratory. This software is free, and versions of Analog 2.0 are available for just about every operating system including DOS, Windows 3.1/95/NT, Mac, and most UNIX systems. You can obtain Analog 2.0 by visiting: http://www.statslab.cam.ac.uk/~sret1/analog/.

Listing 3-1 A Daily Report from Analog 2.0

```
Daily Report
```
```
Each unit (+) represents 100 requests for pages, or part
    thereof.
```

```
       date: pages:
____   __

 1/Apr/97:   2396: +++++++++++++++++++++++++
 2/Apr/97:   1968: ++++++++++++++++++++
 3/Apr/97:   1996: +++++++++++++++++++++
 4/Apr/97:   1619: ++++++++++++++++++
 5/Apr/97:   1057: +++++++++++

 6/Apr/97:   1302: ++++++++++++++
 7/Apr/97:   2167: +++++++++++++++++++++++
 8/Apr/97:   2003: ++++++++++++++++++++++
 9/Apr/97:   1777: +++++++++++++++++++
10/Apr/97:   1858: ++++++++++++++++++++
11/Apr/97:   1939: ++++++++++++++++++++
12/Apr/97:   1424: +++++++++++++++

13/Apr/97:   3723: ++++++++++++++++++++++++++++++++++++++++
14/Apr/97:   4200: ++++++++++++++++++++++++++++++++++++++++++++
15/Apr/97:   4319:
   +++++++++++++++++++++++++++++++++++++++++++++++
16/Apr/97:   3867: +++++++++++++++++++++++++++++++++++++++++++
17/Apr/97:   3279: +++++++++++++++++++++++++++++++++++
18/Apr/97:   2482: ++++++++++++++++++++++++++
19/Apr/97:   1957: ++++++++++++++++++++

20/Apr/97:   1952: ++++++++++++++++++++
21/Apr/97:   2570: +++++++++++++++++++++++++++
```

Tracking Software on the Server and on the Desktop

Beyond graphics or text-based representations of the data compiled by tracking software are two other categories of tracking software:

- ✪ Tracking software that runs on your desktop PC
- ✪ Tracking software that runs on the server

Tracking Software That Runs on Your Desktop PC

Some tracking software is designed to be run from your desktop. Unlike tracking software installed on the server, desktop tracking software generally does not run automatically. This means that you are responsible for starting the software, telling it to retrieve the access log for the server, and then compiling the types of reports that you want to see.

net.Analysis is an example of tracking software that runs on your desktop. When you start net.Analysis, the first thing that you must do is retrieve the current log file, which net.Analysis calls *importing* the file. Your modem speed and the size of the log file determines how long retrieving the log file takes; the time can very from a few minutes to several hours.

After retrieving the log file, the tracking software examines the file and optimizes it. The optimization process typically involves removing or commenting out references to image files as well as indexing the file for quicker searching later. Your CPU speed and memory determine how long the optimization takes.

The final step is when you tell the software what type of reports you want to generate. For net.Analysis, each report is generated individually, meaning that you tell the software to create a report, wait until it finishes, and then go on to the next report.

Most tracking software that runs on your desktop isn't free. Still, you can usually obtain free trial versions of the software by visiting the developer's Web site.

Tracking Software That Runs on the Server

Most tracking software is installed as an add-on for a Web server. The job of server-side tracking software is to build periodic reports that can be stored for later access by users or sent directly to users. By running on the server, the software can take advantage of the tremendous power of the server and reduce the amount of work that you as a publisher must do.

Analog 2.0 is an example of tracking software that runs on a Web server. When you install Analog 2.0, you configure the software to generate specific types of reports at designated intervals, such as every week. From then on, Analog 2.0 generates the specified reports automatically. If you later decide that you want a different set of reports, you need to reconfigure the software. Fortunately, the whole process of reconfiguring the software and generating new reports takes only a few minutes.

Because the tracking software is installed on the server, the log files do not need to be transferred to a different system and can be read and interpreted right on the server, which drastically reduces the amount of time that generating reports takes. As a Web publisher, you will notice the speed difference immediately. For example, retrieving a 10MB access log and creating four reports with net.Analysis took over two hours, yet I created similar reports running Analog 2.0 on the server in less than 60 seconds.

As you can see, tracking software that runs on the server has a definite advantage over tracking software that runs on the desktop, yet you may not have permission to install this type of software on the server. For this reason, you should ask your Internet service provider whether it has already selected some type of tracking software that you can use, or whether installing your own tracking software is okay.

Most Internet Service Providers that offer virtual domains or cater to the needs of business customers rather than individual users already have tracking software installed on their Web servers. To access this software, you usually just need to ask. If your Internet Service Provider doesn't have tracking software installed on the server, you may want to point your provider in the direction of Analog 2.0, which is arguably the most versatile tracking software anywhere that doesn't cost a dime.

Other good choices that you'll want to tell your ISP about include:

- getstats: Freeware that works with the following Web server software: CERN, NCSA, Plexus, GN, and MacHTTP. You can obtain getstats at:

  `http://www.eit.com/software/getstats/getstats.html`

FIND IT ▶
ONLINE

- MKStats: Extremely versatile and free for noncommercial use. Because MKStats uses Perl, it is designed to be run on UNIX or Linux systems. You can obtain MKStats by visiting:

  `http://www.mkstats.com/`

⚙ wwwstat: Fairly versatile freeware that also uses Perl. You can obtain wwwstat by visiting:

```
http://www.ics.uci.edu/pub/websoft/wwwstat/
```

Finally, You Know What Pages Are Popular; Now What?

Regardless of whether you track your site's stats by hand or use tracking software, the result is that you now have a better understanding of who is visiting your Web site and why. You should also have answers to many of the big-picture questions. These answers can help you make your Web site a better place to visit and will also help you increase traffic to your Web site.

Right about now, you are probably wondering why I keep saying that you can use the stats to make your Web site a better place to visit as well as to increase traffic to your Web site. After all, the title of the book is *Increase Your Web Traffic In a Weekend*, not *Make Your Web Site a Better Place to Visit In a Weekend*.

The simple truth is that the long-term success of your Web site is based upon understanding your site's good points and bad points. By understanding your site's good points, you learn how to market the Web site to the world. By understanding your site's bad points, you learn what you need to do to fix the problems. If you don't fix the problems at your Web site, you may lose readers just as fast as you find new ones.

The steps to follow to make your Web site a better place to visit include:

⚙ Directing users to popular areas

⚙ Cleaning up unused pages

⚙ Avoiding dead-ends

⚙ Fixing errors

After you take a close look at your Web site, you can move on to the next step, which is to find your niche in cyberspace and formulate a plan that uses your niche to market your Web site to the world.

Directing Users to Popular Areas

Every road sign you can add to the Web makes cyberspace just a little bit more enjoyable, so why not create a few road signs that direct users to popular areas at your Web site? Your road signs don't need to be extravagant. You can use plain-old text to create links to other pages at your Web site, but you need to tell visitors that those other pages exist.

Obviously, you don't want to tell visitors about every single Web page you've published. Instead, you want to direct users to the popular areas of your Web site by creating links to the top-level page within the specific areas that you want to promote. The idea here is that people visiting your sports information page, for example, may also be interested in your sports equipment page. They can't get to the sports equipment page if you don't tell them it exists, however.

Say that your site's stats show that seven pages at the Web site get the most traffic. The URLs for these pages are the following:

http://www.cooldays.com/ - Your main home page

http://www.cooldays.com/summer/ - A page that promotes summertime activities

http://www.cooldays.com/summer/water-skiing.html - A page within the summertime activities area that covers water skiing

http://www.cooldays.com/summer/surfing.html - A page within the summertime activities area that covers surfing

http://www.cooldays.com/equipment/ - A page that discusses where you can look on the Web to get the best bargains in sports equipment

http://www.cooldays.com/equipment/forsale.html - A page that lets people post ads to sell their sports equipment

http://www.cooldays.com/equipment/tips.html - A page that provides tips for getting the best value for your money when you buy sports equipment

When you examine the seven most visited pages, you see that three specific areas of the Web site are getting the most traffic:

- The main home page
- The summertime activities area
- The sports-equipment area

The home page is the place to toot your horn about the main areas at your site, but you also need to do so on the top-level pages within the site. Although you may think that most visitors start on the site's home page, this isn't always true. In fact, most people probably start their visit on some other page. For this reason, you should tell anyone visiting the summertime activities area that you have this wonderful sports-equipment area, and vice versa.

By promoting both areas, you increase page views at your site and let readers know that your site really does have a lot to offer. On the Web page at http://www.cooldays.com/summer/, you add a clear road sign that directs visitors to the sports equipment area (see Figure 3-2). The markup for the road sign is as follows:

```
<HR SIZE=5>
<H3><A HREF="http://www.cooldays.com/equipment/">Sports
  Equipment</A></H3>
<UL>
<LI>Find the best bargains on the Web
<LI>Read tips for buying sports equipment that will save you
  a bundle
<LI>Get great deals on used equipment or post your own for
  sale ad
</UL>
```

Then, on the Web page at http://www.cooldays.com/equipment/, you add another road sign that directs visitors to the summertime activities area (see Figure 3-3). The markup for the road sign is as follows:

```
<HR SIZE=5>
<H3><A HREF="http://www.cooldays.com/summer/">Fun In the
```

Figure 3-2

Directing visitors to
the sports
equipment area.

```
Sun</A></H3>
<P>Interested in summer-time sports like scuba diving,
water skiing and surfing? Why not stop by
our Fun in the Sun headquarters?
```

Cleaning Up Unused Pages

After studying your Web site to see how you can direct traffic to popular
areas, you should take a hard look at pages that rarely get visitors. Although
your first impulse may be to delete the page or stop updating the page, this
may not be the right solution. Rather than remove or neglect the page, you
should ensure that other pages at your Web site have clear road signs that
tell people what the page is all about. You may also want to consider combining the information on this page with information on another page.

Say that your site's stats show two pages at the Web site rarely receive visitors. The URLs for these pages are as follows:

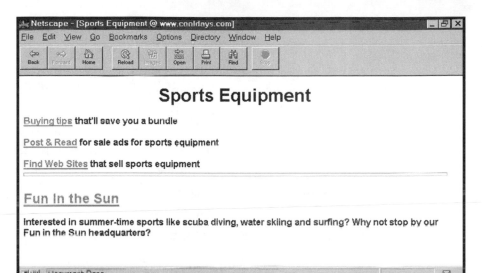

Figure 3-3

Directing visitors to the summertime activities area.

http://www.cooldays.com/summer/background.html - A background page for the summertime activities area.

http://www.cooldays.com/summer/scuba/deepwater.html - A page that promotes deep-water scuba diving

After examining the background page, you may discover that you can summarize the information and place it directly on the top-level page for the summertime activity area. In this way, visitors to this area of the Web site get a quick summary without having to visit the background page. By adding the information to the top-level page, you make the area a better place to visit.

Next, you look at the page that promotes deep-water scuba diving. Your scuba diving pages are broken down into three categories: fresh water, salt water, and deep water. Although the fresh water and sea water scuba pages get lots of visitors, the deep-water page rarely gets a visitor. The problem here may be organizational; perhaps your top-level page needs to explain that deep water refers to deep-sea scuba diving with submersibles and that you also feature video from the Galapagos undersea expedition.

Avoiding Dead Ends

Dead ends are show stoppers. All your Web pages should end with links that lead back to a main page, the previous page, or the next page in a series of pages. Links at the bottom of a Web page are subtle reminders that the Web site has more to offer. By adding appropriate links to the bottom of your Web pages, you can make navigating your Web site easier, thereby increasing traffic to your Web site. Remember, if readers visit your sports-related Web site, they are interested in sports, so why not help them find the information they are looking for?

Links at the bottom of a Web page can be as basic as the one shown in Figure 3-4. The markup for the link is as follows:

```
<HR SIZE=5>

<P><A HREF="/summer/">Back to Fun in the Sun</A></P>
```

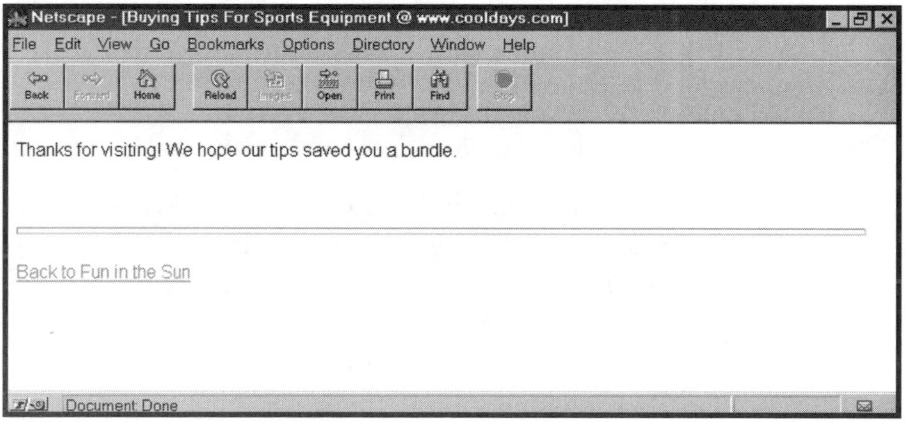

Figure 3-4

Avoiding dead ends with a basic link.

You can also use mini menus that tell readers about other areas of your Web site, such as the one shown in Figure 3-5. The markup for this mini menu is as follows:

```
<HR SIZE=5>
<P><A HREF="/">Our Home Page </A> ||
<A HREF="/summer/">Fun in the Sun</A> ||
<A HREF="/equipment/">Sports Equipment</A></P>
```

Netscape - [Buying Tips For Sports Equipment @ www.cooldays.com]

File Edit View Go Bookmarks Options Directory Window Help

Back | Forward | Home | Reload | Images | Open | Print | Find | Stop

Thanks for visiting! We hope our tips saved you a bundle.

Our Home Page ‖ Fun in the Sun ‖ Sports Equipment

Document Done

Figure 3-5

Avoiding dead ends
by ending the page
with a mini menu.

Another form of dead end is a page that causes the reader to lose interest in your Web site. For example, a page full of errors or inconsistencies may make the reader think that the rest of your Web site isn't worth visiting. For this reason, you may want to look for pages that are often the last page that people visit, and see whether they need updating.

A Last Look at Error Correction

Whenever you have bad references in your Web pages, you risk losing visitors. If you haven't taken the time to examine the errors in the server log's files, you may want to do so now. Refer to the Saturday Morning section under "Gaining Lost Readers from the Error Logs" for help with this.

Understanding Your Niche

After tracking your site's stats, you should have a clearer understanding of the resources that attract visitors to your Web site. These resources help define your niche in cyberspace. Understanding your niche and using it to your advantage are the keys to success when you try to promote your Web site to the world. By taking the time to learn exactly why people visit your Web site, you save yourself a barrel full of heartaches.

Before they started tracking their stats, the creators of www.cooldays.com thought that the underwater video sequences they published online were the main events at their Web site. As it turned out, the Web pages covering deep-sea scuba diving were the least visited. Although you could say that the problem was poor organization, it turns out that the Web site had lots of other things to offer visitors.

Thus, although the creators of the Web site started out to build a resource for scuba divers, they ended up with a Web site that covered many different water sports, including water skiing and surfing. They also created a wonderful guide to buying sports equipment online. Looking back, they saw that their niche covered two different areas: resources for anyone who loved water sports; and resources for buying and selling sports equipment online.

Unfortunately, the site's banners and logos promoted the site as "A great place for anyone who loves scuba diving." Worse, the developers of the site used this same slogan whenever they had an opportunity to promote the Web site. When they registered with search engines, they hyped their great scuba-diving center and forgot about the other areas. When they traded links with other sites, they told the publisher to be sure to tell people about the site's scuba-diving resources. Even though they did indeed attract visitors who were interested in scuba diving, they missed out on many other opportunities to increase the traffic to their Web site.

As you can see, the creators of www.cooldays.com should have taken the time to put together a better picture of their Web site before they started promoting their site as a great place for anyone who loves scuba diving. A better description of their Web site would have been the following:

> A terrific site for anyone who loves water sports! We have tons of resources covering scuba diving, water skiing, surfing, and many other water sports. We also have a terrific guide to sites that sell sports equipment. Our buying tips may save you a bundle.

The creators of www.cooldays.com could also create separate descriptions for each popular area at the Web site. This would allow them to promote the Web site as a whole and each area separately. For example, the next time they register in a search engine, they could use the combined description and then register each area separately as well. You'll learn all about search engines in the next part, under "Capitalizing on Search Engine Fundamentals."

Wrapping Up and Looking Ahead

Before you continue, create descriptive blurbs for your Web site. Start by identifying the most popular areas at your Web site, and then use the subjects that these areas cover to come up with a brief description that identifies your site's niche. Afterward, create separate descriptions for each popular area at your Web site. For the remainder of this afternoon, you discover more ways to use this information when you promote your Web site to the world.

Capitalizing on Search Engine Fundamentals

Finding Web sites would be nearly impossible without sites that let you quickly and easily search for information. These so-called search engines provide a service that puts all the resources of the Web within reach. Search engines allow Web publishers to register their Web pages so that the pages will be added to the list of resources the search engine knows about. Search engines allow Web users to find the pages listed in the search engine using keywords and phrases that identify the information that the users want to find.

Although search engines are one of the primary means of getting your site noticed by users around the world, few people truly understand how search engines work. That is, people rarely get the most out of the search engine and often waste their time and resources when they register their site with search engines. In this part of this section, you will learn how search engines do what they do and how you can make the most of the techniques that search engines use to index and reference your Web site.

Millions of Users Are But a Search Away

More than 50 million people are just a click away from your Web site. They just need to follow the references that lead to you. The only problem is that your Web site probably doesn't show up in the results retrieved by the search engine they are using, and on the rare occasion when the results show your site, the information that users need to make the decision to visit your site is lacking. At that point, they head off to some other site. Day in and day out, this scenario plays out at the hundreds of search engines on the Web. The result is that your Web site doesn't get the level of traffic it deserves.

Because few people truly understand how search engines work, Web publishers often get frustrated when they try to attract visitors using search engines. Usually, the Web publisher will register the site with a few search engines, and then sit back and wait for the visitors to come. When the visitors don't come, the publisher then registers with more search engines. Eventually, the publisher may even turn to commercial services that promise to bring visitors to the Web site.

Search engines are one of the least understood Internet tools, and anytime there is a lack of understanding, someone out there is going to try to make a buck at your expense. You'll find services trying to sell you the Holy Grail for hundreds of dollars. These services tell you that they will register your site with every search engine available; get your site listed in the top 10 search results every time; or trick search engines into displaying your site more often than not. To all that, I say: Don't spend a dime. Instead, take the time to learn how search engines work and use this information to get your site noticed by the millions of Web users.

Indexers, Spiders, Crawlers, and Other Web Beasties

In the early days of the Web, search engines were simple tools for finding information using indexes. Much like the index of your favorite computer book, the purpose of the index was to make finding information possible by using keywords. Rather than the page references used in traditional indexes, Web indexes had hypertext links that you could click on to access the information at Web sites around the world.

Over the years, search engines evolved. Today, the best search engines are complex applications that use advanced techniques to put millions of Web pages at the fingertips of Web users. Often, these advanced search engines have descriptive names that hint at the techniques the search engine uses to index Web pages, such as *spider* or *crawler*.

Working with Search Engines

No matter what label you use to identify a search engine, the fundamental purpose of a search engine is generally to index Web sites in a way that allows people to use keywords to find Web pages that interest them. To do this, search engines rely on an indexer, spider, or crawler to ferret out the pages at your site and then create indexed references to those pages in the search engine's database. After the pages are indexed in the search engine's database, anyone can use the front-end search process to find the pages.

If you jaunt over to Lycos at `http://www.lycos.com/`, you find two input fields. As shown in Figure 3-6, the first input field asks what area you want to search and the second input field asks what you want to search for. These two fields represent the basic search process at Lycos. When you click on the Go Get It button, the search engine uses the parameters that you've entered to find matching references in the Lycos database.

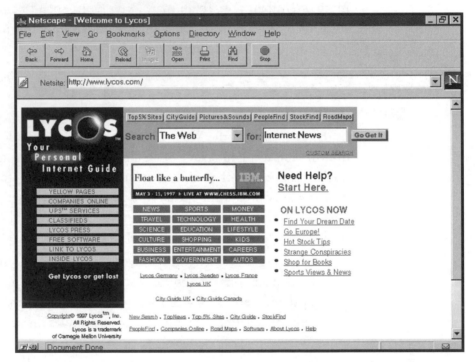

Figure 3-6

Using a search engine.

When you search using the keywords *Internet News*, you get a list of results like those shown in Figure 3-7. As you can see, the results of a search are usually displayed according to their relevancy to the search parameters that you entered. Here, the probability that the first listing is a match is 100 percent, with two out of two of the search words found. The probability that the second listing is a match is 81 percent, with two out of two of the search words found.

Remembering that you searched for the words *Internet News*, the results state that both words were found in the listed documents. Thus, two out of two search words were found in these documents. Further, the search engine maintains that the probability of a match for the first document is 100 percent, meaning that the search engine believes this document is a very strong match for your search. Generally, the probability of a match is based on the number of times your search words occur in the associated document, the position of the words within the documents, and several other factors.

Most search engines display references to the top 10 or 20 pages that match your search parameters. Successive groups of matching pages are also available, but you have to follow a link to another results page. At Lycos, you can click on the Next Page link found at the top and bottom of the results page to see additional pages that might be a match for your search.

Often, the matching pages are described using the page title and a brief description taken from the page itself. Most commercial search engines allow you to customize the search and how search results are displayed. The search engine at Lycos lets you customize the search to display summary information or detailed information rather than the standard results. You can also specify how strictly you want the search engine to match your parameters to Web pages and the number of possible matches to display in each results page.

Comparing Search Engines and Directory Lists

Search engines and directory lists are very different. When you look for information with a search engine, you use keywords. When you look for information at a directory listing, you search by following links to pages within the directory site. Your search starts by clicking on a broad category, such as entertainment, and you eventually drill down to a very specific subject, such as movie reviews.

One of the best known directory lists is Yahoo! (http://www.yahoo.com). When you visit the Yahoo! home page (shown in Figure 3-8), you are greeted by a listing of the top-level categories of information available at the site. Under the top-level categories are more focused categories of information. If you select the News and Media category, you end up on the page shown

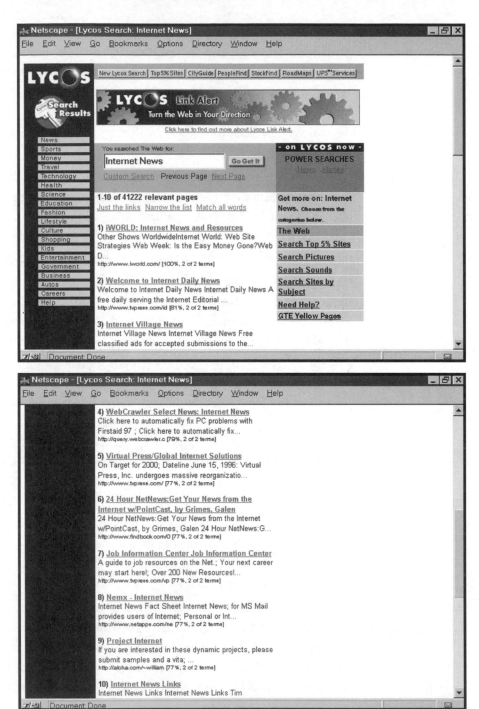

Figure 3-7

The results of a
search.

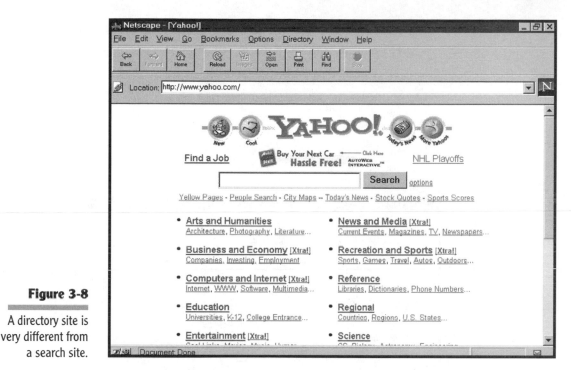

Figure 3-8

A directory site is very different from a search site.

in Figure 3-9. As you can see, this page shows many different broad categories of news. By selecting another link, you can get to a more narrowly focused category, such as business news or technology news.

Yahoo! also makes use of a search engine. Whereas the Lycos search engine lets you search the Web, the Yahoo! search engine finds pages within Yahoo!'s own Web site that contain references to the information you seek. In this way, you can find information faster, without having to spend time following links from a broad category to a narrowly focused category. Directory lists are covered extensively later on Saturday afternoon under the heading, "Submitting Your Web Site to the Top Guides, Lists, and Directories."

Search Engine Fundamentals

Although we've come to think of search engines as giant applications that find information, a search engine is really three different applications that work together to find and retrieve information. These applications consist of the following:

    ✿   An indexer: The back-end application that finds and indexes pages for inclusion in a database; other names for this type of application include *spider*, *crawler*, and *robot*

    ✿   A database: The application that stores the indexed references to Web pages

    ✿   A query interface: The application that handles the queries submitted by users

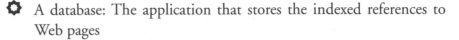

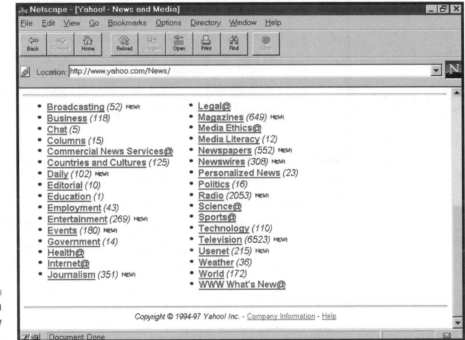

Figure 3-9

Accessing a broad category of information.

Search engines can't find or index your Web site without a little help, which is why people register their sites with search engines. Another way for a search engine to find your Web site is through a link to one of your pages from someone else's site. After a search engine finds your Web site, the search engine uses the links within your pages to find additional pages at your Web site. In this way, the search engine crawls through your Web site one link at a time.

What Do Search Engines Look For?

Search engines don't store all the data in your pages. Instead, search engines create indexed references to your pages. Most of the time, this indexed reference contains the following information:

- ✿ **Page title:** From the TITLE element of your Web page

- ✿ **Page URL:** The absolute URL to your Web page

- ✿ **Summary description:** A description taken from the page itself

- ✿ **Keyword list:** A list of keywords taken from the page itself; accompanied by a relevancy index that explains how relevant each indexed word is to other indexed words and, often, how relevant the indexed words are to the page title as well

Although most search engines create indexed references to your Web pages, just about every search engine gathers this information from different areas of your Web page. Whereas one search engine may gather the summary description for your page from the first few hundred characters, another search engine may look for common words or phrases in the page to use in the summary description.

The various search engines use the summary information in different ways as well. Some search engines make all the information available to user queries. Other search engines store all of the information categories, yet user queries are performed only against specific categories of data, such as the page title and keyword list.

What Does the Indexed Reference Look Like for a Real Web Page?

To get a better understanding of what indexers do, I give you a look at a real Web page and point out what an indexed reference for the page looks like. Figure 3-10 shows the page in a Web browser. The source for the page is shown in Listing 3-2.

As you examine the sample Web page, note the title and the use of the <META> tag to describe the page and identify keywords. Also note that the page contains lots of text.

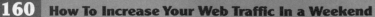

Listing 3-2   A Sample Web Page

```
<HTML>
<HEAD>
<TITLE>Writer's Gallery: Resources for Writers and Readers</
    TITLE>
<META NAME=description" CONTENT="Writer's Gallery is a place
    for anyone who loves the written word. You'll find links to
    hundreds of writing-related resources as well as new works
    of fiction published at our site. ">
<META NAME="keywords" CONTENT="writing, reading, write, read,
    book, author, story, fiction, nonfiction, literary, mythol-
    ogy, medieval, biblical, renaissance, library, Dante,
    Dickens, Faulkner, Shakespeare, news, world news, enter-
    tainment news, business news, current events, publishing,
    dictionary, encyclopedia, bookshelf">

</HEAD>
<BODY BGCOLOR="#000080" text="#ffff00" link="#fffbf0"
vlink="#808000" alink="#ff0000">

<IMG SRC="wgttl2.jpg" ALT="Writer's Gallery" BORDER=0
    ALIGN=LEFT>
<CENTER>
<H1>A place for anyone who loves the written word!</H1>
<H3>Over 250 New Resources!</H3>
</CENTER>
<FONT SIZE=-1><P><A HREF="vpspons.html">We're looking for
    sponsors.</A>
<P>Brought to you by the Original Virtual Press — Fine Publi-
    cations, Community Service and Much More Since March, 1994.
If you'd like more information about <A HREF="vpbg.html">The
```

```
Virtual Press</A> or would like to post information to the
Writer's Gallery:  Send e-mail to <A
  HREF="mailto:wg@tvpress.com">wg@tvpress.com</A></FONT></P>


<P><IMG SRC="bboard.gif" ALIGN="BOTTOM" ALT="* ATTN *">Put a
  bookmark here.
Come back and visit!</P>
<BR CLEAR=ALL>
<H2><A HREF="vpwfeat.html">Writer's Gallery Features</A></H2>
<P>Find hundreds of zines, thousands of books and links to
all good things related to writing!  </P>
<H2><A HREF="vpwlite.html">Writer's Gallery Literary Re-
  sources</A></H2>
<P>If you need a literary reference look here.  From Greek
mythology to the Renaissance.  From medieval to biblical.
From the 9th century to the 19th century.  This page covers
it all.</P>
<H2><A HREF="vpwauth.html">Writer's Gallery Great Authors</
  A></H2>
<P>If  you are looking for information on great writers from
history, look here.  You'll find information on writers from
Dante, Dickens, Faulkner, Shakespeare and more!</P>
<H2><A HREF="wcurrent.html">Writer's Gallery Guide to Current
  Events</A></H2>
<H3><A HREF="http://tvpress.comhttp://www.tvpress.com/idn/"
  TARGET="_parent">
Internet Daily News</A> || <A HREF="wcurrent.html#usnews">US
  News</A> ||
<A HREF="wcurrent.html#worldnews">World News</A> ||
<A HREF="wcurrent.html#busnews">Business News</A> ||
<A HREF="wcurrent.html#entnews">Entertainment News</A> ||
<A HREF="wcurrent.html#finnews">Finance News</A></H3>
```

```
<H2><A HREF="vpwcomp.html">Writer's Companions</A></H2>
<P>Dictionaries, encyclopedias & more!  All the reference
 works you wish were on your bookshelf.</P>
<H2><A HREF="vpwresou.html">Writer's Resources</A></H2>
<P>A comprehensive resource list for writers!  The Writer's
 Resource includes Virtual Libraries, Meta Indexes, Web
  Databases and more!  Dozens of them . . . </P>
<H2><A HREF="vpnewgp.html">Newsgroups for Writers</A></H2>
<P>Looking for a great way to meet fellow writers?
Join a discussion group!</P>
<H2><A HREF="vppubl.html">Who's Who in Publishing on the
  WWW&#153;</A></H2>
<P>Find publishers on the Web</P>
<H2><A HREF="vpwart.html#art">Art</A></H2>
<P>Interested in finding art resources?  Try these
  resources.</P>
<H2><A HREF="vpwart.html#movies">Movie &amp; Industry
Information</A></H2>
<P>Movie reviews & great movie information</P>
<HR SIZE=4>

<FORM METHOD="POST" ACTION="mailto:wg@tvpress.com">
<P>Help us grow add a link to Writer's Gallery!</P>
<P><TEXTAREA NAME="writer's galery links" COLS="40" ROWS="1">
</TEXTAREA></P>
<P>Please describe the link.</P>
<P><TEXTAREA NAME="writer's galery description" COLS="40"
  ROWS="1">
</TEXTAREA></P>
<P><INPUT TYPE="SUBMIT"> <INPUT TYPE="RESET"></P>
</FORM>
<HR SIZE=4>
```

```
<P>Questions or comments pertaining to the TVP Web site can
   be directed to
<A HREF="mailto:webmaster@tvpress.com">
<IMG SRC="mail.gif" ALIGN="MIDDLE" ALT="*e-mail*">
webmaster@tvpress.com</A></P>
<P>This page, and all contents, are <A HREF="vpcopy.html">
Copyright (C) by The Virtual Press, USA.</A>
</P>

</BODY>
</HTML>
```

Figure 3-10

A sample Web page
from the Writer's
Gallery.

When different search engines index this Web page, they will come up with different results. For search engine A, an indexed reference to the page could look like the following:

- **Page title:** Writer's Gallery: Resources for Writers and Readers

- **Page URL:** `http://www.tvpress.com/vpwg.html`

- **Summary description:** A place for anyone who loves the written word! Over 250 new resources! We're looking for sponsors.

- **Keyword list:** Author, biblical, books, bookshelf, business news, comment, community, companion, current events, database, entertainment news, events, finance news, gallery, Greek mythology, history, index, industry, information, library, literary, medieval, movie, mythology, news, newsgroup, press, publication, question, reference, renaissance, resource, service, sponsor, virtual, word, world news, writer, writer newsgroup, writing, written word

Here, the search engine takes most of the information that it needs directly from the body of the Web page. Because of this, each word in the page is weighed for relevancy and inclusion in the keyword list. You learn more about relevancy later in this section. Also, note that the summary description for this page is truncated at a pre-set number of characters, which means that the last sentence isn't complete in this case.

For search engine B, an indexed reference to the page could look like this:

- **Page title:** Writer's Gallery: Resources for Writers and Readers

- **Page URL:** `http://www.tvpress.com/vpwg.html`

- **Summary description:** Writer's Gallery is a place for anyone who loves the written word. You'll find links to hundreds of writing-related resources as well as new works of fiction published at our site.

- **Keyword list:** Author, biblical, book, bookshelf, business news, current events, Dante, Dickens, dictionary, encyclopedia, entertainment news, Faulkner, fiction, fiction works, library, literary, medieval, mythology, news, nonfiction, publishing, read, reader, reading,

renaissance, resource, Shakespeare, story, world news, write, writer, writing, written word

Here, the search engine obtains the page description from the `<META>` tag and then combines the keyword information provided in the `<META>` tag with words used in the page to come up with a keyword list. Although this technique may seem unusual, many search engines that take advantage of meta information combine the description and keywords that you provide with information taken from the body of the page.

NOTE Don't worry, I cover more about the `<META>` tag and meta information later in the section. Look for the heading, "Getting the Most from Keywords and Meta Information."

For search engine C, an indexed reference to the page could look like this:

- ✪ **Page title:** Writer's Gallery: Resources for Writers and Readers

- ✪ **Page URL:** `http://www.tvpress.com/vpwg.html`

- ✪ **Summary description:** A place for anyone who loves the written word! Over 250 new resources! We're looking for sponsors.

Here, the search engine only makes use of the page title and a summary description obtained from the first 100 characters of text found in the page. Although the streamlined entries in the database aren't desirable for the publisher, the search engine designers probably chose this format because it drastically reduces the size of the database, which in turn reduces overhead and speeds up database queries.

What Happens After Your Web Site Has Been Indexed?

Indexing a Web site is not a one-time deal. After the search engine initially indexes your site, your site is usually scheduled for re-indexing at periodic intervals. By re-indexing Web sites, search engines are able to keep up with the ever-changing face of the Web. That said, not all search engines automatically re-index your site, and some search engines re-index your

Web site so infrequently that you end up with outdated references.

Additionally, the way that a search engine re-indexes your Web site may not be what you expect. Some search engines simply check to see whether the page still exists, but don't update the actual reference to the Web page. Other search engines check the page header to see whether the page has changed, so if you changed text at the bottom of the page, the search engine won't re-index the page. Still other search engines use the modification date on the page to determine whether the page should be re-indexed. The search engine then either re-indexes the page immediately or schedules the page for re-indexing at a later date.

Another problem with search engines is that pages you deleted months ago may still be listed. Although some search engines let you remove outdated references from the database, the best way to solve these and other problems that you may encounter is to periodically resubmit your Web site to the search engine. For problems related to pages that you've moved to different locations, you may also want to use placeholder documents and the redirection techniques examined in the Saturday morning section under "Gaining Lost Readers from the Error Logs." In this way, you direct readers from the old page to the new page and eventually the search engine will pick up on this and update the references to your Web site.

Boosting Visits with Ordinary Descriptions

To a search engine, text is the most important part of the page. Search engines use ordinary text to describe the page, to build the keyword list, and to determine the relevancy of the page to particular subjects. Although search engines may treat text in different ways, they share some common themes concerning how text is indexed and referenced.

Understanding Summary Descriptions

Whenever results are displayed by a search engine, the main thing that sells your page to the reader is the summary description, which usually comes from the first 100 to 200 characters in the Web page. When you look at your Web pages to see what the description may look like, be sure to include all text in headers, paragraphs, and other text elements on the page.

Because some search engines have very specific parameters for obtaining the summary description, text at the top of the page is usually given more weight than text at the bottom of the page. Thus, if you have a short description at the top of your page followed by several graphic elements, tables, or linked lists, the search engine may not use text from the later sections of the page. By understanding this, you can see why some page descriptions are really short and others fill out the full 100 to 200 characters used by the search engine.

To help your Web site get noticed, create clear summary statements for your key Web pages, which includes the home page and top-level pages at your Web site. The summary statement should be the first text element in the page, perhaps directly following your graphical banner. If you keep the summary statement short but descriptive, it usually flows well with the rest of the page.

TIP

Whenever possible, try to end your summary statement with proper punctuation. Believe it or not, a few search engines look for complete statements. Phrases without punctuation are considered ambiguous, and phrases with punctuation are considered relevant.

Understanding Relevancy

The position of text in your Web page often determines its relevancy. Because of the variations in how search engines use text, relevancy is one of the hardest search engine terms to pin down. In general terms, the relevancy of text describes:

 How a word relates to other words

 The proximity of one word to another

 The position of the word within the page

 Whether the word is presented as part of a complete statement

 How many times the word is used in the page

The concept of relevancy explains why some of the techniques that publishers use to get their pages listed at the top of search results lists have little effect, and also explains why a technique may work for one search engine and not for others. In the end, the varying definition of relevancy makes optimizing your Web pages for each and every search engine almost impossible. In fact, you'd probably be wasting your time if you tried to optimize your Web pages for all the search engines.

Have you ever come across a Web page that repeated a word over and over again, and wondered why? Well, the publisher was probably trying to get the page listed as the top choice when a user searched using this keyword. Although this technique may have worked for a particular search engine, most other search engines would have completely ignored the repeated use of the word, which caused the page to appear lower in their search results lists.

Have you ever come across a Web page that used phrases that didn't seem to fit in the Web page, yet there the phrases were just the same? Here, the publisher was probably trying to get the page to show up when someone searched for a hot topic, such as news, entertainment, or sports. Again, this technique may have worked for a particular search engine, but other search engines would have given the entire page lower relevancy because it was full of ambiguous phrases and didn't seem to have a common thread.

Rather than haphazardly repeat keywords or use ambiguous phrases in your Web page, use sound organizational techniques that bolster the relevancy of your page's theme. Focus your attention on your home page as well as your top-level pages first. When you look at your home page or top-level page, ask yourself these questions:

- Is the subject of the page clear?
- Can I weave the main subject(s) of the page throughout the main text in such a way that it builds relevancy?
- Does the page build the relationship between the main subject and related topics?
- Can I add descriptions to lists of links to clearly define what the link points to?

✪ Are the statements made in the page clear and complete?

✪ Can I transform ambiguous phrases into clear statements that relate to the main theme of the page?

Using Page Titles to Your Advantage

A good page title will bring visitors to your Web site. Most search engines display Web pages according to their title, making the page title one of the most important elements for bringing visitors to your Web site. Additionally, your browser displays the title prominently at the top of its window, and when you bookmark a page, the title is used to differentiate the page from other pages that you've marked.

Beyond its job of grabbing the reader's attention, the title also plays an important role in determining the relevancy of the Web page to the reader's search parameters. Specifically, the keywords in the title often receive greater emphasis than other keywords on the page.

The best titles describe the subject of the page in a clear and meaningful way. Instead of a title that says, "Welcome to my home page," use a title that says "Bill's Home Page: Find Sports Memorabilia, Sports Records, & Player Stats." In this way, search engines that use the page title to determine relevancy will have a clear understanding of the page's subject and the most important keywords.

Getting Your Frame-Enhanced or Graphics-Intensive Page Noticed

Pages with frames, scripts, and lots of graphics present special problems to publishers and search engines. With frame-enhanced pages, the main document usually contains only references to the files that a browser loads into each frame. With scripts, the code is in the place of the all-important text at the top of the page. With graphics-intensive pages, the text on the page is limited.

Although some search engines are smart enough to understand and properly handle frame-enhanced pages, scripts, and graphics-intensive pages, such search engines are more the exception than the rule. Fortunately, you can get your page noticed without eliminating frames, scripts, or your wonderful graphics. You use meta-information to do this. The next section provides more details on the <META> tag.

Getting the Most from Keywords and Meta Information

Meta information is data that is included in a Web page header but is hidden from the reader. Usually, meta information contains instructions or special notes for Web clients, such as your browser or the indexer used by a search engine. To provide meta information to a Web client, you use the <META> tag. The information that you can provide to search engines with the <META> tag includes a very specific description of the page as well as additional keywords for the page.

Working with Meta Information

Before you add meta information to your Web pages, you should know that not all search engines make use of the <META> tag. A search engine that doesn't use the meta information simply ignores the information. Additionally, most of the search engines that use meta information still index the entire contents of your Web page. Thus, you use the <META> tag to give search engines additional information, not to replace the information that they've already gathered from the Web page.

You use the following two main attributes when you use the <META> tag :

 NAME: Used to describe the type of meta information that you are providing, such as NAME="description" or NAME="keywords"

 CONTENT: Used to supply the actual meta information, such as the description of your Web page or a list of keywords for the Web page

You can add a description to your page using meta information as follows:

```
<META NAME="description" CONTENT="Writer's Gallery is a place
    for anyone
```

who loves the written word. You'll find links to hundreds of writing-related resources as well as new works of fiction published at our site. ">

You can add a keyword list to your page using meta information as follows:

```
<META NAME="keywords" CONTENT="writing, reading, write, read,
book, author, story, fiction, nonfiction, literary, mythol
ogy, medieval, biblical, renaissance, library, Dante,
Dickens, Faulkner, Shakespeare, news, world news, entertain-
ment news, business news, current events, publishing, dictio-
nary, encyclopedia, bookshelf">
```

In a Web page, the meta information is always added to the page header inside the <HEAD> and </HEAD> tags, as in the following example:

```
<HTML>
<HEAD>

<TITLE>Writer's Gallery: Resources for Writers and Readers</
  TITLE>

<META NAME="description" CONTENT="Writer's Gallery is a place
for anyone who loves the written word. You'll find links to
hundreds of writing-related resources as well as new works of
fiction published at our site. ">

<META NAME="keywords" CONTENT="writing, reading, write, read,
book, author, story, fiction, nonfiction, literary, mythol-
ogy, medieval, biblical, renaissance, library, Dante,
Dickens, Faulkner, Shakespeare, news, world news, entertain-
ment news, business news, current events, publishing,
  dictionnary, encyclopedia, bookshelf">


</HEAD>
<BODY>
 . . .
</BODY>
</HTML>
```

Using Meta Information in Your Web Page

The description of your page in the <META> tag is every bit as important as the summary description in the main text of the page. The advantage to describing a page in the <META> tag is that you provide the exact description that you want to use, rather than have the search engine extrapolate the description from the main text of the page. A good <META> tag description summarizes the main selling points of the page in 200 characters or less. Because some search engines use page descriptions that are fewer than 200 characters, try to put the most relevant information first.

When it comes to finding your Web page in a search engine, a <META> tag keyword list gives your Web page a definite edge over a page that doesn't use meta information. The main thing to remember is that the <META> tag keyword list is normally used in addition to the keywords that the search engine gathers from the main text of the page. Thus, rather than simply repeat keywords that appear in the main text, you may want to concentrate on related topics or variations of the primary keywords. For example, if the keyword is *writer*, you can use variations such as *write, writing*, and *written*.

You can also create various combinations of keywords or phrases in the keyword list. When I say various combinations, I don't mean that you should repeat the keyword several times. Instead, create word combinations, such as business news, entertainment news, and sports news. Keep in mind that some search engines penalize you for repeating specific keywords too many times. In fact, the search engine may disregard the keyword list entirely if you repeat keywords too many times, as in the following:

```
<META NAME="keywords" CONTENT="news, news, news, news, news,
   news, news, news, news, news,
business, business, business, business, business, business,
business, entertainment, entertainment, entertainment,
entertainment, entertainment, entertainment, sports, sports,
sports, sports, sports, sports, sports">
```

The following example instead uses word combinations and variations of the topic for the keyword list:

```
<META NAME="keywords" CONTENT="news, business, entertainment,
    sports, current events, business news, entertainment news,
    sports news">
```

Just as the length of your description is important, the length of your keyword list is important as well. Generally speaking, limit the keyword list to fewer than 1,000 characters. Further, try to restrict the number of times that you repeat any word in the keyword list. A good rule of thumb is to use a keyword or a word combination that uses the keyword no more than seven times. In the previous example, the keyword *news* was repeated four times.

After you update your home page and top-level pages with meta information, consider adding meta information to the rest of your Web pages. Although this may be a mammoth undertaking, the payoff makes the time investment worthwhile. I recommend tailoring the meta information to the individual page rather than the site as a whole.

A Last Look at Search Engine Fundamentals

As you have seen, you can do many things to improve the odds of someone finding your Web page through a search engine. The idea here is not to trick the search engine into displaying references to your pages. Instead, you are structuring your pages so that search engines can clearly identify the subjects that your pages cover and index the appropriate keywords for those subjects. You are also using techniques that make identifying the subjects your pages cover easier for your readers. Figure 3-11 shows the main design concepts to follow when you optimize your Web pages for search engines.

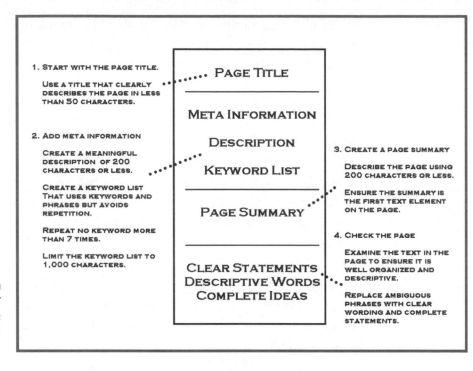

Figure 3-11

Optimizing your
Web page
for search engines:
step by step.

Wrapping Up and Looking Ahead

By capitalizing on search engine fundamentals, you ensure that your Web pages receive the attention they deserve. Before you continue to the next part of this section, take a few minutes to apply the techniques discussed in this section to your home page and other top-level pages at your Web site. By doing so, you will be ready to submit your Web site to the search engines covered in upcoming sections.

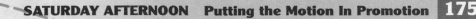

Registering with the Top Search Engines on the Planet

Now that you've optimized your Web pages for indexing, you are ready to submit your Web pages to search engines. Although hundreds of search engines are out there, trying to submit your Web site to every single one of them is not practical or worthwhile. Instead, you should start by registering your site with the major search engines. Because the search engines covered in this part index tens of millions of Web pages, they are the ones used most often to search the Web, and you can make the most of your time and resources by focusing your efforts on these search engines.

To find the top search engines on the planet, I visited, compared, and tested more than 500 different ones. I came up with a list of the best search engines available on the Web, and you will find them featured in this and other sections in this book. The idea was to do the hours of legwork for you so that you could get the most out of your promotion efforts with the least amount of work.

Submitting Your Site to a Search Engine

When you register with a search engine, you let the search engine know that your Web site exists. Many search engines take a preliminary look at your site immediately after you submit your site and, in doing so, verify that the address you provided is valid. Afterward, the search engine schedules your site for indexing.

Although several days may pass before the indexing begins, the actual time that you have to wait to get into the database depends on the backlog of new sites waiting to be entered into the database and the efficiency of the indexer. Some search engines may index your Web site within hours. Other search engines may not index your Web site for weeks.

How Does Indexing Work?

Most search engines use the URL that you submit to find other pages at your Web site. If you give the search engine the URL to your home page at the following:

```
http://www.your_isp.com/~you/
```

the indexer uses this page as a launching pad to all the other pages at your Web site. Generally, the indexer creates an indexed reference to the current page and then searches all the links on the page one by one. If the first link that the indexer finds is to a page called `background.html`, the indexer accesses the `background.html` page, creates an indexed reference, and then searches all the links on this page one by one. Eventually, the indexer crawls through every page at your Web site.

TIP If an area of your Web site is not linked from a main page that the indexer can find, that area will not be indexed. The solution is to add a link to the page on a top-level page that the indexer can find, or to register the area separately.

How Can You Exclude Directories and Pages?

Although indexing your site is a good thing, sometimes you might not want the search engine to index your entire site. You can control what pages are indexed and what pages aren't by using a robot exclusion file. The exclusion file is a plain-text file placed in the main directory of your Web site. In the exclusion file, you specify the directories or pages that search engines are not allowed to index. The name of the exclusion file must be robots.txt.

Because you will generally want the exclusions to apply to all search engines, the first line of the file should read as follows:

```
User-agent: *
```

After you specify the search engines to exclude, you specify the directories or pages to exclude. You can exclude an entire directory as follows:

```
Disallow: /cgi-bin/
```

or

```
Disallow: /images/
```

You can exclude a single page as follows:

```
Disallow: /prg/webstat.html
```

You can put all these entries in an exclusion file as follows:

```
User-agent: *
Disallow: /cgi-bin/
Disallow: /images/
Disallow: /prg/webstat.html
```

> **TIP**
>
> If you publish a large Web site or publish your Web site as part of a larger domain, you should strongly consider using an exclusion list. With so many Web pages, search engines are finding it harder and harder to index everything at a Web site. For this reason, some search engines index only 500–750 pages per domain.

How Often Is Your Site Re-Indexed?

Indexing your Web site is not a one-time deal. Most search engines periodically re-index your pages. By re-indexing your pages, the search engine verifies that the pages still exist and can update the indexed reference to your page if necessary.

In an ideal world, search engines would rapidly remove references to pages that no longer exist and just as rapidly create references to new areas that you build. In reality, search engines do not remove pages or find new areas as quickly as we would like.

The reason search engines don't immediately remove pages that can't be found is that the dreaded 404 -File Not Found error occurs all too often. Whenever your site is busy, down, or can't respond to a request, the search engine simply marks the page and moves on. If the server can't find the page on several occasions, the page is removed from the database.

Search engines don't add new areas as fast as we would like because they often don't re-index the entire site and all its contents. Instead, the search engine may check only for changes by comparing page headers or modification dates. The result is that the search engine may need several visits to find and index a new area of your Web site.

Why Won't This Search Engine List Your Site?

Sometimes you register with a search engine only to find, days or weeks later, that you can't find the site anywhere in the search engine's database. A search engine may not list your site for several reasons, but the main reason is usually that the URL you provided couldn't be read or used. To avoid this problem, ensure that you type the complete URL to your Web site. Because URLs are case sensitive, ensure that your URL uses the proper case. For example, the URLS `http://www.tvpress.com/HOME.htm` and `http://www.tvpress.com/home.htm` refer to different documents.

You should also watch the syntax of the URL. Some search engines will not use an URL that includes reserved characters, such as:

= The equal sign

$ The dollar sign

? The question mark

Another reason for a search engine not indexing your site is that you use frames and the search engine doesn't know how to deal with them. To ensure that the search engine can find your page links, add a `<NOFRAME>` area to the page that contains the main text and links (see Listing 3-3).

Listing 3-3 Using a <NOFRAME> Area in a Web Page

```
<HTML>
<HEAD>
<TITLE>Las Vegas Virtual Tour Guide</TITLE>
<HEAD>

<FRAMESET ROWS="25%,*" BORDER=0>
     <FRAME SRC="side.htm" NORESIZE>
     <FRAME SRC="main.htm" NORESIZE>
</FRAMESET>

<NOFRAMES>
     <BODY>
```

```
    Add text and links here for version of Web page without
frames.
    </BODY>
</NOFRAMES>

</HTML>
```

Scripts and graphics-only pages can also present problems to search engines. To ensure that your page has a description and keywords, use the techniques discussed previously this afternoon under "Capitalizing on Search Engine Fundamentals."

Additionally, if you don't have your own domain, a robots.txt file may be the cause of your problems. As discussed previously, the robots.txt file can be used to keep search engines out of specific directories. To check the contents of the robots.txt file for your domain, use the following URL:

```
http://www.your_domain.com/robots.txt
```

in which `your_domain` is your actual domain. If the robots.txt file excludes your directory or all public directories on the server, you've found the cause of the problem. If you find that your files are excluded in the robots.txt file, definitely ask the server administrator whether this can be changed.

Increasing Your Web Traffic with the Top Search Engines

The focus of this section is on the top search engines, not all the search engines available on the Web. Registering with the major search engines is the best way to increase traffic to your Web site. You will find that you get the most out of your time investment when you register your site with the major search engines.

If you've followed the techniques for optimizing your Web site for search engines as discussed previously under the heading "Capitalizing on Search Engine Fundamentals," you should see marked improvements in your Web traffic simply by registering with the search engines listed in this section. Don't expect a great flood of traffic the day after you register your Web site, however; rather, you should see a steady increase in the level of traffic that your Web site receives over time. The actual level of traffic increase that you see will depend on the subject of your site, the size and quality of your Web site, and your use of search engine optimization techniques.

Although you could use the techniques that I discuss here to register with hundreds of other search engines, the reward for all your hard work usually isn't worth the effort. Millions of people use the major search engines to find what they need. Every day, these search engines collectively handle about 90 percent of the searches performed by general search engines. Obviously, this means that the hundreds of other general search engines handle only about 10 percent of the search transactions. Do you really want to spend countless hours registering with hundreds of other search engines when you can potentially reach the vast majority of users simply by registering with the most-used search engines? Probably not.

As you read this section, I suggest that you apply it as you go. Register your Web site with each of the search engines discussed in the section. To make the task of registering your Web site easier, you may want to visit the companion Web site for this book. Use the following URL:

`http://www.tvpress.com/promote/search.htm`

NOTE Keep in mind that I am talking about general search engines, not specialized or category-specific search engines. In upcoming sections, I show you how to increase your traffic using other types of search engines. Note also that there are many popular alternatives to search engines, such as directories and guides, which I discuss later in the book as well.

Registering Your Site with AltaVista

With tens of millions of accesses every day and tens of millions of indexed pages, AltaVista (`http://www.altavista.digital.com`) is one of the busiest and largest search engines on the Web. From the main page at AltaVista, you can search the Web, USENET newsgroups, and more (see Figure 3-12). Beyond the basic keyword search, you can also perform complex searches with multiple parameters and options using an advanced query page.

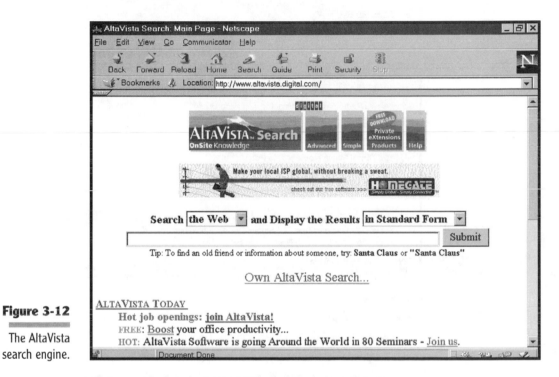

Figure 3-12

The AltaVista
search engine.

What Does AltaVista Look For?

Although search engines allow you to customize the results of a search, most users rely on the default search options. With this in mind, you can learn an awful lot by examining the results of searches using the default search options. When I visited AltaVista, the default style of result listings was the way it appears in Figure 3-13. As you can see, AltaVista displays search results by page title. Beneath the page title is a brief description of the page, followed by the page URL, file size, and modification date.

Although AltaVista supports page descriptions defined in <META> tags, you can see that none of the pages listed here uses these descriptions. As a result, the page summaries are extracted from the first 100–200 characters of text found in the page.

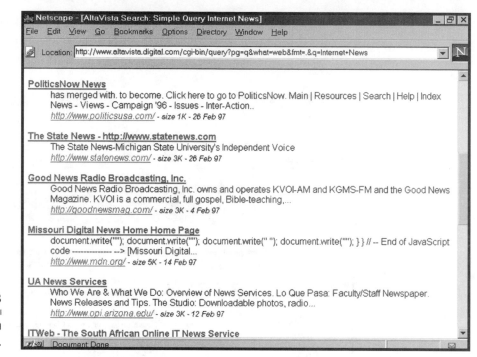

Figure 3-13

Search results from AltaVista.

NOTE

In working with AltaVista, I noted that the search engine seemed to place strong emphasis on the keywords in the title and the summary. Generally, if the keyword for which you searched was in the page title and the page summary, the page was listed high in the results.

Submitting Your Site to AltaVista

FIND IT ▶
ONLINE

You can submit your site to AltaVista using the submission page shown in Figure 3-14. The URL for this page is as follows:

```
http://www.altavista.digital.com/av/content/addurl.htm
```

NOTE

Page URLs often change. If the submission page is changed, all you need to do is visit the main home page for AltaVista and follow the links that say Add URL or Submit Your Page. I also publish a resource list for search engines at the Web site for this book at:

```
http://www.tvpress.com/promote/search.htm
```

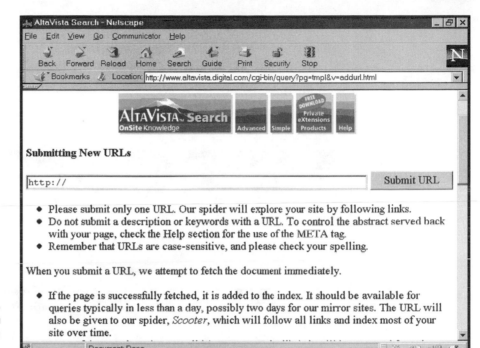

When you submit your site to AltaVista, use your home page URL. After
you submit your URL, the AltaVista indexer immediately examines the
URL to ensure its accuracy and then schedule a full indexing of your Web
site. To keep pace with the ever-changing face of the Web, AltaVista re-
indexes Web sites more often than most other search engines. AltaVista
determines the number of times that it performs re-indexing based on the
frequency of updates that you make to your pages. The indexer does this
by comparing modification dates for the page. For this reason, a page that
changes every day may indeed get re-indexed every day. Similarly, a page
that rarely changes will rarely get re-indexed.

Submitting Your Site to Excite

Excite maintains a huge database of well over 60 million Web pages, making its search engine one of the largest on the Web. Like many other search

engines, Excite also compiles lists and guides from its database. These lists allow users to search for Web sites by categories rather than keywords.

Excite's home page is shown in Figure 3-15. You can access this page using the following URL:

```
http://www.excite.com/
```

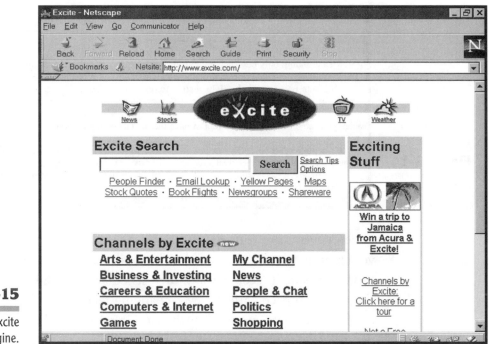

Figure 3-15

The Excite
search engine.

What Does Excite Look For?

When you search at Excite using the basic search option, you will see results similar to those shown in Figure 3-16. Excite lists pages by relevancy, title, URL, and summary. Having worked with Excite, I have the impression that the actual contents of the page receive more emphasis than the title or summary.

Excite is one of the few major search engines that doesn't use meta information, and it's not because the search engine isn't keeping up with current trends. Rather, the developers of Excite believe that meta information can

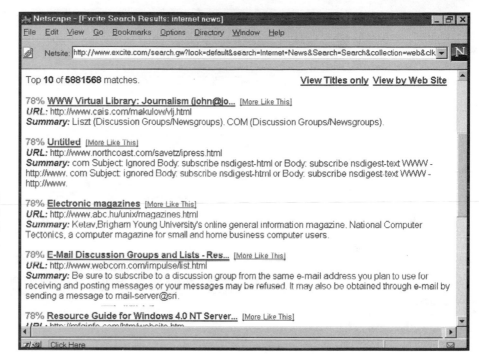

Figure 3-16

Search results
from Excite.

be misleading; therefore, they've made the search engine rely on the actual text of the page instead. When Excite indexes your site, the full text of your pages is stored in the database. From these pages, Excite extracts a summary by looking for repeated ideas and common threads.

Adding Your Site to Excite

To add your site to Excite, use the submission page shown in Figure 3-17. The URL for this page is as follows:

```
http://www.excite.com/Info/add_url.html
```

When you submit your site to Excite, enter your home page URL and your e-mail address. The Excite Guide is a guide to the best sites on the Web. Because the Excite Guide gives Web users another way to find your site, you might as well take a few extra minutes and fill out the optional information.

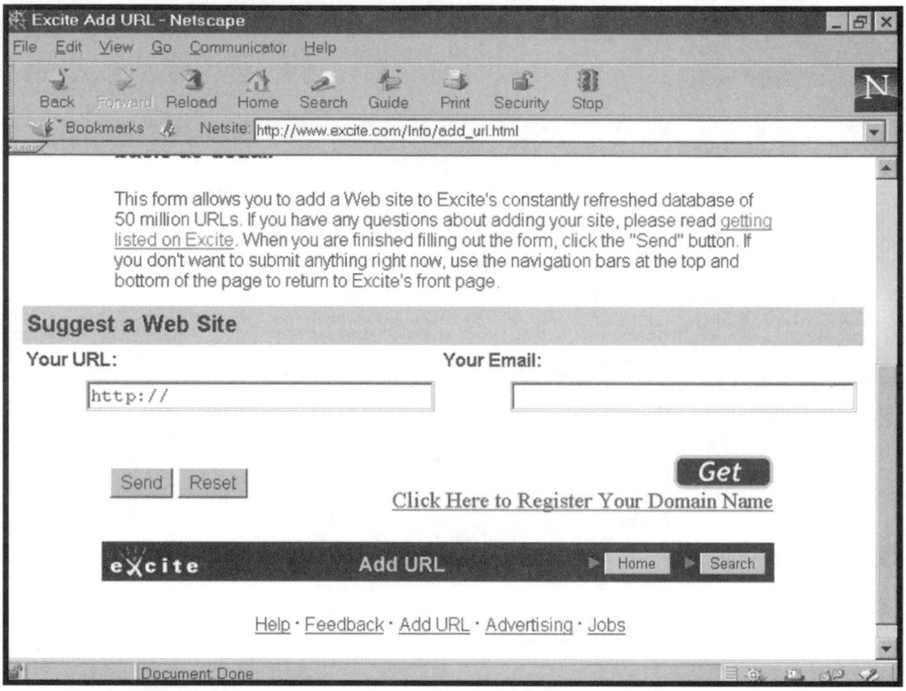

Figure 3-17

The submission page at Excite.

NOTE You can find tips for submitting your Web site to guides, lists, and directories a little later, under the heading "Submitting Your Web Site to the Guides, Lists, and Directories."

Excite doesn't index new sites immediately. Instead, Excite adds the site to a list of sites to be indexed. The actual indexing of your site takes place in about two weeks, after which Excite then re-indexes your site on a regular basis, which is normally monthly.

Entering Your Site in HotBot

HotBot is a testament to how rapidly the Web changes. Before 1996, few people had ever heard of this search engine, and then HotBot stormed onto the scene, sporting millions of pages in its database. Driven by its

strong relationship with *Wired* magazine, HotBot quickly became one of the most popular search engines on the Web. Today, HotBot is a clear winner for its diversity and versatility.

Figure 3-18 shows the home page for HotBot (http://www.hotbot.com). As you can see, the search interface at HotBot lets you easily set options for the search and results.

What Does HotBot Look For?

The results of a search at HotBot are shown in Figure 3-19. As you can see, the default search setting yields fairly descriptive results that are organized by relevancy and page title. Following the title is a summary description, the page URL, the byte size of the page, and the modification date of the page.

Although HotBot supports meta information, HotBot does not rely exclusively on this information to create the indexed reference for Web pages. With HotBot, there are several different elements that can be combined to create strong emphasis. Thus, the best way to achieve strong results is to

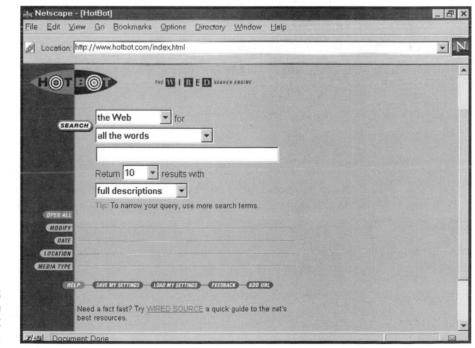

Figure 3-18

The HotBot
search engine.

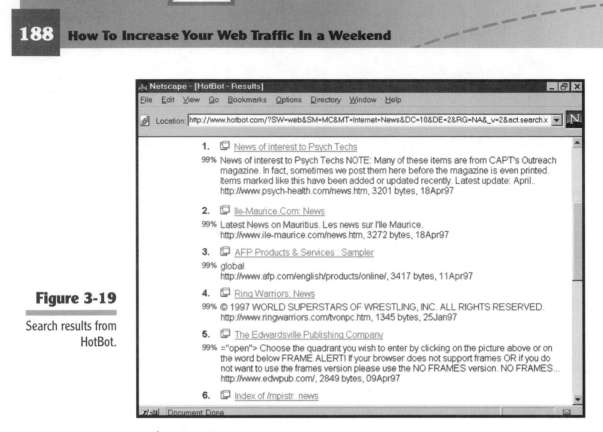

Figure 3-19

Search results from HotBot.

follow the advice that I gave you previously, in the part called "Capitalizing on Search Engine Fundamentals."

Submitting Your Site to HotBot

The submission page for HotBot is shown in Figure 3-20. The URL for this page is as follows:

FIND IT ▶ ONLINE

`http://www.hotbot.com/addurl.html`

When you submit your site to HotBot, you enter your home page URL and your e-mail address. Like Excite, HotBot doesn't index new sites immediately. Instead, HotBot adds the site to a list of sites to be indexed. The actual indexing of your site takes place in about three weeks.

Adding Your Site to InfoSeek

Not only does Infoseek maintain one of the largest search engines, it has one of the largest Web directories as well. This combination allows users to

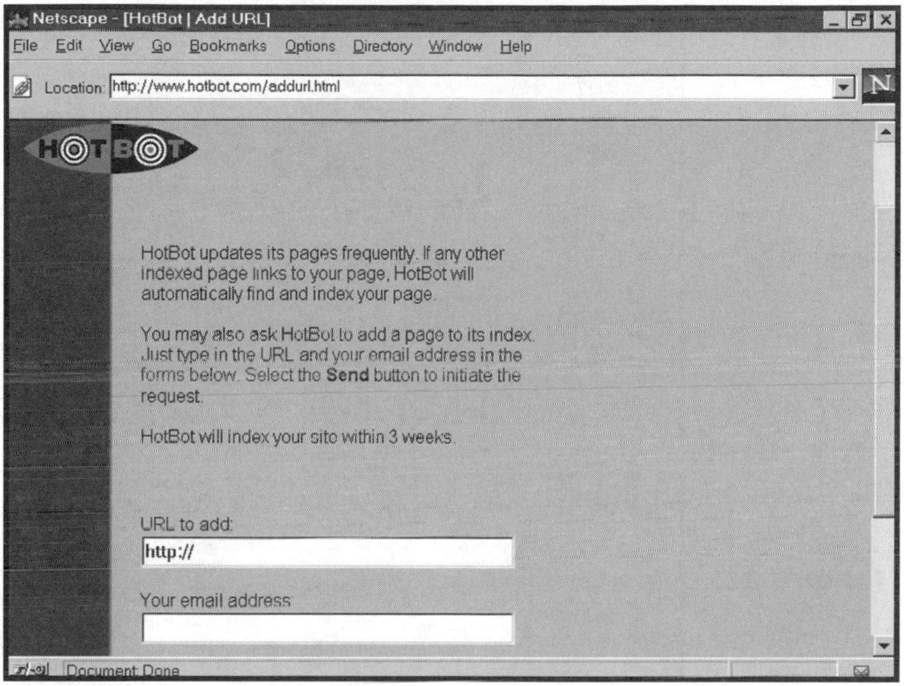

Figure 3-20

The submission page at HotBot.

FIND IT ▶
ONLINE

search for specific topics and to wander through the listings by category. You can access the Infoseek search engine and directory from the page shown in Figure 3-21. The URL for this page is as follows:

```
http://www.infoseek.com/
```

Using Infoseek, you can search the Web, Usenet newsgroups, current news items, and much more. Although much of this information is gathered from Infoseek's database, some of the information comes from databases maintained by other sites, such as White Pages or Yellow Pages directories. For example, if you use the e-mail address search, you will access one of the White Pages directories.

What Does Infoseek Look For?

A basic search at Infoseek yields results similar to those shown in Figure 3-22. As you can see, Infoseek lists pages by title and summary, followed by

Figure 3-21

The Infoseek
search engine.

a relevancy indicator, the page URL, and the file size. The results suggest that Infoseek places strong emphasis on the page title as well as the actual text or meta keyword list for the page.

NOTE   Although you can add your site to the Infoseek search engine, you cannot submit your site directly to the Infoseek directory. Instead, the staff at Infoseek periodically examines sites for inclusion in the directory listing.

Infoseek is one of the few search sites that openly admits that frames, scripts, and graphics-intensive pages cause problems during indexing. To get a clear summary description for your page at Infoseek, use meta information. You also can use meta information to define additional keywords for the page. Because Infoseek checks the keywords for relevancy to the actual text on the page, you should ensure that the keywords relate strongly to the theme of your page.

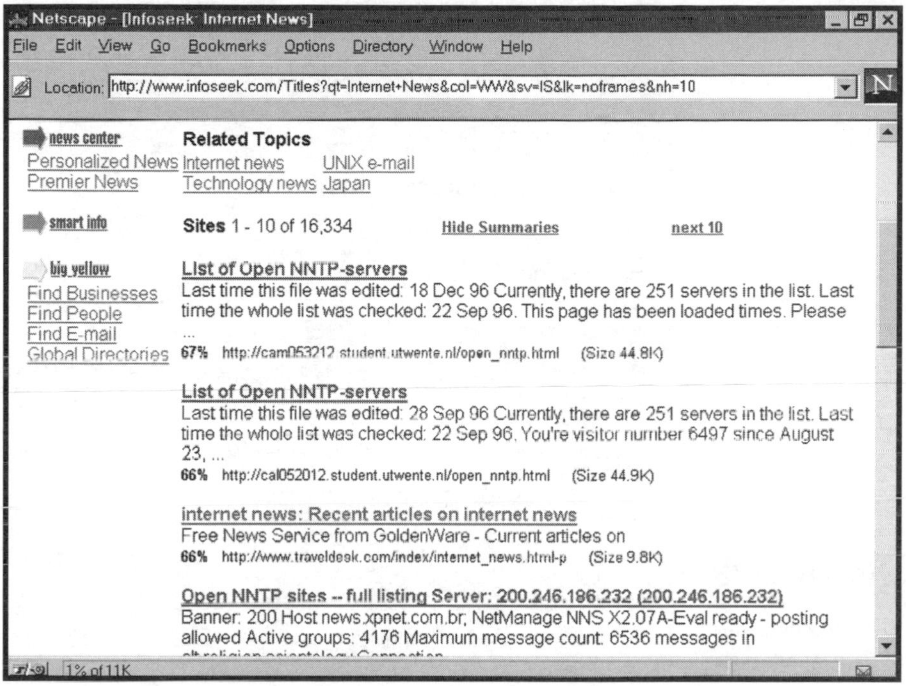

Figure 3-22

Search results
from Infoseek.

Interestingly, Infoseek also looks at the ALT attribute of the <IMG> tag. For
this reason, if you have lots of graphics on your page, you should describe
the images using the ALT attribute.

Submitting Your Site to Infoseek

Infoseek maintains its place as one of the most preferred and most up-to-
date search engines on the Web by enforcing strict guidelines. Unlike most
other search engines, Infoseek does not index your entire site. Instead,
Infoseek indexes only the pages that you submit using the form shown in
Figure 3-23. The URL for this submission page is as follows:

```
http://www.infoseek.com/AddUrl?pg=DCaddurl.html
```

FIND IT ▶
ONLINE

Although having to submit every page that you want listed in Infoseek is a
lot of work, Infoseek makes up for this tedium by indexing your pages and
making them available to searches within minutes after you submit them.
If you have more than 50 pages to submit to Infoseek, you should submit

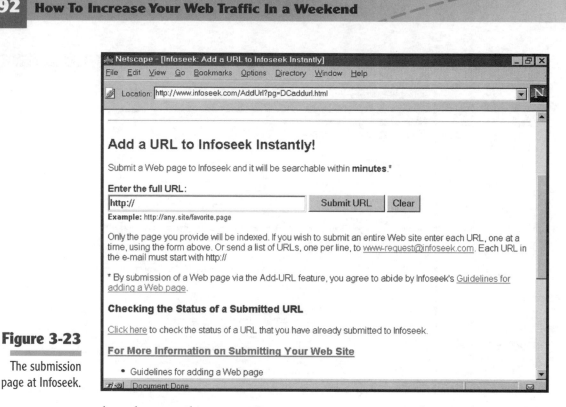

Figure 3-23

The submission
page at Infoseek.

them by e-mail to `www-request@infoseek.com`. Each page that you submit must be listed on a separate line in the e-mail message. You must also include the full URL, such as:

```
http://www.tvpress.com/vpbg.html
```

NOTE The e-mail submission process takes about a week. Still, for mass submissions, being able to send one message is much easier than having to go through the submission process a few hundred times. Note also that if your site covers adult-oriented material, you *must* use the e-mail submission process.

Getting Listed at Lycos

Lycos (`http://www.lycos.com`) maintains one of the best-known search engines on the Web. Like many other search engine sites, Lycos maintains

FIND IT ▶
ONLINE

both directory listings and guides to the Web. The most popular Lycos guide is called the Top 5% Sites, which is a searchable collection of reviews covering the best Web sites. Note the emphasis on the best Web sites rather than all Web sites. Although directories usually list all Web sites, Web guides usually only list the top or best Web sites. You'll find more information on Web guides and directories a little later this afternoon, in the section called "Submitting Your Site to the Top Guides, Lists, and Directories."

The main search interface for Lycos is shown in Figure 3-24. Although the default search is for Web sites only, you also can look for specific information on sounds, graphics and reviews of the sites that Lycos considers to be in the top five percent.

What Does Lycos Look For?

When you search at Lycos using the basic search option, you will see results similar to those shown in Figure 3-25. Lycos lists results by relevancy, page title, summary, and URL. Lycos is one of the few search engines that matches

Figure 3-24

The Lycos
search engine.

all keywords by default. Thus, if you search with several keywords and don't specify explicitly how the search should be conducted using AND/ OR flags, Lycos retrieves pages only with all the keywords for which you are looking.

Figure 3-25

Search results
from Lycos.

Although Lycos didn't support meta information until early 1997, the latest version of the Lycos search engine does support meta information. Using meta information, you can ensure that your pages have a clear summary description. You can also use meta information to define additional keywords for your pages.

NOTE   My work with the Lycos search engine shows that page title and summary receive strong emphasis in the search results. Meta information also plays an important part in determining the relevancy of your page.

Submitting Your Site to Lycos

FIND IT ▶
ONLINE

You can to submit your site to Lycos using the submission page shown in Figure 3-26. The URL for this page is the following:

```
http://www.lycos.com/addasite.html
```

As with many search engines, Lycos requests that you supply your e-mail address along with the URL to your Web page. After you submit your URL, Lycos immediately examines the URL to ensure that it is accurate and not already in the database. Although the Lycos indexer performs a full indexing of your Web site immediately after verifying your URL, your site will not be available at Lycos until the next time that the database is fully updated, which is usually several weeks. After your site is entered into the Lycos database, it will be re-indexed every couple of weeks.

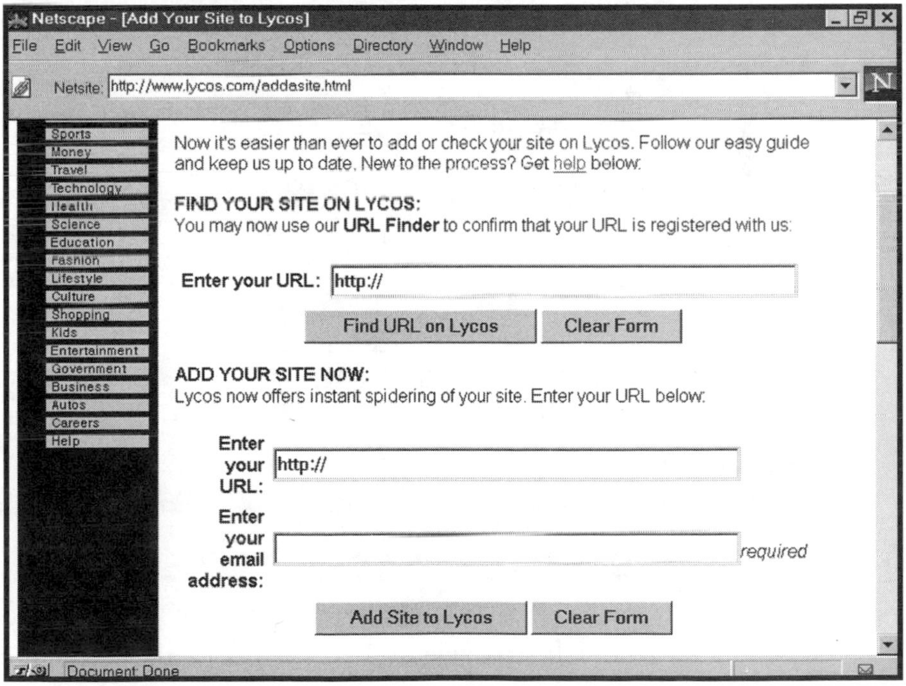

Figure 3-26

The submission page at Lycos.

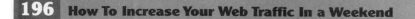

Submitting Your Site to WebCrawler

WebCrawler has a database of several million pages, making it one of the smallest search engine sites listed in this section. Still, WebCrawler is one of the oldest and most used search engines on the Web. WebCrawler also makes up for its relatively small database with value-added resources, such as extensive Web site reviews, the WebCrawler 100, and interactive maps.

FIND IT ▶
ONLINE

You can access the WebCrawler search engine from the page shown in Figure 3-27. The URL for this page is as follows:

```
http://www.webcrawler.com/
```

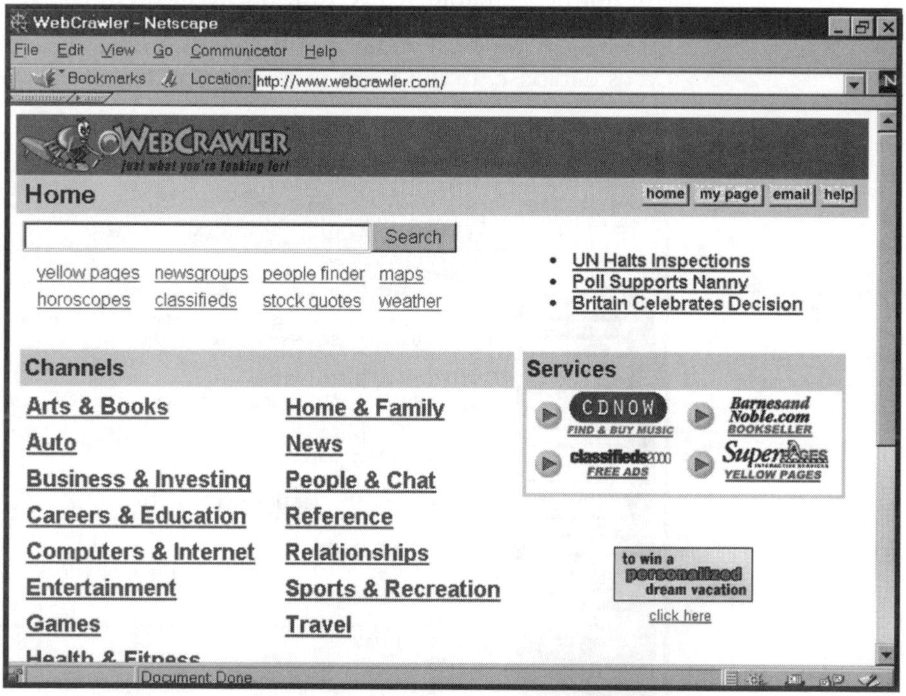

Figure 3-27

The WebCrawler
search engine.

What Does WebCrawler Look For?

If you use the basic search option at WebCrawler, the results will be similar to those shown in Figure 3-28. As you see, the default format at WebCrawler shows only the page titles. When you click on the Show Summaries link or select Show Summaries when performing the search, WebCrawler also displays descriptive summaries, relevancy scores, and URLs.

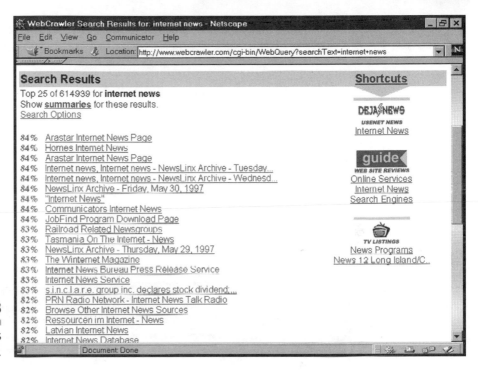

Although WebCrawler does understand meta information, it does not rely on it as extensively as some of the other search engines. Additionally, WebCrawler is very particular about the content of pages. If your pages have material that is not relevant to the topic of the page or you purposely add word lists to the body of the page in an attempt to get it listed higher in the search results, WebCrawler will remove your page from its database.

Although removing pages from the database may seem harsh, WebCrawler uses the frequency of words within documents to determine relevancy and simply cannot maintain the integrity of its database if people try to cheat the system. The more times the search word appears in your document, the higher the relevancy of the document. WebCrawler also looks at how frequently the search word appears in other documents. If the word isn't used often in other documents, then WebCrawler gives your document higher relevancy as well.

Submitting Your Site to WebCrawler

WebCrawler doesn't index your entire site. Instead, WebCrawler indexes only the pages that you submit using the form shown in Figure 3-29. The URL for the submission page is as follows:

```
http://webcrawler.com/Help/GetListed/AddURLS.html
```

Using the form on the submission page, you can submit individual pages for indexing at WebCrawler. If you have many pages, you can save time by omitting the http:// part of the URL. Although WebCrawler will usually index your pages the same day that you submit the page URLs, your pages won't be added to the database for several weeks.

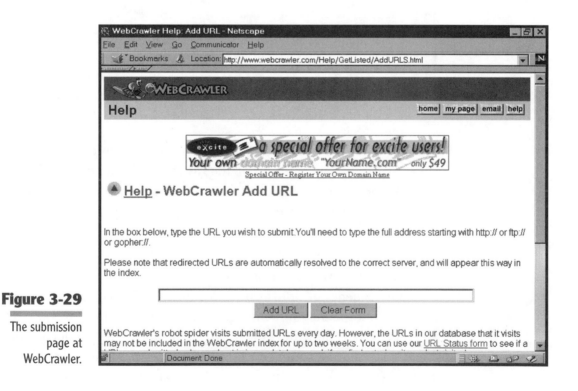

Figure 3-29

The submission page at WebCrawler.

Wrapping Up and Looking Ahead

Registering with search engines is a terrific way to build traffic to your Web site, especially when you consider that millions of people use search engines to find information every day. As you have seen, submitting your site is fairly easy, and all you really need to do is visit the site and submit your URL. Now that you've registered your site with the top search engines on the planet, you can move on to the top guides, lists, and directories covered next.

Submitting Your Web Site to Top Guides, Lists, and Directories

The phenomenal popularity of resource directories such as Yahoo! ushered in whole new era of guides, lists, and directories designed to help people find things on the Web. Whereas the focus of Web guides is usually on the top or best sites, lists and directories focus on categorizing information found on the Web.

Just as hundreds of search engines are available, you can find hundreds of guides, lists, and directories to the Web as well. Unfortunately, trying to submit your site to every guide, list, and directory is a waste of your time and resources. Instead, you should focus on the top resources that you find in this section.

To come up with the list of Web sites featured in this and other parts of the book, I visited, compared, and tested thousands of Web sites—more than 5,000 of them, as a matter of fact. Searching, categorizing, and comparing all these Web sites to produce a list of the ones that would truly help increase your Web traffic took weeks. Fortunately, you don't have to scour the Web; you just need to work your way through this book.

Submitting Your Site to Lists and Directories

Guides, *lists*, and *directories* are all terms used to describe Web resources that provide links to Web pages. Web guides usually provide pointers to the best or top sites. Think of a guide as something that you might buy at the bookstore to help you learn about a country you are visiting. Lists are exactly what the name implies: a list of Web sites that is usually organized into several major categories. Think of a list as something that you might put together before you go grocery shopping. Beyond lists, you will find directories, which usually have rather extensive listings of Web sites divided into many categories. When you think of a directory, think of the Yellow Pages directory, that huge yellow tome that lists tons of businesses.

Although size is usually the major factor that distinguishes a list from a directory, don't get hung up on the terminology. Generally speaking, lists and directories serve the same purpose and, for this reason, I don't dwell on the difference between a list and directory. More often than not, I simply use the words *directory* when I am talking about both lists and directories.

Web site listings in guides and directories are very different from the results returned by a typical search engine. Guides and directories do not index your Web pages at all. They simply use the information that you provide to create a listing for your Web site.

When you submit your Web site to a list or directory, you submit the URL for your home page or other top-level page at your site. Along with the page URL, you usually are asked to submit the page title, a brief description of the page, and a specific category for the page. The page category should always be tailored to the specific directory to which you are submitting your page. Some directory sites have hundreds of narrowly focused categories, such as entertainment news for kids and computer book reviews. Other directory sites have only a few broadly focused categories, such as entertainment and travel.

Most directory sites screen all new submissions rigorously. If the same page has been submitted previously, the site usually disregards the submission. If the page is submitted to the wrong category, the site may disregard the submission for that reason also.

Rather than place your listing in a category that you think is popular, you should place your listing in a category that strongly relates to the topic your site covers. Placing your site in a category that fits your content ensures that readers who are looking for a site like yours will be able to find it.

Trying to submit the same page to multiple categories will usually get you in trouble. Rather than submit the same page to multiple categories, examine the type of content that you publish to see whether different areas of your site fall into different categories. You could, for example, list your home page in one category, your writing area in another category, and your job center in another category. Whenever possible, I recommend that you list each of the major areas at your Web site separately in directories, which gives your Web site a better chance of getting noticed. And the more your Web site gets noticed, the more your Web traffic will increase.

Submitting Your Site to Web Guides

The focus on the top or best sites puts Web guides in a league of their own. When you submit your site to a guide, you are betting that the guide's reviewers will find your site to be useful, informative, or well presented. If the guide's reviewers count your site among the best that they have seen, they will write a review of your site and your site will show up in their database of the Web's top sites. If the guide's reviewers don't like your site for whatever reason, they will move on to the next site in their long list of sites to review.

A typical review rates a Web site in several categories. The Lycos Top 5% Guide rates sites in presentation, content, and the overall experience of visiting the site. NetGuide rates sites in content, design, and personality. These scores are the site's rating. Contrary to what you might think, the Web sites with the fancy graphics and multimedia don't always have the best ratings. In fact, some of the most highly rated Web sites have mostly text.

You can improve your odds of getting your site reviewed by taking the time to learn what the guide looks for and what the guide's reviews look like. When you have gained a clear understanding of how the guide works, submit your site with descriptive information that will catch the eye of the reviewers. Along with the summary information, you may want to include a rating for your Web site. If this rating is realistic, you may give the reviewers a reason to visit your Web site.

Another way to improve your odds with Web guides is to focus on the top-level areas of your Web site. My primary Web site publishes two key resources: Writers Gallery and Internet Job Center. When I submit my site to a guide for review, I submit entries for both of these areas rather than the Web site as a whole. The reason for this is that these areas have very different focuses and can't be realistically rated in the same review.

As a final note, remember that reviewers are real people. With thousands of Web sites to review, several weeks or even a month could elapse before a reviewer gets a chance to look at your Web site. If reviewers don't review your site, there isn't much point in inundating them with e-mail or repeated submissions. Instead, wait a few months and then try again.

How Do People Find Your Listing in the Guide or Directory?

Most guides and directories can be searched in two ways:

- By category
- By keyword

When you search by category, you follow links from a broad category to a progressively more focused category. In a category search, the categories themselves are the main elements driving users to your listing. Yet, when users finally get to the detailed page that shows your listing, it is the page title and summary description that will influence their decision to visit your Web site.

A keyword search in a guide or directory is handled in a very different manner. Rather than follow links, you use a search interface to find categories and listings within the guide. If the keywords that you enter lead to several different categories, you see category headers. If the keywords that you enter lead to a specific listing, you see either the listing itself or the page of which the listing is a part. The main elements driving a keyword search within a Web guide or directory are the category headers and page titles, which are usually the only elements that are indexed.

How Often Is Your Site's Listing Updated?

Unlike search engines that periodically schedule your site for re-indexing, most guides and directories rarely update their listings. The problem with updating listings is a logistical one. To update a listing in a Web guide, a reviewer needs to take another look at the Web site. To update a listing in a directory, the directory site needs to have someone check the validity of the link and the description. Both actions require time and resources that could be directed at new listings.

Don't rely on someone from the guide or directory site to update your listing in six months or a year; take a proactive stance instead. If you move the furniture around a bit or add a new addition to your Web home, let the folks who run the guide or directory site know. Generally, you will want to send a message to the folks who maintain the directory or guide. The key things to tell them are what the old information looked like and what the new information should look like.

TIP　Definitely limit the number of updates that you send to the maintainers of the guide or directory. Here, an annual or semi-annual update message may be just what the doctor ordered.

Increasing Your Web Traffic with Guides and Directories

Getting your Web site listed in a popular guide or directory will definitely increase the traffic to your Web site. As with search engines, you will find that you get the most out of your time investment when you submit your site to the top guides and directories, which is why this part of this section focuses on the best guides and directories.

Although you know that a Web page or area within your Web site will be listed in the directory, there is no assurance that you will get listed in a Web guide. Still, I firmly believe that submitting your site to the guides listed in this section is worthwhile, especially when you consider that getting your site listed in any one of these guides will bring thousands of visitors to your Web site every single day. For many Web sites, an extra thousand visitors a day would effectively double or triple the site's traffic. Doubling or tripling your Web traffic from a single listing may seem like a pipe dream, but the reality is that people often seek out the best that the Web has to offer. After all, do you settle for bronze, when silver, gold, and platinum are waiting in the wings?

As you read this section, you should submit your Web site to the guides and directories that I discuss. You will find that most of the sites I look at are Web guides. The reason for this is that most directories have a specific focus, and specialized directories are discussed later in the book. In the

end, there is a very narrow field of the great directories that have a broad, general focus.

To make the task of registering your Web site easier, you may want to visit the companion Web site for this book. Use the following URL:

```
http://www.tvpress.com/promote/guide.htm
```

 NOTE Any guides or directories that you find at the online site that are not listed in this section are discussed later in the book. In particular, C|Net and JumpCity are covered in Sunday morning's section under "Getting Your Site Listed as the Cool Site of the Day." I recommend that you hold off on registering with these other sites for now.

Getting Listed in the Excite Guide to the Web

The Excite guide (`http://www.excite.com`) features listings and reviews of select Web sites. These listings and reviews are organized within broad categories that Excite calls *channels*. As shown in Figure 3-30, the main way to access the guide is by clicking on a channel heading.

When you access Excite channels, you are searching outside the main Excite database. As you learned previously under the heading "Registering with the Top Search Engines on the Planet," the main database at Excite indexes millions of Web pages. Listings in the Excite guide represent the best of those millions of pages.

What Do Entries in the Excite Guide Look Like?

As with most Web guides, listings in the Excite guide are rated to help readers determine the "best of the best" from the "good but could be better" sites. At Excite, each listing is assigned a star rating (see Figure 3-31). Within their rating, listings are organized alphabetically. That is, the four-

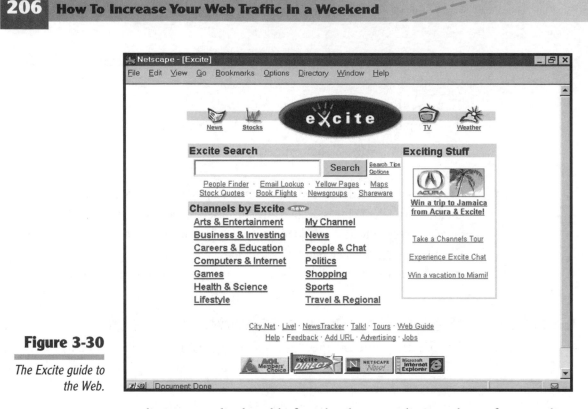

Figure 3-30

The Excite guide to the Web.

star listings are displayed before the three-star listings, but a four-star listing that begins with *A* is displayed before a four-star listing that begins with *B*. Although this rating scale is rather simplistic, the star rating has been used for a long time to rate everything from books to movies.

Anytime that a review for a listing is available, you will see the editor's review link. A typical set of reviews is shown in Figure 3-32. As you can see, the summary paragraph for a review goes a lot further than the one-liner associated with each listing.

Submitting Your Site to the Excite Guide

You can submit your site to the Excite Guide using the submission page shown in Figure 3-33. The URL for this page is `http://www.excite.com/Info/add_url.html`.

Because of the growing trend to create metropolitan and area-specific guides, be sure to specify the city and state information. You should also be sure to select the proper category for your site. If your site covers travel and tour-

Netscape - [Excite: Home > Arts & Entertainment Channel > Kids]

File Edit View Go Bookmarks Options Directory Window Help

Home > Arts & Entertainment Channel > Kids

Books	**Magazines**
Clubs	**Movies**
Comics & Fantasy	**Music**
Games	**TV**
Humor	

★★★★ **Kids & Parents Page** *editor's review*
No kidding around-- there's yummy stuff here for kids from ...
★★★★ **LA CityKids** *editor's review*
This is a fantastic list containing Los Angeles children's ...
★★★ **Canadian Kids Page** *editor's review*
Well, those Canadians have done it again...done the right ...
★★★ **Kids' Space** *editor's review*
Psssst-- hey kids, don't tell your parents about this page, ...
★★★ **KidsAct** *editor's review*
Many organizations are online to help kids improve their ...
★★★ **KidWorld** *editor's review*
Here's a fun site for kids to swap stories, jokes, pictures
★★★ **Oregon County Fair** *editor's review*
For a quarter of a century, this gathering has been taking ...
★★★ **The Children Page** *editor's review*
A frequently visited, text-only kids page that emanates ...
★★★ **The Dog Ate My Homework** *editor's review*
Not only are there plenty of ready-to-use excuses for for ...
★★★ **The Refrigerator** *editor's review*

Document: Done

Figure 3-31

Listings in the Excite guide.

Netscape - [Excite: Kids Reviews]

File Edit View Go Bookmarks Options Directory Window Help

★★★★ **Kids & Parents Page**
No kidding around-- there's yummy stuff here for kids from tots to teens and, yes, for grownups,
too. Kids: contribute a file to Global Show & Tell, share another kid's home page. Dad: read how
fatherhood changes a couple. Mom: check out Totware (software for wee ones). The Web's
version of Families 'R' Us.

★★★★ **LA CityKids**
This is a fantastic list containing Los Angeles children's and youth resources, museums and
attractions, schools and national hotlines. Site comes courtesy of the Youth and Childrens Net in
Oakland, California.

★★★ **Canadian Kids Page**
Well, those Canadians have done it again...done the right thing, that is. This cornucopia of things of
interest to kids -- stories, songs, sounds, and links to all manner of other servers with kids' stuff on
'em -- is operated as a free service by Leslie Owens. As they say, it's for the young, and the young
at heart.

★★★ **Kids' Space**
Psssst-- hey kids, don't tell your parents about this page, or you'll never get on the computer again.
This site is part coloring book, part story book, and you get to play along. Find e-mail pen pals,
submit your own creative work, or just enjoy seeing what other Web kids are weaving.

★★★ **KidsAct**
Many organizations are online to help kids improve their lives, but here's one site where the kids
reverse roles. "Kids Accepting Challenges Today" publishes news about youngsters who do things
for their community, who aid abused kids and the elderly, and who perform other good-neighbor
and good-citizen acts. Begun by a student in South Carolina, there's input from kids nationwide.
Refreshing.

Document: Done

Figure 3-32

Reviews in the Excite guide.

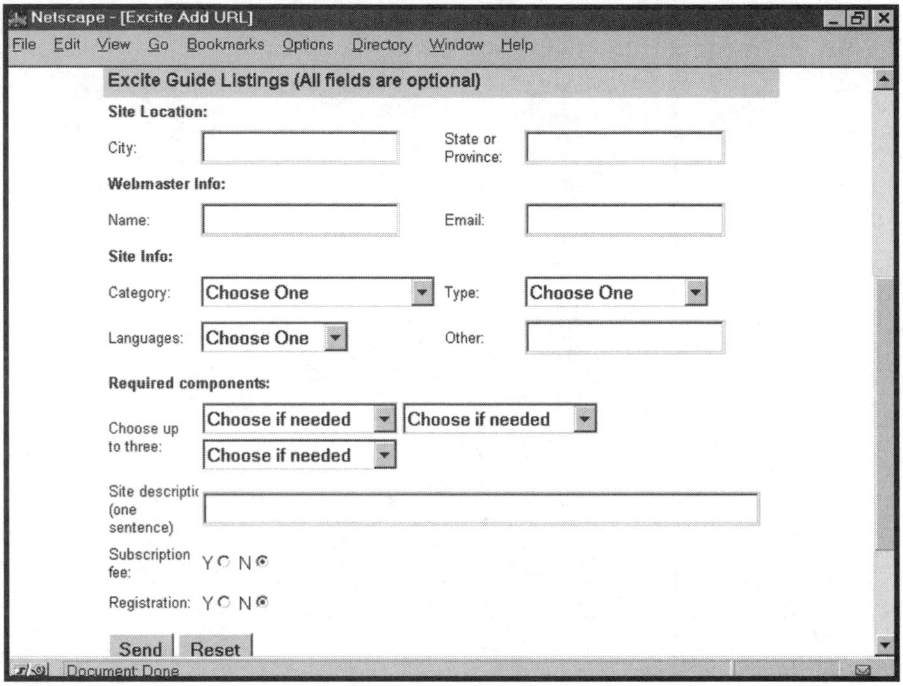

Netscape - [Excite Add URL]

File Edit View Go Bookmarks Options Directory Window Help

Excite Guide Listings (All fields are optional)

Site Location:

City: _____   State or Province: _____

Webmaster Info:

Name: _____   Email: _____

Site Info:

Category: | Choose One ▼ | Type: | Choose One ▼ |

Languages: | Choose One ▼ | Other: _____

Required components:

Choose up to three: | Choose if needed ▼ | | Choose if needed ▼ |
| Choose if needed ▼ |

Site description (one sentence) _____

Subscription fee: Y ○ N ◉

Registration: Y ○ N ◉

Send | Reset

Document: Done

Figure 3.33

The submission page for the Excite guide.

ism, select the travel category. If your site covers business and investing, choose the business category.

NOTE

On Sunday morning, you'll find out more about metro guides in the section called "Directories by Industry and Category."

The required components fields give you a chance to indicate that your site uses cutting-edge technologies. If you designed your site specifically for Netscape Navigator and Internet Explorer, indicate this. If your home page requires Java or ActiveX to get the most out of the page, indicate this as well.

Getting Listed with InfoSpace

FIND IT ▶
ONLINE

InfoSpace (`http://www.infospace.com`) does a great job of pulling together the best features of Yellow Pages and White Pages directories as well as metro guides, making the site a one-stop directory to people, places, and things on the Web. The front door to InfoSpace is shown in Figure 3-34. If you've never worked with very specific types of directories, the organization of InfoSpace will seem very confusing, especially when you discover that InfoSpace uses different search mechanisms to access each of the main types of information available at the Web site.

To make sense of all the information available at InfoSpace, think of each area at the site as a separate directory. If you want to find a business on the Web, use the Yellow Pages. If you want to find a personal home page or information on a specific person, use the White Pages or People area. If you want to find information on a specific city, use the City Information area.

Figure 3-34

The InfoSpace directory to the Web.

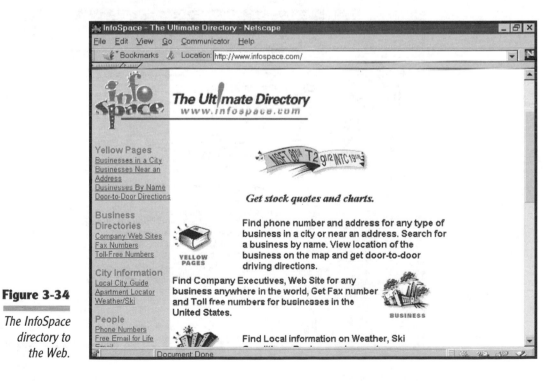

What Do Entries in the InfoSpace Directory Look Like?

Each area within InfoSpace is organized in a different way. Still, if you are seeking information on businesses or people, the results should be similar to those shown in Figure 3-35. In this example, I searched for businesses in Massachusetts that started with the letter *I*.

By clicking on the address information, you can access a detailed listing at InfoSpace. The additional information in the detailed listing includes fax number, e-mail address, contact name, and a summary description.

By clicking on the phone number, you can access an auto dialer, which is definitely an innovation. To use the auto dialer, you hold your touch-tone phone up to your computer's speaker and then click on the dial button in the auto-dialer Web page.

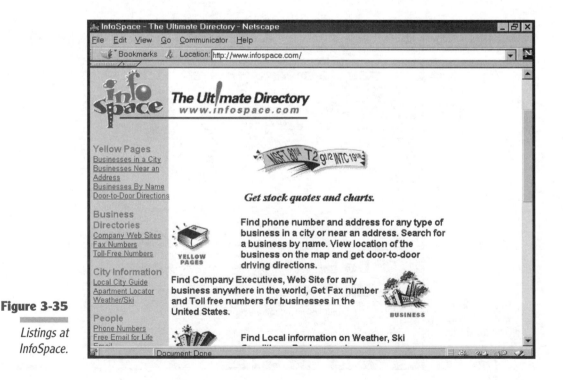

Figure 3-35

Listings at InfoSpace.

Submitting Your Site to InfoSpace

FIND IT ▶ ONLINE

Listings that can be submitted to InfoSpace are separated into two types: business and personal. All business listings are placed in the Yellow Pages area. All personal listings are placed in the White Pages or People area. Although both listings allow you to include your URL and descriptive information, submitting separate entries for your business and personal pages may be worthwhile. The URL for the submission page is the following:

```
http://in-119.infospace.com/info/submit.htm
```

TIP

As shown in Figure 3-36, the submission page asks for a lot of information. Not all of this information is indexed, however. For business searches, the business name and geographic location are the primary items on which you can search. For people searches, the name, geographic location, and e-mail address are the primary items on which you can search. For this reason, don't spend a lot of time entering keywords or descriptive information.

Getting Listed with LookSmart

FIND IT ▶ ONLINE

LookSmart (`http://www.looksmart.com`) is a guide to the best of the Web from *Reader's Digest*. Sites listed in the guide are given the LookSmart Editor's Choice award.

As shown in Figure 3-37, the LookSmart guide is organized into broad subjects through which you can search by clicking on category headings. If you don't feel like exploring LookSmart by category, you can also use a keyword search to find what you are looking for.

What Do Entries in the LookSmart Guide Look Like?

Entries in the LookSmart guide are displayed by site title, which is followed by a summary description. Because the descriptive information is

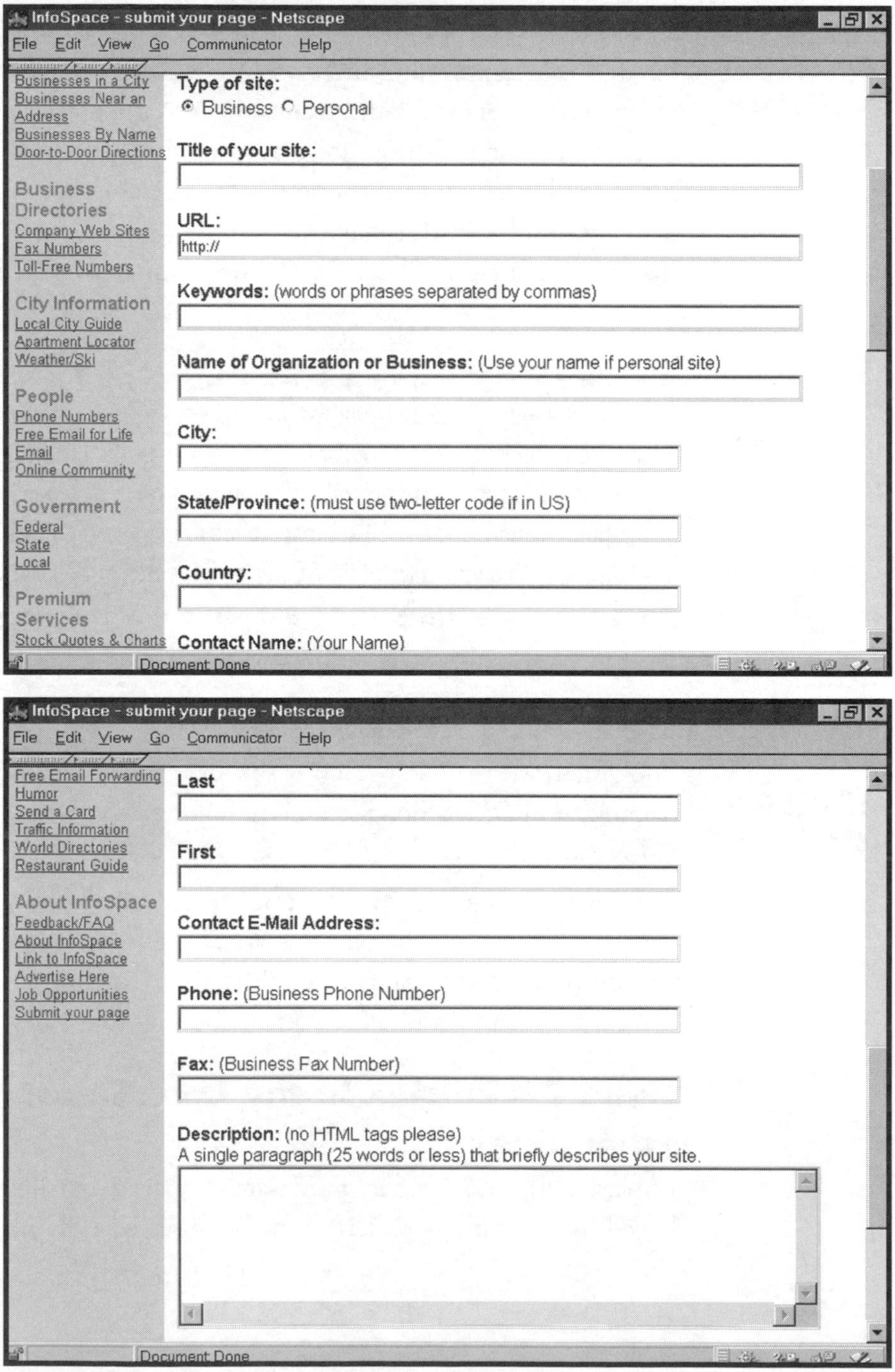

Figure 3-36

The submission page at InfoSpace.

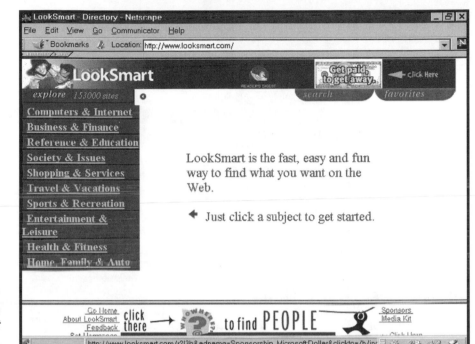

Figure 3-37

The LookSmart guide to the Web.

often taken from the data that you submit, your description really counts. When you submit your site suggestion, use a summary description that is one paragraph of 20 words or fewer.

After wandering through the LookSmart guide for a while, you will find that the listings themselves seem to be organized haphazardly. For example, the listings shown in Figure 3-38 aren't organized alphabetically or by any relevancy indicator displayed with the listing. When 25 to 50 sites are displayed without apparent organization, finding sites of interest is difficult. Still, LookSmart is a popular destination for Web surfers, making it an ideal guide in which to be listed.

Submitting Your Site to LookSmart

FIND IT ▶
ONLINE

You can suggest a site for listing in the LookSmart Guide using the form shown in Figure 3-39. The URL for this page is as follows:

```
http://www.looksmart.com/h/info/submsite.html
```

Figure 3-38

Listings at LookSmart.

Anything you do to make it easier for the folks at LookSmart to categorize and review your Web site will improve your odds of getting listed in this guide. This is why you should find the appropriate place for your site in the LookSmart guide before you fill out the suggestion form. Do this by following the subjects to a page that contains listings that cover topics similar to the ones that your site covers. When you find this page, write down the subjects that you followed to get there. On the suggestion form, you can enter this information in the field that asks: "Do you have a specific recommendation for where the site should be listed?"

Getting Listed in the Lycos Top 5%

The Lycos Top 5% (`http://point.lycos.com`) is a collection of reviews covering the best Web sites. You can explore the Top 5% listings by

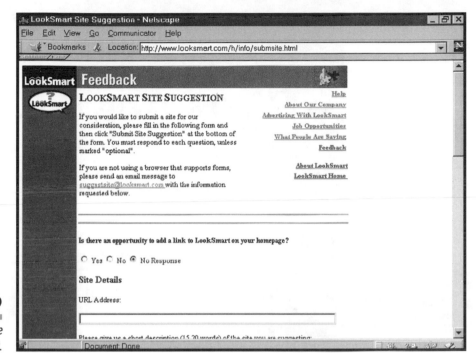

Figure 3-39

The submission page at LookSmart.

category or search the reviews by keyword (see Figure 3-40). Because Lycos also maintains one of the best search engines on the Web, getting listed in the Lycos Top 5% can really boost the amount of traffic at your site.

As the name of the guide implies, Lycos tries to include only the top five percent of all Web sites in the listing. With hundreds of thousands of Web sites publishing hundreds of millions of Web pages, however, the top five percent field is extremely diverse. To narrow the field, Lycos also publishes select lists based on entries in the Top 5% guide, such as the Top 10 sites by category.

What Do Entries in the Lycos Top 5% Look Like?

The Lycos Top 5% guide is not only one of the first Web guides but also one of the best Web guides. All entries in the guide are rated in three cat-

Figure 3-40

*The Lycos Top 5%
guide to the Web*

egories: content, design, and overall experience. As shown in Figures 3-41
and 3-42, these ratings are displayed with the summary listings as well as
the detailed listings.

One of the best features of this guide is that you can sort the summary
listings in many different ways. By default, the summary listings are sorted
from the highest to the lowest overall rating. You can also sort the listings
alphabetically or by individual rating category. Although the summary listing doesn't tell you much about the site's content, the actual review goes
into great detail about what the site is about and why it is one of the best.

Submitting Your Site to the Lycos Top 5% Guide

You can submit your site to the Lycos Top 5% guide by sending e-mail to
top5@lycos.com. To help the folks at Lycos make the decision to review

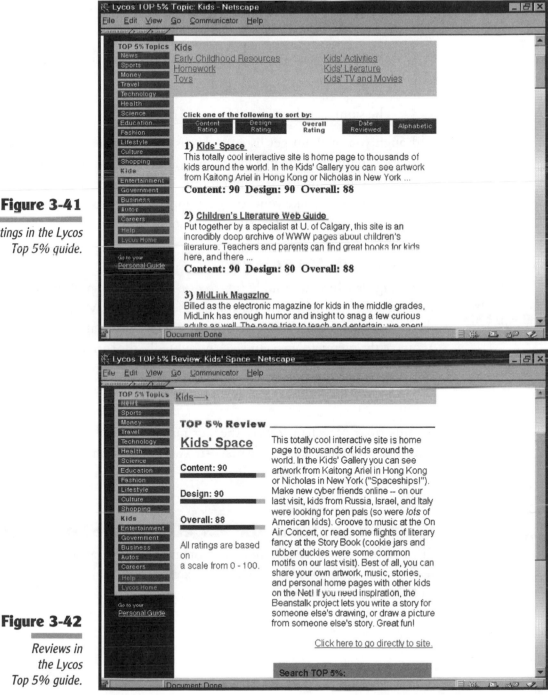

Figure 3-41

Listings in the Lycos Top 5% guide.

Figure 3-42

Reviews in the Lycos Top 5% guide.

your site and list it in the top five percent of the Web, your e-mail should tell the reviewers three things:

1. The specific category into which your site/page fits.

2. The URL to your site or top-level page.

3. The summary description for your resource.

Although you may not get listed in Lycos the first time you try, you can always resubmit your site in a few months. One way to improve your odds is to turn your summary description into a mini-review of your Web site. Who knows—if you rate your resources honestly and provide an interesting review, you may peak the reviewer's interest.

Getting Listed with Magellan

FIND IT ▶ ONLINE

The Magellan Internet Guide (`http://www.mckinley.com`) is one of the oldest guides to the Web. Over the past several years, Magellan has gone through many up and downs, yet it was only recently that the site emerged as one of the premiere Web guides. Undoubtedly, the turnaround was made possible in part by the partnership with Excite. Thanks to this partnership, you can search Magellan and the Web using the same search interface (see Figure 3-43).

Awards from Magellan feature the star rating assigned to your site. Star ratings go from four stars—the best—to two stars. If you receive one of the awards, you will be able to display the Magellan award icon at your Web site.

What Do Entries in the Magellan Guide Look Like?

Listings in the Magellan guide are displayed with a rating and a mini-review (see Figure 3-44). As with the Excite guide, listings are organized alphabetically within their rating.

Figure 3-43

The Magellan guide to the Web.

Figure 3-44

Reviews in the Magellan guide.

Submitting Your Site to Magellan

Because of the partnership with Excite, all submissions to Magellan are handled via Excite. If you want your site to be reviewed in Magellan, you should submit your site to the Excite guide.

Getting Listed with NetGuide

FIND IT ▶
ONLINE

NetGuide (`http://www.netguide.com`) provides comprehensive reviews of the best Web sites. When you visit the NetGuide home page shown in Figure 3-45, the first thing you might notice is the unique approach used at this site. In addition to thousands of reviews, NetGuide features live events, categorized guides that are updated daily, and useful reference material.

Awards from NetGuide include the NetGuide Platinum site and the NetGuide Gold site. Platinum sites represent the very best out of all the sites reviewed. Gold sites represent the best of the Web. In addition to these awards, NetGuide has annual awards for the top site of the year in various categories.

What Do Entries in NetGuide Look Like?

Listings in NetGuide are displayed with a brief summary, and the newest ones are shown first (see Figure 3-46). The listing title is linked to the Web site being reviewed. Along with this information is a Site Details page that shows a more detailed review of the site (see Figure 3-46). Click on Site Details to access the Site Details page.

NetGuide also makes it possible to view the detailed listings for multiple sites without having to access the Site Details page. After you search using a keyword, click on the View Full Text reviews link found at the top of the search results page. Later, you can change back to the mini reviews by clicking on View QuickList reviews.

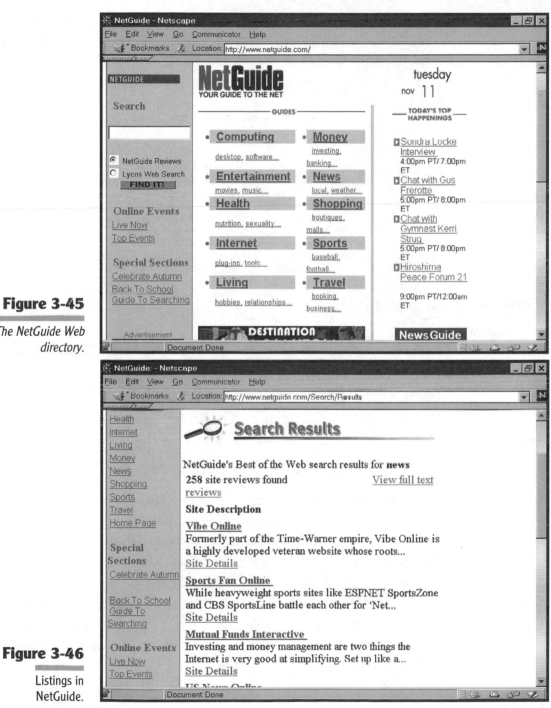

Figure 3-45

The NetGuide Web directory.

Figure 3-46

Listings in NetGuide.

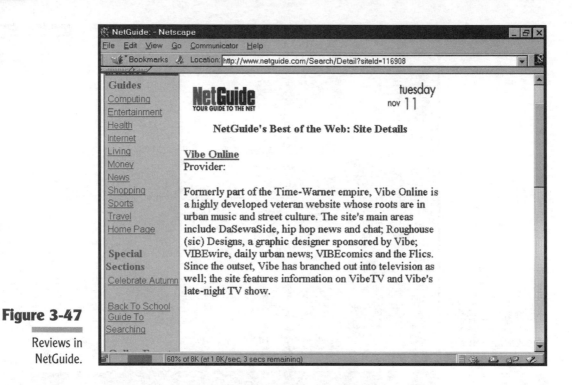

Figure 3-47

Reviews in
NetGuide.

Submitting Your Site to NetGuide

FIND IT ▶
ONLINE

You can submit your site to NetGuide by sending e-mail to `ngreview@ cmp.com`. The information that you provide in the message is important in helping NetGuide determine whether to assign someone to take a look at your site. For this reason, your e-mail should be well planned. Start by telling the reviewers the specific category into which your site fits best. This category should be narrowly focused, and you should be sure that it exists within NetGuide. Next, state the title and URL for your site. Finally, provide a summary description of your Web site.

As stated previously, if you provide several different resources, you may want to tell the reviewers about these resources individually. With this approach, you describe each top-level area rather than the site as a whole. For the best results, try to limit this to the two or three top-level areas that are truly the best your site has to offer.

Getting Listed with Yahoo!

FIND IT
ONLINE

Yahoo! (http://www.yahoo.com) is undoubtedly the most famous Web directory. To say that Yahoo! has been around the block a few times is a huge understatement. In the early days, Yahoo! was nothing more than a collection of links broken down by category. The site didn't even have a search feature. Since then, Yahoo! has remade itself several times and now offers all the bells and whistles that you would expect from one of the Web's biggest success stories.

Like most directories, you can search Yahoo! by keyword or by following links to various categories (see Figure 3-48). Because Yahoo! is so tremendously popular, the directory is divided into many different specialty guides as well. You can find the best of the Web in the Weekly Picks section, and area guides for major metropolitan areas such as Seattle, New York, and Chicago. Yahoo! also offers international guides to countries such as Canada, Japan, and Germany, and even a guide for kids, called Yahooligans.

What Do Entries in the Yahoo! Directory Look Like?

Searching Yahoo! by category is a different experience from most other directory sites, especially because Yahoo! has so many different categories and so many levels of information. Although all the levels of information within Yahoo! allow you to find links to very specific topics, you need to understand this maze before you submit your Web site to Yahoo.

For most subjects, the related pages are divided into three sections: links to related resources published in Yahoo!, links to more specific subjects, and links to other Web sites within the current subject. When you click on a category such as entertainment, you come to a page that lists many different subjects within this specific area. The next topic that you select, such as

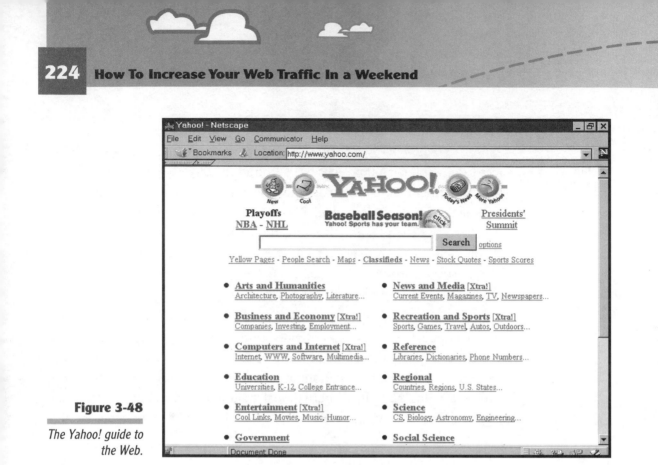

Figure 3-48

The Yahoo! guide to the Web.

movies and films, brings you to another page with more detailed subjects and more detailed information (see Figure 3-49).

If you are interested in movie trivia, you might want to follow the link to trivia from the movies and films page. Although you've already moved through four levels of information, you can still find more topics from which to choose (see Figure 3-50).

After you've wandered the Yahoo! maze, you can target specific categories that relate to your Web site. Ideally, you will have several very specific categories in mind before you try to submit your site. The important thing to know when you find a topic in Yahoo! is how to write down a category reference, which is taken directly from the page's URL.

To come up with the category reference, you just remove the text that reads `http://www.yahoo.com/` from the full URL. For a URL that reads:

`http://www.yahoo.com/Entertainment/Movies_and_Film`

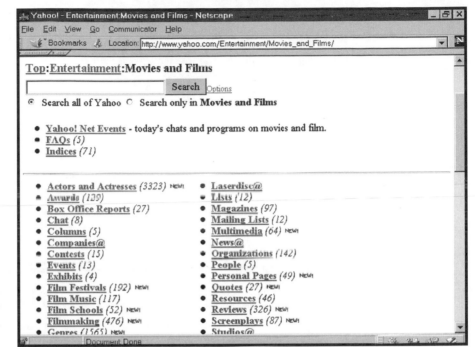

Figure 3-49

The Movies and Films category at Yahoo!.

the category reference is the following:

```
Entertainment/Movies_and_Film
```

For a URL that reads:

```
http://www.yahoo.com/Entertainment/Movies_and_Film/Trivia
```

the category reference is as follows:

```
Entertainment/Movies_and_Film/Trivia
```

Submitting Your Site to Yahoo!

To submit your site to Yahoo!, go to the specific category that best fits your site; then, click on the Add URL icon in the page banner. The submission page, shown in Figure 3-51, appears. Because you are on a specific category page, the category field is filled in for you automatically. Do not make any changes to the category field.

After you fill in your page title and URL, enter references for the additional categories where you think your site should be listed. Any comments that

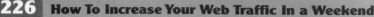

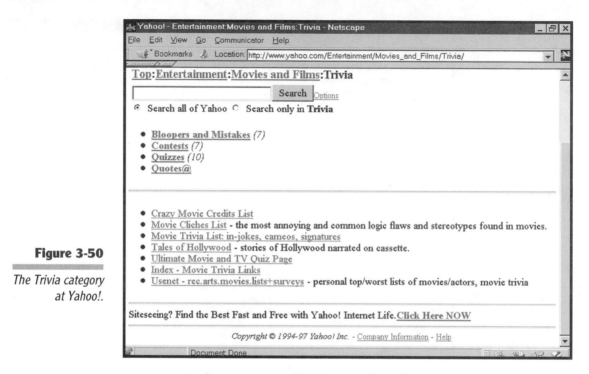

Figure 3-50

The Trivia category at Yahoo!.

you enter in the comments field are used to describe your page. Because Yahoo! listings rarely have more than a few words, you should limit your comments to a single descriptive sentence—the shorter your comments, the more likely they are to be added to your listing.

Internet Subject Index from Nerd World

The Internet subject index from Nerd World Media (`http://search.nerd world.com`) is a comprehensive directory to everything the Web has to offer. Like most directories, the Internet subject index is broken down into many different categories, but Nerd World Media adds a unique twist by dividing all listings into two broad categories called Leisure and Knowledge (see Figure 3-52).

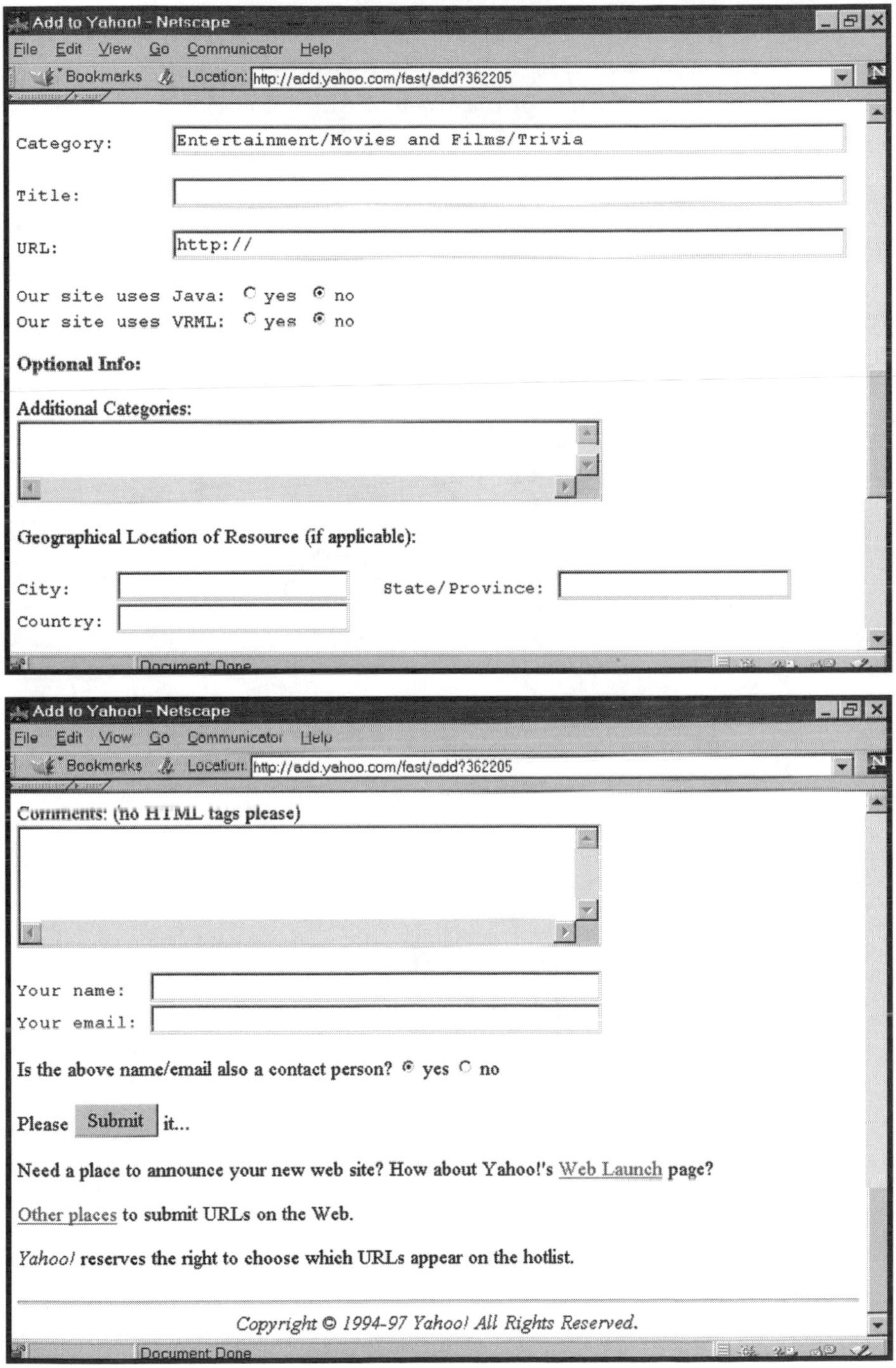

Figure 3-51

The submission page at Yahoo!.

Leisure categories cover anything you might do in your free time, such as music, sports, and travel. Knowledge categories cover anything that you would use primarily at work, school, or to build knowledge, such as resources, reference material, and news.

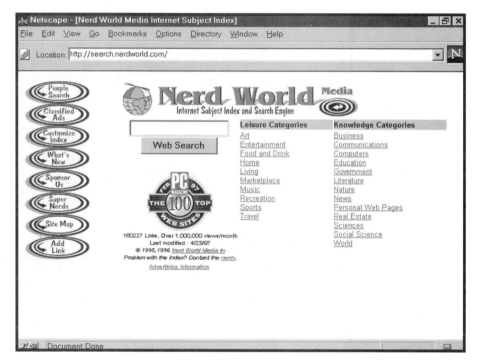

Figure 3-52

An index for the world from Nerd World Media.

What Do Entries in the Internet Subject Index Look Like?

Nerd World currently uses frames to list focused categories within a broad category in a side frame and entries for specific categories in a main frame (see Figure 3-53). Most listings are accompanied by a summary paragraph that describes the listing.

Although you can search the Internet subject index by keyword, the actual descriptions are not indexed. This means that the most important aspects of your listing are category selection and page title.

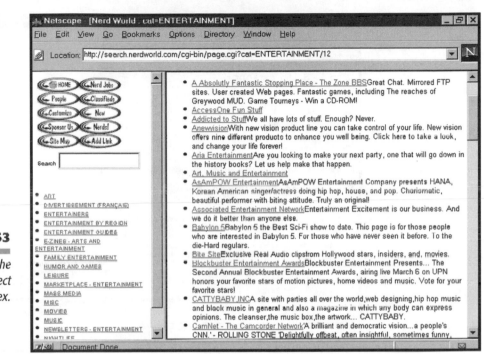

Figure 3-53

Listings in the Internet subject index.

Submitting Your Site to the Internet Subject Index

Before you submit your listing to the Internet subject index, you should have a clear idea of the category that best fits your page. Knowing the category that you want to use will save you time. Because listings in the directory are displayed with summary descriptions, you should carefully consider the description that you will use for the listing. Ideally, your description will be two to three carefully considered sentences of fewer than 25 words altogether.

FIND IT
ONLINE

You can submit your site to Nerd World using the page shown in Figure 3-54. The URL for this page is as follows:

```
http://search.nerdworld.com/nwadd.html
```

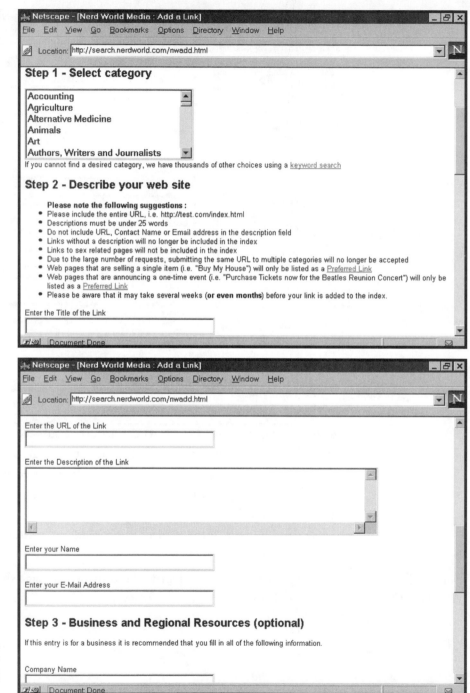

Figure 3-54

The submission page at the Internet subject index.

Your Tool for Success

INTERNET JAVA AND ACTIVEX ADVISOR is the essential tool hands-on Internet developers need by their side. Written by experts, every issue brings you vital information on the latest products and technologies necessary for staying on top of the Internet revolution. Take a look at what you'll get each month when you subscribe today:

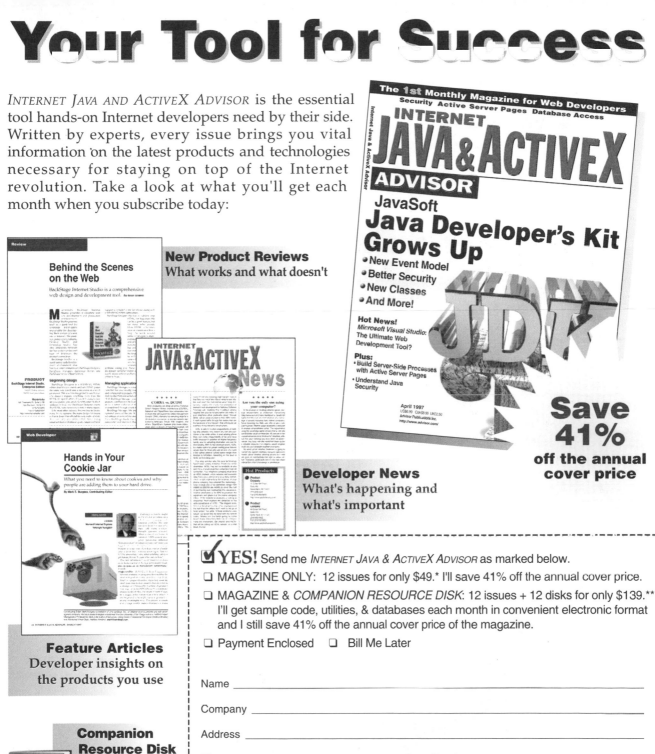

New Product Reviews
What works and what doesn't

Developer News
What's happening and what's important

Feature Articles
Developer insights on the products you use

Companion Resource Disk
Sample code, databases, and utilities in easy-to-use electronic format

The 1st Monthly Magazine for Web Developers
Security Active Server Pages Database Access

INTERNET JAVA & ACTIVEX ADVISOR

JavaSoft
Java Developer's Kit Grows Up
- New Event Model
- Better Security
- New Classes
- And More!

Hot News!
Microsoft Visual Studio: The Ultimate Web Development Tool?

Plus:
- Build Server-Side Processes with Active Server Pages
- Understand Java Security

April 1997
US$6.99 Cdn$9.99 UK£2.50
Advisor Publications Inc.
http://www.advisor.com/

Save 41%
off the annual cover price

Wrapping Up and Looking Ahead

Guides, lists, and directories can really help get your Web site noticed. Although you aren't guaranteed a listing in a guide to the best of the Web, your time is still well spent when you consider that a single award could bring a flood of thousands of visitors to your site. The next section examines the best directories and search engines for business-oriented Web sites.

The Coolest, The Hottest, and the Best

- ✿ The Best Business Search Engines and Yellow Pages Directories

- ✿ Directories by Industry and Category

- ✿ Promoting Your Web Site in Specialty Directories

- ✿ Getting Your Site Listed as the Cool Site of the Day

Several hundred business search and directory sites currently are available, but this part of Sunday morning's coverage focuses on the best of these sites so that you can get the most exposure for your time investment.

I have spent many hours compiling these resources so that you don't have to. If you have time, go ahead and make use of these resources as you learn about them; that is, proceed with the registration process that I describe as you go through this section. If you don't have time to get them all in now, come back when you do. It will be worth your while, I promise.

Later this morning, you'll find out how to vie for awards that help get your site noticed by cyberspace travelers. Awards abound on the Web, and your site can sizzle as Hot Site of the Day or freeze out the competition as Cool Site of the Week. Some awards are more likely to increase your Web traffic than others, though, and this part of the book introduces you to some of the best.

The Best Business Search Engines and Yellow Pages Directories

Business search engines and Yellow Pages directories provide great resources for anyone who offers products, services, or business-related information on the Web. Most business-oriented search engines and directories provide much more detailed information than other search sites and directories. These detailed entries allow you to list your Web site and tout your products and services as well.

Submitting Your Site to Business Search and Directory Sites

Hundreds of thousands of businesses offer products and services on the Web. The sites that help Web users make sense of all these offerings are the business search engines and Yellow Pages directories. Because these search and directory sites are tailored for businesses, you can search for specific businesses by company name, location, and industry as well as the products and services that the companies offer.

Although they are similar to traditional search engines, most business search engines do not index your Web site or the pages that you submit for being listed at the search site. Instead, these search engines create an indexed reference to your site based solely on the information you submit, which doesn't necessarily include the URL to your Web site. In this respect, this type of business search engine is more like a directory listing than a traditional search engine.

Because business search engines don't actually index your site, many business search sites are called Yellow Pages directories. Although some Yellow Pages directories are modeled after the Yellow Pages of your phone book, most Web-based Yellow Pages directories have features of both traditional directory sites and traditional search engine sites.

Due to their very direct focus, business search sites and directories often want a great deal of information from anyone registering with the site. For this reason, before you register with these sites, you should have all the following information planned out:

- How you want the company contact information to read
- Who you will list as the contact name at the company
- What keywords you want to associate with your site
- What page URL you want to be listed at the site
- What e-mail address you want to use for inquiries
- What description you will use for your company, products, and services

You should also know that, by their very nature, business search sites and directories are out to make a profit. The worst of these sites exist only to push paid services at unwitting souls who want to get listed at the site. Again, I recommend that you don't sign up for anything that will cost you money. Plenty of sites are happy just to have your listing and they will list you without charge. These sites get their money from advertising rather than listings.

Increasing Your Web Traffic with Yellow Pages Directories

Just as the top search engines and directories receive millions of visitors every day, so do the top Yellow Pages directories and, accordingly, registering your Web site with Yellow Pages directories will increase the traffic to your Web site. That said, Yellow Pages directories generally don't drive thousands of visitors to a particular Web site; rather, you can reasonably expect relatively modest increases in your Web traffic over time.

By *relatively modest*, I mean that the average Web site, which may have 500 visitors a day at present, may see an additional 50 visitors daily as a result of registering with a popular Yellow Pages directory. The traffic depends, of course, on the types of products and services that you offer. Right now you may be thinking, wow, is it really worth the effort? The answer in this case is a resounding yes if you focus your efforts on the top Yellow Pages directories listed in this section.

Although Yellow Pages directories are popular and they do receive millions of visitors every day, Yellow Pages directories are business-oriented. Visitors to these directories are usually looking for very specific types of information—for example, information on a management consulting service. Furthermore, because Yellow Pages listings contain addresses, phone numbers, and other contact information, people visiting the Yellow Pages directory may not visit your Web site at all. Instead, they may visit your physical storefront or otherwise contact you by phone, fax, or e-mail.

Whether visitors to a Yellow Pages directory go to your storefront, contact you, or visit your Web site, you have managed to bring in the all-important consumers who are actively looking for a business that offers products or services like yours. With a listing in a traditional search engine or directory site, you simply cannot bring in this type of visitor on a consistent basis. Most businesses I know of would much rather have 50 people browsing the aisles, virtual or otherwise, than 500 people racing past the windows on their way to somewhere else.

As you follow along with the discussion, I recommend that you submit your Web site to the search engines and directories found in this section. For anyone who is in a hurry and doesn't have time to register with all the sites I examine, simply start with the first site and register with as many sites as you can. To make the task of registering your Web site easier, you may want to visit the companion Web site for this book. Use the following URL:

```
http://www.tvpress.com/promote/yellp.htm
```

NOTE Any Yellow Pages directories that you find at the online site that are not listed in this part are discussed later in the book. I recommend that you hold off on registering with these other sites for now.

Announcing Your Business at the All Business Network

The All Business Network (`http://www.all-biz.com`) offers many different services to businesses on the Web. From the All Business Network home page shown in Figure 4-1, you can access headline news, a job bank, business information, and much more. Still, the main attraction at this site is the comprehensive business directory.

Business sectors and industry sectors, such as aviation, finance, and accounting, organize listings at the All Business Network. Within the major category, there are many different subcategories. Visitors to the All Busi-

ness Network are able to search through the major categories and eventually the subcategories as well using the main search interface.

Figure 4-1

The All Business Network.

What Do Entries in the All Business Network Look Like?

The All Business Network has one of the best layouts for business listings (see Figure 4-2). All listings are displayed alphabetically by company name. Following the company name is a summary description of the services or products offered.

To get the most out of your listing at the All Business Network, you should provide a fairly descriptive summary of your Web site. A good length for the summary is 35 to 50 words. The summary should provide an overview of the company as well as your products and services. You should also ensure that you provide the URL to one of the main pages at your Web site. The company name will be linked to this page.

ABN Communications - Netscape
File Edit View Go Communicator Help
Bookmarks Location: http://www.all-biz.com/communic.html
Organizations
The American Communications Association - is the national professional organization of scholars, students, and practitioners in the field of communication studies. This site provides information about the ACA, a collection of materials on communication law and First Amendment issues, resources for teaching and research in communication studies, and an extensive reference resource page for scholars and activists.
International Communications Industries Association - ICIArepresents for-profit organizations and individuals who derive revenue from the commercialization or utilization of communications technologies. ICIA's mission is to position itself as the pre-eminent provider of information, training and services to its members and to users of communications technologies. ICIA is an alliance of more than 1,500 communications members selling video, audio-visual and computer products and services to the business and industry, government, education and health markets.
Public Relations Society of America
Document: Done

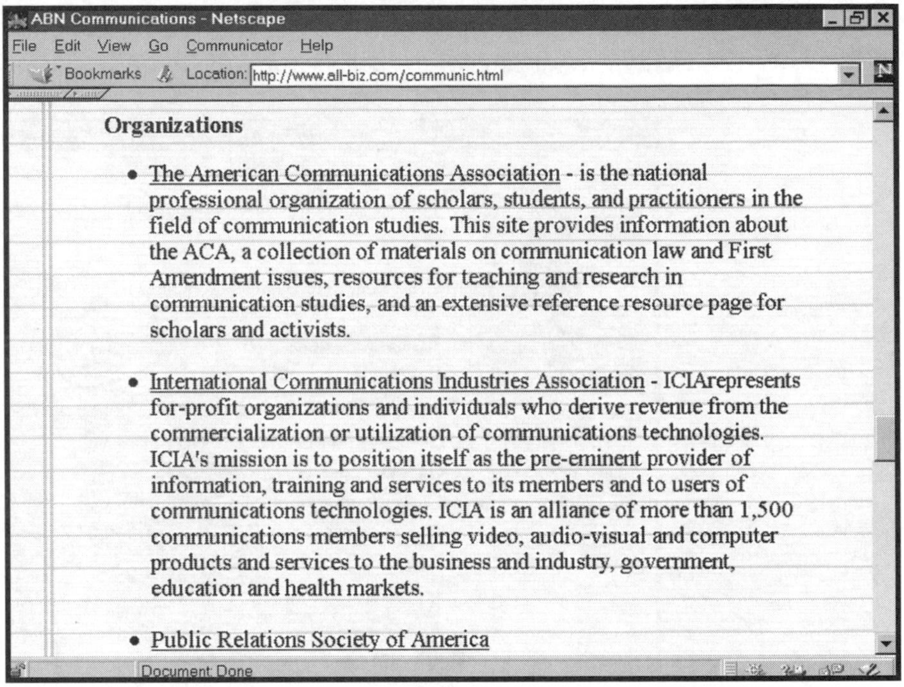

Figure 4-2

Listings at All Business Network.

Placing a Listing at the All Business Network

FIND IT ONLINE

You can submit your site to the All Business Network using the submission page shown in Figure 4-3. The URL for this page is as follows:

`http://www.all-biz.com/directry.htm`

When you arrive at this page, click on the Add button to enter a new directory listing and follow the prompts to create your summary listing. After you fill out all the appropriate information in the form provided, submit it and you are on your way.

In addition to the summary listing, the All Business Network provides a free home page service for businesses, which provides you with another billboard for your cyberspace operations. You can use this billboard to bring visitors to your main home page or Web site. During the submission process, you will be given the opportunity to create and customize this home page. Be sure to write down your user name and password. You will use this information to add information to your page and to update the page in the future.

Because the home page is blank initially, you need to select the Maintenance icon or the Maintenance link to add information to the page. Start by adding general information for the products and services that your company offers. Next, add your URL and other custom features to the page.

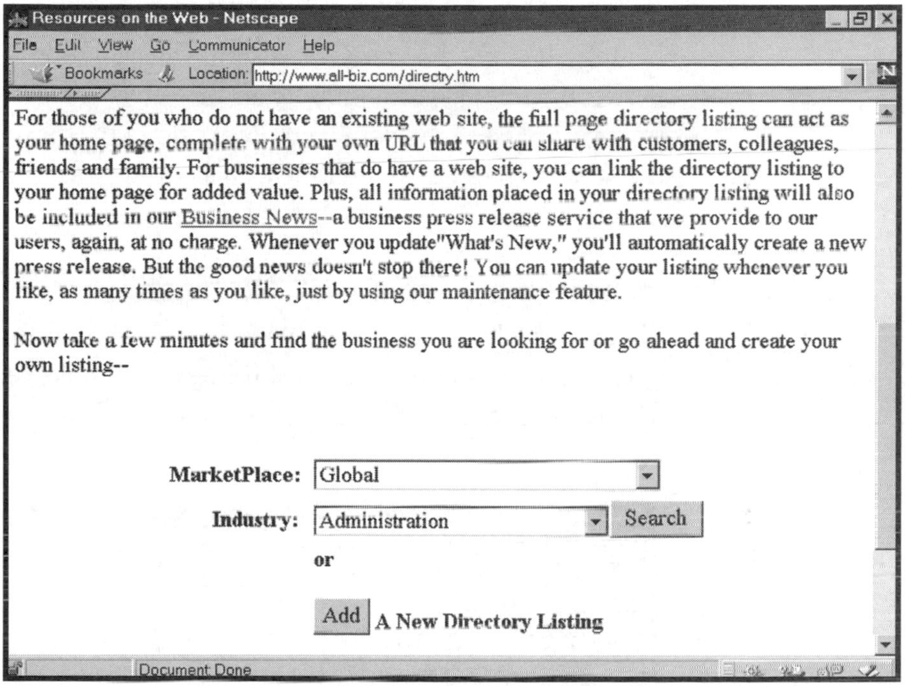

Figure 4-3

The submission page at the All Business Network.

Announcing Your Business at BizWeb

FIND IT ▶
ONLINE
BizWeb (http://www.bizweb.com) offers a fairly comprehensive business directory that is divided into several hundred broad subject categories ranging from Antiques to Web software. Although the BizWeb home page shown in Figure 4-4 doesn't offer a visual feast of graphics, the site is highly regarded for its business listings.

Unlike many other business directories, BizWeb doesn't organize the site by company name or industry focus. Instead, the BizWeb site is organized by the products and services that companies offer. Visitors to BizWeb can search for products and services by using keywords or by selecting one of the category links. Because BizWeb is indexed using categories as well as user-supplied keywords, the BizWeb search engine is fairly efficient and user friendly.

What Do Entries at BizWeb Look Like?

Listings at BizWeb are organized into categories of products and services that companies have announced in the directory (see Figure 4-5). All entries are linked to the home page or catalog URL of the company. Because the BizWeb focus is not on the business as a whole, the listings do not have lengthy summaries.

Placing a Listing at BizWeb

When you add a listing to BizWeb, keep in mind the site's focus on products and services rather than the business as a whole. Also note that BizWeb uses your answers to determine whether your listing is appropriate for the

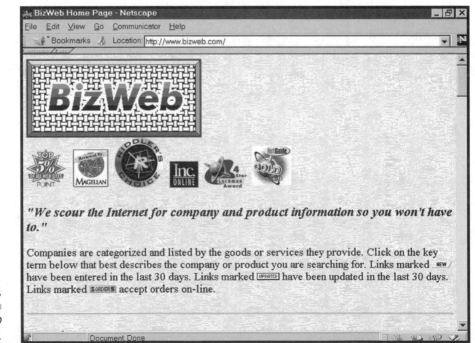

Figure 4-4

The BizWeb directory.

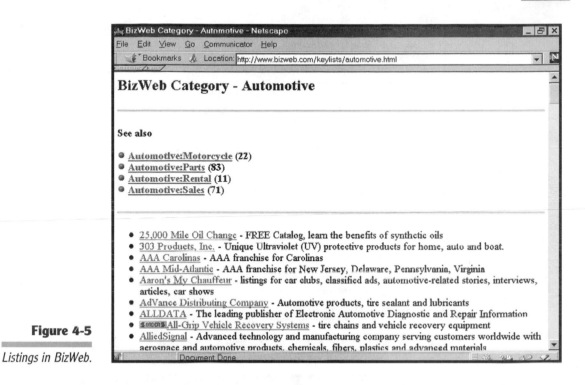

Figure 4-5

Listings in BizWeb.

directory. With this in mind, your entry should have a clear description of the services or products that your company offers. Further, you should answer all the questions regarding your services and products. If you indicate that your site doesn't offer products or services, your entry might be considered a personal listing rather than a business listing, in which case the entry will not be submitted to the database.

Although the BizWeb search engine does make use of your keywords, the keywords aren't used extensively. Still, I recommend providing a sample of the relevant keywords for your Web site. Figure 4-6 shows the submission form at BizWeb. The URL for this page is as follows:

```
http://www.bizweb.com/InfoForm/
```

Announcing Your Business at ComFind

As Figure 4-7 shows, ComFind (`http://www.comfind.com`) claims to be the largest global business directory, and indeed, the ComFind database

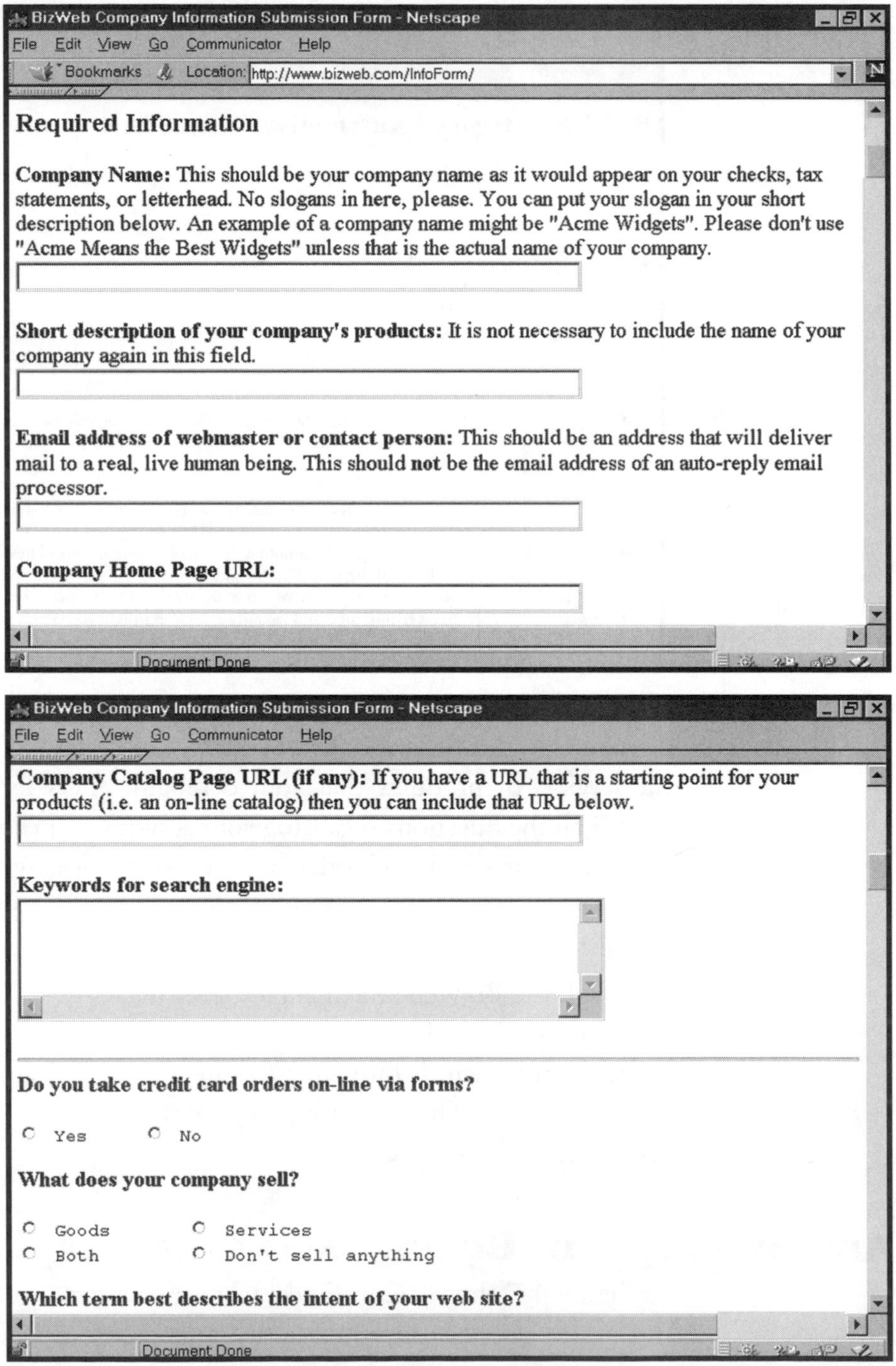

Figure 4-6

The submission page at BizWeb.

does list hundreds of thousands of business around the world. In addition to maintaining a business directory, ComFind also publishes a listing of the Top 100 business sites.

Like other business directories, the ComFind directory is organized by industry-oriented categories that you can search through using keywords. If you search using categories, you will find that ComFind has an extensive search interface that helps you move easily from a broad category topic to a very specific topic. Beyond the standard category search, ComFind also lets you search for companies by name.

What Do Entries at ComFind Look Like?

After you drill down to an actual entry, you will find that listings at ComFind are organized alphabetically in their respective categories (see Figure 4-8). The entries include the company name and contact information. For standard—that is, free—entries, the company name links to the company's Web site. For enhanced entries, the company name links to an advertiser

Figure 4-7

The ComFind business directory.

page or extended listing. As you might expect, enhanced entries cost money. Again, I say don't spend a dime.

Placing a Listing at ComFind

Before you can submit anything to ComFind, you must use the search engine to find the appropriate category for your Web site. On the bottom of the category page, you will find a button labeled Go! Register that allows you to access the submission page shown in Figure 4-9. Alternatively, you can select Add New Listing from the home page and then follow the instructions for finding a category and registering your Web site.

After you find a listing, you will be on Step 2 of the registration process. In this step, you are asked to enter a two-letter designator for your country, such as US, and a local phone number. The phone number that you use is matched against current entries in the ComFind database. If a match is found, you will not be able to create a new entry unless you enter a different phone number.

Figure 4-8

Listings at ComFind.

In Step 3, you enter information related to your business and your Web site. Be sure to fill in all of the required information. Although the URL to your home page is optional, you should fill this in to ensure that readers can easily access your Web site to find more information. You should also enter a keyword list for your site. Because the search engine doesn't use the keywords extensively, you may want to include short descriptive phrases that tell the reader about your Web site. Keep in mind that any keywords provided are displayed with the listing.

CAUTION   Be aware that ComFind does try to sell you an enhanced listing from the submission page. For this reason, you should read all the information that follows the free listing fields.

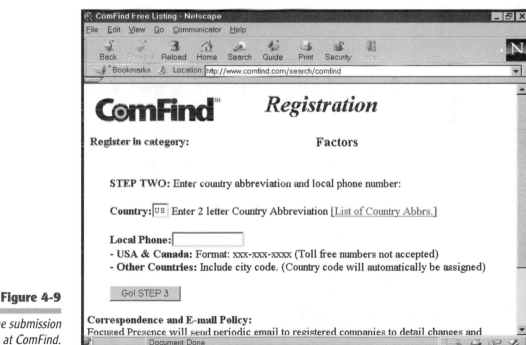

Figure 4-9

The submission page at ComFind.

Announcing Your Business at ProNet

Pronet (http://www.pronett.com and http://www.pronet.ca) is a terrific international business directory that lists sites in English, Spanish, French, and German. So, if you know several languages, you can use Pronet to reach out to a global audience. At the time of this writing, the Pronet database listed about 200,000 companies and was adding more than 1,000 new companies every day.

The directory at Pronet is well thought out and is supported by an extremely versatile search engine. When you perform a search at Pronet, the power of the search engine is clearly evident. You can search not only by category but also by country, company name, and keyword (see Figure 4-10).

What Do Entries at Pronet Look Like?

Pronet is a clear winner when it comes to well-organized and easy-to-read listings (see Figure 4-11). As with most search sites, the company title is linked to the company's home page URL, which is followed by a summary.

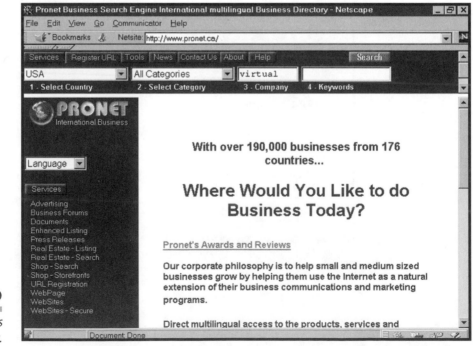

Figure 4-10

The Pronet business directory.

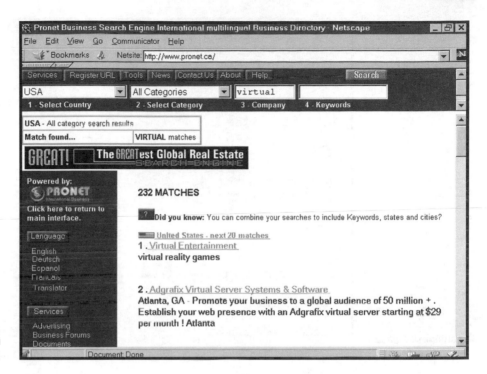

Figure 4-11

Listings at Pronet.

Because Pronet completely indexes its database, the search results are displayed much like the search results you would see at one of the traditional search engines, such as Lycos. Here, the first listing has highest relevancy and the later listings have lower relevancies.

FIND IT ▶
ONLINE

Placing a Listing at Pronet

You can submit your site to Pronet using the submission page shown in Figure 4-12. The URL for this page is as follows:

```
http://pronet.ca/add_url/
```

When you fill out the submission form at Pronet, try to provide as much information as possible. Keep in mind that all the information you supply can be used to include or exclude your company from search results. Pronet even uses the address information to allow searches within specific geographic areas.

Because the Pronet search engine uses your keywords to create the indexed reference to your listing, you should supply an extensive keyword list.

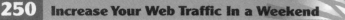

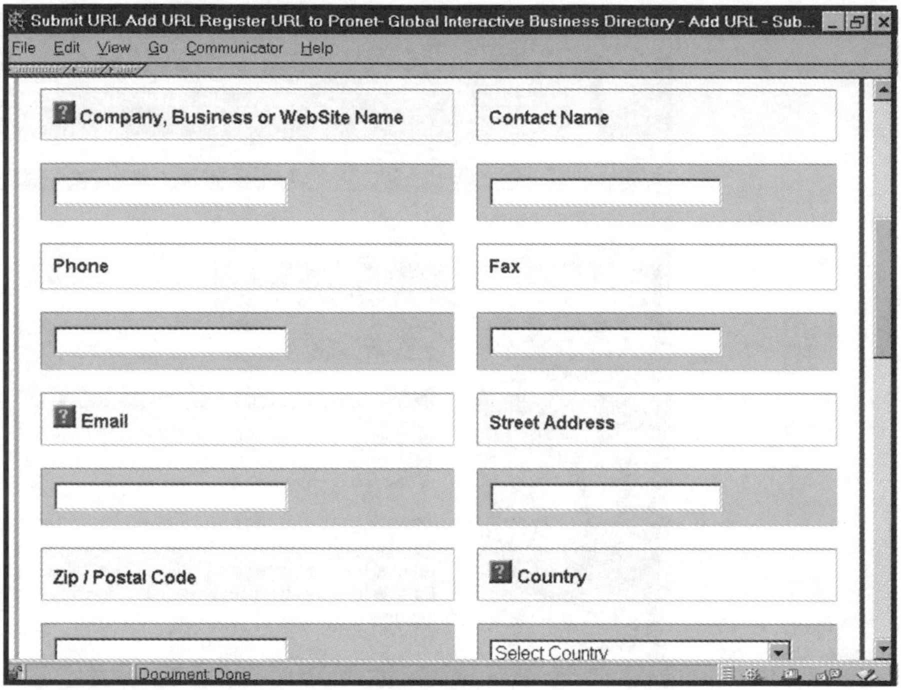

Figure 4-12

The submission page at ProNet.

Additionally, Pronet allows you to provide a fairly detailed summary of your Web site as well as the products and services that you offer, so be sure to take the time to provide a great summary for your Web site.

Announcing Your Business at Where2Go

Where2Go (`http://www.where2go.com`) offers extremely comprehensive business listings and is a true search engine in every sense of the word. Because Where2Go creates indexed references using just about all the information provided with entries, visitors can search on business names, industry, products, services, and even URLs (see Figure 4-13).

What Do Entries in Where2Go Look Like?

The unique approach of Where2Go has attracted thousands of businesses and millions of visitors. Entries in the Where2Go search engine are care-

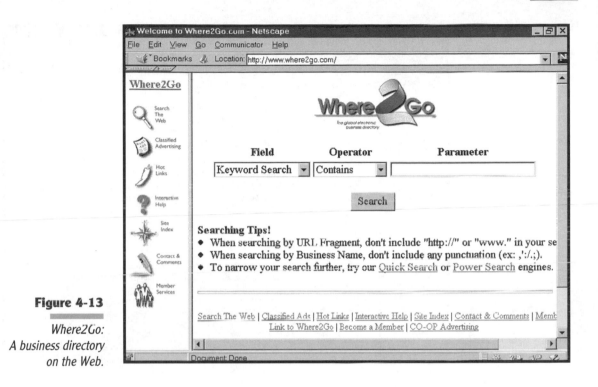

Figure 4-13

*Where2Go:
A business directory
on the Web.*

fully indexed and organized, making Where2Go listings easy to search and read (see Figure 4-14).

Although you can search using keywords at Where2Go, search results are ordered alphabetically rather than by relevancy. Each listing has four key elements: company name, category, products/services, and URL. Unlike most directories that restrict your listing to specific categories, Where2Go simply asks for a general category that would match a Yellow Pages listing for the business.

By clicking on the company name, you access a detailed home page for the company at Where2Go (see Figure 4-15). As you can see from the figure, the home page includes the full contact information for the company and detailed descriptions of the products and services offered.

An interesting addition at Where2Go is the table that follows the products and services listing. The elements in the table are meant to give a snapshot of the type of business that you conduct, such as the type of sales you do,

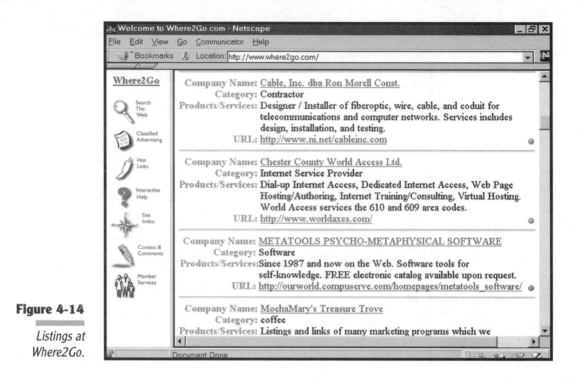

Figure 4-14

*Listings at
Where2Go.*

how you sell your products and services, and the payment options for purchases. Also included in the listing are the company's return policy and number of years in business.

Placing a Listing in Where2Go

Before you can place a listing at Where2Go, you must become a member and accept the use policies for the search engine. Fortunately, the basic membership package doesn't cost anything, except for a few minutes of your time to fill out a form for your listing. The membership form is at:

```
http://www.where2go.com/html/signup.html
```

After you accept the use policies for Where2Go, you can complete an entry form. Although this form asks you to fill in a great deal of information, the payoff in the customized home page is certainly worth the effort.

Be sure to include a comprehensive description of the products and services that you offer, along with a complete keyword list; both are indexed

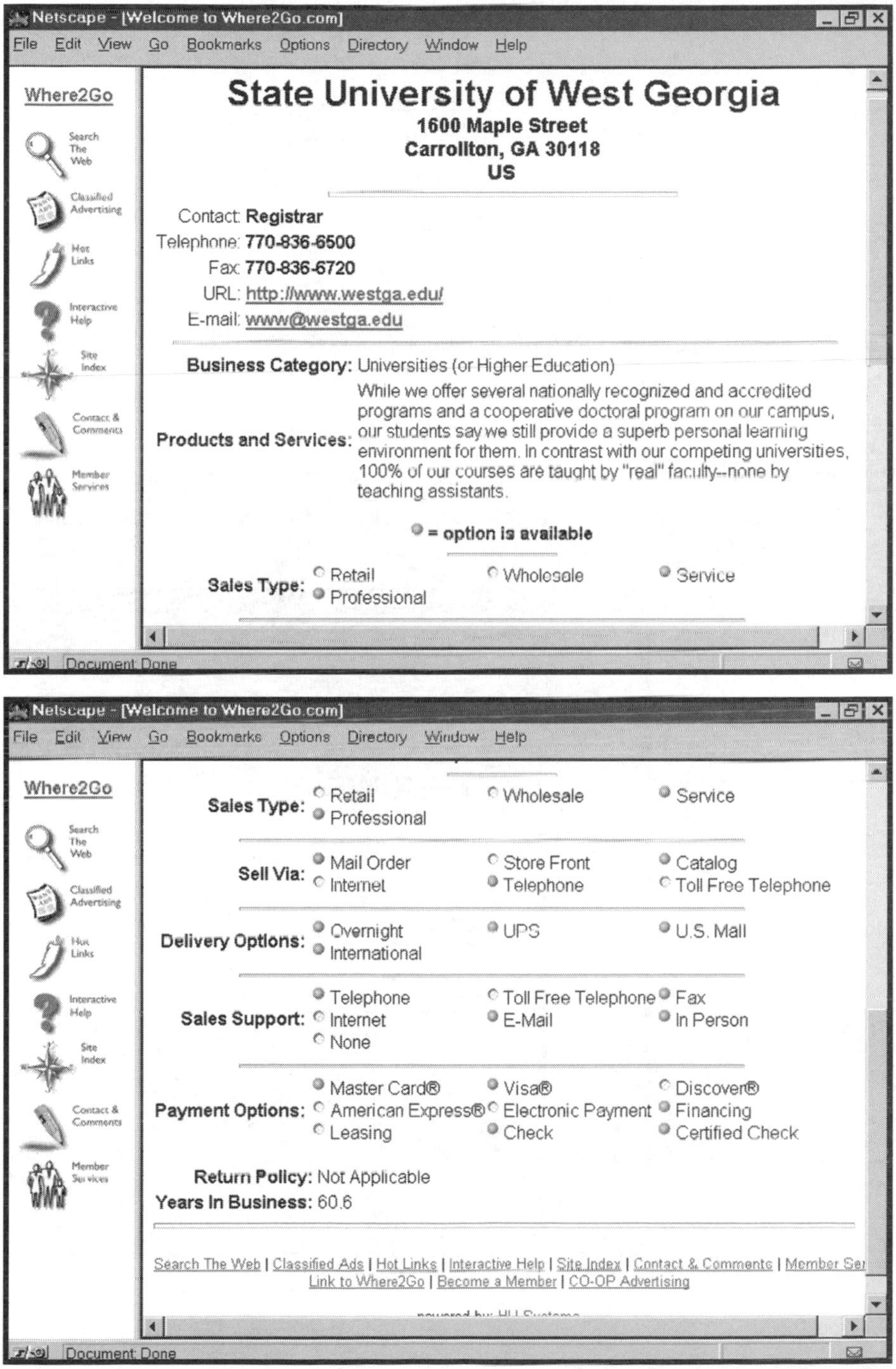

Figure 4-15

The detailed listing at Where2Go.

with your listing. If a visitor performs a brand name search, keywords in the products and services description are used to help determine matches. If a visitor performs a keyword search, your keyword list is used to help determine matches. Other things to watch out for include the e-mail address, which is linked with a mailto: reference on the detailed home page, and the business start date, which is used to calculate the length of time you've been in business.

Announcing Your Business in the YellowNet World-Wide Pages

YellowNet (http://www.yellownet.com) is an international business directory. From the YellowNet home page, you can search for businesses by name, category, and geographic location (see Figure 4-16).

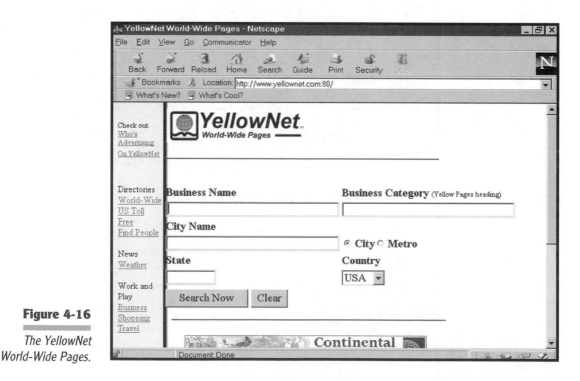

Figure 4-16

The YellowNet World-Wide Pages.

What Do Entries in the YellowNet World-Wide Pages Look Like?

YellowNet is organized like the Yellow Pages in your phone book, which means that entries in the YellowNet directory aren't detailed (see Figure 4-17). Although you can search using business categories and geographic information, search results are ordered alphabetically rather than by relevancy. Each listing has three key elements: company name, phone number, and address.

Placing a Listing in the YellowNet World-Wide Pages

You can submit your site to YellowNet using the submission page shown in Figure 4-18. The URL for this page is the following:

```
http://www.yellownet.com/change.html
```

Because the business category is the primary element that aids the retrieval of your listing, you should spend a few minutes at the site and familiarize your-

```
YellowNet - Netscape                                                _ 8 X
File   Edit   View   Go   Communicator   Help
    Bookmarks    Location: http://www.yellownet.com/cgi-bin/ypcgi?search_name=Technology&search_cat=&sear   N

  ● 20/20 TECHNOLOGY INC
  (910)791-9226 305-F RALEIGH ST WILMINGTON NC

  ● 21ST TECHNOLOGY
  (402)330-3334 275 N 115TH ST OMAHA NE

  ● 2B TECHNOLOGY INC
  (804)747-4849 4222 COX RD GLEN ALLEN VA

  ● 2DAYS TECHNOLOGY
  (402)371-2247 2116 MARKET LN NORFOLK NE

  ● 2ND CHANCE GLASS TECHNOLOGY
  (310)493-9386 PO BOX 30117 LONG BEACH CA

  ● 3 D TECHNOLOGY
  (408)263-9244 MILPITAS CA

  ● 3 D TECHNOLOGY
  (203)371-8500 12 CAMBRIDGE DR TRUMBULL CT

  ● 3 D V TECHNOLOGY
  (312)654-8210 16 W ONTARIO ST CHICAGO IL

  ● 3 FOXX TECHNOLOGY
  (508)534-6000 LEOMINSTER MA

        Document Done
```

Figure 4-17

Listings at YellowNet World-Wide Pages.

self with the categories in use. When you find the appropriate category for your company, fill out the submission form. YellowNet won't post your listing until someone has contacted you by telephone or e-mail to verify the entry.

CAUTION

◆ ◆

Although the YellowNet directory is well maintained and visited by lots of Web users, the company does try to sell many extra services. Be sure to read all the Yes/No elements in the form and respond appropriately.

◆ ◆

Announcing Your Business in the Yellow Pages from BigBook

FIND IT ▶
ONLINE

With millions of listings, BigBook (`http://www.bigbook.com`) is one of the largest directories for businesses in the U.S. As Figure 4-19 shows, you can search BigBook by category, business name, and geographic location.

In addition to standard directory searches, BigBook provides many terrific extras. Using the address book feature, you can create a personalized address book of companies listed in BigBook. With the map feature, you can find companies by clicking on a map of the U.S. You can also rate companies using the voting feature.

Figure 4-20 shows the results of a standard search in the BigBook Yellow Pages. As you can see, companies are listed by business name, address information, and telephone number. As with most other directories, search results are displayed alphabetically rather than by relevancy—even when you do a category search.

When you click on the business name, you access a detailed listing for the business. As shown in Figure 4-21, BigBook follows a fairly unique approach when it comes to the detailed listing. Not only does the listing show your hours of operation, it allows you to add extras such as directions, cross streets to look for, and foreign languages spoken. In this way, BigBook helps build traffic to your physical storefront as well as your virtual storefront.

ADD NEW LISTING INFORMATION:

• Enter the **new** information to appear in YellowNet. (USA listings only)
• Listing an 800 number requires the **purchase of an extra line.**

BUSINESS:

ADDRESS:

CITY: STATE: ZIP:

TEL: No 800 Numbers. Numbers only, no ".-

BUSINESS CATEGORY:

• Enter the specific YellowNet business category name.

CATEGORY:

CONTACT INFORMATION: All information will be verified by telephone prior to posting. Complete all information:

YOUR NAME:

EMAIL:

TEL: Numbers only, no ".-()".

FAX: Numbers only, no ".-()".

Leave blank if this is the same as above.

MARKETING CONTACT:

TEL: Numbers only, no ".-()".

○ Yes ○ No I currently have a web site.

○ Yes ○ No In a key word search I have to go through several pages of web links to find myself listed on other search engines?

○ Yes ○ No Links must be purchased. I would be interested in purchasing a link if it guaranteed the easy location and priority display of my link.

○ Yes ○ No I would be interested in purchasing expanded links which appear in a variety of business categories (headings), particularly if I could create my own heading.

○ **Yes** ○ No I would be interested in multi location or heading package programs and/or the discount for placing a reciprical link to YellowNet on my web site

Figure 4-18

The submission page at the YellowNet World-Wide Pages.

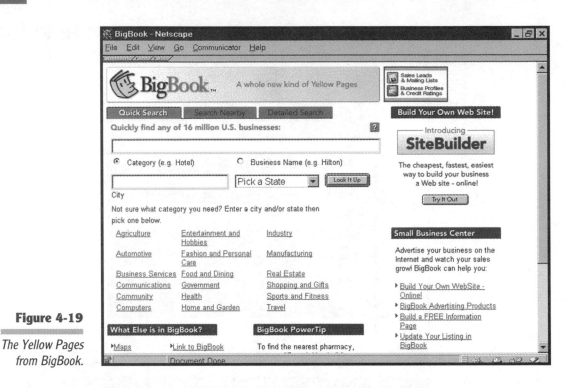

Figure 4-19

The Yellow Pages from BigBook.

Placing a Listing in the BigBook Yellow Pages

When you add your listing to BigBook, you set up a free account in the BigBook directory. As with your Internet account, you need to choose a user name and password for the BigBook account. You will use this user name and password to update your entry at BigBook.

To create an account, follow the links to the business center; then, click on the set-up free account link. This will take you to the page shown in Figure 4-22. After you fill out the fairly comprehensive submission form and provide personal verification information, you can submit the form for validation. If you've provided all the required information, you have one last chance to check the information as it will read in the BigBook database. Provided that all the information is correct, you can continue with the account creation process.

Next, BigBook verifies that you don't already have an account in the system. If you've never submitted an entry to BigBook before, select the None

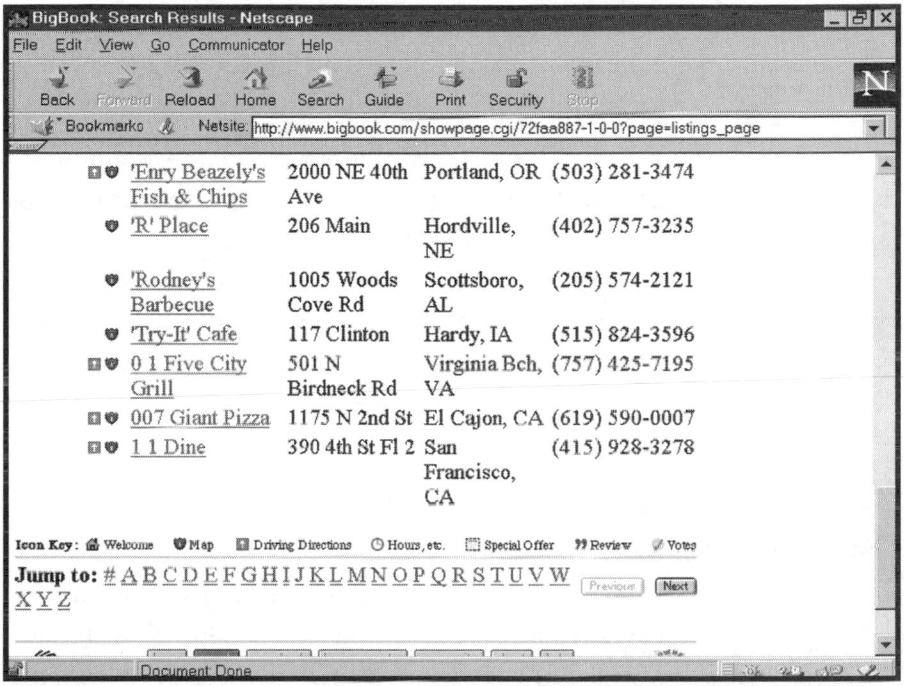

Figure 4-20

Listings in the Yellow Pages from BigBook.

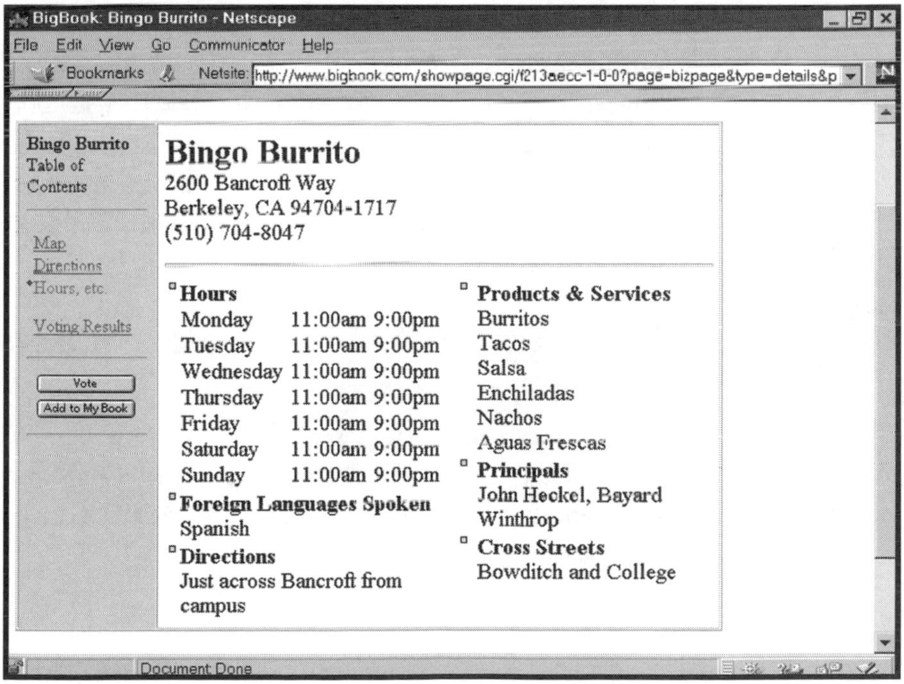

Figure 4-21

Detailed listings in the BigBook Yellow Pages.

of the Above radio button and press the Submit button. The setup process continues through category selection and the submission of additional information for the detailed listing page.

NOTE After you finish the rather lengthy account setup process, BigBook sends you an e-mail message. When you reply to this message, all you need to do is quote the text of the message. If your e-mail program is set up to quote messages automatically, you just click on the Reply button and then the Send button in your e-mail program. Otherwise, you have to copy the body of the original message and paste it into a new message.

Announcing Your Business in the New Riders Yellow Pages

FIND IT ▶
ONLINE

If you want to get listed in a print publication, the New Riders Yellow Pages is a great choice. The New Riders Yellow Pages (`http://www.wwwyp.com`) are provided as a searchable directory online and an annual print edition sold through bookstores.

Offline, you can check out your entry in the annual print edition of the directory. Online, you can search the New Riders Yellow Pages by keyword and by category (see Figure 4-23). Because the directory indexes all the information provided with a listing, keyword searches are matched against company name, URL, and summary description as well as the actual keywords provided.

What Do Entries in the New Riders Yellow Pages Look Like?

Although category searches are organized alphabetically in the New Riders Yellow Pages, search results are organized by relevancy (see Figure 4-24). Each entry is listed with six key fields: title, URL, keyword, description, date of submission, and relevancy.

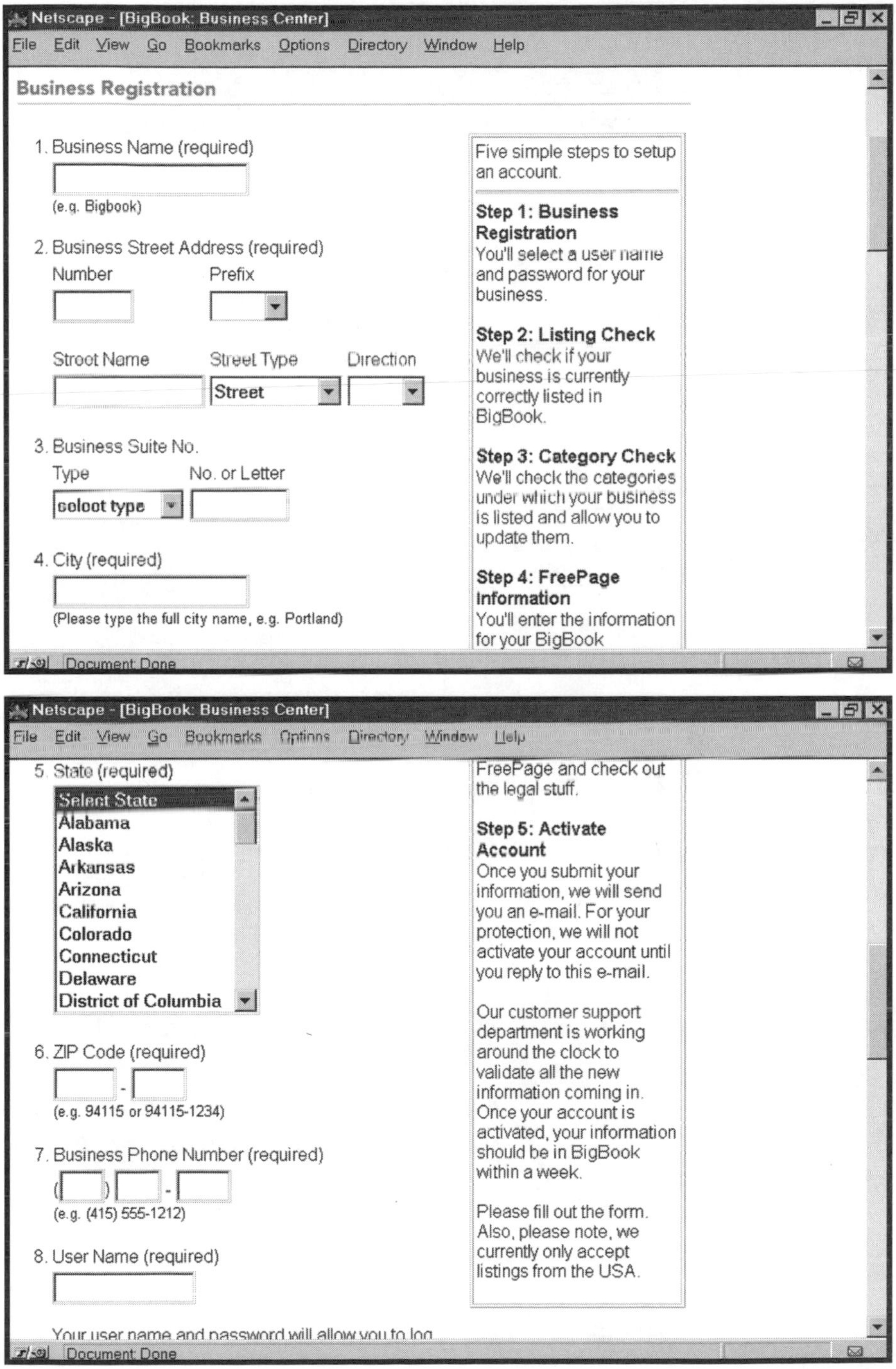

Netscape - [BigBook: Business Center]

File   Edit   View   Go   Bookmarks   Options   Directory   Window   Help

Business Registration

1. Business Name (required)

(e.g. Bigbook)

2. Business Street Address (required)

Number

Prefix

Stroot Name   Street Type   Direction

Street

3. Business Suite No.

Type   No. or Letter

seloct type

4. City (required)

(Please type the full city name, e.g. Portland)

Five simple steps to setup an account.

Step 1: Business Registration
You'll select a user name and password for your business.

Step 2: Listing Check
We'll check if your business is currently correctly listed in BigBook.

Step 3: Category Check
We'll check the categories under which your business is listed and allow you to update them.

Step 4: FreePage Information
You'll enter the information for your BigBook

Document: Done

Netscape - [BigBook: Business Center]

File   Edit   View   Go   Bookmarks   Options   Directory   Window   Help

5. State (required)

Select State
Alabama
Alaska
Arkansas
Arizona
California
Colorado
Connecticut
Delaware
District of Columbia

6. ZIP Code (required)

(e.g. 94115 or 94115-1234)

7. Business Phone Number (required)

( )   -

(e.g. (415) 555-1212)

8. User Name (required)

Your user name and password will allow you to log

FreePage and check out the legal stuff.

Step 5: Activate Account
Once you submit your information, we will send you an e-mail. For your protection, we will not activate your account until you reply to this e-mail.

Our customer support department is working around the clock to validate all the new information coming in. Once your account is activated, your information should be in BigBook within a week.

Please fill out the form. Also, please note, we currently only accept listings from the USA.

Document: Done

Figure 4-22

The submission page at the Yellow Pages.

Placing a Listing in the New Riders Yellow Pages

New Riders has a rather lengthy submission form for new entries (see Figure 4-25). The URL for the submission page is the following:

`http://www.mcp.com/directories/submit.html`

All entries at New Riders must be placed in a specific category. Although the category is important, your listing is indexed on just about everything that you supply with the listing, making the keywords and summary description much more important than the category of your listing.

In addition to the standard information about your Web site, you are also asked to fill out contact information. The e-mail address that you provide will be used to send a confirmation for your new entry. Additionally, unless you deselect the check box pertaining to the Yellow Pages mailing list, periodic messages regarding the directory will be e-mailed to you.

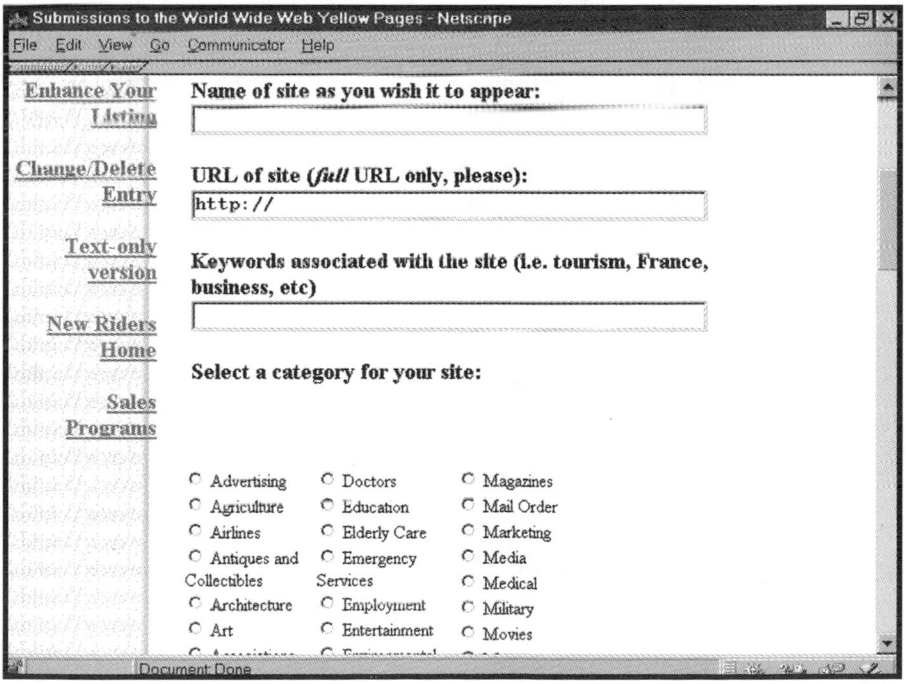

Figure 4-25

The submission page at the New Riders Yellow Pages.

Announcing Your Business at USYellow.Com

FIND IT ▶
ONLINE

U.S. Yellow Pages (`http://www.usyellow.com`) provides a directory to businesses in the U.S. As Figure 4-26 shows, you can search USYellow.Com by industry category, business name, and geographic location.

What Do Entries at USYellow.Com Look Like?

Figure 4-27 shows the results of a category search in the USYellow.Com directory. Companies are listed by business name, address information, and telephone number. As with most other directories, search results are displayed alphabetically rather than by relevancy.

When you click on the business name, you access a detailed listing for the business. As shown in Figure 4-28, USYellow.Com provides additional information on the products and services that the company offers. The detailed

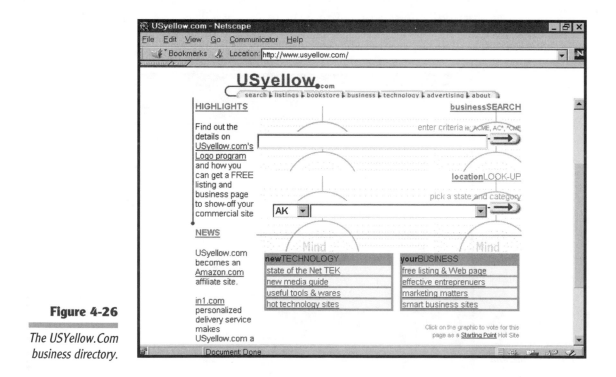

Figure 4-26

The USYellow.Com business directory.

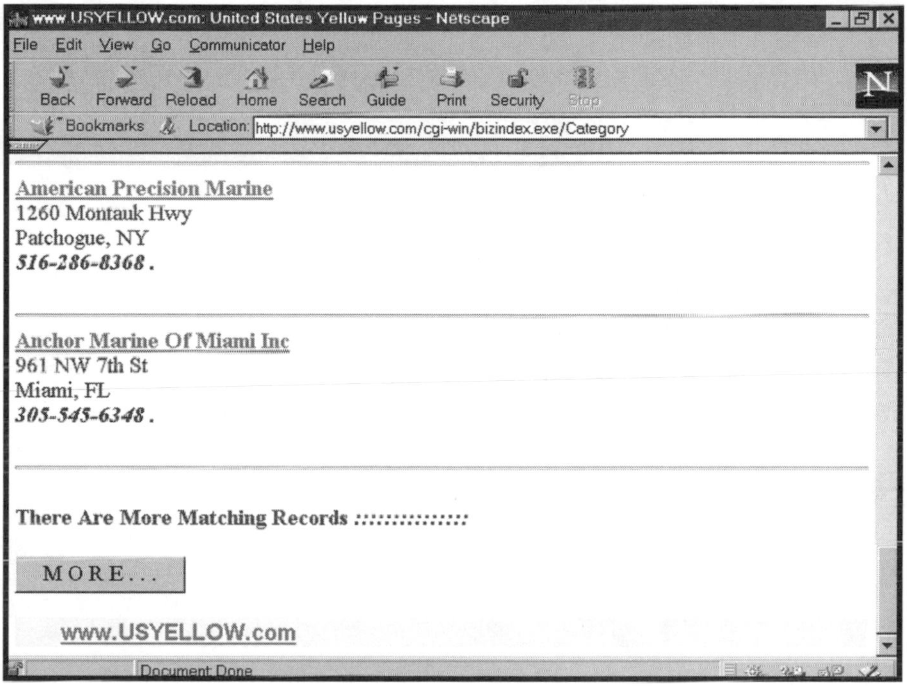

Figure 4-27

Listings at USYellow.Com.

listing also links to the company's Web site and provides an easy way to send your company representative an e-mail message.

Placing a Listing at USYellow.Com

USYellow.Com provides two different ways to get a free listing in its Yellow Pages directory: a basic listing and an extended listing. As shown in Figure 4-29, the submission form for the basic listing allows you to enter standard company contact information but doesn't include your URL, e-mail address, product information, or service information. To get the additional information added to your listing, you must agree to display the USYellow.Com logo at your Web site, which is really a small price to pay for the extra visibility.

If you want a basic listing, you can use the submission form at:

```
http://www.usyellow.com/add.htm
```

If you want an extended listing, you can use the submission form at:

```
http://www.usyellow.com/logo.htm
```

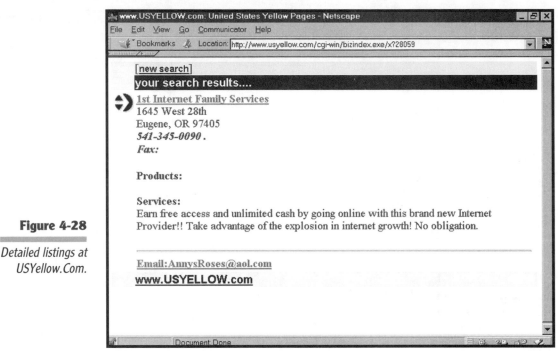

Figure 4-28

Detailed listings at USYellow.Com.

Announcing Your Business at Business Seek

Business Seek (http://www.businesseek.com) is a search engine for businesses located throughout the world. Because of its international focus, listings at Business Seek are published in several different languages. Although entries can be in several different languages, no way exists to search for entries in a specific language, which is perhaps the only shortcoming of this well-organized site.

Using the main search form at Business Seek (see Figure 4-30), you can search by company name, geographic location, and keyword. The results of your search will be organized by relevancy to the keywords that you supply.

What Do Entries at Business Seek Look Like?

Business name, keywords, business activity, and description index entries in the Business Seek search engine. Unlike other search sites that supply

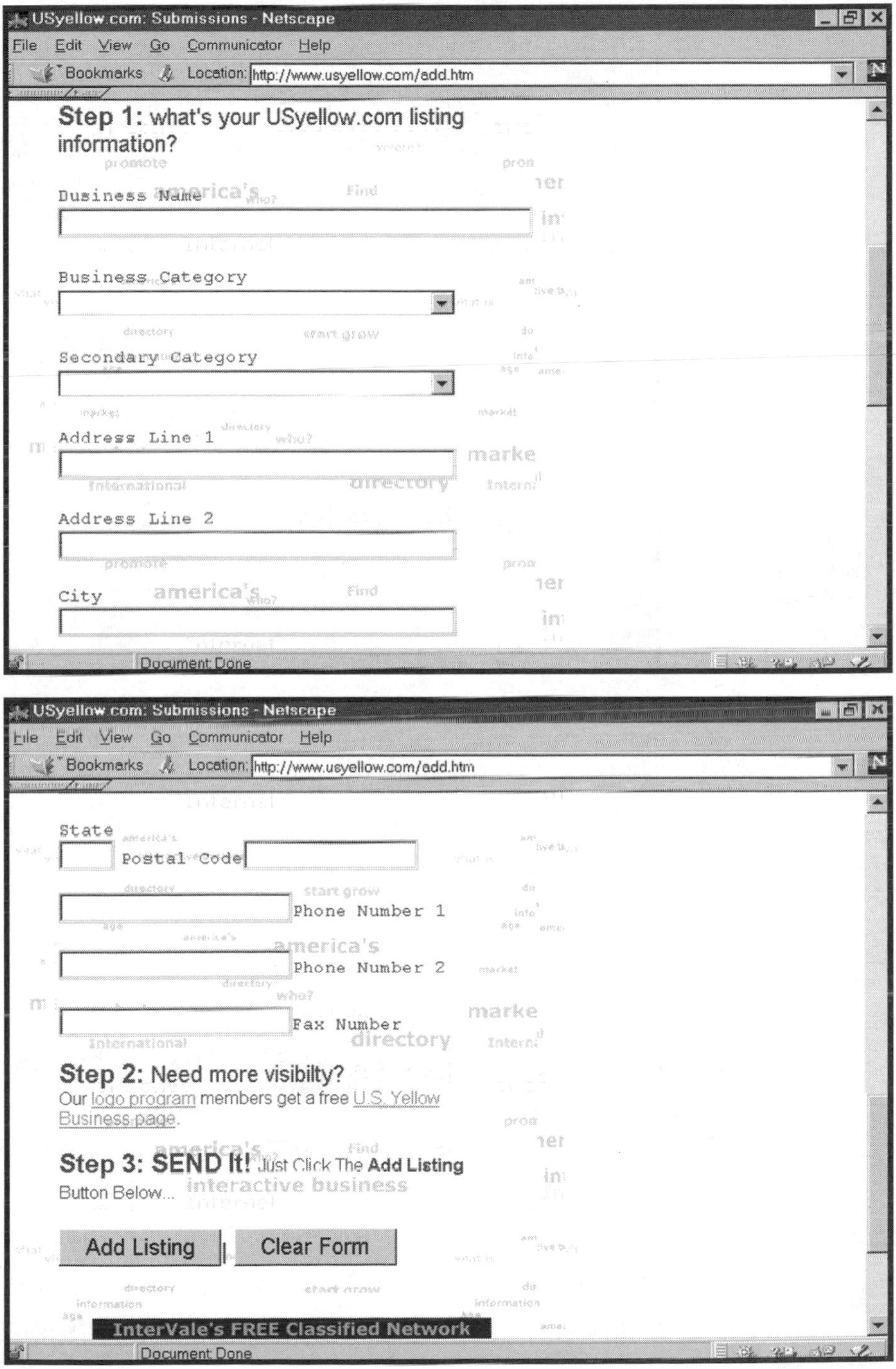

Figure 4-29

*The submission
page at
USYellow.Com.*

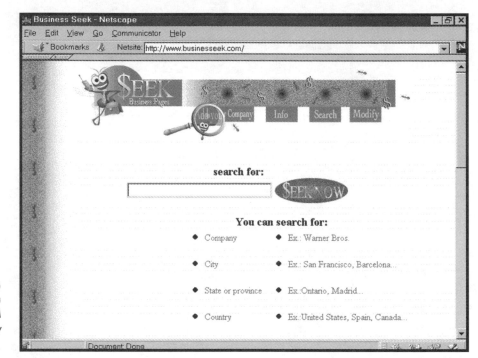

Figure 4-30

Business Seek: A business directory on the Web.

only summary information for matches, Business Seek returns extended listings for all matching entries.

As shown in Figure 4-31, companies are listed with a plethora of information that includes business name, URL, several e-mail addresses, and full contact information. Also listed are some interesting statistics for the business, such as primary activities, number of employees, annual income, and languages spoken.

Placing a Listing at Business Seek

FIND IT ▶
ONLINE

If you want to list your site in English, you can submit your listing to Business Seek using the submission page shown in Figure 4-32. The URL for this page is as follows:

```
http://www.businesseek.com/business/engalta.htm
```

Although the submission form asks for a great deal of information, much of this data is optional. Still, you should fill in the important information

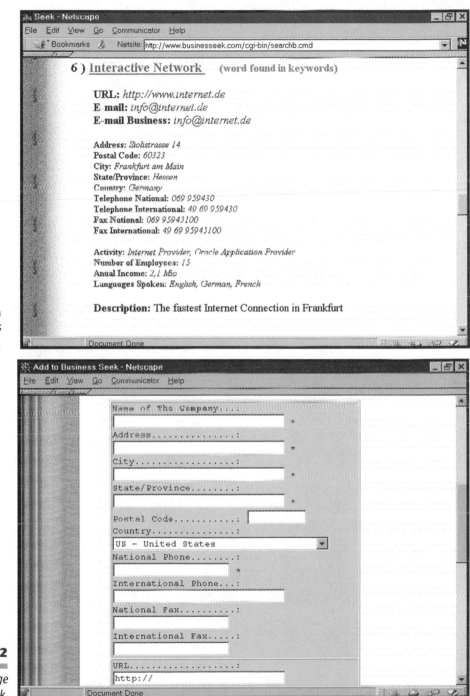

Figure 4-31

Listings at Business Seek.

Figure 4-32

The submission page at Business Seek.

such as your full contact information, business description, and a detailed keyword list.

Wrapping Up and Looking Ahead

If you offer products, services, or business information at your Web site, you should definitely list your site at business search sites and directories. Business search engines and Yellow Pages offer a unique place to get your business and your business-oriented Web site noticed. After submitting your site to these search engines, you should go on to submit your site to search engines and directories that focus on specific industries. You will learn all about industry-oriented search engines and directories in the next part of this section.

Directories by Industry and Category

The major search engines and directories are great for getting your Web site noticed by the masses, but you also want your site to be accessible to people looking for specific types of information, which is where industry and category-specific directories come into the picture. Whether your site covers fine dining in Seattle, outdoor sports activities in Australia, or one of thousands of other topics, there are directories devoted to your subject, and this part shows you how to find and use them.

Getting the Most Out of Industry and Category Directories

Whereas industry directories focus on major industries, such as the real estate and travel industries, category directories focus on specific topics, such as resources for writers, or outdoor sports. Because of their narrow focus, industry and category directories are sought out by people who are looking for specialized or tailored information, making these directories the perfect place to get your Web site noticed.

As with most directories, industry and category directories focus on pages rather than entire Web sites. Thus, you generally submit the URL to a specific page or area that strongly relates to the topic of the directory. Along with the URL, you usually submit the page title and a summary description. Although the description of your page may not be published with your listing, the directory maintainer uses the description to determine whether the page is appropriate for the directory.

Because industry and category directories have a very specific focus, they are great for increasing the traffic to your Web site. In a way, getting listed in these directories is like being able to conduct an advertising campaign that targets readers who are interested in the exact type of site that you publish.

Before you submit your site to industry or category directories, you should take a few minutes to plot out the industries or categories that fit your Web site. Although the first industry or category that you think up is probably the best, a typical Web site will fit into several categories or industries. Your collection of articles on Spain would probably fit in perfectly with a travel and tourism directory. But you could also look for metro or city guides that cover Spain. Additionally, your articles may cover the best restaurants in Madrid, making these pages suitable for a listing in a directory to restaurants, fine dining, or food.

City and Metro Guides

City and metro guides are becoming increasingly popular. The idea is that by focusing a directory on a specific city, state, or country, users will be able to find information directly relating to an area of the world in which they are interested. If you want to find an Italian restaurant in Denver, you access a city guide featuring Denver. If you want to find a Web design firm in the Seattle area, you access a guide to the Seattle metropolitan area.

Every single Web site in cyberspace has a place in a city or metro guide. After all, we all live somewhere. For this reason, you should register your site in a directory that covers your city or metro area. To make finding the right directory for you easier, the best city and metro guides are covered in this section. Online, you will find the city and metro guide listings at:

http://www.tvpress.com/promote/metro.htm

Creating a Listing in GeoCitie

GeoCities (http://www.geocities.com) is a different kind of city guide. Instead of focusing on your actual location in the real world, GeoCities focuses on virtual communities of interest. The BourbonStreet community is a tribute to the Big Easy. The CapitalHill community covers politics and government. The MotorCity community is for racing fans and car enthusiasts everywhere. In all, more than 30 virtual communities exist that cover dozens of topics.

The home page for GeoCities is shown in Figure 4-33. As the figure shows, GeoCities is home to more than a half million Web users. To enter GeoCities or publish a page within GeoCities, you must become a member. Fortunately, membership is currently free. As you might expect, there is a catch. GeoCities displays an awful lot of advertising that you have to wade through when you visit and work with your Web page.

What Do Entries in GeoCities Look Like?

GeoCities is organized into dozens of virtual communities. Each page within a community has an address—sort of like your street address. Anytime an address has a vacancy, a new homesteader—you, for example—can create and customize a home page within the community. Figure 4-34 shows the main page in Area 51, a virtual community for sci-fi and fantasy fans.

Because everyone can create a customized home page within GeoCities, no standard look to the pages exists. Your home page in GeoCities can be the doorway to your Web site. Your home page in GeoCities can also be a separate outlet for your creativity. Either way, you can use the home page in GeoCities to attract readers.

Figure 4-33

The GeoCities home page.

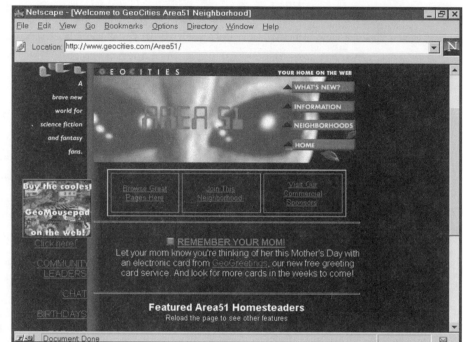

Figure 4-34

Area 51 at GeoCities.

Placing a Listing at GeoCities

Before you can place a listing in GeoCities, you must become a member. When you become a member, you can create a home page. Start by visiting the virtual community of which you would like to become a part, and then follow the links to the free home page or vacancies area (see Figure 4-35). Just as with any service provider, your home page can be a single page or a collection of pages. Currently, your home page is limited to 2MB of disk space.

From the vacancies page for the community, you can search for unoccupied pages within specific areas of the community. When you find a page that is vacant, you can set up shop. To save time and eliminate frustration, ensure that you follow the guidelines of GeoCities and that the topic you plan to cover strongly relates to the theme for the virtual community.

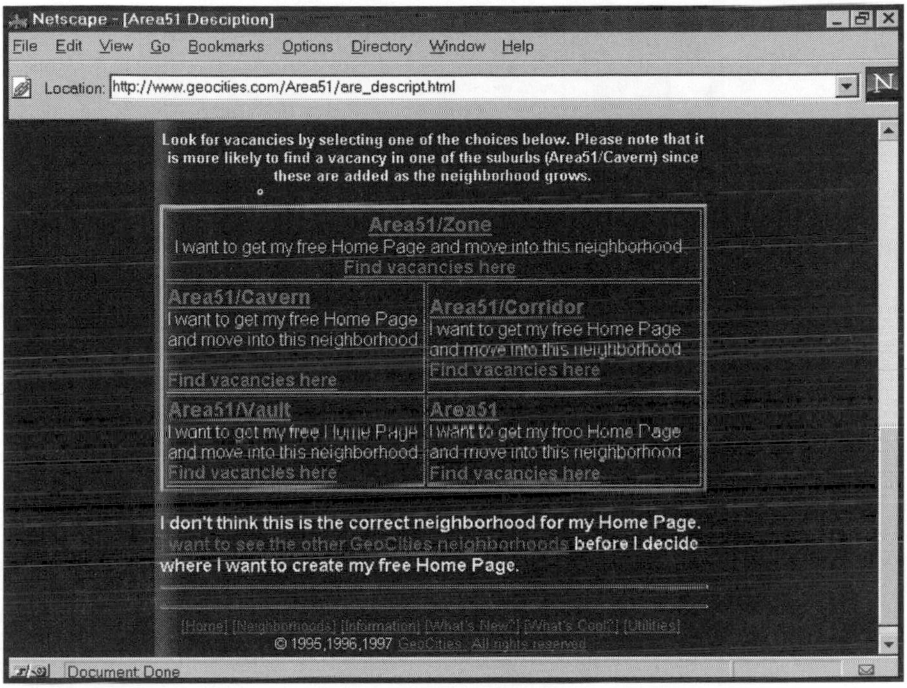

Figure 4-35

Finding vacancies at GeoCities.

Getting Listed at Metroscope

Metroscope (http://www.metroscope.com) is an international guide to major metropolitan areas. Although most major metropolitan areas have their own pages within Metroscope, the guide also looks at states within the U.S. and countries throughout the world (see Figure 4-36). For example, Alaska and Hawaii have their own areas within the guide.

Because Metroscope is a guide to the best sites rather than a guide to all of the available sites, the directory listings within Metroscope aren't extensive. The focus on the best is what makes Metroscope a great place to give your Web site additional visibility.

What Do Entries in Metroscope Look Like?

As shown in Figure 4-37, entries in Metroscope are organized into specific categories. All listings are displayed alphabetically by company name or site title. Because no descriptive text accompanies the listing, the category and the listing title are the only elements that can help bring traffic to your Web site.

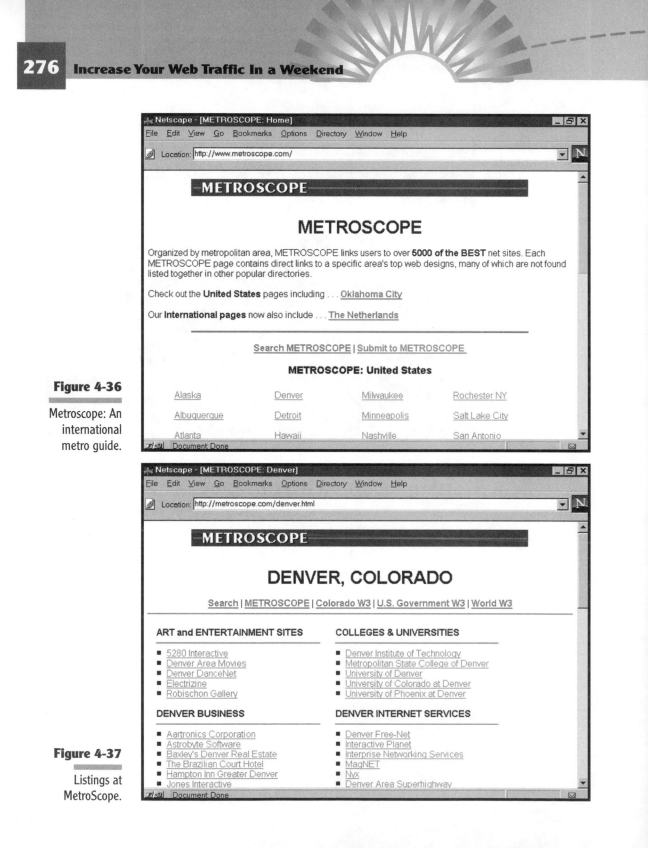

Placing a Listing at Metroscope

FIND IT ▶
ONLINE

You can submit your site to Metroscope using the submission page shown in Figure 4-38. The URL for this page is as follows:

```
http://metroscope.com/addsite.html
```

Before you submit a listing to Metroscope, you should examine the metro areas within the directory to determine where your site should be listed. If you live near a major metro, you should enter the name of this metro in the City and State, or Country, field. Additionally, when you describe your site, you should think in terms of the specific categories used in Metroscope. If you have a Web site dedicated to arts and entertainment, simply state that your site covers arts and entertainment.

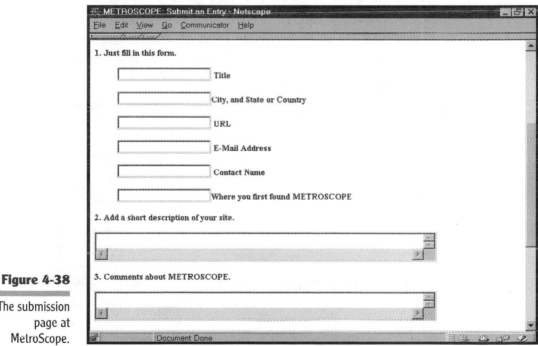

Figure 4-38

The submission page at MetroScope.

Getting Listed at USA CityLink

USA CityLink (http://www.usacitylink.com) is a city guide that focuses primarily on travel and tourism. Because of this narrow focus, most of the listings in USA CityLink focus on state- and city-specific information from government and state sources, such as visitor information published by the state. Yet you can also find information on vacation tips, tourist attractions, convention centers, airports, and many other topics that relate to travel and tourism.

The home page for USA CityLink is shown in Figure 4-39. From the home page, you can get on overview of the site or you can jump straight to the directory listings.

What Do Entries in USA CityLink Look Like?

Although USA CityLink is a city guide, it is organized by state rather than by individual cities. Each state within the U.S. has its own area within the guide (see Figure 4-40). These areas are divided into broad categories, such as state information and city information.

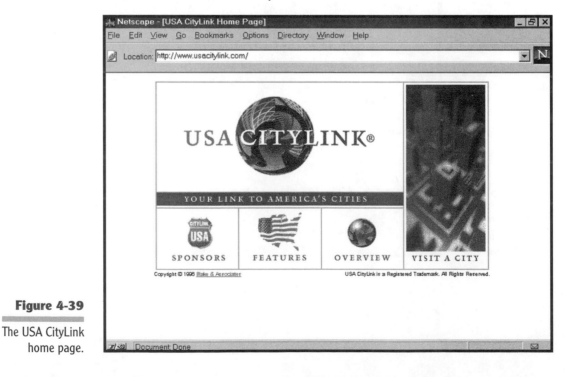

Figure 4-39

The USA CityLink home page.

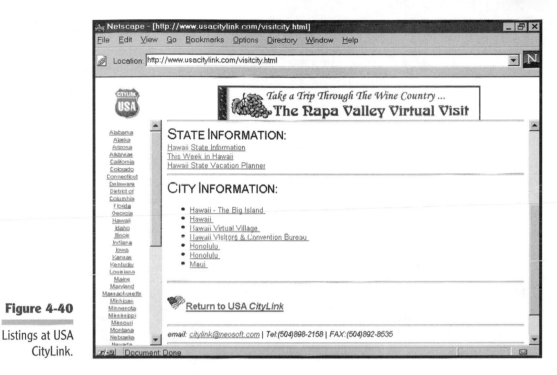

Figure 4-40

Listings at USA CityLink.

Placing a Listing at USA CityLink

USA CityLink is another site that you should definitely browse before you submit anything. First, make sure that your listing fits in with USA CityLink's strong focus on travel and tourism information. If your site does, then you should submit your site using the submission page shown in Figure 4-41. The URL for this page is as follows:

```
http://www.usacitylink.com/addcity.html
```

To get the most out of your listing, you should fill out the form completely, including the optional information such as the name of your organization. Because listings in USA CityLink are so terse, the name of your organization is usually the only thing that distinguishes your listing from another listing that covers a similar topic.

Other City and Metro Guides

Millions of people are lost in the endless sea of the Web. They are looking for tailored information that they can access easily and quickly, which is

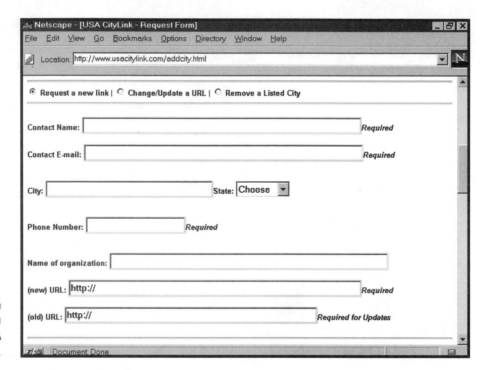

Figure 4-41

The submission page to USA CityLink.

exactly what city guides provide. The growing trend to tailor information based on geographic boundaries is clearly evident when you visit the major search sites. Just about every major search site has a city or metro guide.

The Lycos City Guide (`http://cityguide.lycos.com`) is shown in Figure 4-42. When you visit the top-level page in the Lycos City guide, you see a map of the world. You can click on the map to visit areas within the city guide dedicated to specific countries. By following maps and links, you will eventually end up on a page with listings dedicated to a specific city or metro area. Although you cannot place listings directly in the Lycos City Guide, you can register your site with the Lycos search engine, which then places you in the Lycos database. (To learn more about Lycos, see the Saturday Afternoon section and look under "Registering with the Top Search Engines on the Planet."

Not to be outdone, Excite also has a city guide called the Excite Travel Channel (`http://www.city.net`). Originally, the Excite Travel Channel

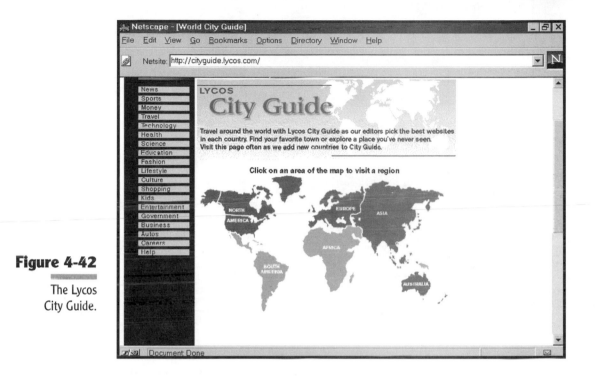

Figure 4-42

The Lycos
City Guide.

was an independent city guide called City.Net. When Excite took over City.Net, Excite changed the name to City Net Travel. The home page for City.Net Travel is shown in Figure 4-43. Just as with the Lycos Travel Guide, you cannot submit listings directly to City.Net Travel. Instead, you must register your site in the main Excite database.

Although Excite and Lycos use their extensive databases to create city guides, Yahoo! has taken a completely different approach to creating city guides by setting up separate Web sites for major metros and countries throughout the world. The Web site for Yahoo! Seattle (http://seattle.yahoo.com) is shown in Figure 4-44 If you want to register your Washington-based business or Web site in the Seattle metro guide, visit Yahoo! Seattle and go through the same submission process that you do for the main Yahoo! directory. If you want to register your Web site in any other Yahoo! city guide, you visit the city guide and go through the submission process as well.

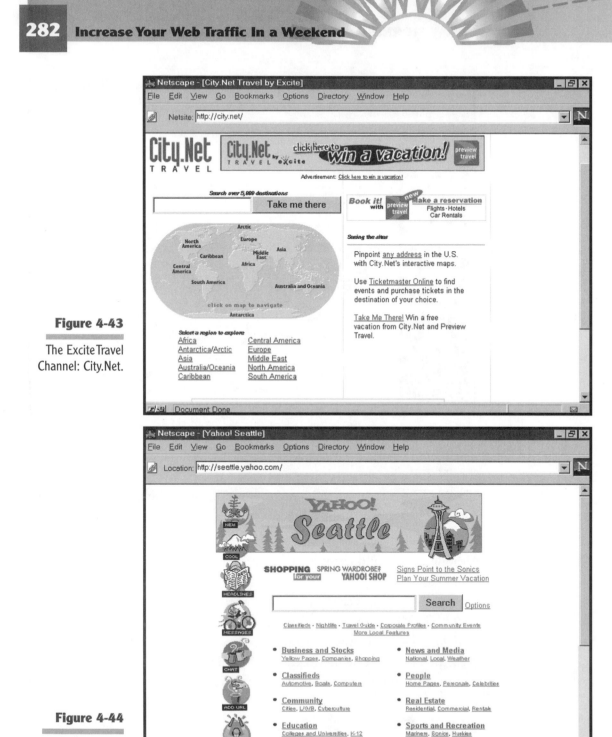

Figure 4-43

The Excite Travel Channel: City.Net.

Figure 4-44

The Yahoo! metro guide for Seattle.

The Seattle metro guide is only one of many other Yahoo! metro guides. Some of the other Yahoo! metro guides include:

Yahoo! Atlanta	atlanta.yahoo.com
Yahoo! Austin	austin.yahoo.com
Yahoo! Boston	boston.yahoo.com
Yahoo! Chicago	chi.yahoo.com
Yahoo! Washington DC	dc.yahoo.com
Yahoo! Dallas/Fort Worth	dfw.yahoo.com
Yahoo! Los Angeles	la.yahoo.com
Yahoo! New York	ny.yahoo.com
Yahoo! San Francisco	sfbay.yahoo.com

Some of the Yahoo! national guides include:

Yahoo! Canada	www.yahoo.ca
Yahoo! France	www.yahoo.fr
Yahoo! Germany	www.yahoo.de

To find a complete list of Yahoo! city and country guides and their URLs, visit Yahoo!'s main Web site at www.yahoo.com.

Real Estate Directories and Guides

When you think of real estate, you probably think of real estate agents and brokers. Although agents and brokers are the cornerstones of real estate, the real estate industry encompasses many other professions and organizations. At one end of the spectrum are the construction companies, developers, engineers, planners, workers, and service organizations whose efforts create the homes in which we live and the office buildings in which we work. At the other end of the spectrum are the property managers, asset managers, trust companies, and holding companies that manage the construction and the properties. In between are the financial institutions, the appraisers, the investors, and the property owners who make the construction possible.

Because dozens of professions and organizations are a part of the real estate industry, the fact that this industry has a dominant presence in cyberspace is no surprise. In fact, real estate directories are some of the best-designed sites that you'll find online. If your Web site or business covers any of the professions or organizations related to the real estate industry, you should add a listing to the directories in this section. Further, if you publish any information that relates to the real estate industry, you should consider adding a listing in real estate directories as well. Online, you will find the real estate directory listings at:

```
http://www.tvpress.com/promote/real.htm
```

Getting Listed at CenterNet

CenterNet (`http://www.centernet.com`) is a commercial real estate directory published by Net Properties Corporation. As shown in Figure 4-45, the directory covers many different aspects of the commercial real estate industry. You'll find listings of real estate companies, retailers, products, and services. You'll find listings of trade journals, news sources, and associations that are related to the industry as well.

FIND IT ▶
ONLINE

Net Properties Corporation maintains a sister site to CenterNet called HomeNet. The HomeNet (`http://www.homenet.com`) directory focuses on the residential real estate industry but also provides relocation information. This directory contains listings of real estate agencies, brokers, mortgage and lending services, and industry news. Because of the focus on relocation assistance, you will also find listings for schools, census information, and career markets for various areas throughout the U.S. and the world.

What Do Entries at CenterNet/HomeNet Look Like?

Although CenterNet and HomeNet primarily cover the U.S. real estate industry, they also provide fairly extensive listings for the international market. All listings in the directory are organized geographically and by topic, such as real estate companies, agencies, and related services. These sites provide separate areas for each state within the U.S. Listings within most states are further divided by county.

After the U.S., the real estate market best represented is Canada. The sites offer listings for each province.

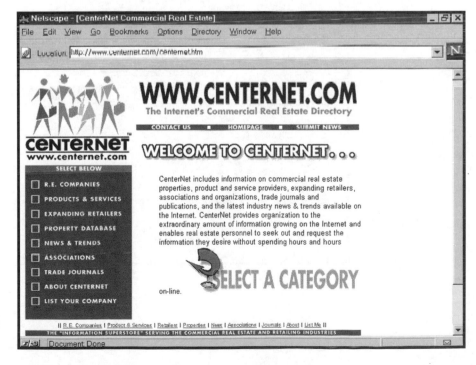

Figure 4-45

The CenterNet home page.

As with most directories, CenterNet and HomeNet list only the title of the company or service (see Figure 4-46). The title is linked to the home page of the company or service.

Placing a Listing at CenterNet

CenterNet and HomeNet accept listings for real estate companies, agencies, and brokers. Whether you register your site with CenterNet or HomeNet, the form that you use will be similar to the one shown in Figure 4-47. To register with CenterNet, you can use the following URL:

```
http://www.netprop.com/comm/misc/listme/wsite.htm
```

To register with HomeNet, use this URL:

```
http://www.netprop.com/gif/addurl.htm
```

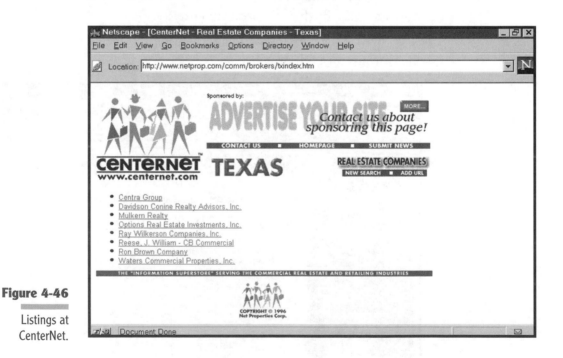

Figure 4-46

Listings at CenterNet.

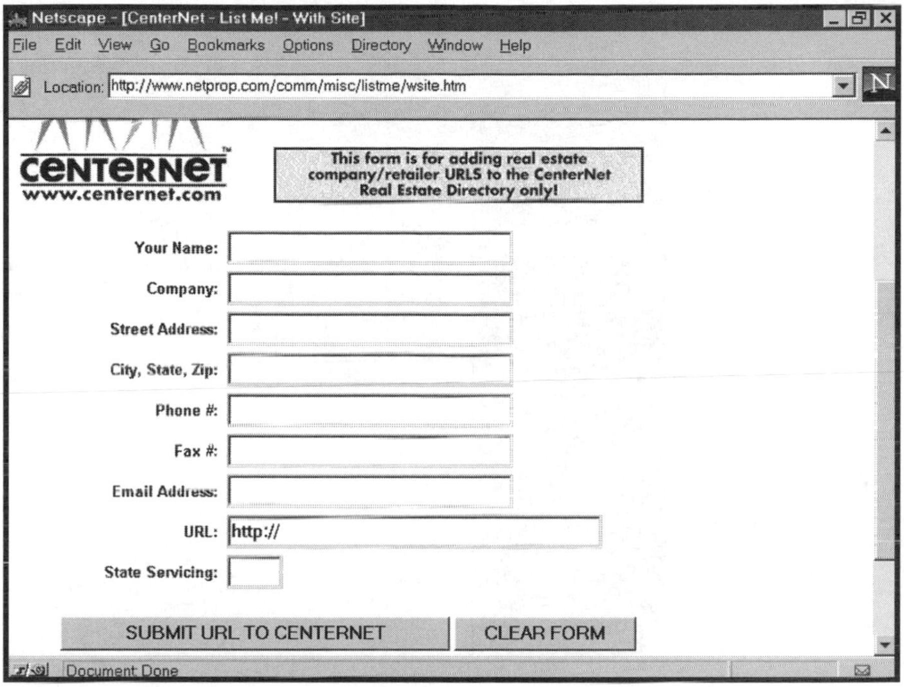

Figure 4-47

The submission page for CenterNet.

Getting Listed in Estates Today

Estates Today (http://www.estatestoday.co.uk) is a terrific directory for the commercial and residential real estate industry. Although the primary countries covered in the directory are the UK and the U.S., Estates Today also has comprehensive listings for many other countries.

Unlike some real estate directories that focus only on companies, agencies, and brokers, Estates Today covers every aspect of the industry (see Figure 4-48). In addition to the very diverse directory, Estates Today also publishes lists of the top sites by country and category.

What Do Entries in Estates Today Look Like?

The Estates Today directory has a terrific design that allows you to find information in many different ways. You can find comprehensive listings by category for various countries, or zero in on specific states and provinces. Estates Today also organizes listings by category for cities within the U.S.A. and major international cities.

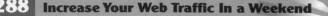

Figure 4-48

The Estates Today
home page.

As shown in Figure 4-49, listings in Estates Today appear by company name. Following the company name is a summary description of the services, products, or resources provided.

Placing a Listing at Estates Today

Estates Today accepts listings from a broad spectrum of areas that relate to the real estate industry. Because of this wide focus, you can list just about any type of Web site or company that relates to real estate, including agencies, appraisal companies, asset managers, construction services, consultants, developers, financial services, legal services, and property managers.

Before you submit a listing, you should find the category that fits your Web site or company. After you find the specific category that best fits you, submit e-mail to `estates@estatestoday.co.uk`. The message should provide the following information:

✪ Company or Web site title

✪ Category

⚙ Summary description

⚙ Address

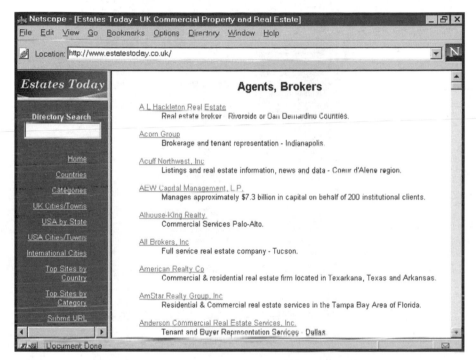

Estates Today

Directory Search

Home
Countries
Categories
UK Cities/Towns
USA by State
USA Cities/Towns
International Cities
Top Sites by Country
Top Sites by Category
Submit URL

Agents, Brokers

A L Hackleton Real Estate
  Real estate broker   Riverside or San Bernardino Counties.

Acorn Group
  Brokerage and tenant representation - Indianapolis.

Acuff Northwest, Inc
  Listings and real estate information, news and data - Coeur d'Alene region.

AEW Capital Management, L.P.
  Manages approximately $7.3 billion in capital on behalf of 200 institutional clients.

Althouse-King Realty.
  Commercial Services Palo-Alto.

All Brokers, Inc
  Full service real estate company - Tucson.

American Realty Co
  Commercial & residential real estate firm located in Texarkana, Texas and Arkansas.

AmStar Realty Group, Inc
  Residential & Commercial real estate services in the Tampa Bay Area of Florida.

Anderson Commercial Real Estate Services, Inc.
  Tenant and Buyer Representation Services - Dallas

Document Done

Figure 4-49

Listings at
Estates Today.

Getting Listed in the International Real Estate Digest

The International Real Estate Digest (http://www.ired.com) is a comprehensive directory to the real estate industry. The goal of IRED is to be a one-stop shop for real estate information. As an actual online digest, the site features current news covering the real estate industry.

The home page for the U.S. version of the International Real Estate Digest is shown in Figure 4-50. You can also access IRED's real estate digests covering Europe (http://www.ired-europe.com) and Asia (http://www.ired-asia.com).

Figure 4-50

The International
Real Estate Digest.

What Do Entries in the International Real Estate Digest Look Like?

The International Real Estate Digest has thousands of listings from more than 85 countries. You can browse the listings in several ways, including by world region and country. As shown in Figure 4-51, individual listings appear with titles and summary descriptions. Most listings also have graphical icons that depict the kinds of information you will find at the Web site.

Placing a Listing in the International Real Estate Digest

The International Real Estate Digest accepts listings from many different types of organizations that relate to the real estate industry. Some of these organizations include agencies, appraisal companies, brokers, builders, construction services, education, inspectors, financial services, and legal services. You can add a listing to IRED using the following URL:

```
http://www.ired.com/dir/addme.htm
```

When you get to the `addme.htm` page, select the type of listing that you wish to add. Then, you will see a form similar to the one shown in Figure 4-52.

Figure 4-51

Listings at the International Real Estate Digest.

To get the most out of your IRED listing, be sure to carefully consider the graphical icons that may pertain to your site. Each icon that you select will be displayed with your listing. In the remarks sections, you should add a brief description of your Web site; doing so should ensure that your listing is displayed with a summary description.

Other Real Estate Directories

Although I've focused on the top directory sites for the real estate industry, many other real estate directories exist. Some of the other real estate directories that you may want to consider include the Real Estate Cyberspace Society and Open House America.

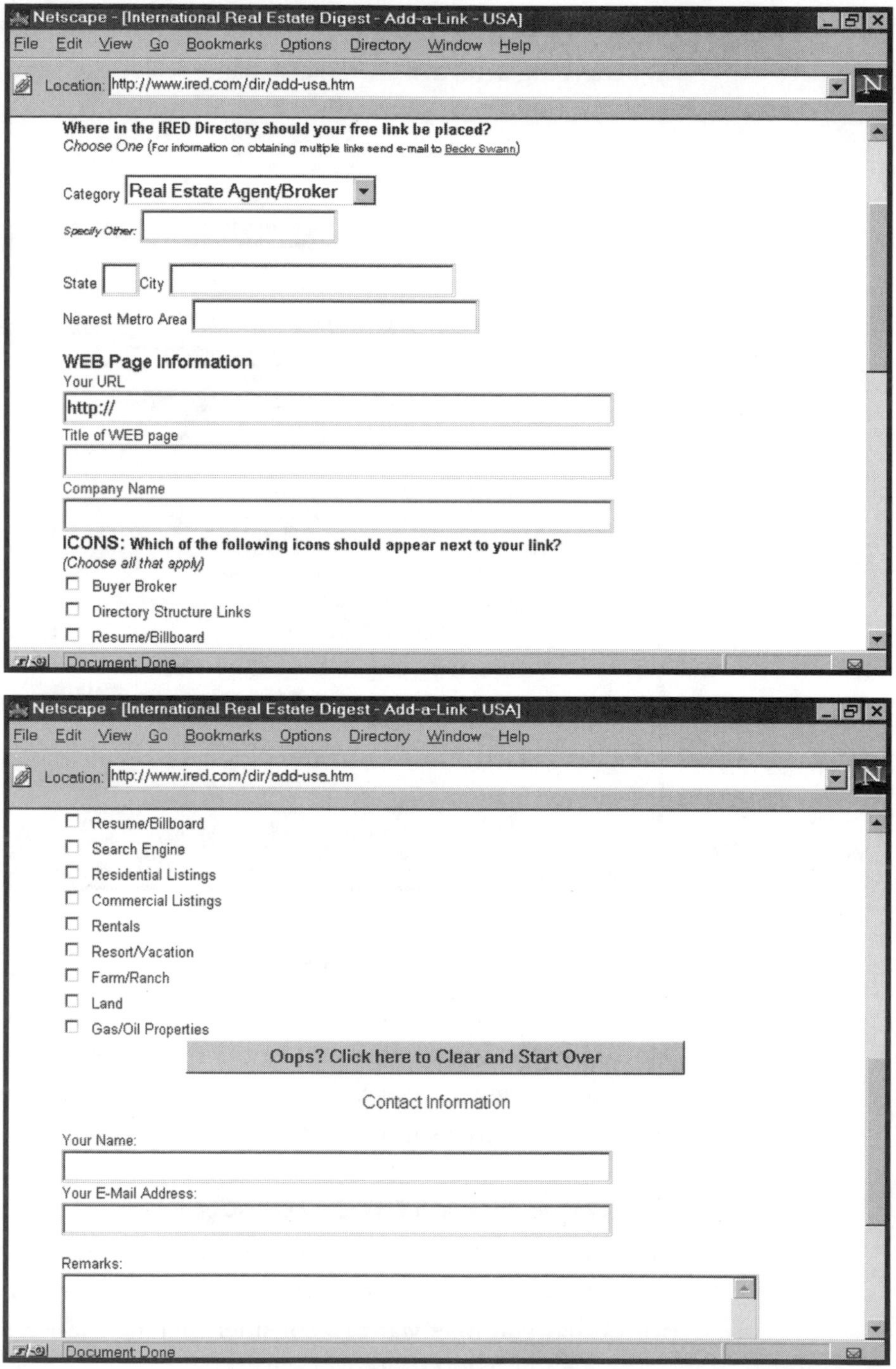

Figure 4-52

The submission page for the International Real Estate Digest.

FIND IT ▶
ONLINE

The Real Estate Cyberspace Society (`http://www.recyber.com`) provides services for real estate professionals. The home page for this site is shown in Figure 4-53. You can submit your site to the Real Estate Cyberspace Society directory at:

`http://www.recyber.com/links/links.html`

Open House America (`http://www.openhouse.net`) is a site for home buyers that includes directories for realtors, financial services, and general real estate-related listings. The home page for this site is shown in Figure 4-54. You can submit a listing to Open House America at:

`http://www.openhouse.net/realtor_register.html`

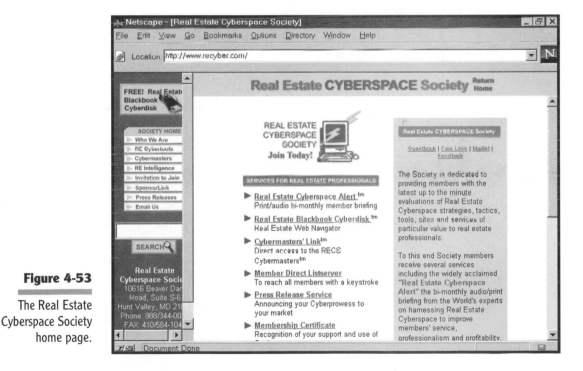

Figure 4-53

The Real Estate Cyberspace Society home page.

Travel and Tourism: Guides and Directories

The travel industry covers many different professions and organizations. Travel agents book tickets; airlines, cruise lines, train companies, and bus companies provide transportation; hotels offer a place to stay; car rental

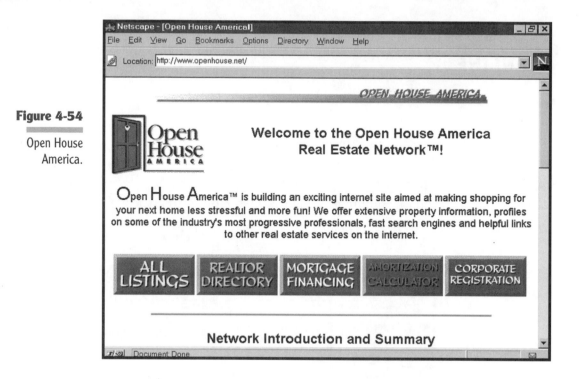

Figure 4-54

Open House
America.

agencies give you flexible mobility; recreation and amusement businesses provide entertainment.

Because travel and tourism is big business, the industry is well represented online. As with the real estate industry, many high-profile travel directories can help you build traffic to your Web site. If your Web site covers any of the professions or organizations related to the travel industry, you should consider adding a listing to the directories in this section. If you publish any information that relates to travel and tourism, you should consider adding a listing in travel directories as well. Online, you will find the travel and tourism directory listings at:

```
http://www.tvpress.com/promote/travel.htm
```

Getting Listed in Hotels and Travel on the Net

Hotels and Travel on the Net (http://www.hotelstravel.com) is an international directory for the travel and tourism industry. This comprehensive directory contains hundreds of thousands of listings, all neatly organized.

You can search Hotels and Travel by keyword or by following links to specific categories of information (see Figure 4-55). Categories within the directory include hotels, airlines, airports, travel-related products, travel-related services, and travel references. Most of the major hotel chains have areas within the site as well.

What Do Entries in Hotels and Travel on the Net Look Like?

Entries in Hotels and Travel cluster around hotels, airports, and airlines. Figure 4-56 shows listings for hotels, which are organized into state-wide directories, local directories, maps, and tourist information. The site indexes most of the entries according to city names.

Figure 4-55

The Hotels and Travel on the Net home page.

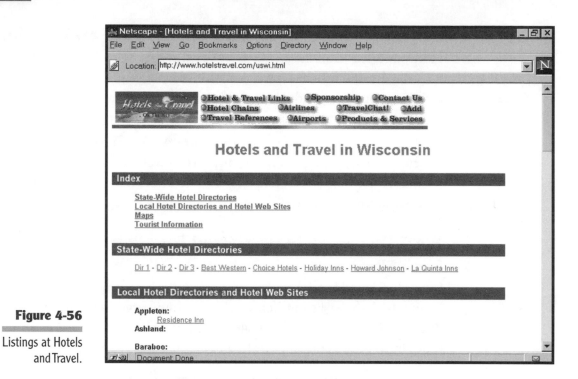

Figure 4-56

Listings at Hotels
and Travel.

Placing a Listing in Hotels and Travel on the Net

If your site features travel-related information, you can add a listing to Hotels and Travel using the form shown in Figure 4-57. The URL for this page is as follows:

```
http://www.hotelstravel.com/add.html
```

Fill out only the information that pertains to your Web site. If you are submitting a travel-related site, be sure to specify the city, state, or country that your site serves.

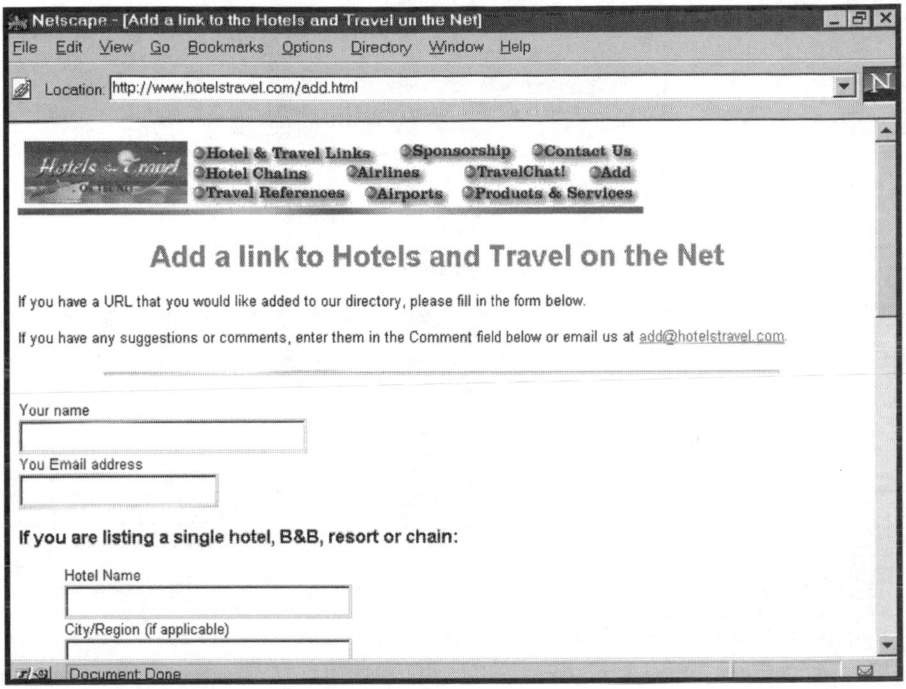

Figure 4-57

The submission page
for Hotels and Travel
on the Net.

Getting Listed in Ecotravel

Ecotravel (http://www.ecotravel.com) is an exceptional international directory to outdoor sports and travel. The home page for this site is shown in Figure 4-58.

The Ecotravel directory contains much information on outdoor activities and travel destinations for the adventurous. Because of its focus on eco-tourism, the site includes listings on conservation, wildlife information, and outdoor education. It also carries listings for sites that sell outdoor equipment, sites that cover outdoor sports, and sites that describe the latest events in outdoor sports.

What Do Entries in Ecotravel Look Like?

Entries within the Ecotravel directory are organized by category, such as destinations and activities. Within specific categories, the directory is divided by country. Figure 4-59 shows the U.S. destinations page. The actual listings are displayed with a title and a summary description.

Figure 4-58

The Ecotravel
home page.

The unique focus of the Ecotravel directory gives anyone who publishes information related to outdoor sports and travel a great opportunity to be noticed. If you publish outdoor sports information or travel information, you should be listed in this directory. If you sell sports gear or publish information related to sports gear, this directory is ideal for you as well.

Placing a Listing in Ecotravel

Before you submit your site, you should familiarize yourself with the categories within this directory. The Conservation area focuses on wildlife information, environmental issues, and outdoor education. The Gear area focuses on outdoor equipment manufacturers and sites that sell this equipment or publish related information. The Activities area focuses on outdoor activities, such as backpacking and kayaking. The Destinations area focuses on worldwide locations for outdoor sports and travel. The Events area focuses on upcoming events in outdoor sports. Other areas cover general travel and hotel information.

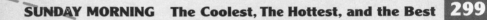

Figure 4-59

Listings at Ecotravel.

FIND IT ONLINE

The submission page for Ecotravel is shown in Figure 4-60. The URL for this page is as follows:

```
http://www.ecotravel.com/addalink/
```

Other Travel and Tourism Directories

After you submit listings to the Hotels and Travel directory and the Ecotravel directory, you may want to try other travel directories as well. After all, you want to build traffic to your travel-related Web site, and the best way to do this is to spread the word about your Web site through the key directories for the travel industry. Some of the other travel directories to which you may want to submit your site include SETII, TravelHub, and the Rec. Travel Library.

FIND IT ONLINE

The Search Engine for Travel Information on the Internet (`http://www.setii.com`) provides a search interface to thousands of travel and tourism listings in its international travel directory. Most of the listings in the directory cover travel-related areas such as travel agencies, airlines, cruise lines, vehicle rentals, travel clubs, and resorts. To submit a listing to this

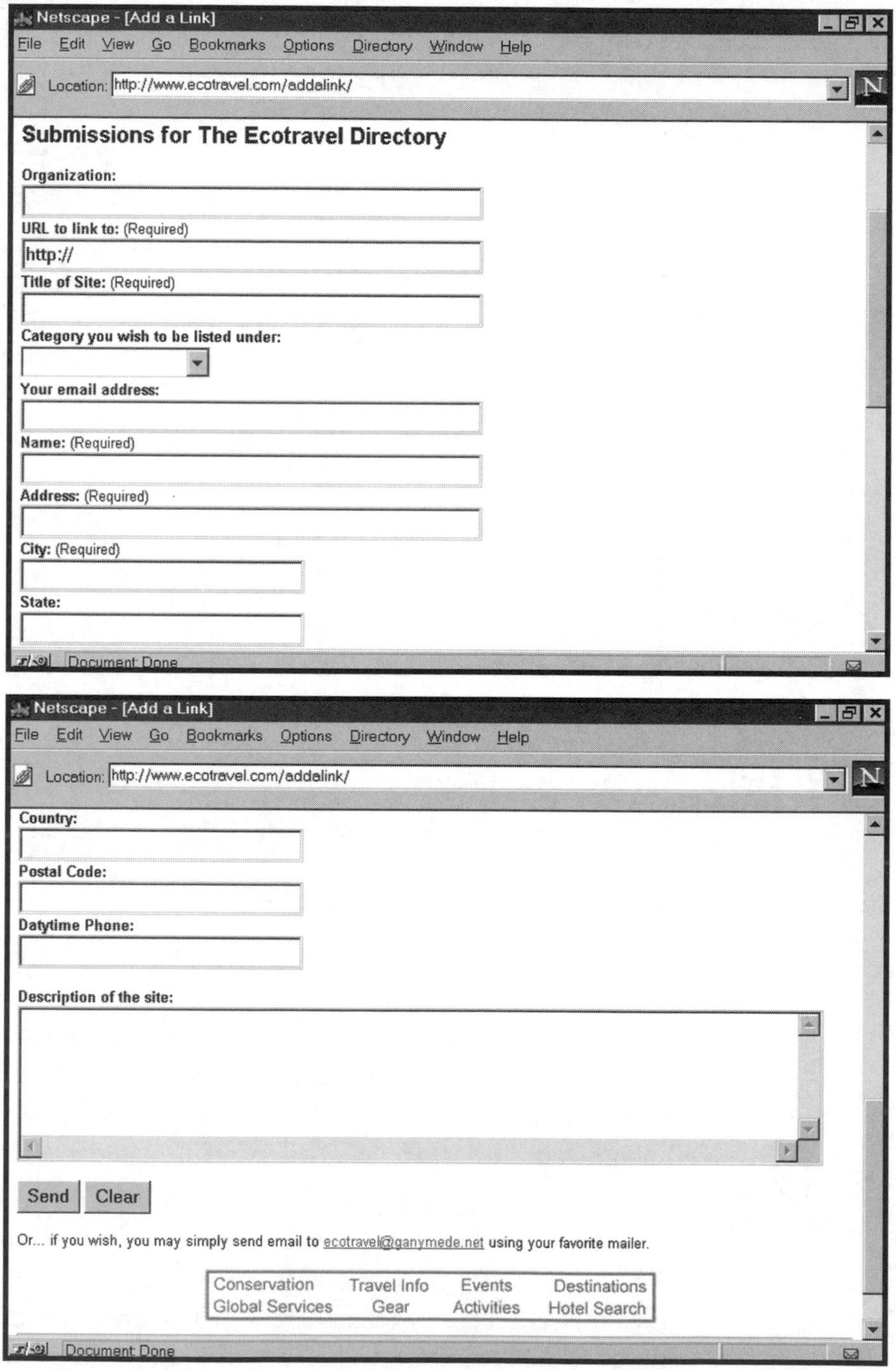

Netscape - [Add a Link]

File Edit View Go Bookmarks Options Directory Window Help

Location: http://www.ecotravel.com/addalink/

Submissions for The Ecotravel Directory

Organization:

URL to link to: (Required)

http://

Title of Site: (Required)

Category you wish to be listed under:

Your email address:

Name: (Required)

Address: (Required)

City: (Required)

State:

Document Done

Netscape - [Add a Link]

File Edit View Go Bookmarks Options Directory Window Help

Location: http://www.ecotravel.com/addalink/

Country:

Postal Code:

Datytime Phone:

Description of the site:

Send   Clear

Or... if you wish, you may simply send email to ecotravel@ganymede.net using your favorite mailer.

| Conservation | Travel Info | Events | Destinations |
| Global Services | Gear | Activities | Hotel Search |

Document Done

Figure 4-60

The submission
page for Ecotravel.

site, visit the home page shown in Figure 4-61 and click on the Add button or follow the links to the free listing area.

FIND IT ▶
ONLINE

TravelHub (http://www.travelhub.com) is a directory to travel agencies. If you are a travel agent, TravelHub provides a number of free services that can help you build traffic and boost your company's bottom line. The home page for TravelHub is shown in Figure 4-62. To find out how you can get listed in this directory, visit the following address:

http://www.travelhub.com/info.html

The Rec. Travel Library (http://www.Travel-Library/) is a complete reference resource for travelers. If you publish travel-related information, find the specific area within the Rec. Travel Library that fits your site and then submit e-mail to lucas@travel-library.com. Your e-mail message should include the title of your site, a summary description, and a suggestion for where to place your listing within the Rec. Travel Library (see Figure 4-63).

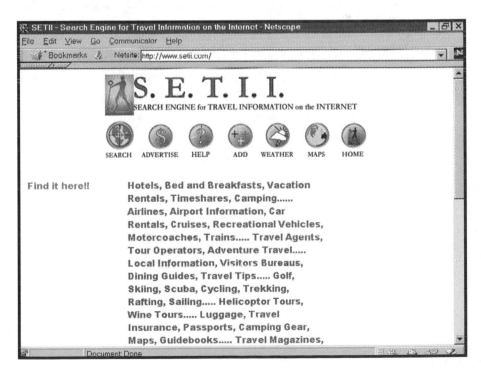

Figure 4-61

The Search Engine for
Travel Information
home page.

Figure 4-62

The Travel Hub Home page.

More Guides and Directories by Category

Category-specific guides and directories are great ways to get your site noticed. The usefulness of category guides is apparent when you want to find specific types of information without having to wade through search engine results. Because category guides are so useful, they are also extremely popular. The Web contains thousands of category-specific guides covering every imaginable topic. If you are looking for a very specific category guide, one of the best places to find it is shown in Figure 4-64. The URL for this page is the following:

FIND IT ▶ ONLINE

```
http://www.yahoo.com/Business_and_Economy/Companies/
    Directories/
```

Before you go on to the next part in this section, look for additional directories that relate to topics or industries discussed at your site. Rather than try to submit your site in dozens of categories, focus on the top three

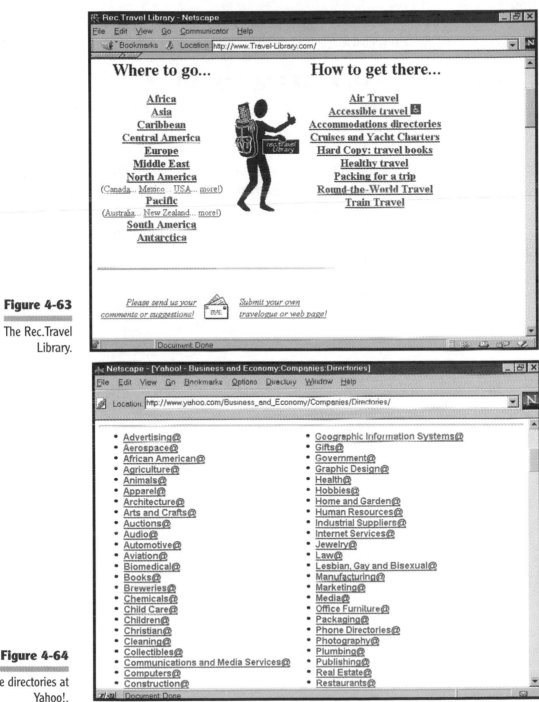

Figure 4-63

The Rec.Travel Library.

Figure 4-64

More directories at Yahoo!.

categories. After you've identified these categories, submit your site to the best directories related to these categories.

Wrapping Up and Looking Ahead

Submitting your site to category-specific guides and directories will help you reach users who are looking for tailored information. Category guides can also help your Web site stand out from the crowd, especially when you consider that the major category guides attract millions of visitors, yet have considerably fewer listings than mainstream directories such as Yahoo!

The next part of this section of the book covers promoting your Web site in specialty directories. Specialty directories include announcement sites, White Pages directories, and Internet malls.

Promoting Your Web Site in Specialty Directories

Beyond the traditional and category-specific directories, two key types of directories are frequently used to find information on the Web. The first type of directory is called a White Pages directory, which is a guide to people rather than businesses. The second type of directory is a What's New? directory, which is a guide to new sites and resources on the Web. I call these *specialty directories* because they have unique focuses that set them apart from other types of Web directories.

Boosting Traffic with White Pages Directories

Millions of people are connected to the online world. They have phone numbers, e-mail addresses, and home pages. Finding out who's wired in and who's not is what White Pages directories are all about. Unlike the White Pages of your phone book, which have listings for your local area only, Web-based White Pages directories cover entire countries, allowing you to search the world without having to know the area code or country code of the person you are trying to reach.

Although the White Pages contain business listings, White Pages directories are primarily about people. Just as traditional White Pages directories are moving beyond phone numbers and addresses, so are Web-based White Pages directories. You might find not only someone's phone number in these directories but also his or her e-mail address and home page URL.

Because White Pages directories make finding people anywhere in the world so easy, their popularity is rivaled only by that of the major search engines and the best Web guides. Needless to say, putting a listing in the top White Pages directories can definitely help build traffic to your Web site.

White Pages directories have their drawbacks just as any other types of directories or search sites do. With millions of listings in a typical directory, you will usually find multiple listings for the same name, which means that you generally have to rely on geographic information to find the person you are looking for. Furthermore, because our world isn't static, information about people changes every day, which means that sometimes you encounter outdated listings. When you create an entry in a White Pages directory with the intent of increasing your Web traffic, you want to ensure that your information is up-to-date and accurate at all times.

To follow along with the discussion, I recommend that you submit your Web site to the White Pages directories found in this part of the book. If you are in a hurry and don't have time to register with all the sites that I examine, submit your site to the top three White Pages directories and skip the other White Pages directories for now. Online, you will find the listings for the White Page directories at:

```
http://www.tvpress.com/promote/whitep.htm
```

Exploring the Four11 Directory

The Four11 directory (`http://www.four11.com`) is the premiere White Pages directory on the Web. With millions of page views every single day, Four11 is also one of the busiest sites on the Web. In fact, for 1996, the site was rated as one of the 25 Web sites most frequently visited.

FIND IT ▶ ONLINE

Four11 has a program to distribute the directory to industry partners, which allows you to search Four11 at other sites. Some of the major partners include BigYellow (`http://www.bigyellow.com`), Yahoo! (`http://www.yahoo.com`), InfoSeek (`http://www.infoseek.com`), and NetGuide (`http://www.netguide.com`).

FIND IT ▶ ONLINE

As shown in Figure 4-65, the main search interface at Four11 is quite advanced. You can search for e-mail address and home page URLs by name, geographic location, company, and domain. Telephone numbers and addresses have a similar search interface.

Tuning in to Listings at Four11

The two main directories within Four11 are the e-mail and telephone directories. When you search Four11 for telephone numbers, it returns the

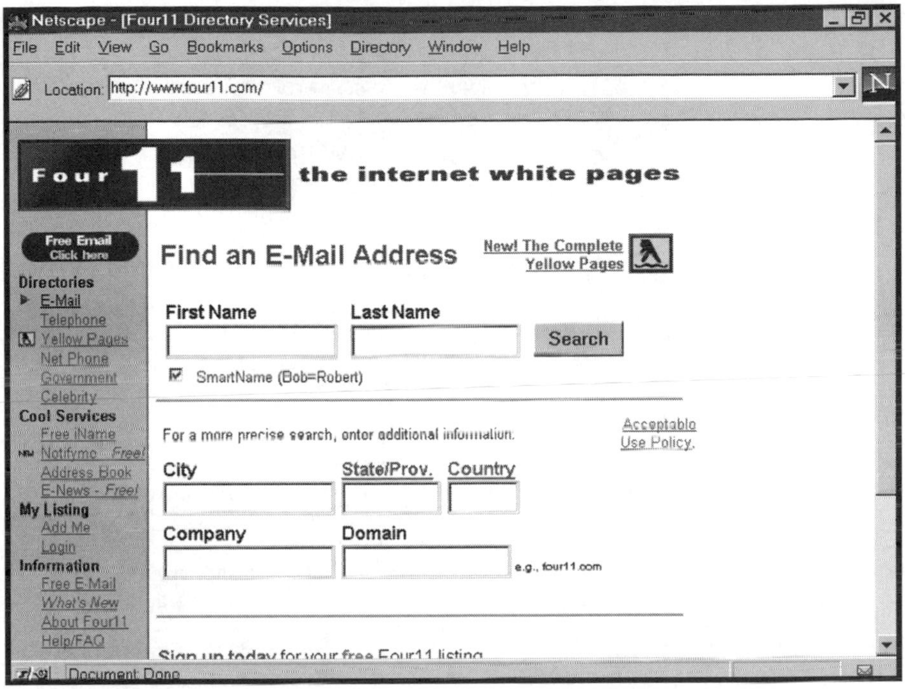

Figure 4-65

The Four11 directory.

results in a two-line summary format that shows names and addresses. When you search Four11 for e-mail addresses, it returns the results in a one-line summary format that shows names and e-mail addresses.

In both cases, Four11 links the user names to detailed listings within the Four11 directory. Whereas the detailed listing for telephone numbers shows only the full name, address, and telephone number, the detailed listing for e-mail addresses shows much more information. You see not only the person's e-mail address but also his or her home page URL, previous e-mail addresses, and personal data (see Figure 4-66).

Creating a Listing in the Four11 Directory

Before you can add a listing to the Four11 directory, you need to verify that your e-mail address isn't already in the system. You do this by following the My Listing or Add Me links from the Four11 home page. Doing so takes you to a page like the one shown in Figure 4-67. Simply enter your e-mail address and click on the Register button. If your e-mail address isn't in the system, you can create a new listing.

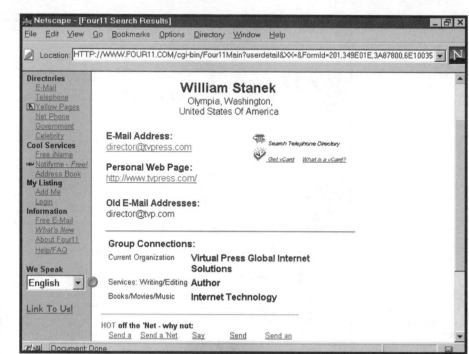

Figure 4-66

A listing in the
Four11 directory.

The primary information that is indexed within Four11 is your name, physical address, and e-mail addresses. Four11 makes finding people in several other ways possible as well, however. For this reason, be as detailed as possible when filling out the submission form. Also, be sure to list any additional or old e-mail addresses that you have and enter the URL to your personal home page.

In the current organization field, enter your business or the company for which you work. In the fields for past connections, you can describe organizations with which you are associated or things that interest you. If you examine Figure 4-67, you will see that in the first Past Connections field, I selected Writing/Editing and described this with the word *Author*. In the second Past Connections field, I selected Books/Movies/Music and described this with the phrase *Internet Technology*. Although this information isn't essential, it does serve to identify me and also provides additional keywords for retrieving my listing.

The next-to-last step is to choose a password. Definitely choose a password that is unique to this directory and then write it down. You need this password if you want to update your listing at a later date. After you select a password, submit the listing.

NOTE For the Group Connections information, a check box following the field lets you toggle on or off the option of having the information displayed automatically with your listing. If you want the information to appear with your listing, leave it in the checked position. If you want the information to appear only when a match occurs based on this field, deselect the check box.

Figure 4-67

Submitting your listing to the Four11 directory.

Exploring WorldPages

FIND IT ▶
ONLINE

WorldPages (http://www.worldpages.com) is a combined White Pages and Yellow Pages directory (see Figure 4-68). With more than 100 million listings for the U.S. and Canada, WorldPages is one of the largest directories of its kind. You can search WorldPages for directory information related to businesses, people, and government agencies.

Most of the information in WorldPages comes from traditional sources such as your local phone company, which is why the directory focuses on names, addresses, and phone numbers. Through partnerships with other directory services, WorldPages does associate e-mail addresses and home page URLs with search results whenever possible.

Tuning in to Listings at WorldPages

Results of a White Pages search at WorldPages are shown in Figure 4-69. As you can see, WorldPages uses icons to show whether additional information is available for a listing. Selecting any of these icons takes you to a results page at a partner site, such as Four11 or AltaVista.

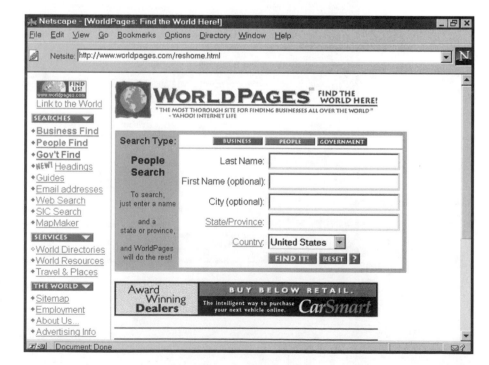

Figure 4-68

WorldPages: A combined White Pages and Yellow Pages directory.

By clicking on an Email search link, you can look for an e-mail address related to a particular listing. Click on the Map link to get a detailed listing that shows the person's full name, address, and phone number. Usually, a digital map accompanies the detailed listing; this map pinpoints the address associated with the listing (see Figure 4-70).

Creating a Listing in the WorldPages Directory

Anyone who lives in the U.S. or Canada should search WorldPages for his or her listing before trying to add one. With more than 100 million listings, the odds are fairly good that you already have a listing in this wonderful directory. Still, if you are not listed, you can ask the folks at WorldPages to add a listing using `http://www.worldpages.com/feedback.html`. Your message should include your full name, street address, e-mail address, and phone number.

FIND IT ▶ ONLINE

To get the most out of your listing in WorldPages, you should register with partner sites, such as Four11 (`http://www.four11.com`) and AltaVista

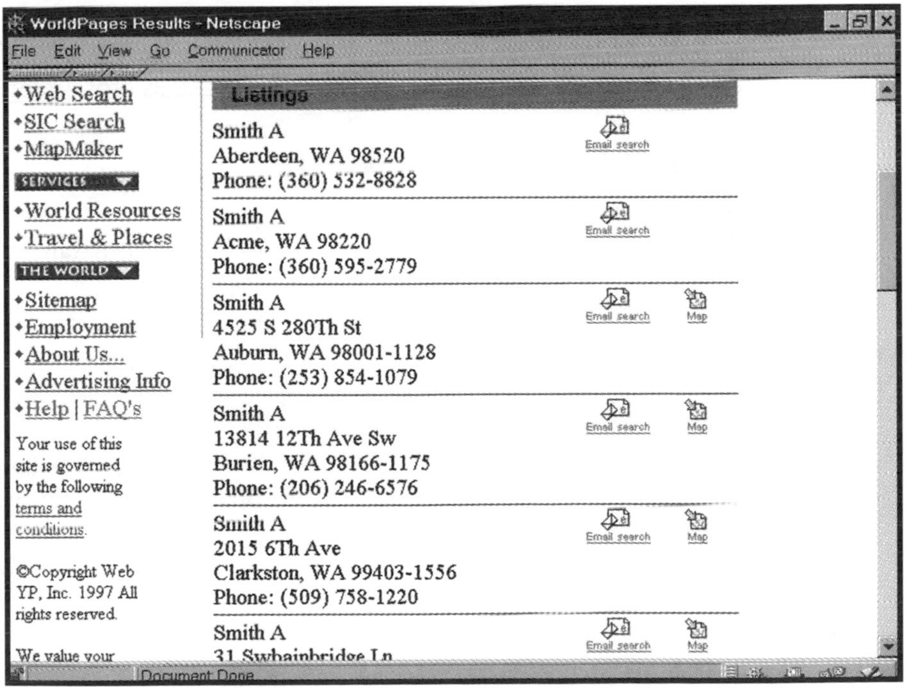

Figure 4-69

A listing at WorldPages.

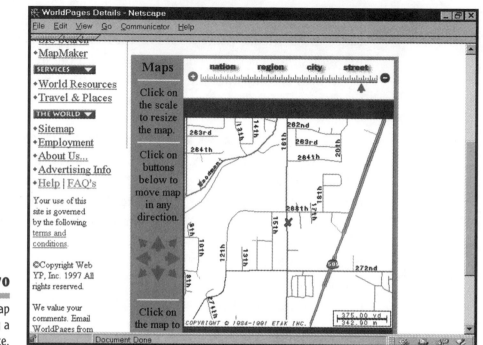

Figure 4-70

A digital map
pinpointing a
person's residence.

(http://www.altavista.digital.com). If your information is available
in one of these other databases, WorldPages cross-references your listing.

Exploring WhoWhere

WhoWhere (http://www.whowhere.com) is an extensive White Pages
directory for the U.S. One of WhoWhere's outstanding features is its extensive search interface that allows you to search by name,
e-mail address, and telephone number (see Figure 4-71). You can also search
for people who share interests similar to yours.

The WhoWhere directory is also branching out into the international arena.
You can access international listings in several languages, including French
(http://french.whowhere.com) and Spanish (http://spanish.whowhere.com).

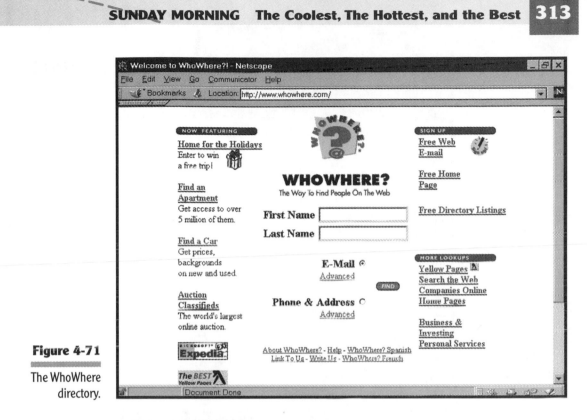

Figure 4-71

The WhoWhere
directory.

Tuning in to Listings at WhoWhere

Listings in WhoWhere are both extensive and diverse. For this reason, the results that you see depend on the type of search that you perform. Figure 4-72 shows the results of a search for e-mail addresses. If a user has taken the time to fill out additional information, the listing will have a link that allows you to see more details.

Detailed listings at WhoWhere are the best you will find in any White Page directory. Beyond the user's general information, the directory provides many extras related to work place, associations, personal interests, and a comprehensive personal profile—all of which are entered by the user.

Creating a Listing in WhoWhere

Creating a listing in WhoWhere is a multistep process that begins when you visit the page shown in Figure 4-73. The URL for this page is as follows:

```
http://www.whowhere.com/cbs/cbsadd.html
```

Figure 4-72

A listing in
WhoWhere.

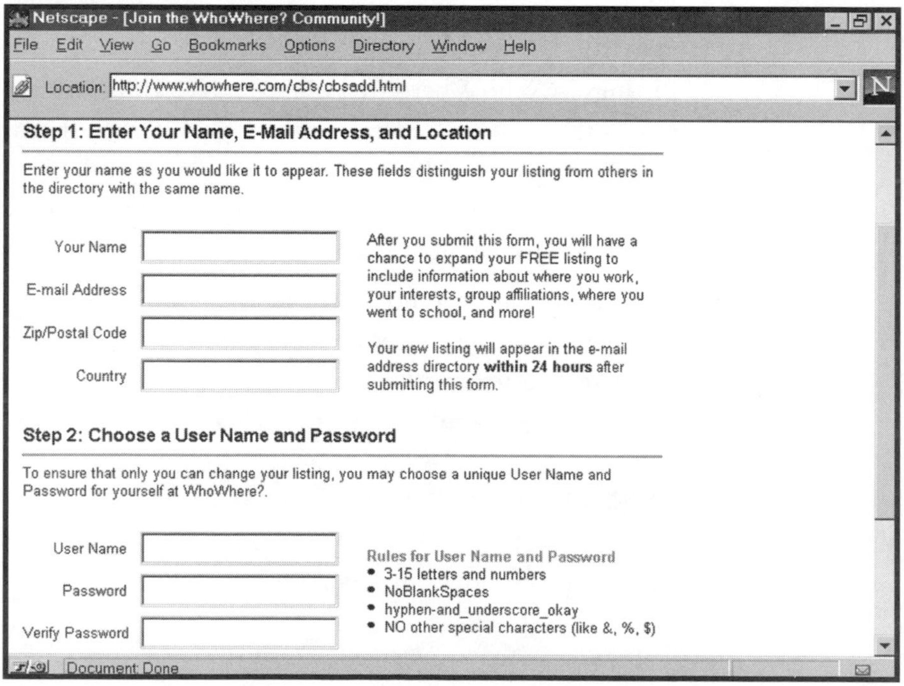

Figure 4-73

Submitting your
listing to
WhoWhere.

The initial information that you enter is used to determine whether you already have a listing within WhoWhere, as well as to create a summary listing for new accounts. As with some other White Pages directories, you must select a user name and password for the WhoWhere directory. Because you will use this information to update your listing in the future, ensure that you write down this information. To protect your information, use a unique user name and password.

After you enter the preliminary information, submit the form. WhoWhere checks the database and then creates a new listing if you have entered unique information. You can now go on to create the detailed listing for the directory. Because your goal is to increase traffic to your Web site, take the time to create the detailed listing.

Your expanded listing should include your home page URL and any additional or previous e-mail addresses. If you are selling products or services on the Web, don't miss the opportunity to get in another URL for your business-oriented home page.

■■■

Before you enter any information in the personal profile area, spend a few minutes considering what you want to place here. The personal profile area is an open section that can contain HTML markup, meaning that you can create a mini-home page complete with hypertext links and images. Ideally, you would use markup and text straight from your primary home page.

■■■

Start by loading your home page into a word processor or text editor. Determine the section that you want to paste into the personal profile area; then, update this section so that all hypertext links, images, and other references use absolute URLs that point to your site. For example, if the SRC attribute for an image pointed to:

```
image/home.gif
```

you would change the reference to:

```
http://www.you.com/image/home.gif
```

After you have updated the section, copy and paste it into the text area for the personal profile. When you are ready, submit the expanded listing. Don't worry—you will have an opportunity to view the listing and correct it if necessary.

Other White Pages Directories

I selected three of the top White Pages directories to cover extensively in this book, but many other such directories exist as well. A few others to which you may want to submit listings are 411Locate, the World Email Directory, and the SuperPages from GTE. Brief descriptions of these directories follow.

411Locate (`http://www.411locate.com`) is a White Pages directory for the U.S. In addition to phone numbers and addresses, 411Locate also lists e-mail accounts and home page URLs. The main page at 411 Locate is shown in Figure 4-74. Because the primary directory services for 411Locate come from LookUpUsa (`http://www.lookupusa.com`), most of the information in 411Locate comes from traditional sources like phone book directories. Still, you can submit new listings directly to 411Locate using this URL:

`http://www.411locate.com/cregister.htm`

FIND IT ▶
ONLINE

The World Email Directory (`http://www.worldemail.com`) is a comprehensive directory of people, places, and things on the Web. Although this international directory has millions of residential and commercial listings, the focus of the site is on finding e-mail addresses (see Figure 4-75).

When you create a listing for this directory, you can add detailed personal and business-related contact information, all of which is indexed within the database. Be sure to add a simple keyword list and select a category for your listing. Because the URL to the submission page changes frequently, you should visit the World Email Directory home page and follow links for adding a listing. Usually this link is labeled Add, Change, or Remove your free listing.

FIND IT ▶
ONLINE

The GTE SuperPages (`http://superpages.gte.net`) are definitely one of the great finds on the Web. As you would expect from GTE, the SuperPages directory is quite extensive. The home page for the main SuperPages Web site is shown in Figure 4-76. You will find the White Pages directory at `http://wp.gte.net` and the Yellow Pages directory at `http://yp.gte.net`.

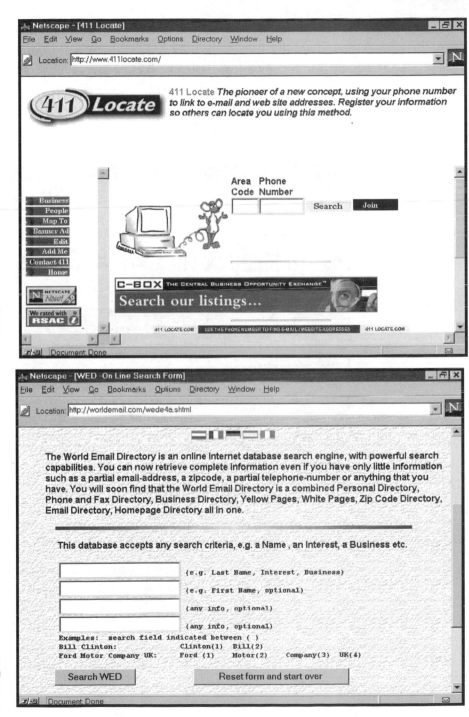

Figure 4-74

The home page for 411Locate.

Figure 4-75

The World Email directory.

Despite the fact that GTE publishes a White Pages directory, the SuperPages are all about business, so unless GTE changes the current policy, you will not find personal listings in the SuperPages. To add a listing to the GTE SuperPages, visit the Yellow Pages directory and follow the Add Listing links. GTE enhances this listing by allowing you to associate business categories with your listing.

Figure 4-76

The GTE SuperPages directory.

More Mileage in What's New? Directories

Announcement sites are an effort to capture the euphoria surrounding the exponential growth rate of the Web, and simultaneously tap into the usual excitement over things that are new and fresh. One of the first What's New? directories was maintained by NCSA—the same folks who gave the world the Mosaic browser. The list at its peak received thousands of submissions for new Web sites every day. Today, the list is no longer updated but NCSA maintains the list for its historical value. After all, by reading the list archives, you can roll back time and truly get a sense of how fast the Web grew in the early days.

Although NCSA no longer updates its What's New? list, many other sites publish extensive What's New? directories. When you visit the major What's New? lists, you will find that these well-maintained Web sites are tremendously popular. This popularity will help drive visitors to your Web site. What's New? directories are organized much like other directories, with specific broad categories such as business and entertainment. Listings within a specific category are usually arranged alphabetically by title and often chronologically as well.

NOTE What's New? lists are by nature guides to new sites. Still, if you've never submitted your site to a specific list before, your site is new to the list and you can therefore certainly submit a listing.

When you register with What's New? directories, you will generally see short-term increases in your Web traffic. The reason for this is that your site usually will be featured in the What's New? directory for only one or two days. Afterward, your listing will appear only in the site's archive files—provided that the site has archive files. If you are interested in short-term increases in Web traffic, What's New? directories are definitely for you. Considering that people often bookmark sites they like, a listing in a What's New? directory can provide modest increases in traffic over the long haul as well.

I recommend that you submit your Web site to the What's New? directories found in this part of the book. If you are in a hurry and don't have time to register with all the sites that I examine, I recommend that you submit your site to the top three What's New? directories and skip the other What's New? directories for now. At the companion Web site for this book, you will find the listings for What's New? directories at:

http://www.tvpress.com/promote/new.htm

Exploring the Starting Point Directory

Starting Point (http://www.stpt.com) is a directory service that has re-made itself several times over the last few years. Whereas Starting Point once strove to become a major directory à la Yahoo, the service now fo-cuses on making a search of hundreds of Web databases easier using its central search resource called PowerSearch. Using the PowerSearch inter-face, you can search individual databases all over the Web by category and keyword.

Despite the change of focus, Starting Point still maintains one of the best guides to new sites (see Figure 4-77). The Starting Point What's New? list (http://www.stpt.com/general/newsite.html) is organized into 12 cat-egories that range from business to weather. On the average day, Starting

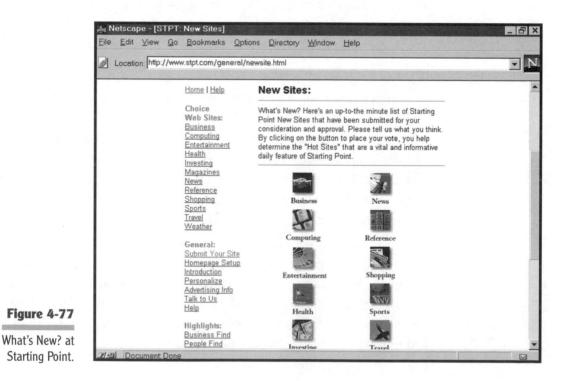

Figure 4-77

What's New? at Starting Point.

Point receives several thousand submissions for new sites and enhances the directory by allowing visitors to vote for new sites that should be featured as the Hot Site of the Day.

Tuning in to What's New? at Starting Point

All Web sites that are submitted to Starting Point are displayed in the What's New? directory. Within each of the 12 categories, listings are organized chronologically, with the most recent listings displayed first. Because Starting Point receives so many submissions, the directory displays only the most recent listings.

Each listing has a page title and a summary description (see Figure 4-78). To get the most out of your listing, be sure to select a category that fits your Web site. You should also provide a descriptive title and a clear summary for the listing.

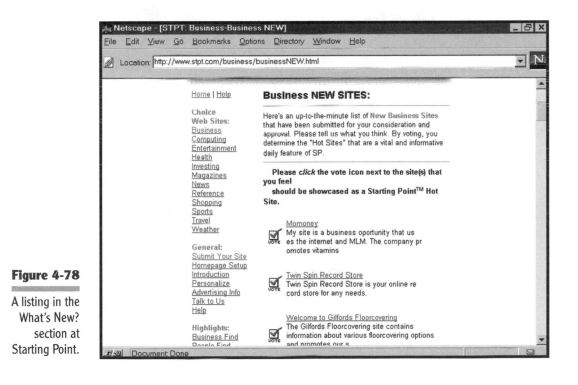

Figure 4-78

A listing in the What's New? section at Starting Point.

Creating a Listing in What's New section at Starting Point

You can submit your site to Starting Point using the submission page shown in Figure 4-79. The URL for this page is the following:

```
http://www.stpt.com/general/submit.html
```

When you examine the Starting Point submission form, the first thing that you may notice is that the site requests a great deal of information. Most of this information isn't used in the directory, however, which is why I recommend entering only the mandatory information. You should also note that you will be signed up for Starting Point's Web Notification Service by default. If you don't want additional e-mail from Starting Point, deselect the check box for the notification service.

Exploring the What's New on the Internet Directory

What's New on the Internet (`http://www.whatsnew.com`) is a small but popular directory for new sites maintained by Emap Computing. Rather than organize the site by category, the site's developers chose to organize it geographically, allowing you to access new sites in the U.S., Europe, U.K., or from around the world. The home page for What's New on the Internet is shown in Figure 4-80.

When I last visited What's New on the Internet, the site was beginning to collect information for categories. The dozens of categories ranged from agriculture sites to weird sites. Thus, by the time you read this, the site may supplement the geographic organization with these categories.

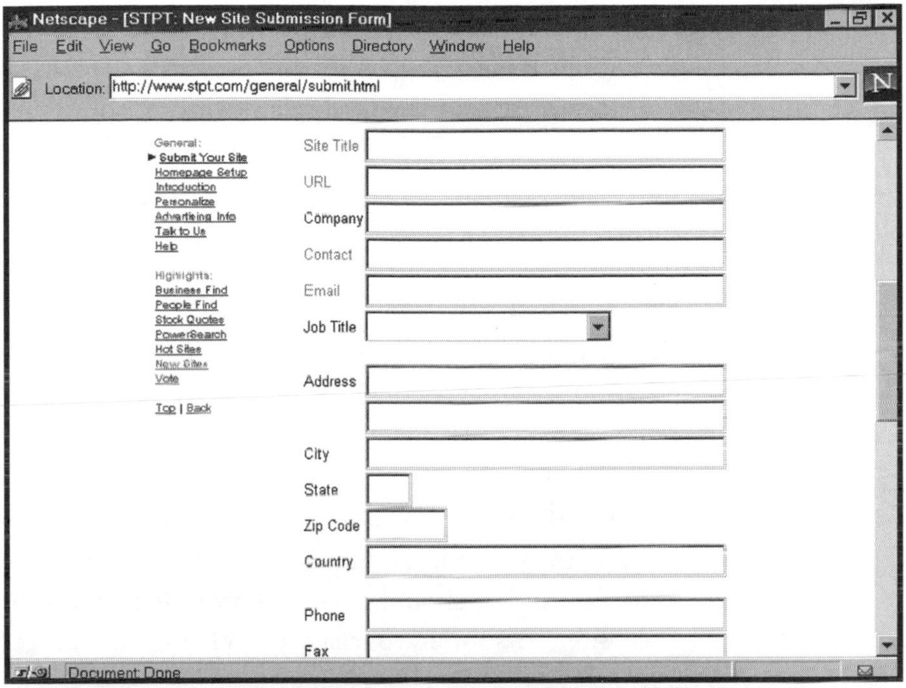

Figure 4-79

Submitting your
listing to
Starting Point.

Figure 4-80

What's New on
the Internet.

Listings at What's New on the Internet

Listings in What's New on the Internet are organized chronologically, with the most recent submissions displayed first. As shown in Figure 4-81, listings display the page title, summary, submission date, and country designator. Several times a day, old listings move to a current archive file. At the end of the day, the listings move to an archive of the previous day's listings.

Creating a Listing in What's New on the Internet

Before you submit a listing to What's New on the Internet, you should check to see whether the site's publishers have implemented the new category structure. If they have implemented the category structure in the directory, browse the listing to get a good feel for the types of sites published in the various categories.

FIND IT ▶
ONLINE   Because the site indexes the page title and description for its search engine, your description should contain keywords that will help users find your Web site. To submit your site to What's New on the Internet, use the

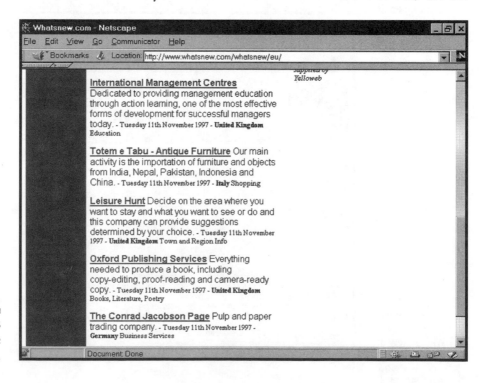

Figure 4-81

A listing at What's New on the Internet.

submission page shown in Figure 4-82. The URL for this page is as follows:

```
http://www.whatsnew.com/whatsnew/submit/
```

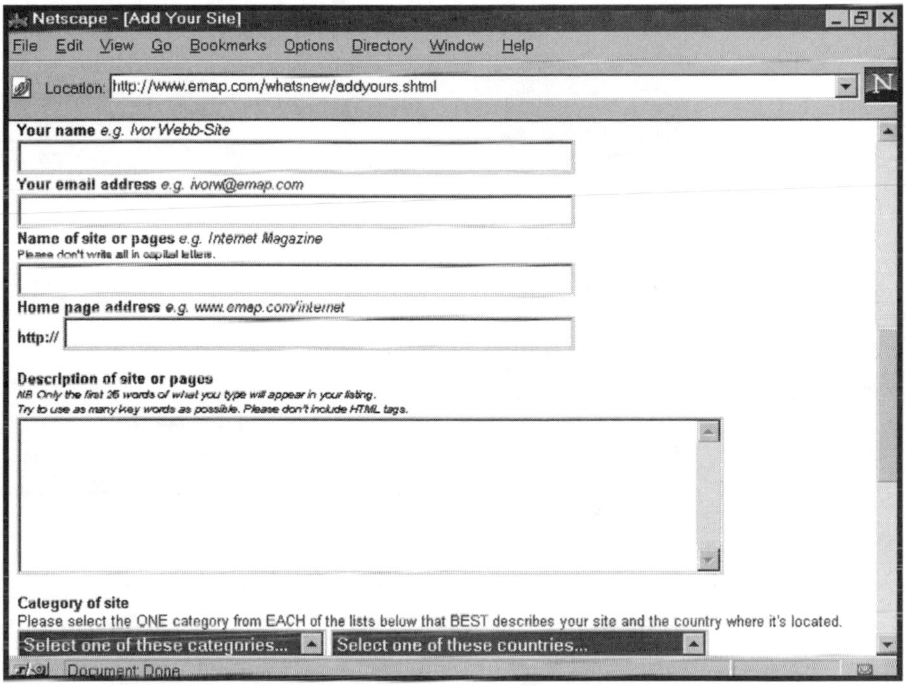

Figure 4-82

Submitting your listing to What's New on the Internet.

Exploring What's New from Whatsnu.Com

What's New from WhatsNu.Com (`http://www.whatsnu.com`) is a comprehensive What's New? site that receives thousands of new listings every day. Unlike other What's New? sites that are primarily directories, Whats Nu.Com provides access to listings via a search engine, allowing you to search the database by keyword and category (see Figure 4-83). When you search the database, you will find that all listings are archived, allowing you to retrieve listings for old and new announcements.

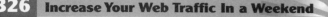

Figure 4-83

The Whatsnu.Com
home page.

Tuning in to Listings at Whatsnu.Com

Because the site archives listings within the primary database, your submission to Whatsnu.Com will be available for quite some time. This feature is great for increasing visibility and attracting visitors to your Web site. Listings in the database appear by title, category, description, URL, and submission date (see Figure 4-84).

As with most search engines, the Whatsnu.Com search engine returns listings according to relevancy. The search engine bases relevancy upon keywords used in the page title and the description.

Creating a Listing at Whatsnu.Com

To get the most out of your listing in Whatsnu.Com, you should use a title and description with keywords that strongly relate to your site's topic. This topic should also strongly relate to the category in which you submit your

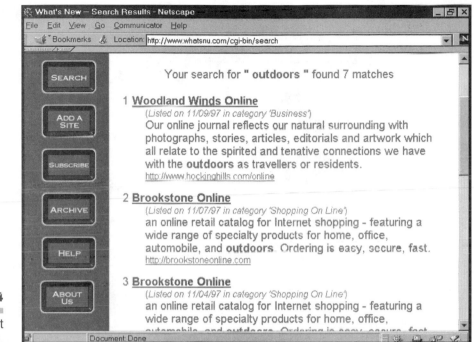

Figure 4-84

A listing at
Whatsnu.Com.

site. After you've plotted out the description and category that you want to use, submit your site using the form shown in Figure 4-85. The URL for this page is the following:

```
http://www.whatsnu.com/add.html
```

Other What's New? Directories

Finding the new and the interesting is what announcement directories are all about. Two additional What's New? directories for you to consider submitting your site to are What's New Too and Go2WhatsNew.

What's New Too (`http://newtoo.manifest.com`) has been around since the early days of the Web (see Figure 4-86). The name comes from the fact that the site was another choice for announcing what's new in addition to NCSA's famous What's New? directory. Ironically, What's New Too continues to endure although the original What's New? is no longer updated.

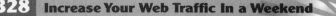

Figure 4-85

Submitting your
listing at
Whatsnu.Com.

Because the directory is archived and searchable, you will find that What's New Too is a great choice for announcing your site. The URL for the submission page at What's New Too is as follows:

```
http://newtoo.manifest.com/submit.html
```

Go2WhatsNew (`http://www.go2whatsnew.com`) offers comprehensive announcements for new products and services, making this site perfect for people who use their own Web site to promote products and services (see Figure 4-87). Listings in Go2WhatsNew are organized into broad product and service-oriented categories, such as consumer electronics and gifts.

Go2WhatsNew follows an advertising approach in which each product or service has a comprehensive ad rather than a summary listing within the directory. You can create a free ad within Go2WhatsNew using this URL:

```
http://www.go2whatsnew.com/freead.htm
```

Figure 4-86

The What's New Too directory.

Figure 4-87

Go2WhatsNew on the Web

Wrapping Up and Looking Ahead

This part of this section focused on White Pages directories and What's New? directories. White Pages directories are great for helping people find your personal information, e-mail address, and home page URL. What's New? directories are great for announcing your site to the world. But directory-based promotion doesn't end with these specialty directories. You can also promote your Web site by getting it listed as the cool site of the day, and the next part tells you how to do that.

Getting Your Site Listed As the Cool Site of the Day

One of the most famous awards on the Web is the Cool Site of the Day award. Getting named the Cool Site of the Day is an accomplishment that gets your site noticed. But the Cool Site of the Day award is only the icing on the cake as far as awards go. There are dozens of other awards that range from the fleeting to the everlasting. Making sense of all these awards and finding the awards that truly make a difference is what this part of this section is all about.

Want to Be Named Cool Site of the Day?

Nothing makes your site stand out from the crowd like an award. Awards are stamps of approval that tell the masses your site is worth their time. Not just any old award will do, though. The Web has more than a thousand different types of site awards. These awards range from Bubba's Cool Site of the Day to the Web 500 Best of the Web. Although Bubba's award may do wonders for your ego, the actual award itself will do very little for your site's traffic. On the other hand, an award like the Web 500 Best of the Web can dramatically increase traffic to your Web site.

NOTE   At the time of this writing, there's no award called Bubba's Cool Site of the Day—I just made it up to make a point.

Wandering the Maze of Web Awards

Over the years, my sites have received hundreds of awards—hey, I've been around for quite some time and have created dozens of Web sites. I've discovered that awards can work miracles when it comes to building traffic to your Web site, but they can also be mere self-serving trophies that you place in a glass case to brag about your achievements. The simple truth is that displaying your awards prominently doesn't build traffic to your Web site, no matter what the sites granting the awards want you to think.

The number of awards doesn't matter, either. You could have hundreds of Bubba and Bubba-clone awards and it wouldn't make a difference as far as your site's traffic is concerned. The reality is that these days it seems everyone is offering a Web award of some type or another. There are more than a hundred Cool Site of the Day awards. There are awards for Cool Site of the Moment, Cool Site of the Hour, Cool Site of the Week, Cool Site of the Month, and Cool Site of the Year as well. Beyond the cool site awards, there are the Hot Site of the Day, Hour, Week, Month, and Year awards. Next come the Crazy Site of the Day, Hour, Week, Month, and Year awards. There are so many awards that Web neophytes have started offering backward awards such as the Mediocre Site of the Day, the Ugly Site of the Day, and the Bottom 95% of the Web.

If displaying your awards or the number of awards doesn't matter, you are probably wondering what does matter. Well, the true equalizers are the underlying meaning of the award and the strength of the award giver's announcement medium. When an organization such as *PC Magazine* recognizes your Web site as one of the Top 100 of the Year, you can expect your traffic to skyrocket. Again, the reason for this isn't so much the award itself as the significance of the award and the channels through which it is announced.

FIND IT
ONLINE

PC Magazine is well respected in the industry. The Top 100 of the Year award (`http://www.zdnet.com/pcmag/special/web100/_open.htm`) is bestowed upon sites only after thorough research and extensive review. The list of recipients of the Top 100 is published in *PC Magazine*, which has several million readers. After publishing the list in its print edition, *PC Magazine* publishes the list in its online edition, where it is available to the Web community throughout the year. The longevity of the print edition coupled with the continued traffic to *PC Magazine*'s Web site and the Top 100 list itself are what drives traffic to the Web sites of the recipients.

Finding the Right Award

The right award can make all the difference in the world when it comes to increasing traffic to your Web site. To find the right award, you really need to visit the home of the organization or person granting the award. When you get to the Web site, spend some time reviewing the site and the techniques used to display awards.

Ideally, current awards will be showcased at the site for at least a day and then later put into an archive that can be searched. In this way, the award isn't fleeting but is rather lasting and meaningful because the visitors to the award site can find your award today, tomorrow, or next month. Because the popularity of the award site is also important, you should try to gauge the level of traffic at the Web site. The busier the award site, the better the chances that it will increase traffic to your Web site.

All this talk of finding the right award may seem strange. After all, these sites are giving away an award and I have the audacity to ask whether the award is meaningful and worthwhile. Unfortunately, with more than a thousand different organizations offering awards of one type or another, you really do need to make sure that the award is meaningful and worthwhile before you take the time to submit your Web site. Fortunately, I've already done the legwork for you. After searching through more than a thousand award sites, I came up with the list of sites featured in this section of this book.

Submitting Your Site

Receiving an award depends largely upon the personal tastes of the reviewer and the philosophy of the award site as a whole. Some award sites look for truly cool sites based on graphic design or coverage of zany issues. Other award sites look for great resources, with no consideration going to whether the site uses mostly text or a cutting-edge graphic design. Because personal opinion weighs heavily in the decision, truly great sites are sometimes passed by.

To improve your odds of being selected, take the time to get to know the types of sites that the reviewers prefer. If they review mostly entertainment sites and you have a business-oriented site, the odds are high that you will get passed by. So, rather than submit the URL of your main business page, submit the URL for that fun area where you let customers interact with your products online, or highlight this area in the summary description that you supply with the submission.

You can also improve your odds of winning by submitting each of the key areas within your site separately. If your site has three different areas, you might submit each of these areas. Ideally, these areas would cover unrelated topics, such as sports memorabilia, music singles from the '50's, and multimedia CD-ROMs for the Mac. In this way, you are truly submitting something different.

The old adage of "If at first you don't succeed, try, try again," certainly applies to awards. Don't abuse the submission process by submitting your site every few days or weeks, though. Instead, wait a few months before trying to submit your site again. In the interim, you may also want to work on the design, flow, and content of your Web site.

As you read this part, I suggest that you apply the information as you go. Submit your Web site to each of the awards that I discuss. To make the task of submitting your Web site easier, you may want to visit the companion Web site for this book. Use the following URL:

```
http://www.tvpress.com/promote/award.htm
```

Cool Site of the Day

Cool Site of the Day is one of the most popular awards. Hundreds of different organizations offer this award. To help you make sense of these offerings, you will find the top Cool Site of the Day awards in this section. These sites are the best of the best when it comes to the Cool Site of the Day award because they follow the guidelines for a good award discussed previously. For the most part, the awards are showcased for at least a day. Then, because they are archived, the awards can continue to generate traffic to your site over the long haul. The sites are also popular and, as I stated earlier, the busier the award site, the better the chances for increasing your Web traffic.

FIND IT ▶
ONLINE
Infi.Net (`http://cool.infi.net`) offers one of the original Cool Site of the Day awards. Along with the Cool Site of the Day award, Infi.Net has many other features that make the site a great destination (see Figure 4-88). All sites that receive the Cool Site of the Day are showcased on the day of the award. Afterward, they move to a page featuring sites picked that

week, and then later move to an archive featuring all past awards. Infi.Net also gives a Cool Site of the Year award.

You can submit your cool home page or Web site to Infi.Net by sending e-mail to `cool@infi.net`. Your message should contain the page title, page URL, and a description of the page you are submitting.

Project Cool (`http://www.projectcool.com`) is another hip site that recognizes the coolest sites on the Web. Project Cool features its current Cool Site of the Day in a section called Sightings (see Figure 4-89). You can access the cool sites for the current month in the Coolest on the Web section. Project Cool supplements its cool site picks with a Web site developer area and a reader discussion area. A lot of Web developers visit the developer area but end up browsing just because this site is so wonderfully designed. You can submit your site to Project cool using a submission page found at:

`http://www.projectcool.com/sightings/submit.html`

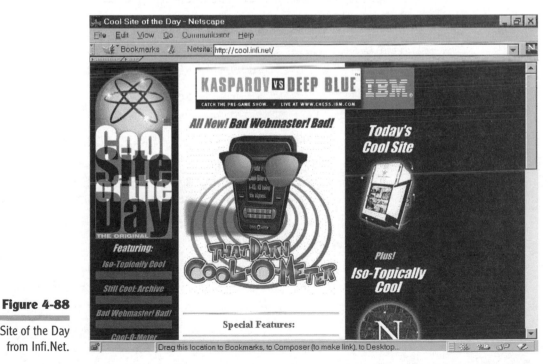

Figure 4-88

Cool Site of the Day from Infi.Net.

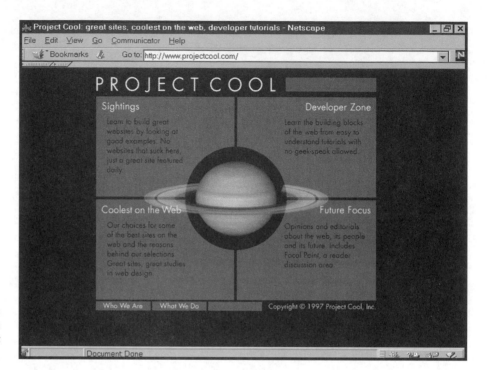

Figure 4-89

*Project Cool's
Sightings.*

You can get Cool Site Central's stamp of approval as the cool site of the day by visiting Cybermut's Cool Continuum (see Figure 4-90). You will find this site at:

http://www.coolsitecentral.com

Although Cybermut's Cool Continuum is not as polished as the previous award sites in this category, the site does a great job of presenting the awards and making an extensive list of past winners available. You can submit your site to Cybermut's Cool Continuum by sending e-mail to Submit@cool sitecentral.com or by using a submission form found at http://www.coolsitecentral.com/submit.htm.

Dr. Webster (http://www.drwebster.com) prescribes the latest cool sites every day with the Cool Web Site of the Day award. This site produced by 123Go has many extras that make the site a fun place to visit (see Figure 4-91).

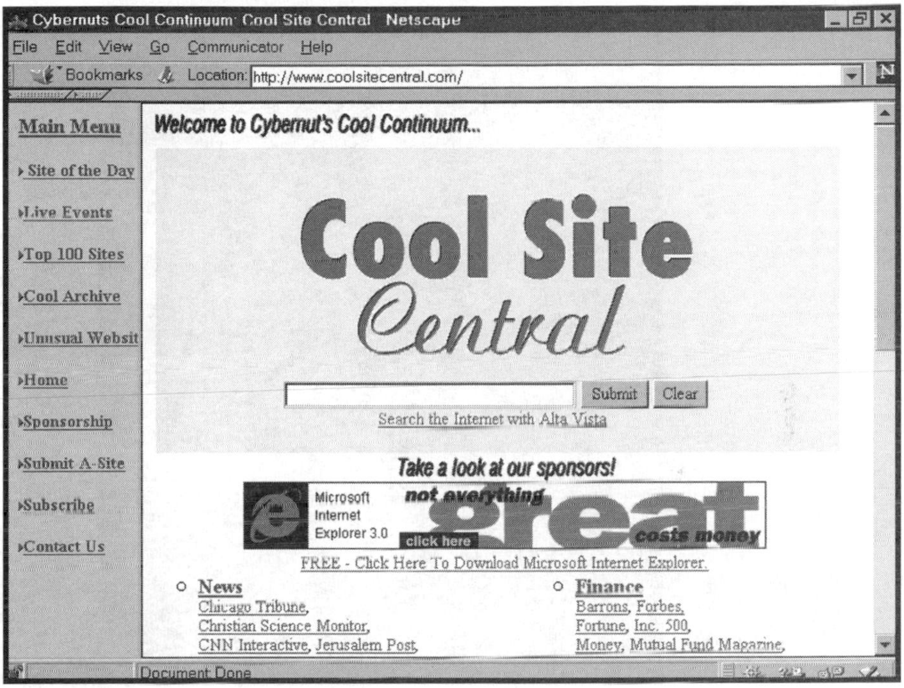

Figure 4-90

Cybermut's Cool Continuum Site of the Day.

Be sure to check out the X of the Day area, where you'll find links for items such as Letterman's list of the day and the Dilbert cartoon of the day.

The current cool site is featured in Dr. Webster's zany prescription of the day style. Afterward, the cool site of the day is moved to an archive that you can browse by month and day. To submit your Web site to Dr. Webster's Cool Web Site of the Day, visit the Dr. Webster home page and follow the Submit a Site link.

Hot Site of the Day

The words *hot site* imply as much as the words *cool site*, so it makes sense that there are Hot Site of the Day awards. When you round up all the entries in this category, you find that most aren't as polished as the sites that started the cool craze. Still, two awards sites stand out from the crowd. These sites are Cybersmith's Hot Site of the Day and HotSpots from *Windows Magazine*.

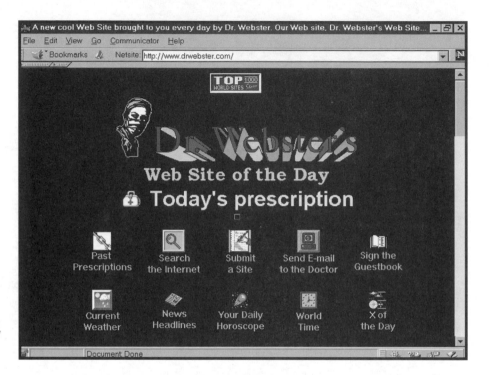

Figure 4-91

*Dr. Webster's Cool
Web Site of the Day.*

Cybersmith (http://magneto.cybersmith.com) is a chain of coffee houses for the wired generation. At the home page for Cybersmith's well-trafficked Web site, you will find links to lots of interesting areas within the site that promote the company and its stores. Cybersmith also publishes online features such as the Hot Site of the Day and CD-ROM Sizzlers, which is a list of the top multimedia CD-ROMs.

As shown in Figure 4-92, the current Hot Site of the Day is highlighted on the hot sites home page (http://magneto.cybersmith.com/hotsites/). You can access mini-reviews of the current week's hot sites or monthly archives of hot sites as well. You can submit your site to Cybersmith using a form found at:

http://magneto.cybersmith.com/hotsites/suggestsite.html

Windows Magazine (http://www.winmag.com) publishes a list of what it calls *hotspots*, with a new hotspot featured every day. Because of the tremendous popularity of *Windows Magazine*, the site and the HotSpots page

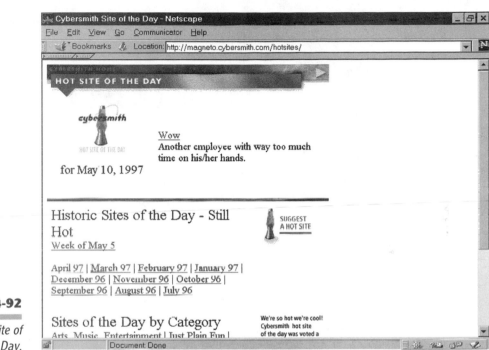

get lots of visitors, making the Windows Hotspot award something that will definitely increase traffic to your Web site (see Figure 4-93). To access the HotSpots page, visit the following address:

```
http://www.winmag.com/flanga/hotspots.htm
```

You can suggest your site to *Windows Magazine* by sending e-mail to `hotspots@langa.com` or follow the Suggest a New HotSpot link. Your message should contain the title, URL, and description of the page that you are submitting.

Wild, Crazy, and Zany Site Awards

Take a walk on the wild side with the wild, crazy, and zany site of the day awards. Although these types of awards are offshoots of the original Cool Site of the Day concept, this category has several terrific award sites.

FIND IT ▶
ONLINE

Too Cool (`http://www.toocool.com`) offers the Too Cool award. As shown in Figure 4-94, the featured site appears directly on the home page, accompanied by a graphic and a quick review. Although the graphics are what

Figure 4-93

Windows Magazine's
HotSpots.

make this site terrific, lists of all sites that have received the award are archived with and without graphics. In addition to the Too Cool award, you can also use the Leave-a-Link service, which allows you to submit a link to a category-specific directory maintained at the site.

You can submit your site for consideration for the Too Cool award by sending e-mail to `webmaster@toocool.com`. To add your link to the Leave-a-Link directory, use the submission form found at:

`http://toocool.com/guest/cool_add.htm`

Very Crazy Productions (`http://www.verycrazy.com`) offers an award for the craziest site of the week (see Figure 4-95). As the name implies, the award is for sites that are fun and wild. You can access the awards page directly at:

`http://www.verycrazy.com/crazysites/craziestsite.shtml`

Unlike other sites that simply archive lists of previous recipients, Very Crazy Productions adds an interesting twist by allowing visitors to tour the sites

Figure 4-94

Too Cool daily awards.

of previous recipients. The actual tour is handled by a script that randomly selects the first site on the tour. Then, using an innovative browsing interface at the bottom of the featured page, you can wander through other award-winning sites.

To submit your site to Very Crazy, use the submission page found at:

`http://www.verycrazy.com/crazysites/submitsite1.html`

Another interesting twist on the traditional cool site of the day is That's Useful, This Is Cool (`http://www.usefulcool.com`). As the name of the site implies, the folks at That's Useful, This Is Cool offer awards for useful sites and cool sites. In this way, if you have a great resource that isn't necessarily hip, cool, or zany, you can get a That's Useful site of the day award.

As shown in Figure 4-96, each site that receives an award is highlighted with a fairly extensive review. Snippits from the reviews are displayed in the weekly archives. You can submit a site for That's Useful by sending e-mail

Figure 4-95

Craziest Sites on the Planet daily awards.

to useful@usefulcool.com. You can submit a site for This Is Cool by sending e-mail to cool@usefulcool.com. Although submitting the same page for both awards is tempting, the developers of That's Useful, This Is Cool ask that you submit to one category only.

Site of the Week

Just as daily awards are popular, so are weekly awards. The great thing about weekly awards is that you get more up-front exposure, which in turn drives more traffic to your Web site over a longer period of time.

Cool Central (http://www.coolcentral.com) from Athenia Associates offers many different awards, including Cool Site of the Moment, Cool Site of the Hour, Cool Site of the Day, and Cool Site of the Week (see Figure 4-97). Although being recognized as cool site of the moment or hour is an ego booster, the awards aren't that great for building traffic; the site simply doesn't showcase the award recipients long enough. Cool Central's Site of

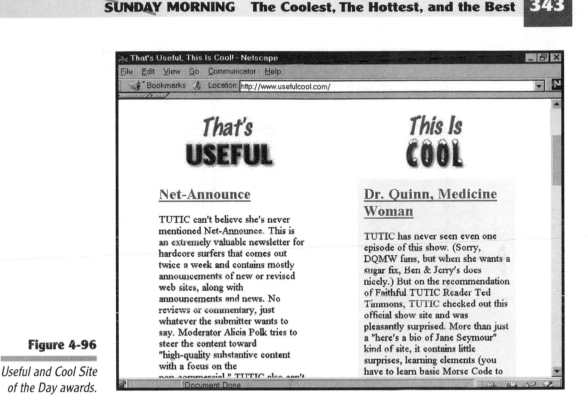

Figure 4-96

Useful and Cool Site of the Day awards.

the Day award, however, is great for increasing traffic, but the best award is the site of the week because it gets so much attention.

A terrific extra is the listings for runners-up as well as the award recipient in the site of the day and site of the week categories. Cool Central also maintains a comprehensive archive of listings for award winners. You can submit your site to Cool Central using a submission form found at:

http://www.coolcentral.com/suggest.cgi

Computer Currents Interactive (http://www.currents.net) recognizes outstanding sites by designating them as the link of the week. Unlike other sites that grant only a single award, the Link of the Week award usually goes to several sites that cover different topics, such as entertainment, sports, and humor (see Figure 4-98). With multiple awards being offered each week, you have a better chance of receiving an award. Lists of past winners are available in an archive that you can search by category.

You can submit your site to CCI by sending e-mail to mmc@compcurr.com.

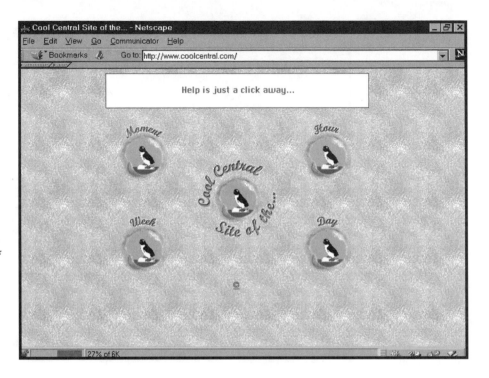

Figure 4-97

Cool Central's Site of the Week.

The URL for the awards page is at the following address:

`http://www.currents.net/resources/link/linkweek.html`

Another great award site is Yahoo!'s Weekly Picks (`http://www.yahoo.com/picks/`). Winners of the Yahoo! Weekly Pick award are showcased in a feature article that covers about a dozen different Web sites (see Figure 4-99). All the Weekly Pick columns are archived for easy browsing.

In addition to the weekly picks, Yahoo! has a daily pick award on its What's New? page (`http://www.yahoo.com/new/`). Unlike the weekly picks, daily picks are listed by title with a one-line summary. The daily picks are archived with the What's New? page.

You can submit a page to Yahoo!'s daily and weekly picks by sending e-mail to `suggest-picks@yahoo-inc.com`. Your message should contain the page title, page URL, and a description of the page that you are submitting.

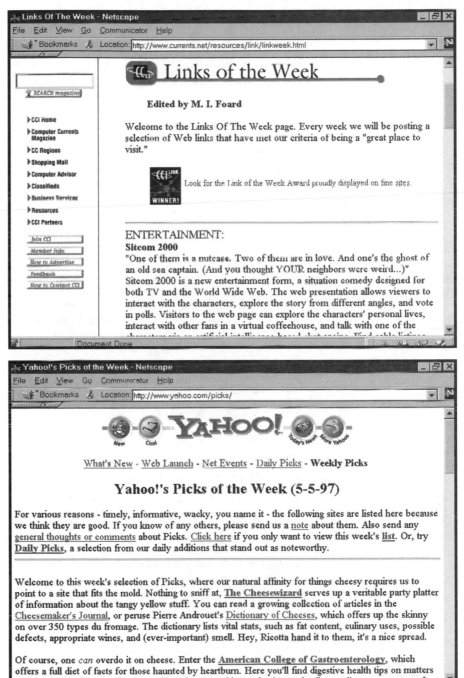

Links Of The Week - Netscape

Figure 4-98

Links of the Week from CCI.

Figure 4-99

Yahoo! Picks of the Week.

Best of the Web

Truly great sites are designated as the best of the Web. As I've discussed previously, many Web guides offer insights into the best sites on the Web. Here, you will find additional Web guides to check out and, of course, to submit your site.

CINet (`http://www.cnet.com`) is well known for its technology news and reviews. As a tremendously popular destination, CINet gets millions of visitors every week. It is this overwhelming flow of traffic that makes being recognized as CINet's Best of the Web so wonderful. The Best of the Web at CINet is featured in Figure 4-100. You can find reviews of the current week's winners at:

`http://www.cnet.com/Content/Reviews/Bestofweb/`

The reviews of previous weeks are archived so that you can search them alphabetically and by category. You can submit your site for possible review by CINet using the submission form found at:

`http://www.cnet.com/Content/Reviews/Bestofweb/feedback.html`

Before you can submit a site, you must become a member of CINet. Although membership is free, it will take you a few minutes to fill out the forms, which you can do at:

`http://registration.cnet.com/`

JumpCity (`http://www.jumpcity.com`) reviews the best sites on the Web (see Figure 4-101). Although the top pick of the week is showcased in the Features area, other areas such as Web Watch allow you to quickly find interesting sites. All reviews within JumpCity are indexed in the main database, allowing you to search by keyword and special category codes called *jump codes*.

Not only are the top Web sites featured online, but JumpCity selections are also featured in books such as *What's On the Web* and *What's On the Internet* published by Internet Media Corporation. You can submit your site to JumpCity using a submission form found at:

`http://www.jumpcity.com/send-page.html`

The Web 100 (`http://www.web100.com`) focuses on the top 100 Web sites (see Figure 4-102) Each site featured has a mini-review and is searchable by

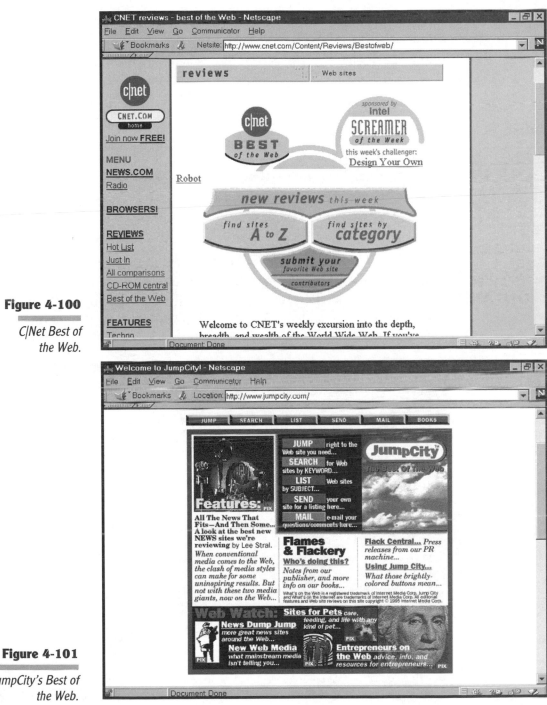

Figure 4-100

C|Net Best of the Web.

Figure 4-101

JumpCity's Best of the Web.

position within the list as well as by keyword and category. Sites selected in the Web 100 are voted onto the list by users. Because the visitor rating is interactive, the Web 100 is constantly changing, making it a great place to get listed.

You can submit your site to the Web 100 using the submission form found at:

```
http://www.web100.com/other/submit.html
```

The Web 500 (`http://www.web500.com`) ranks the top sites in more than 20 categories (see Figure 4-103). Although the top 10 sites in a category are ranked and reviewed, other sites listed in a category are displayed by title only. You can submit your site to the Web 500 by sending e-mail to `info@accelerated.com`. Your e-mail should contain the title, URL, and description of the page you are submitting.

FIND IT ▶
ONLINE

In an attempt to outdo the other top-of-the-Web sites, Web Side Story (`http://www.websidestory.com`) publishes a list called the World's Top 1000 Web pages. Unlike other top of the Web lists, the Top 1000 at Web

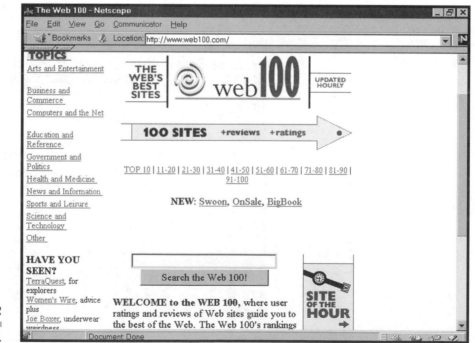

Figure 4-102

The Web 100.

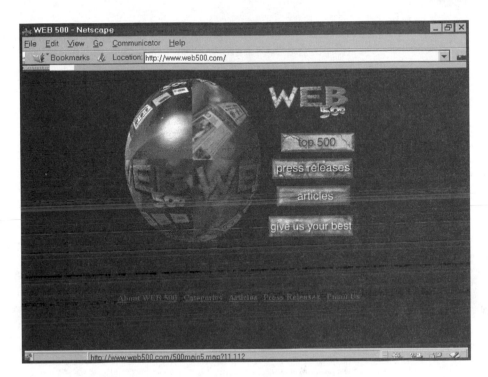

Figure 4-103

The Web 500.

Side Story is a list of the top 1,000 sites in each of more than 35 categories (see Figure 4-104). Although having a thousands sites in each category at your fingertips may seem overwhelming, Web Side Story has done a nice job of neatly organizing the listings.

The diversity of the Top 1000 gives Web publishers a chance to really get noticed. You can submit a listing to the Top 1000 by visiting the following address:

```
http://www.hitbox.com/wc/hitbox.html
```

Wrapping Up and Looking Ahead

Thousands of organizations are offering Web awards. Web awards range from daily awards, such as the Cool Site of the Day award, to yearly awards, such as *PC Magazine*'s Top 100. When you work your way through the maze of Web site awards, you find that there is a tremendous difference between Bubba's Site of the Day award and an award from a well-respected, well-trafficked Web site. At the start of the next section, you learn how to submit your site to many search engines and directories simultaneously. As always, the focus is on using resources that are cost free so that you don't have to spend a dime.

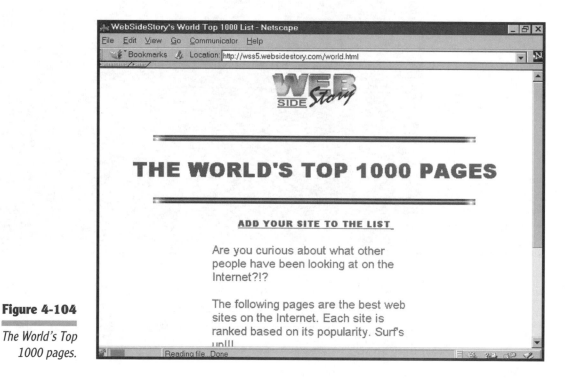

Figure 4-104

The World's Top 1000 pages.

Attracting the Masses

- ⚙ Registering with Lots of Search Engines and Lists Simultaneously
- ⚙ Selling Your Web Site through E-Mail
- ⚙ Attracting the Masses with Freebies, Reciprocal Links, and More
- ⚙ Cost-Free Banner Advertising: No Joke
- ⚙ Reviewing Your Progress and Planning More for Next Weekend

More than a dozen organizations offer services that allow you to register with multiple search engines and directories. These so-called registration services are great if you want to quickly spread the word about many different page URLs. You'll spend this afternoon learning about these and other valuable means of promoting your Web site.

After you've made your way through this afternoon's material, take a break—have some fun this evening. You've earned it. On the other hand, you might be enjoying some creative brainstorms so much, with all the resources at hand to apply them, that you'll want to keep at it for a while.

Registering with Many Search Engines and Directories Simultaneously

Just as search engines and directories have different submission processes, so do registration services. This part of the Sunday Afternoon section covers registration services: how they operate, what to watch out for, and how to use these services without paying a dime.

Introducing Web Registration Services

Registration services are one of the most innovative types of Web services to come along. The idea is that instead of having to register with search engines and directories one by one, you can use the registration service to register with many different search engines and directories. Although one central interface for registering your Web site is wonderful, you still have to go through a rather lengthy submission process.

Before you get started, I cannot stress enough how important it is to go through the submission process yourself first. When you work hands-on with a search engine or directory site, you get a clear idea of how the site works. When you work with a registration service, you rely on the service to take advantage of how a site works, which doesn't always happen.

Using Registration Services

The registration process usually starts with you entering information into a form. This information includes all the elements that you would normally enter into the submission form of a search engine or directory, such as the page title, page description, and personal contact information. Next, you select the search engines and directories to which you want to submit your site. Afterward, you begin the submission process, which almost always involves having to register each site separately by clicking on individual submission buttons that will send your information to a specific search engine or directory.

Because most search engines and directories use unique categories or require you to fill out other information, you usually enter this additional information during the submission process. Before you can submit your page to the Nerd World Internet directory, you need to select a category. Before you can submit your page to What's New on the Internet, you must select a category and state where the page is located. Before you can submit your page to Pronet, you have to enter state, country, and category information.

All these intermediate stops along the road mean that the registration process isn't as easy as the registration services would like you to believe. Still, the process is an improvement over manual submission if you are in a rush. Generally, it takes about 30 minutes to submit your site to 20–25 search engines and directories using a registration service, which shaves 10 to 15 minutes off the time that submitting your site manually would take.

Working with Registration Services

Like any service-oriented business, registration services are for-profit enterprises. You can't blame these services for trying to make a buck off their hard work. The cost of registering your site can run into hundreds of dollars, however, and most registration services base their charges on the number of URLs that you want to register and the number of places to which you submit your URLs. For example, a registration service may charge $30 to submit a single URL to 50 search engines, $60 to submit two URLs to 50 search engines, or $100 to submit one URL to 150 search engines.

Although these rates were much higher in the past, the influx of new registration services is forcing the market to be competitive, resulting in wholesale pricing and better registration engines. But before you shell out your hard-earned cash or corporate money, you should know what you are buying. Table 5-1 shows a sample of the search engines and directories most commonly used by registration services.

The first thing you may note when you examine the table is that you've probably never heard of most of these sites—well, some of them I had never heard of either. You should note that some of these sites are personal home pages with very little Web traffic at all. Some of these sites weren't even functioning, yet a few registration services claimed to have registered your site with these nonfunctioning search engines and directories nonetheless.

Additionally, you should note that many of the listings are for restricted types of search engines and directories. You will find Yellow Pages directories that take only business listings. You will find directories for Web sites covering specific geographic areas such as Canada, Europe, or Asia. You will also find specialty directories, such as What's New? directories, award sites, and guides to the best of the Web.

In the end, whether you can register with 50 or 500 search engines doesn't really matter. What matters is the number of search engines that you can use out of those available. With a cost of about $1 per search engine or directory registered, most Web publishers simply cannot afford to throw money away. Fortunately, the best sites are usually those included in the first 50 or so available. Because of this, you get more bang for your buck if you stick to the basics—and the ultimate in giving you your money's worth are the free services covered in the rest of the chapter.

TIP If you are truly gung-ho about going all out with your promotion efforts, I highly recommend that you stick with the freebies and register with any sites you may have missed on your own. To do this, use the URLs listed in Table 5-1.

TABLE 5-1	SAMPLE SEARCH ENGINES AND DIRECTORIES USED BY REGISTRATION SERVICES	
Site Name	**Site URL**
2ask Internet Directory	http://www.2ask.com
411Locate	http://www.411locate.com
555-1212.COM Yellow Pages	http://555-1212.com
A1 Free Directory	http://www.a1co.com
AAA Matilda	http://www.aaa.com.au
ABAWEB European Directory	http://www.abacom.com
AltaVista	http://www.altavista.digital.com
Apollo Search Engine	http://apollo.co.uk
ASOURCE Web Listings	http://www.asource.com
AT&T Business Bookmarks	http://www.bnet.att.com

TABLE 5-1 **SAMPLE SEARCH ENGINES AND DIRECTORIES USED BY REGISTRATION SERVICES** *(CONT.)*

Site Name	Site URL
BC-I Business Classifieds	http://www.bc-i.com
Beatrice's Web Guide	http://www.bguide.com
Been There, Done That	http://www.channel1.com/usbbs/
BigFoot Web Directory	http://www.bigfoot.com
BigYellow Business Directory	http://www.bigyellow.com
BizCom	http://www.bizcom.com
BizWeb	http://www.bizweb.com
BizWiz	http://www.clickit.com/bizwiz/bizwiz.htm
Buy It Online	http://www.buyit.com
Brian's Revised Internet Yellow Pages	http://www.mindport.net
CanVest Business Directory	http://www.canvest.com/canlink/
CERN registry of WWW Servers	http://www.w3.org
Clockwatchers' Classifieds	http://www.clockwatchers.com/classifieds
ComCom Commercial Search Engine	http://www.comcomsystems.com/s_page.html

TABLE 5-1   SAMPLE SEARCH ENGINES AND DIRECTORIES USED BY REGISTRATION SERVICES (CONT.)

Site Name	Site URL
ComFind Business Directory	http://www.comfind.com
Crest Internet Index	http://www.deltamedia.com/crest
Cyber Search Express	http://www.reynoldsenterprises.com
CyberNet Yellow Pages	http://www.wbm.ca
Darren's Free for All Links	http://sys.uea.ac.uk/Research/ResGroups/SIP/dmh/links.html
Delta Cool Sites	http://www.deltacool.com
DeltaDirect Business Directory	http://www.delta-design.com
DEWA Web Directory	http://www.dewa.com
EBORCOM New Page	http://www.eborcom.com
EINET Business Directory	http://lmc.einet.net
Excite	http://www.excite.com
Family Jewels Link Members	http://www.spectropolis.com/tfj/tfjlm/
Four11 White Pages	http://www.four11.com
Galaxy	http://galaxy.einet.net/galaxy.html

Table 5-1	Sample Search Engines and Directories Used by Registration Services (cont.)
Site Name	**Site URL**
Global Online Directory	http://www.god.co.uk
GTE Superpages Directory	http://superpages.gte.net
HotBot	http://www.hotbot.com
Housernet Web Listings	http://www.housernet.com
I-Explorer Directory	http://www.i-explorer.com
I-Guide Net Reviews	http://www.iguide.com
Infohiway Web Listings	http://www.infohiway.com
InfoSeek	http://www.infoseek.com
InfoSpace	http://www.infospace.com
Interactive Yellow Pages	http://www.netcenter.com/yellows.html
Int'l Small Business Consortium	http://www.isbc.com
Internic Net Happenings	http://www.mid.net/NET/
IntIndex	http://www.silverplatter.com
iWORLD Web Pointers	http://webpointer.iworld.com
Jayde On-line	http://www.jayde.com

TABLE 5-1	SAMPLE SEARCH ENGINES AND DIRECTORIES USED BY REGISTRATION SERVICES *(CONT.)*
Site Name	**Site URL**
LexiConn Business Directory	http://www.lexiconn.com/dir/
LinkCentre	http://www.linkcentre.com
LinkMonster	http://www.linkmonster.com
LinkStar	http://www.linkstar.com
LookSmart	http://www.looksmart.com
Lycos	http://www.lycos.com
Mallpark Internet Mall	http://www.mallpark.com
Mamma Search Engine	http://www.mamma.com
Manufacturers' Information Net	http://www.mfginfo.com
MARCO's Worldmap of Homepages	http://www.xs4all.nl
Media Online Yellow Pages	http://www.webcom.com
Mega International	http://www.netway.net
Metroscope	http://www.metroscope.com
Microsoft Library	http://library.microsoft.com
Movie BBS, Inc. Web Listings	http://www.moviebbs.com

TABLE 5-1	SAMPLE SEARCH ENGINES AND DIRECTORIES USED BY REGISTRATION SERVICES *(CONT.)*
Site Name	**Site URL**
Myanmar Free For All Links	http://www.myanmar.com
NedSite's Free Links	http://www.nedsite.nl
Nerd World Internet Directory	http://www.nerdworld.com
Nerve Centre, Canada Listings	http://www.nervecentre.com
Net Mall	http://www.netmall.com
NetSearch	http://www.ais.net
New Rider's WWW Yellow Pages	http://www.wwwyp.com
NewPageList	http://www.web-star.com
NYNEX Interactive Yellow Pages	http://www.niyp.com
One World Plaza	http://www.owplaza.com
On'Village Web Listings	http://www.onvillage.com
Open Market	http://index.openmarket.net
Orientation, Asia's Web Directory	http://www.orientation.com
Paparazzi Web Listings	http://www.measoft.com
Pathways Internet Directory	http://www.host1.com

TABLE 5-1	SAMPLE SEARCH ENGINES AND DIRECTORIES USED BY REGISTRATION SERVICES (CONT.)
Site Name	**Site URL**
Peekaboo Web Listings	http://www.peekaboo.net
Pronet Business Directory	http://www.pronett.com
Recyclinx	http://www.amsmain.com
Rex's List of Web Businesses	http://rex.skyline.net
Shaun's Free Links Page	http://www.mugc.cc.monarch.edu.au/ ~shaund/h/links.html
Starting Point What's New	http://www.stpt.com
Thousand Points of Sites	http://inls.ucsd.edu
Totem Pole Web Listings	http://www.totempole.com
TrekNet Internet Directory	http://www.treknet.net
URL Centrifuge	http://www.keytech.com/~weavers/ centrifuge.shtml
Web 100	http://www.web100.com
WebArrivals New Sites	http://www.webarrivals.com
Webcrawler	http://www.webcrawler.com
WebDirect!	http://www.wdirect.com

TABLE 5-1	SAMPLE SEARCH ENGINES AND DIRECTORIES USED BY REGISTRATION SERVICES *(CONT.)*

Site Name	Site URL
What's New On the Internet	http://www.emap.com/whatsnew/
What's New Too	http://newtoo.manifest.com
What-U-Seek search engine	http://www.whatuseek.com
Who Where	http://www.whowhere.com
World Wide Web Worm	http://wwww.cs.colorado.edu/wwww/
World Wide Yellow Pages	http://www.yellow.com
Yahoo	http://www.yahoo.com
Yellow Pages Online	http://www.ypo.com
Yellow Net World-Wide Pages	http://www.yellownet.com
Yellow Web Business Directory	http://www.yellowwweb.com
Yellow Web Europe	http://www.yweb.com

The most important thing to consider when you use registration services is the type of site with which you are registering. As you learned in previous chapters, there is a huge difference between a search engine and a Web directory.

Search engines use the single URL that you specify to crawl through your entire site and will usually schedule your site for periodic re-indexing. Because search engines re-index your site, you need to register with a search engine only once. Because search engines crawl through your entire site, the only URL that you need to register with a search engine is the URL to your top-level home page.

On the other hand, Web directories create a listing only for the page that you specify, and rarely update the listing in the future. Because Web directories focus on pages rather than entire sites, you can register multiple URLs for the same site. The URLs that you submit should be for separate areas that cover different topics, however.

Because Web directories rarely update listings, you are responsible for updating your listing in the directory if you move the furniture around at your Web site, which doesn't necessarily mean that you should re-register with the directory. Instead, you should check the directory to see whether it has an update or change process. To make life easier on yourself and avoid having to submit changes for your listings, you can use the redirection techniques discussed in the Saturday Morning section under "Gaining Lost Readers from the Error Logs."

In the end, if you use a registration service, don't waste your time re-registering with search engines and directories that you've already used. Concentrate on the search engines and directories with which you haven't registered yet. Online, you will find the registration service listings at:

```
http://www.tvpress.com/promote/reg.htm
```

Using Submit-It! to Register with Multiple Search Engines

FIND IT ▶
ONLINE

Submit-It! (`http://www.submit-it.com`) is the original Web registration service. Although Submit-It! got its start by offering freebies, the service today is largely a commercial for-profit operation. A software version of Submit-It is even available for your PC. Regardless of whether you purchase the Submit-It! software or use the service on the Web, you will pay a premium for each URL you submit.

An alternative to the Submit-It! premium service is Submit-It! Free (`http://free.submit-it.com`), which is produced by the same folks who created the original Submit-It! site. The main page for Submit-It! Free is shown in Figure 5-1. Using Submit-It! Free, you can submit your site to 20 different search engines and directories without spending a dime. The key difference between the paid service and the free service is simply the number of different search engines and directories sites to which you can submit your Web site.

At the time of this writing, the 20 free search engines and directories included:

AAA Matilda	Pronet
Alta Vista	Starting Point
Apollo	The Web Magazine
Bizwiz	Starting Point
ComFind	WebCrawler
Infoseek	WebDirect!
InfoSpace	What's New on the Internet
LinkStar	What's New Too
Mallpark	Yellow Pages Online
Nerd World Media	

Preparing for the Submission Process at Submit-It! Free

Before you can submit your site using Submit-It! Free, you need to select the search engines and directories with which you want to register. By default, all of the search engines and directories are selected (see Figure 5-2). If you have a business-oriented Web site, you will probably want to use all of these selections. If you have a personal home page or nonbusiness Web site, you will probably want to deselect the business-only listings, which include the following: BizWiz, ComFind, LinkStar, Pronet, Yellow Pages Online, and WebDirect.

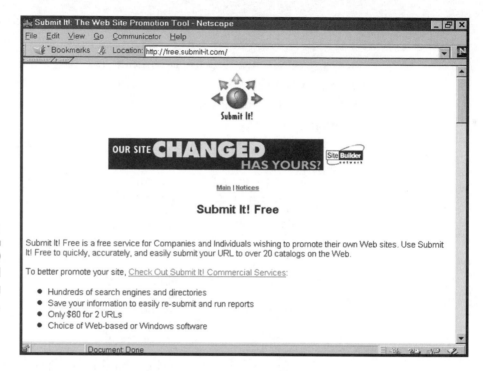

Figure 5-1

Register with 20
search engines and
directories using
Submit-It! Free.

Note also that four of the listings are primarily announcement directories.
These directories include the following: AAA Matilda, Starting Point, What's
New on the Internet, and What's New Too.

Figures 5-3 and 5-4 show the remaining fields in the submission form.
Although you may want to skip the fields for personal and business information, keep in mind that some directories, especially business directories,
will not place your listing without this information.

As when you are registering your site directly, the most important fields are
the ones that describe your Web page. Use the techniques discussed in
previous chapters to select your page title, keywords, and page description.

Submit-It suggests limits on the length of your descriptive information.
These limits are based on the least common denominator, such as a site
that allows your descriptions to have only 255 or fewer characters. Although you can get away with adding more than the suggested limit, you
may have problems when you try to submit your site. You may also find
that the information is simply truncated when necessary.

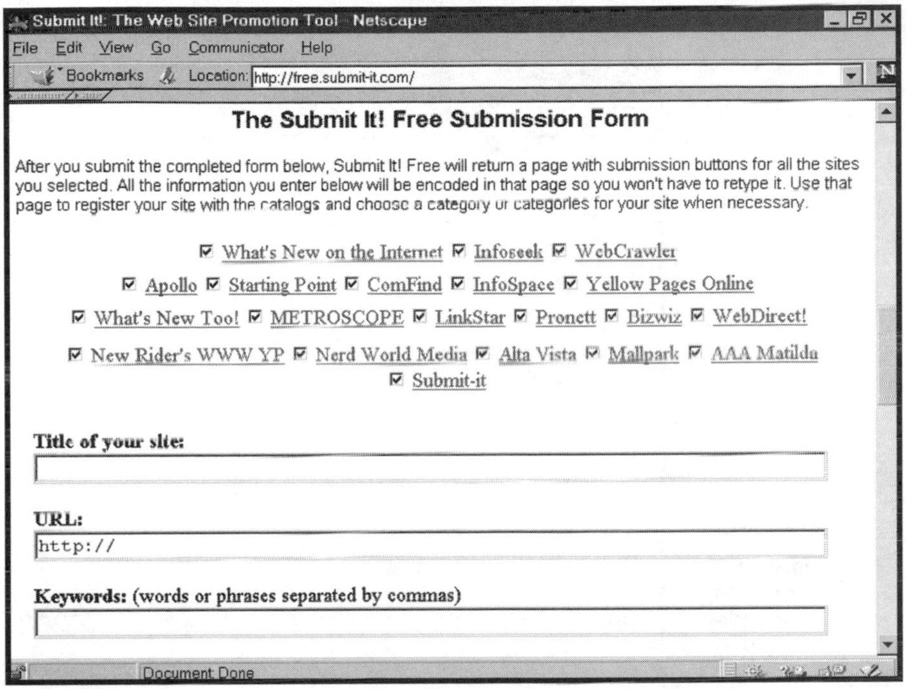

Figure 5-2

Starting the submission process.

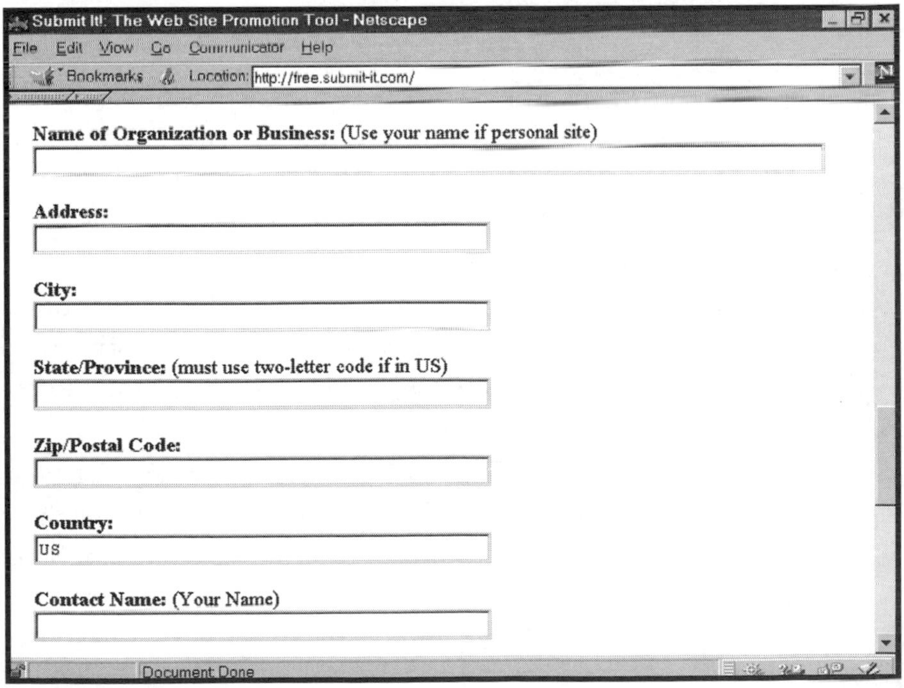

Figure 5-3

Filling out contact information.

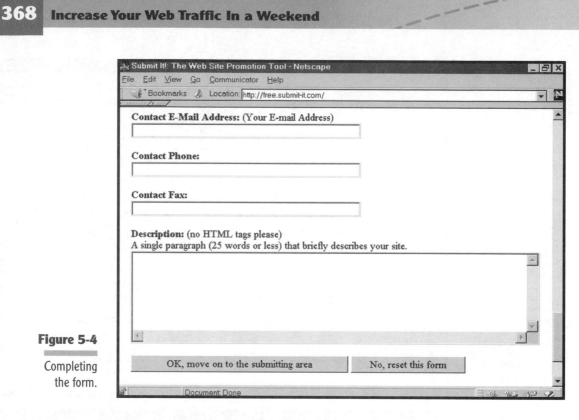

Figure 5-4

Completing
the form.

Registering Your Site

After you fill out and submit the form, Submit-It! Free will load a page that allows you to verify your submission and register your site with the selected search engines and directories. All the information that you entered in the form is stored in hidden fields in the registration page.

If you find a mistake when you are verifying the data, you can use your browser's Back button to return to the fill-out form. When you change the fields containing errors, resubmit the form by clicking on the submission button. When you are satisfied with the information, start the registration process.

As shown in Figure 5-5, the registration page has submission buttons for each search engine and directory that you selected. If no other information is required for registration, you just click on the submission button. Doing so takes you to the search site, where you will usually see a page that confirms your registration. Some sites require you to verify the registration, which adds a few extra steps.

Each time you submit your site, you need to use your browser's Back button to return to the registration page. Doing so enables you to continue through the registration process.

As you know, most directories require you to fill in additional information, such as a category or the location for your Web site. In this case, you have to fill in this additional information before you can register your Web site with the directory. As shown in Figure 5-6, Submit-It puts these fields directly in the registration page, which makes the registration process go smoothly.

After you submit your site to all the search engines and directories that you selected, you're done. If you have additional sites or pages to register, you can go back to the original submission form and start again.

Working with Addme!

FIND IT ▶
ONLINE
Addme! (http://www.addme.com) offers a comprehensive registration service. Unlike most other registration services, the developers of Addme! are

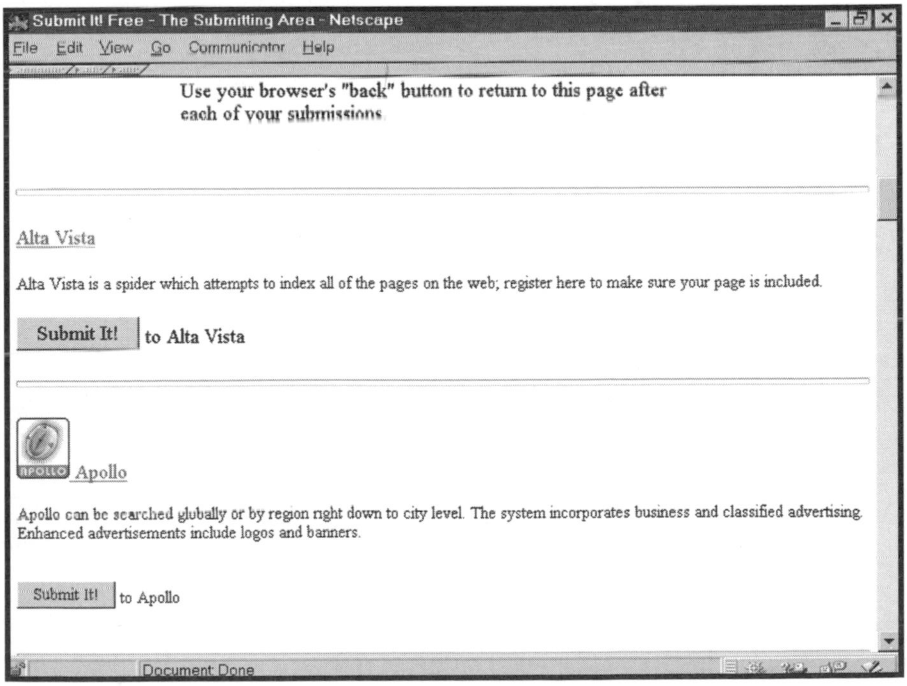

Figure 5-5

Submitting your site to search engines and directories.

hoping that advertising dollars will supplement their service and continue to allow them to provide the service without charge. The home page for Addme! is shown in Figure 5-7.

Using Addme!, you can submit your site to 34 different search engines and directories without spending a dime. At the time of this writing, these search engines and directories included:

411 Locate	Matilda
555-1212	New Rider's Yellow Pages
Alta Vista Search	ON'VILLAGE
Apollo	Open Text
Bigfoot	Peekaboo
Excite	Pronet
Four11	ProsperNet
Global Online Directory	REX
HotBot	Starting Point
InfoSeek	USA Online
InfoSpace	WebArrivals
Jayde Online	What's New
LinkMonster	What's New Too
LinkStar	What-U-Seek
LookSmart	WhoWhere?
Lycos	WWW Worm
Magellan	Yahoo!

Preparing for the Submission Process at Addme!

Before you can submit your site using Addme!, you need to fill out the listing information shown in Figure 5-8. Although Addme! doesn't suggest size limits for the descriptive fields, keep in mind that limits do apply in

Figure 5-7

Register with more
than 30 search
engines and
directories using
Addme! Free.

most cases. As stated previously, if you submit a field with too many characters, you may have problems when you try to submit your site. The information in the offending field may also be truncated.

Starting the Submission Process

After you fill out and submit the listing information, Addme! loads a page that allows you to verify your submission. If you find a mistake, you can use your browser's Back button to return to the listing information page. When you change the fields containing errors, resubmit the form by clicking on the submission button. When you are satisfied with the information, you can click on the Next button to continue with the registration process.

Rather than put all the entries on a single page, Addme! breaks the submission process down into a series of pages that allow you to register with one or more search sites. When no other information is required for registration, you see a page like the one shown in Figure 5-9. Here, you need only click on each submission button. This takes you to the search site where

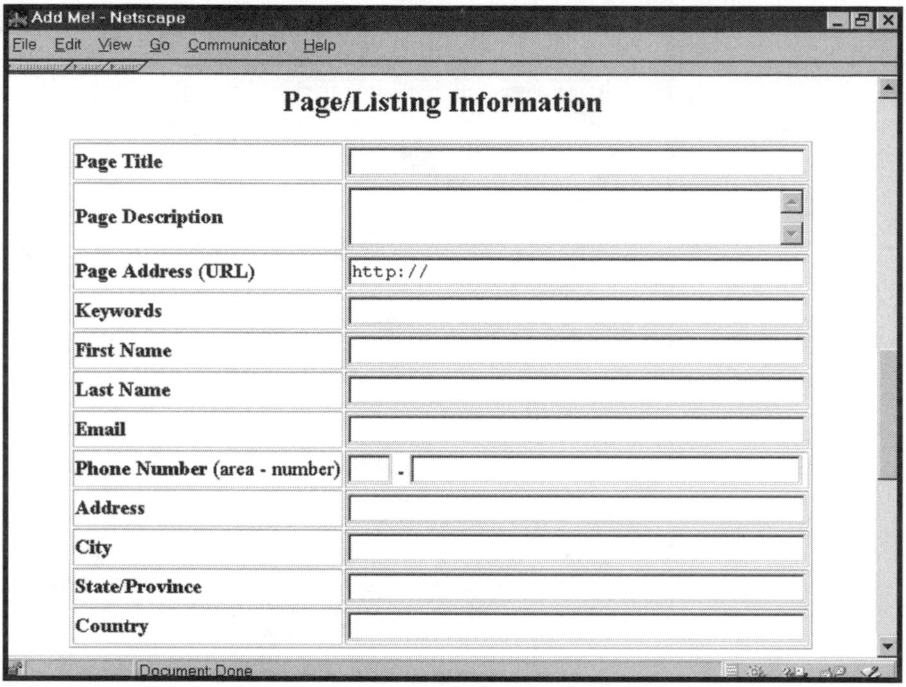

<image name="Netscape browser window">
Add Me! - Netscape

File Edit View Go Communicator Help

Page/Listing Information

Page Title	
Page Description	
Page Address (URL)	http://
Keywords	
First Name	
Last Name	
Email	
Phone Number (area - number)	[ ] - [ ]
Address	
City	
State/Province	
Country	

Document: Done
</image>

Figure 5-8

Filling out contact
information.

you usually see a page that confirms your registration. If the search site requires you to verify the registration, you may have to go through a few extra steps before you can register your site.

Keep in mind that many of the search engines and directories in Addme! have a very specific focus. For this reason, you probably don't want to submit your site to every single one of the available sites. Instead, pick the sites that make sense.

Out of the 34 sites, six focus on business listings. These are as follows: 555-1212.Com, LinkStar, New Rider's Yellow Pages, USA Online, REX, and Pronet. Three sites are White Pages listings. These sites are the following: 411Locate, Four11, and WhoWhere. Five of the sites are primarily announcement sites, as follows: AAA Matilda, Starting Point, WebArrivals, What's New on the Internet, and What's New Too.

Each time that you submit your site, you need to use your browser's Back button to return to the Addme! Web site. After you've submitted your site

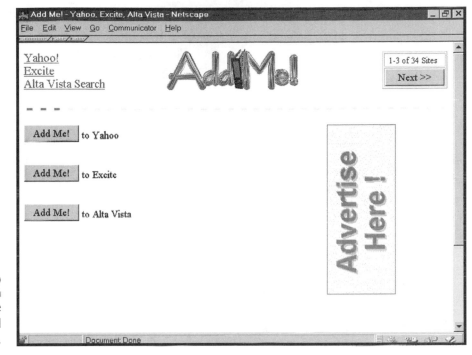

Figure 5-9

Submitting your site to directories and search engines.

to the desired search engines on a particular page, use the Next button at the top of the page to continue through the registration process.

The individual pages within Addme! make customizing the registration process easier for each search engine, which is one of the strong points of this service. Figure 5-10 shows a page that lets you add detailed information when you register with LinkStar. Figure 5-11 shows a page that lets you set up an account with WhoWhere.

After you've moved through all the registration pages, you will see a final page confirming that you are finished with the submission process. If you have additional sites or pages that you want to register, you may want to use your browser's history list to go back to the first entry for Addme!, which contains the submission form that you filled out at the beginning of the registration process. Alternatively, you can simply reenter the URL to the Addme! Web site in your browser's Location field.

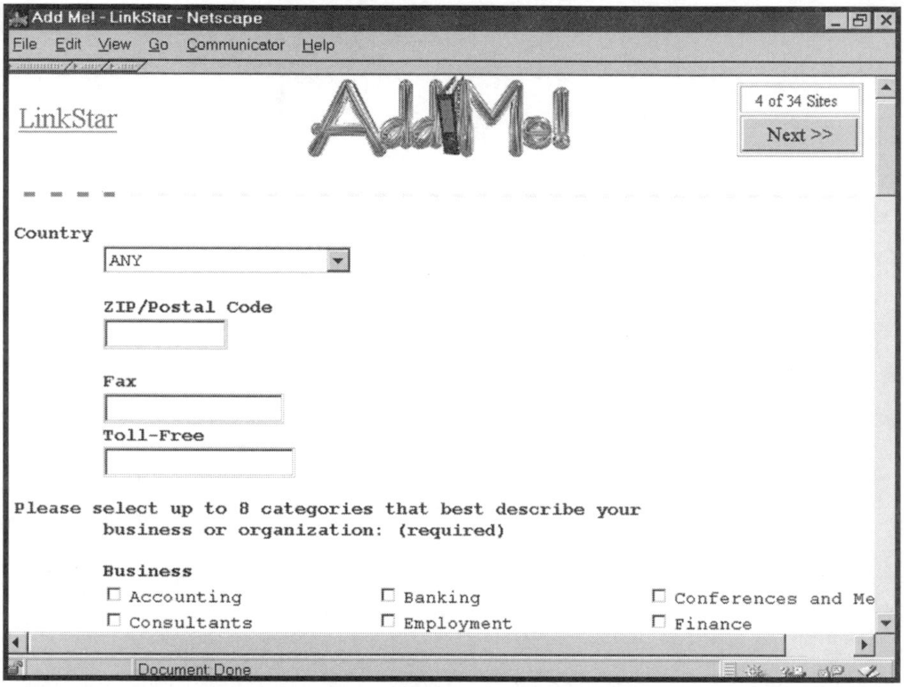

Figure 5-10

Supplying directory-specific information.

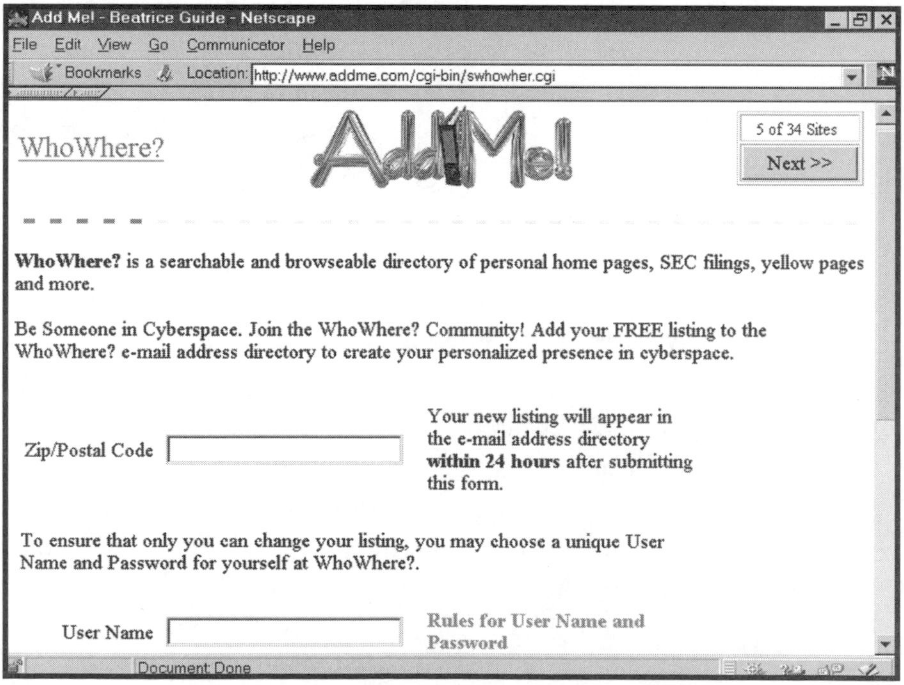

Figure 5-11

Creating an account for your Web site using the registration service.

Submitting Your Site with Register-It

FIND IT ▶
ONLINE

Register-It (http://www.register-it.com) is one of the premiere registration services. You can use Register-It to submit your site to search engines, directories, and awards sites (see Figure 5-12). Fees at Register-It are based on the number of URLs you want to register and the number of places you submit your URLs.

Fortunately, Register-It provides a free service that allows you to register with 17 different search engines and directories. At the time of this writing, these search engines and directories included:

Alta Vista	Starting Point
Excite	The Yellow Pages
Infoseek	TradeWave Galaxy
Infospace	Web411
Lycos	WebCrawler
Magellan	WhoWhere?
Northern Light	WWW Worm
Open Text	Yahoo!
	Yellow Pages Superhighway

Creating an Account at Register-It Free

A powerful feature of Register-It (see Figure 5-13) is the capability to create an account in the registration database. Because of this account-based system, most of the information that you enter is retained in the database, where you can retrieve it if you use the service to register your site at a later date.

To get started, follow the links to Register-It Free from the Register-It home page. Doing so takes you to an area where you can set up a new account or access an existing account. Although the e-mail address that you use for the account should be your actual e-mail address, the password should be unique to Register-It. After you enter an e-mail address and password, click on the Create New Account button to proceed with the registration process.

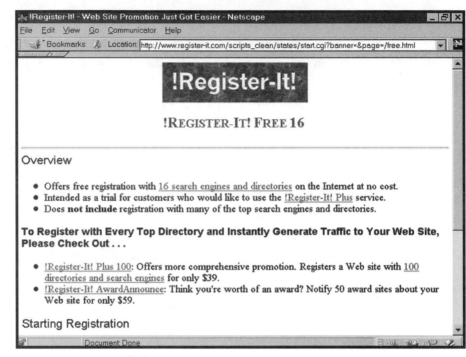

Figure 5-12

Submit your site to 17 search engines and directories using Register-It Free.

NOTE Although Register-It states in its home page that you can use the service to register with 16 search engines and directories, the actual number at the time of this writing was 17.

Next, you need to enter information for your account profile. As shown in Figure 5-14, most of the registration fields in the account profile pertain to your personal contact information.

The form also contains entries for account preferences. Unless you want to receive the Register-It Newsletter or other e-mail from the folks at Register-It, deselect the first two fields before you proceed.

The third account preference field allows you to withhold personal information from the sites with which you are registering. By default, your personal contact information is supplied to those sites that require or use it. If you don't want to give out personal information, change this preference to no.

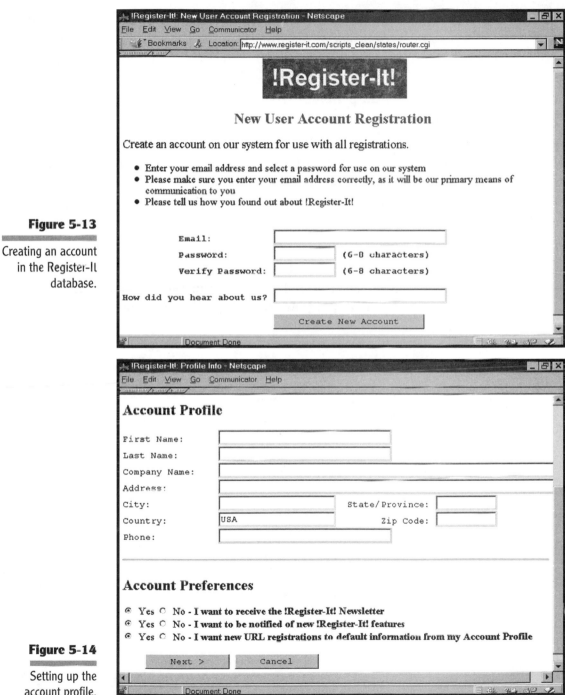

Figure 5-13

Creating an account in the Register-It database.

Figure 5-14

Setting up the account profile.

Afterward, you need to specify the URL that you want to promote and the Register-It service that you plan to use (see Figure 5-15). Be sure to note that by default, the premium service is selected. You need to deselect this manually and then select the free service. Otherwise, you will enter the paid premium service area and be asked to enter credit card information.

After you enter the URL that you want to promote, you need to enter information related to the URL. Register-It calls this Step 1 of the registration process (see Figure 5-16). Although the registration process usually has six distinct steps, the actual number of steps depends on the type and number of sites with which you register.

Each keyword field should contain a single word or phrase without punctuation. The keywords and description that you enter in this step can later be extracted to create a <META> tag for your page. To access the <META> tag generator, you need to complete the registration process and then log in to your account.

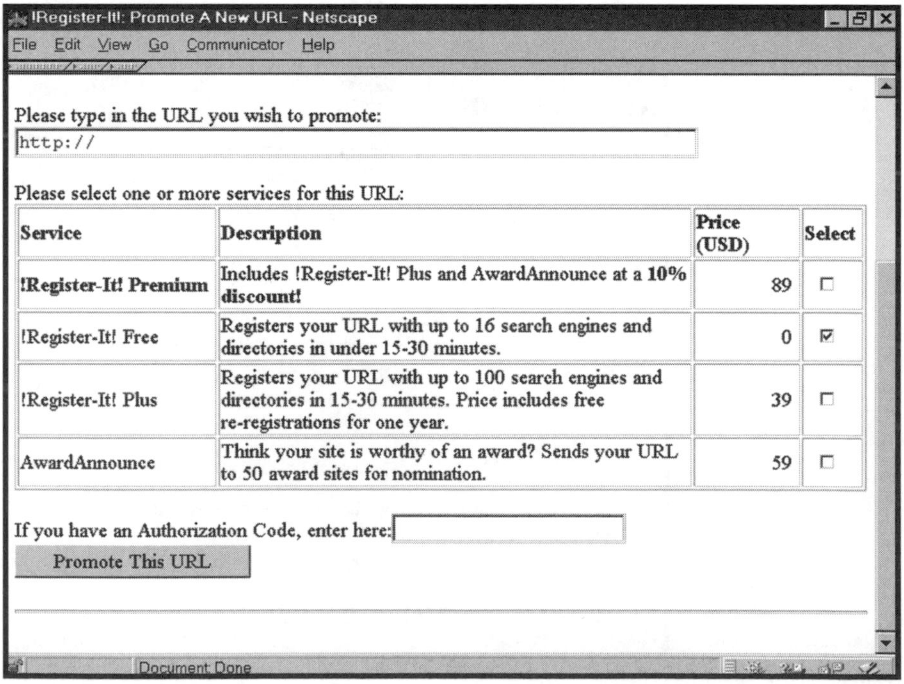

Figure 5-15

Selecting the service that you want to use and the URL that you want to promote.

Verifying the information is Step 2. When you submit the form, Register-It will load a page that allows you to verify the information. You can use your browser's Back button to return to the fill-out form if you find a mistake. After you correct the error, resubmit the form by clicking on the submission button. When you are satisfied with the information, you can go on to the next step.

In Step 3, you select the sites for registration. As shown in Figure 5-17, you do this by selecting the search engines and directories individually. By default, none of the sites is selected. A quick way to select all of the sites in a particular category is to click on the Select Category button. When you click on the Next button, Register-It will automatically register you with sites that don't require any additional information.

In Step 4, you provide additional information for each specific directory and search engine that requires it (see Figure 5-18). Register-It simplifies this process by placing all the necessary fields on a single page whenever possible. Clicking on the Next button automatically registers you with these sites.

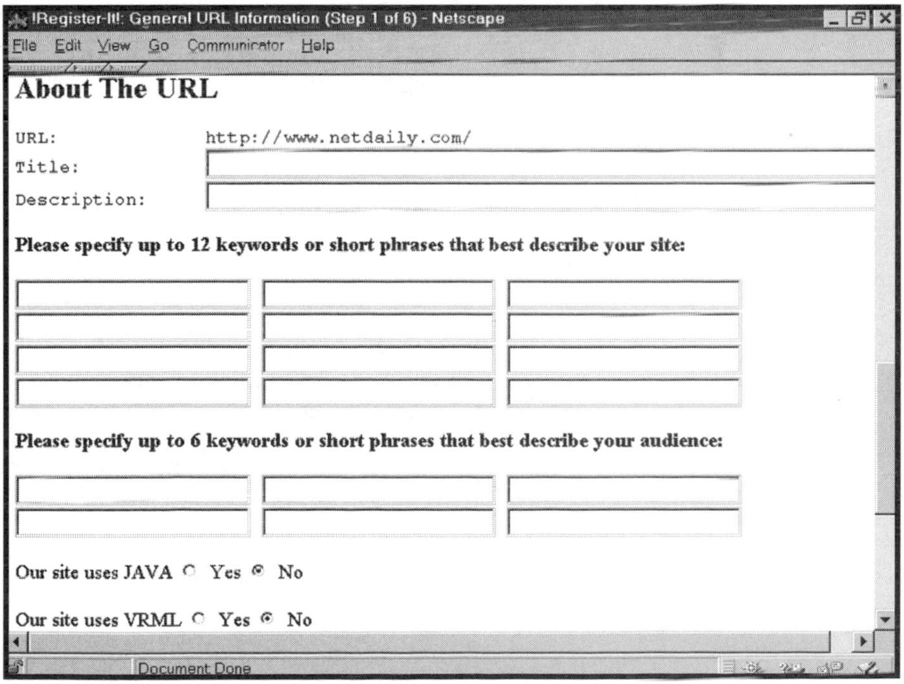

Figure 5-16

Describing the page.

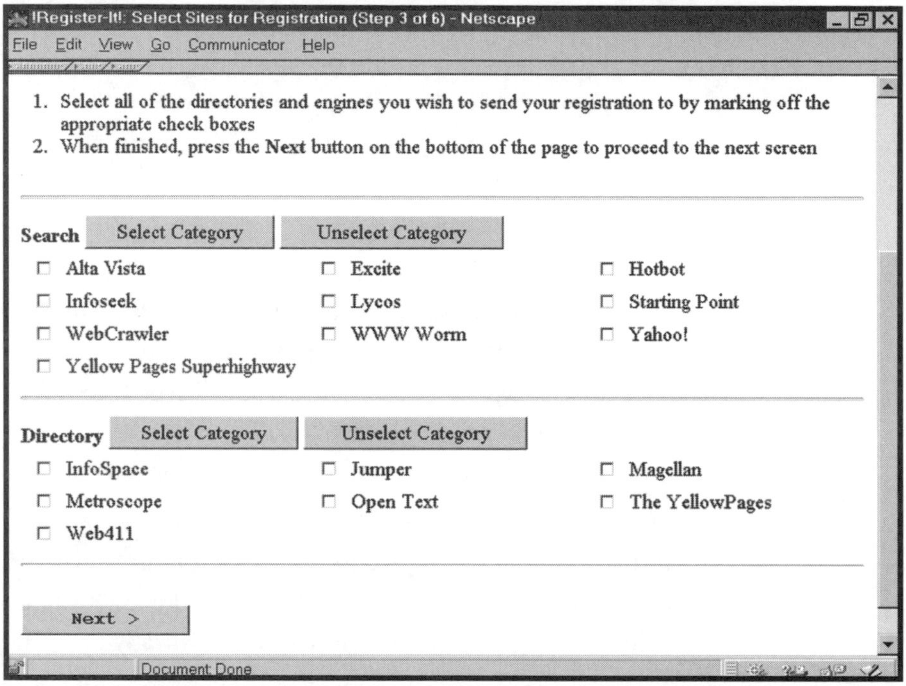

Figure 5-17

Selecting the search
engines and
directories that you
want to use.

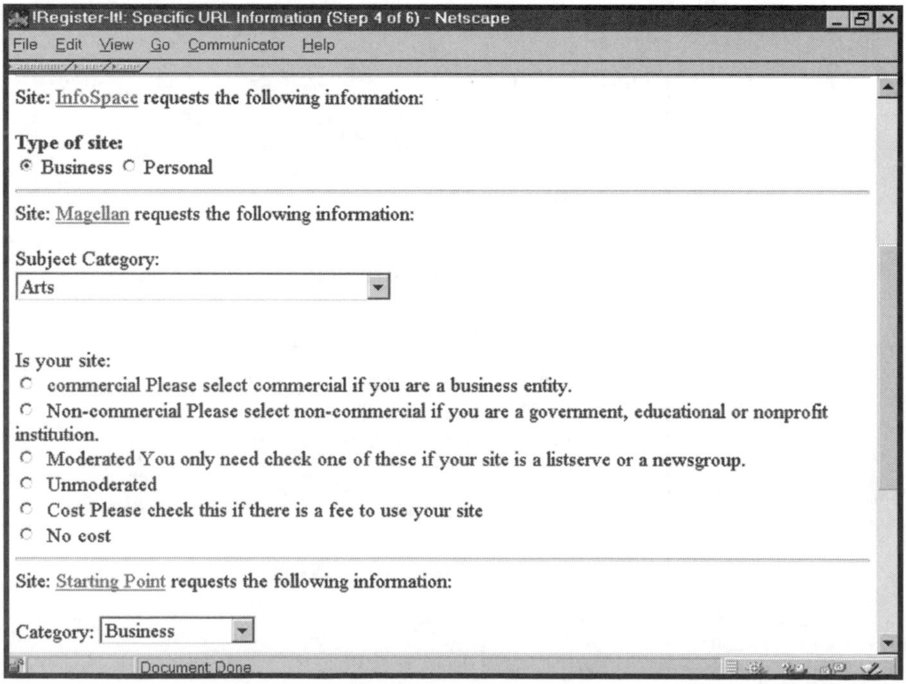

Figure 5-18

Supplying directory-
specific information.

Step 5 is for sites that require manual registration. As shown in Figure 5-19, Yahoo! is one of the sites that you will have to register manually. Clicking on the Next button takes you to each of the sites that requires manual registration.

The final step is simply a page verifying that the registration process is completed. From this page, you can send feedback to the developers of Register-It or register another URL.

Figure 5-19

Manually submitting sites.

Wrapping Up and Looking Ahead

Registration services are great for submitting your site to multiple search engines and directories. Although you could spend hundreds of dollars to register your site, the freebies are usually just what the doctor ordered. By using the free registration services, you can easily submit your site to 16, 20, or even 34 different directories and search engines. In the next chapter, I show you how you can promote your Web site through e-mail.

Selling Your Web Site through E-mail

Plain old e-mail is an extraordinary means of promoting your Web site. Every day, people send more messages by e-mail than by standard mail, and why not? Messages sent by e-mail are usually cost free. The millions of daily e-mail messages bounce around the globe in one of three forms: messages sent from person to person, messages posted to a newsgroup, and messages submitted to a mailing list.

In your promotion efforts, you can use all three ways of distributing e-mail to promote your Web site. Nothing will get you into hot water quicker than sending unsolicited or unwanted e-mail, however. To help you steer clear of the pitfalls of e-mail promotion and get the most out of your e-mail promotion efforts, this chapter shows you the right ways to sell your Web site through e-mail.

Web Site Promotion through Direct E-mail, Newsgroups, and Mailing Lists

Not only has e-mail been around since the earliest days of the Internet but also it is quickly becoming the most used electronic communication method. The widespread popularity of e-mail comes from the fact that it is so compulsively usable. Unlike standard mail, you can use e-mail to quickly and easily send the same message to hundreds, thousands, or even millions of recipients. Unlike the phone, you can send your message at any time of the day or night without fear of waking the recipient. Unlike the fax, you can send a message without having to worry whether the recipient has stocked the fax machine with paper or the fax line will be busy.

Just as most people don't want to receive calls from telemarketers, unsolicited faxes, or junk mail, most people don't want to receive unsolicited e-mail either. In the world of electronic mail, no four-letter word is more odious than *spam*. Spamming is the electronic equivalent of junk mail, and anytime you send unsolicited or unwanted messages, you are guilty of spamming. Sure, Web advertising agencies will try to sell you on the concept of bulk e-mail by telling you that the word *spam* applies only to unsolicited messages sent to multiple recipients, multiple discussion groups, or multiple mailing lists. In the end, however, an unsolicited message is an unsolicited message no matter whether it is sent to one or a thousand recipients.

As anyone who has ever sent unsolicited e-mail will tell you, the consequences can be severe. Your e-mail box may be bombarded with hate mail. Your Internet Service Provider may pull your account. You may even run into legal difficulties. Despite these potential pitfalls, people all over the world continue to spam the electronic byways. The reason is the tremendous value of being able to send messages to anyone, anywhere, at anytime.

Although you can certainly take the haphazard approach for Web site promotion through e-mail, there are ways to work within the system and current guidelines for newsgroups and mailing lists without rocking the boat. Working within the guidelines allows you to tap into the wonderful potential of e-mail, newsgroups, and mailing lists while minimizing the risk of backlash.

NOTE I say that you can work within the system while minimizing the risk because you can't please all of the people all of the time. The simple truth is that some people like to huff and puff. When you encounter someone who cries foul for no apparent reason, you should do one of two things: simply ignore the person, or send a brief apology and then move on.

The following offers a look at how you can effectively promote your Web site through direct communications, newsgroups, and mailing lists.

Promoting Your Web Site Directly

When you send a message to people using their e-mail address, you are using the most direct method of sending e-mail: person to person. As a rule, you should never send e-mail directly to anyone who doesn't want it. Instead, you should put together a promotional campaign that is responsive rather than proactive. This means that you ask visitors to your Web site and anyone else who contacts you whether they want to receive promotional material, rather than send the material to them unsolicited.

Sending Promotional Material

Promotional material that you send to subscribers can take many different forms. For a straightforward marketing approach, you can use advertisements and press releases pertaining to your organization as well as your products and services. You can also use an approach that focuses less on marketing and more on information. With this approach, you send subscribers information on what's new at the Web site, clips from recently published pages, or highlights of interesting places within the Web site.

The best way to invite participation is to add a subscription field to the HTML forms that are already at your Web site. In previous chapters, you saw that many forms used by search sites and directories have subscription fields. These fields ask whether you want to receive information or other promotional material by e-mail.

Subscription fields are often selected by default, which in itself isn't a bad thing, but some search sites go out of their way to ensure that most people who submit their forms join the subscription service. It is a deceptive practice to try to hide the subscription field or to blur the wording so that it isn't clear that the field is obscured.

Tips for Direct Mailings

To ensure that you receive subscriptions only from people who are truly interested in what you have to offer, place the subscription field so that it can be clearly seen, use clear wording, and deselect the field by default. Doing so makes subscribing an active process that requires a conscious effort from the reader.

If you use forms at your Web site to allow visitors to submit comments, sign a guest log, or enter any other type of data, consider adding a subscription field. The subscription field can be as simple as the Yes/No field shown in Figure 5-20. Here, the subscription field asks visitors whether they want to receive information on free promotions and contest updates. Some other subscription field descriptions that you may want to use include the following:

✪ Can we send you press releases related to our company?

✿ Would you like to receive advertisements and promotional material from our sponsors?

✿ Do you want to receive notification when this page is updated?

✿ Would you like to receive weekly updates on what's new at our Web site?

✿ Can we send you weekly highlights of interesting areas within our Web site?

Promoting Your Web Site through Newsgroups

Newsgroups are popular gathering places for people with common interests. When you send a message to a newsgroup, you are submitting the message to a discussion area where everyone who follows the newsgroup may see it. Newsgroups, like Web sites, cover just about every imaginable subject, and whether your Web site discusses cats or conspiracy theories, a newsgroup relating to your topic exists.

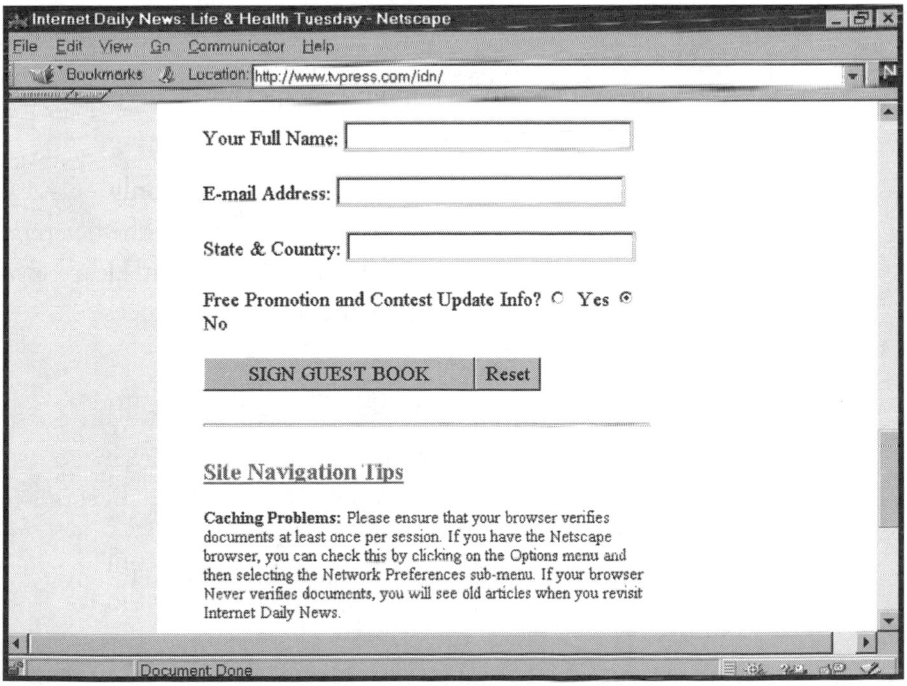

Figure 5-20

A subscription field used at Internet Daily News.

Finding Newsgroups That You Can Use to Promote Your Web Site

FIND IT ▶
ONLINE

With thousands of newsgroups available, trying to find newsgroups without a little help is very time consuming. Rather than browse newsgroups individually, you should visit a newsgroup archive site such as Deja News (see Figure 5-21). At Deja News (`http://www.dejanews.com`), you can search through millions of current postings to newsgroups by keyword. Click on the Interest Finder button. You can now use the search field provided to search by topic of interest.

If your Web site discussed cats, you could enter the keyword *cats* in the topics of interest search field. As shown in Figure 5-22, you would find many related newsgroups. By clicking on the newsgroup names, you could access recent postings to all newsgroups that discussed the topic, and doing so would turn up other newsgroups that discuss cats as well. Some of these newsgroups are as follows:

- ✿ rec.pets
- ✿ rec.pets.cats.announce
- ✿ rec.pets.cats.misc
- ✿ rec.pets.cats.rescue

Because all newsgroups follow a specific hierarchy, you can use the newsgroups that you've found so far to find other related newsgroups. To do this, visit the top-level hierarchy page at Deja News (see Figure 5-23). The URL for this page is the following:

`http://www.dejanews.com/info/toplevel.shtml`

From the top- level hierarchy page, you can browse from the broad category newsgroups at the top of the hierarchy to the narrowly focused newsgroups at the bottom of the hierarchy. Because most of the matches for the sample search are in the rec* newsgroup hierarchy, click on the keyword rec to see next level within this hierarchy.

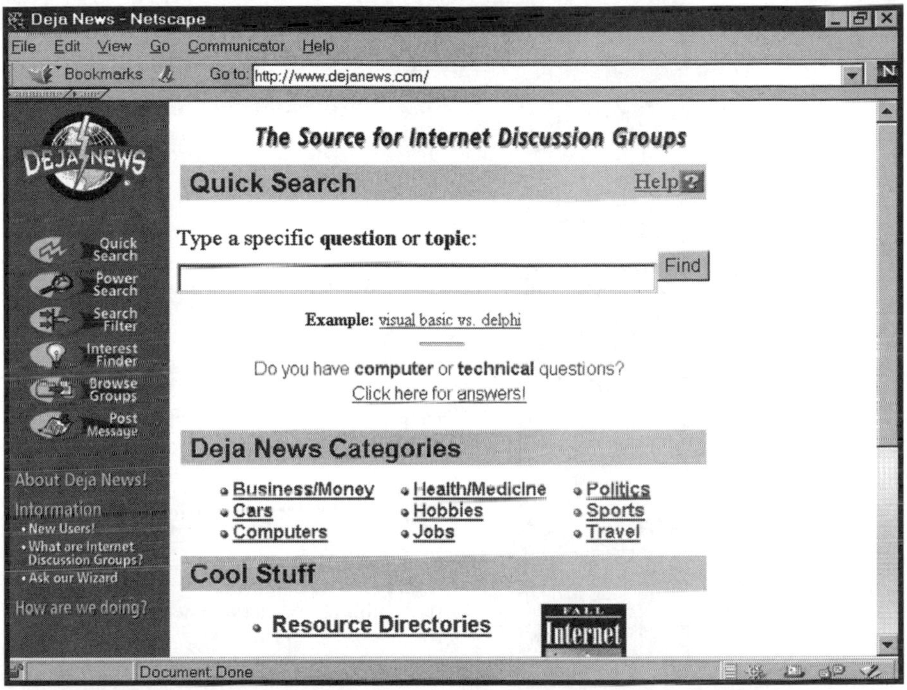

Figure 5-21

Finding newsgroups
at Deja News.

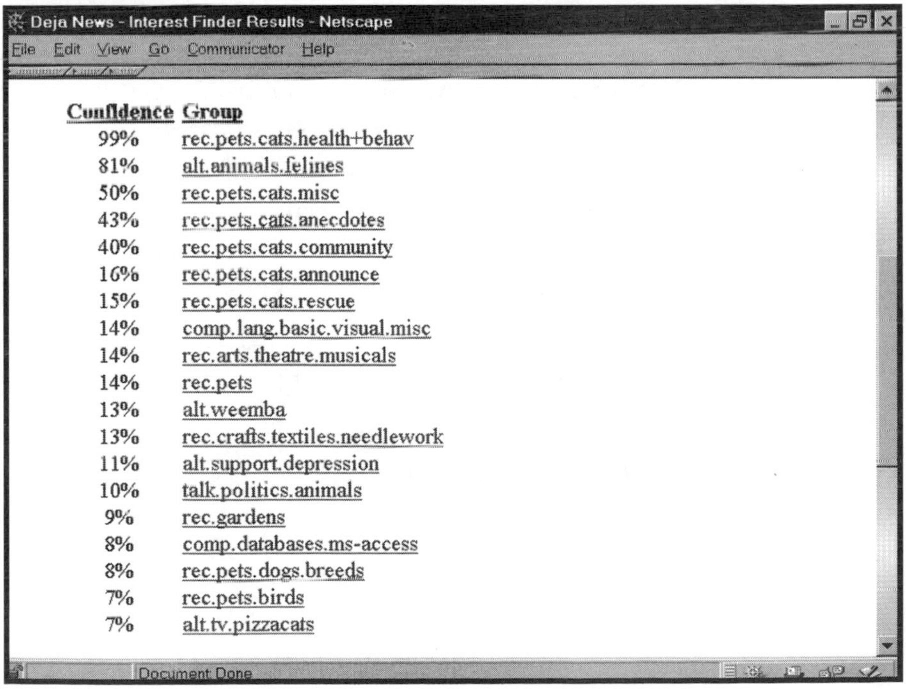

Figure 5-22

Matching topics
to specific
newsgroups.

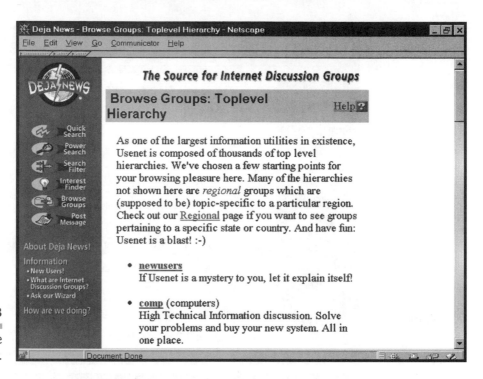

Figure 5-23

Browsing the
newsgroup hierarchy.

When you move down the page showing the second level of the rec*
newsgroup hierarchy, you will find that rec.pets has four branches. To get to
the branch for rec.pets.cats, you need to select the keywords in the last column. On the next level of the hierarchy, you find that rec.pets.cats has six
branches. You can see these branches by selecting the keywords in the last
column. By following this branch, you find that there are no more branches,
meaning that you've finally reached the lowest level within this hierarchy.

Write down all the newsgroups that you've found on the search through
the newsgroup hierarchy. For this search, the list of possible newsgroups
has grown to include:

rec.pets

  rec.pets.cats

    rec.pets.cats.anecdotes

    rec.pets.cats.announce

    rec.pets.cats.community

rec.pets.cats.health

rec.pets.cats.misc

rec.pets.cats.rescue

Now that you've reached the final level of the current newsgroup hierarchy, you can repeat the process to search through other newsgroup hierarchies or other branches within the current hierarchy. For example, you could go back to the page for rec.pets and follow the branch for rec.pets.dogs, or you could go back to the top level page and follow the path for the alt* newsgroup hierarchy.

NOTE The alt* newsgroups make up an alternative hierarchy. To browse this and other nonmainstream hierarchies, use the search field at the bottom of the top-level page (http://www.dejanews.com/toplevel.html).

Posting Tips for Newsgroups

After you have compiled a list of all the newsgroups that may be of interest, you should familiarize yourself with the groups by reading some of the recent postings. Nothing enrages newsgroup participants more than a promotional message that doesn't relate to the topic at hand. Going a step further, some newsgroup participants loathe all advertisements. For this reason, you should:

- Spend some time getting to know the newsgroup
- Ensure that your promotional message strongly relates to the subject at hand
- Use a conversational style without a lot of hype
- Keep the promotional message short, a few paragraphs at most
- Post a message to a specific group one time and one time only; if people are interested, they'll respond

As with direct promotion to individual users, you may want to focus less on marketing and more on information. For example, if a newsgroup participant asks about feline pneumonia and you have a terrific article on this very subject at your Web site, you may want to reply with a message like this:

> Feline pneumonia is a serious illness that affects thousands of cats every year. Because my own cat nearly died from pneumonia, I put together an article detailing the symptoms that pet owners can look for and the treatments that my veterinarian discussed with me. You can find this article at: `http://www.pets.com/felines/pn.htm`.

Promoting Your Web Site through Mailing Lists

Mailing lists are similar to newsgroups but are organized in a different way. Whereas a message sent to a newsgroup goes to a central discussion area, mailing list messages go directly to all the people who have joined the list. Because of the way mailing lists work, you must subscribe to a list before you can participate in the list. After you subscribe to a list, you can read messages posted to the list and post your own messages.

The simple act of posting a message to a mailing list doesn't ensure that it will be sent to the list members. Many mailing lists have moderators who review messages before they are actually distributed to the list members. If the moderator finds an inappropriate message, the moderator may cut out parts of the message or remove the message entirely.

Finding Mailing Lists That You Can Use to Promote Your Web Site

You can find mailing lists by visiting one of the many mailing list archive or index sites. One of the best mailing list directories is Liszt (`http://www.liszt.com`). You can search through the directory using keywords, or browse lists by subject (see Figure 5-24).

When you search or browse through the mailing list directory, you will notice that mailing lists aren't organized into hierarchies. In place of hierarchies, mailing lists use a naming system based loosely on the topic of the list or the name of the organization sponsoring the list. If you browse the philosophy category at Liszt, you will find over a dozen mailing lists that cover this topic in various ways. The mailing list maintained by the American Philosophical Association is called APACIC-L. The mailing list maintained by the Society for Women in Philosophy is SWIP-L. Other philosophy-related mailing lists are devoted to the works of specific philosophers.

When you find a mailing list in Liszt, you will see a brief summary of the list as well as the information that you need to subscribe to the list (see Figure 5-25). Using the links provided, you can get additional subscription details and more information on the list.

Mailing lists are one of the most fluid resources on the Internet. Every day, dozens of new mailing lists are born and dozens of old mailing lists fade away into oblivion. Keeping up with this constant change is a chore made possible only with help from the list creators and moderators. Because of the constant changeover in mailing lists, I recommend that you check several different mailing list directories before making a decision about which you would like to participate in and possibly use to promote your Web site.

Another good guide to mailing lists is America Online's Internet Mailing

Figure 5-24

America Online's
Internet Mailing List

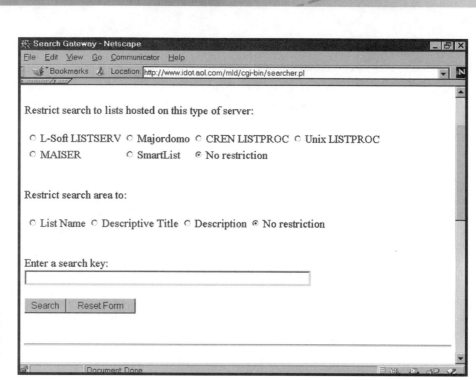

Figure 5-25

Exploring the philosophy category at Liszt.

List Directory (`http://ifrit.web.aol.com/mld/production/`). You can search the directory by keyword using the search engine interface shown in Figure 5-26. The URL for this page is the following:

FIND IT
ONLINE

`http://www.idot.aol.com.mld/cgi-bin/searcher.pl`

Although being able to search by keyword is useful, I found that looking for specific topics by browsing the subject index is easier. You can find the subject index at the following address:

`http://ifrit.web.aol.com/mld/production/mld-master-index.html`

Posting Tips for Mailing Lists

As with newsgroups, you should read some of the postings to a mailing list before you submit anything. With thousands of people on the receiving end of your promotional message, you have to be very careful about the marketing approach you use. Nothing will generate hate mail faster than a blatant advertisement posted to a mailing list.

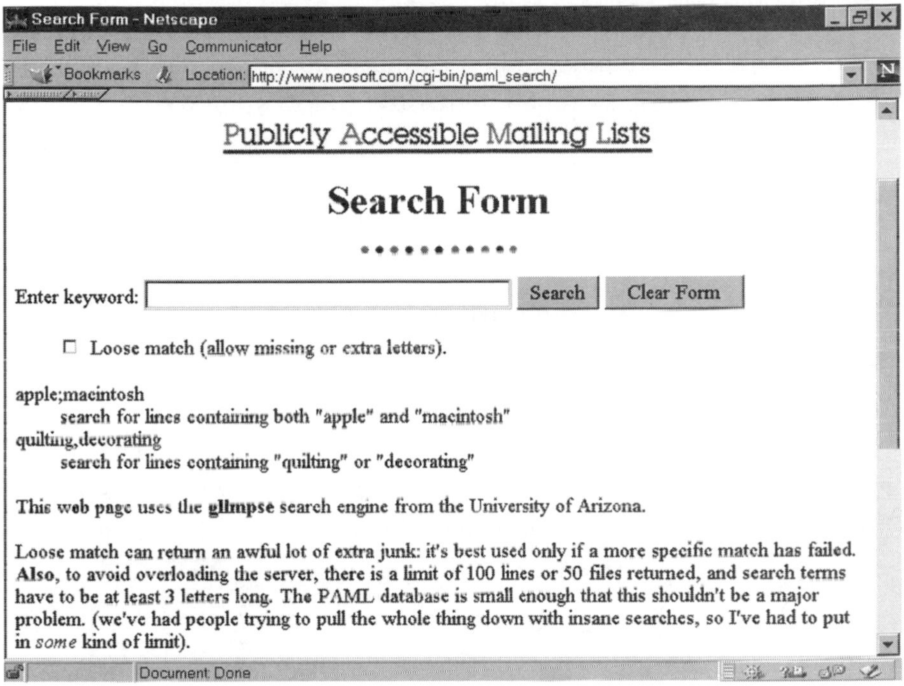

Figure 5-26

The Publicly
Accessible Mailing
Lists directory.

Rather than post an advertisement, you may want to focus more on information. Ideally, your posting will be helpful and useful to those who read it. For specific tips on creating your posting, refer back to the posting tips for newsgroups.

Just about every mailing list out there has a set of rules. Usually, these rules are outlined in a FAQ (Frequently Asked Questions) for the list. Definitely try to find and read the FAQ before you participate in a mailing list. To make it easier to know and follow the rules, most mailing lists send out a confirmation message after you subscribe. In this confirmation message, you will usually find a list of the rules and lots of other good information. Save this message; you may need it later.

Announcing Your Web Site, Products, and Services by E-Mail

Promoting your Web site through topical discussions is a terrific way to build traffic over the long term. Another way to build traffic is to announce your Web site, products, and services through e-mail. Although you can certainly announce your Web site in newsgroups and mailing lists that discuss topics similar to those at your Web site, you can use several additional avenues for making announcements. These avenues include:

- Using newsgroups and mailing lists specifically for announcements
- Using business-oriented newsgroups
- Using marketplace, commerce, and for sale newsgroups and mailing lists

FIND IT ▶
ONLINE

You can browse current postings to any of the newsgroups discussed in this section by visiting Deja News (`http://www.dejanews.com`). After you read some of the postings and are sure that the list is right for you, you can post your announcement. The key is to style your message in a way that is appropriate for the discussion group or mailing list.

When you make an announcement, you may want to organize your message like a press release that covers your Web site or the products and services that you discuss at your Web site. Ideally, your message will be only a few paragraphs long and fewer than 500 words. Brevity is important because most readers won't spend more than a few seconds glancing at your message.

You should work the URLs to your Web site or area within your Web site that you are promoting into the body of the message. Repeating an URL at the top and bottom of the message, or directing readers to different URLs within the Web site, is often a good idea. In this way, anyone scanning the message can zero in on the all-important URLs.

Announcement Newsgroups and Mailing Lists

Just as you can list your Web site in a What's New? directory, you can list your Web site in discussion groups and mailing lists that are devoted to Web announcements. Although most announcements groups and lists focus specifically on announcements for new Web sites, some discussion groups and lists focus on products and services.

Newsgroups that you can use to announce your Web site include:

```
comp.infosystems.www.announce

comp.internet.net-happenings

misc.news.internet.announce

pnet.www.announce

biz.infosystems.www

biz.infosystems.wwwannounce

misc.entrepeneurs
```

Mailing lists that you can use to announce your Web site include:

net-happenings	NET-HAPPENINGS-Request@ LISTS.INTERNIC.NET
Net-announce	nalist@erspros.com
Weekly Bookmark Plus	info@weeklyb.com

Newsgroups that you can use to announce software products related to specific operating systems include:

comp.os.linux.announce	comp.sys.newton.announce
comp.os.ms-windows.announce	comp.sys.next.announce
comp.os.netware.announce	comp.sys.sgi.announce
comp.os.os2.announce	comp.sys.sun.announce
comp.sys.amiga.announce	
comp.sys.atari.announce	
comp.sys.ibm.pc.games.announce	
comp.sys.mac.announce	
comp.sys.mac.games.announce	

Newsgroups that you can use to announce products and services include:

```
comp.newprod

eunet.newprod

fj.net.infosystems.announce
```

Newsgroups that cover specific Web-related products, such as browsers and servers, include:

```
comp.infosystems.www.authoring.html

comp.infosystems.www.authoring.images

comp.infosystems.www.authoring.misc

comp.infosystems.www.browsers.mac

comp.infosystems.www.browsers.misc

comp.infosystems.www.browsers.ms-windows

comp.infosystems.www.browsers.x

comp.infosystems.www.misc

comp.infosystems.www.servers.mac

comp.infosystems.www.servers.misc

comp.infosystems.www.servers.ms-windows

comp.infosystems.www.servers.unix

comp.os.os2.networking.www

alt.www.hotjava

alt.fan.mozilla

comp.infosystems.www.authoring.cgi
```

Business Newsgroups for Making Announcements

Anyone who has ever wondered whether a place exists where blatant advertising and capitalism rule the day need look no further than the biz.* newsgroup hierarchy. In the biz.* newsgroup hierarchy, you will find dozens of newsgroups devoted to announcements for products and services. Although many of the announcements in biz.* newsgroups are filled with hype, the most successful announcements are the ones that focus less on marketing and more on information.

The primary newsgroups in the biz* hierarchy that may be of interest in your promotion efforts include:

```
biz.americast
biz.books.technical
biz.comp
biz.comp.accounting
biz.comp.hardware
biz.comp.jobs
biz.comp.misc
biz.comp.services
biz.comp.software
biz.entrepreneurs
biz.generalbiz.market
   place.non-computer
biz.infosystems
biz.marketplace
biz.marketplace
```

```
biz.marketplace.computers
biz.marketplace.computers.discussion
biz.marketplace.computers.mac
biz.marketplace.computers.other
biz.marketplace.computers.pc-clone
biz.marketplace.computers.workstation
biz.marketplace.discussion
biz.marketplace.international
biz.marketplace.services
biz.marketplace.services.computer
biz.marketplace.services.computers
biz.marketplace.services.discussion
biz.marketplace.services.non-computer
biz.misc
```

More Newsgroups and Mailing Lists for Announcements

With thousands of discussion groups available, the listings in this chapter are only the tip of the iceberg. If you know what to look for, you can find dozens of other places to post announcements. Before you get started, though, keep in mind that I searched out the best of the bunch already— you know, that old legwork stuff designed to save you time and effort.

With newsgroups, you will find that searching the hierarchy listings for keywords is usually the best way to find what you are looking for. You can do this at Deja News by visiting the top-level hierarchy page for newsgroups (`http://www.dejanews.com/toplevel.html`) and using the group/hierarchy search field at the bottom of the page.

To find business-related newsgroups that may accept your announcements, the keywords you may want to use in your search include:

announce

biz

business

commerce

forsale

marketplace

www

For mailing lists, the directories at PAML or LISZT make searching by keyword easy. The reason for this is that the directories contain only the listings rather than the actual postings. To find mailing lists that may accept your announcements, the keywords that you may want to use in your search include:

announce

business

commerce

marketplace

Creative Signature File

An e-mail signature is an extra that you can add to the end of your e-mail messages. This trailer can help you promote your Web site as well as your products and services anytime that you send an e-mail message. Your signature can be styled as a mini-promotion for your Web site or anything else that you want to highlight.

Although you may see e-mail signatures that run 10–20 lines, most signatures are fewer than 5 lines. As a rule of thumb, 3–5 lines is usually a good length for an e-mail signature. Because your e-mail signature will go out with all your mail unless you delete the signature, keeping the signature free of hype is a good idea.

A sample of actual e-mail signatures that I've used in the past is shown in Listing 5-1. This should give you an idea of how you can create a signature that is effective yet doesn't look like an advertisement.

Listing 5-1   Sample E-Mail Signatures

```
—

William R. Stanek
Editor in-Chief, Internet Daily News — http://
  www.netdaily.com/
Author of several tech books — http://www.tvpress.com/writing/
—

William R. Stanek
Executive Director, Virtual Press Global Internet Solutions
  (www.tvpress.com)
Providing global solutions to the Internet community since
  March, 1994

Tune in to Internet Daily News — http://www.netdaily.com/


—

William R. Stanek
Founder & Director of Virtual Press Global Internet Solutions
  (www.tvpress.com)
```

```
Looking for something new? Why not visit: the Writer's Gallery
(www.tvpress.com/vpwg.html) or the Internet Job Center
   (www.tvpress.com/jobs/)
```

Most e-mail applications allow you to create a signature file using an ordinary text file. After you create and save the signature file, you can use the standard features of your favorite e-mail application to add the e-mail signature to all your outgoing messages.

In Netscape Navigator 3, you add an e-mail signature as follows:

1. Select Options, Mail and News Preferences.

2. Click on the Identity Tab. You will find that the signature file is the last field in this tab.

3. In the signature file field, enter the file path to the signature file or use the browse button to help you find the file.

In Netscape Navigator 4, you add an e-mail signature as follows:

1. Select Edit, Preferences.

2. Double-click on the Mail & Groups category.

3. When you select the identity subcategory, you will find that the signature file is the next-to-last field in this tab. Enter the file path to the signature file or use the browse button to help you find the file.

Wrapping Up and Looking Ahead

E-mail is a great way to promote your Web site. Although your promotion efforts can be directed at specific individuals, newsgroups and mailing lists help you reach large groups of people with similar interests. Whenever you post messages to newsgroups and mailing lists, be sure that you follow the rules and that your message makes sense for the topic of the discussion. Your e-mail promotion campaign can also include a simple signature file that is included in all your e-mail correspondence. In this part, you used the signature file to help get your Web site noticed. The next part explores ways to attract the masses using freebies, reciprocal links, and more.

Attracting the Masses with Giveaways, Contests, Sweepstakes, and More

Traditional marketers have used giveaways, contests, and sweepstakes for years to make their sponsors stand out from the crowd. The simple truth is that we all love the chance to win something for nothing, and whenever we have the opportunity to enter a contest or giveaway, we usually go for the gusto. Web advertisers have pushed traditional giveaways and contests onto the World Wide Web, where the quest for freebies can truly bring the masses to the sponsor's Web site.

Can't Get 'Em Any Other Way, Give It Away

Giving things away is a great way to build traffic to your Web site. Whether you want to pass out bumper stickers or trips to Europe, people will want to enter your giveaway. Beyond outright giveaways are contests and sweepstakes that ask the participants to answer questions or enter a creative work, such as a poem or jingle for a commercial.

Giveaways, contests, and sweepstakes promoted on the Web are often direct tie-ins to similar promotions running in print media. If your organization is already planning a giveaway or contest, advertising it on the Web can bring your message to an eager audience of millions.

Figure 5-27 shows a sweepstakes for the television show "Hercules: The Legendary Journeys." The sweepstakes was promoted on three different episodes of the TV show. Contestants were asked to watch each episode and answer a sweepstakes question related to the episode. The grand prize was a free trip to Universal Studios Florida.

Promotional tie-ins between your Web site and a giveaway or contest running in the print media work well if you have the clout of a major corporation behind you. But even if you are not part of a major corporation, you can benefit tremendously from running a contest or sweepstakes at your Web site.

The Fictech for novelists Web site runs a monthly sweepstakes that gives away best-selling works of fiction (see Figure 5-28). To enter the Bestseller Sweepstakes at Fictech, you just fill out a questionnaire. The questionnaire

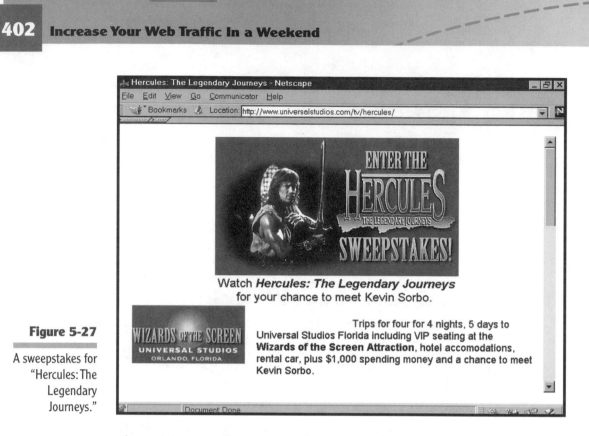

Figure 5-27

A sweepstakes for
"Hercules: The
Legendary
Journeys."

asks aspiring novelists a series of questions about their reading and writing
habits. In this way, Fictech gets more bang for its buck. The sweepstakes
not only attracts visitors but helps to build a database profile of the site's
audience.

Although many traditional promotional campaigns center around giveaways, contests, and sweepstakes, savvy marketers know that the interactive
and dynamic nature of the Web opens doors, removing the traditional
boundaries and restrictions of print media. On the Web, your giveaway
can become part of an interactive trivia quiz with questions that change
dynamically each time the page is visited. You can even create an interactive treasure hunt with clues scattered throughout your Web site.

The Web allows you to conduct other types of promotions as well, such as
online games that give something away to participants with the best scores.
With an online game, contestants get to have fun while trying to win prizes.
Online games can range from simple puzzles and teasers to actual video
games programmed in Java or another programming language.

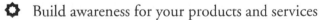

Figure 5-28

A sweepstakes at Fictech that gives away bestsellers.

Figure 5-29 shows the online games available at the Headbone Zone. Kids can not only play the games at Headbone Zone (http://www.headbone.com) but also win prizes by doing so.

Using a giveaway, contest, or sweepstakes to increase traffic to your Web site is a good idea, but definitely not the only reason to give things away. You can use the giveaway, contest, or sweepstakes to accomplish the following:

- Build awareness for your products and services

- Familiarize readers with other areas at your Web site

- Build a profile of your readers based on a survey or questionnaire that is part of the submission form

Later in this section, I examine each of the various types of giveaways and contests that you may want to use in your promotion efforts. These include:

- Free-for-all giveaways and sweepstakes

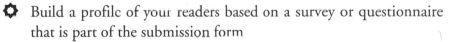

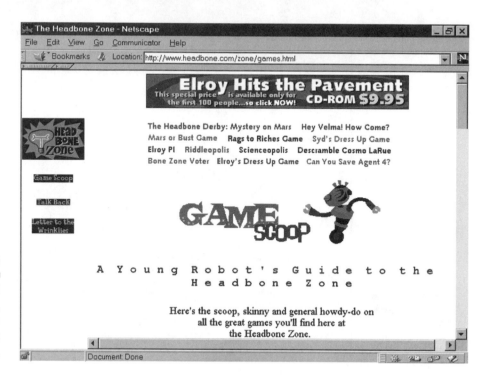

Figure 5-29

Online games at the Headbone Zone, where kids can play games and win prizes.

- Contests for artists, writers, and other creative people
- Trivia quizzes, games, puzzles, and teasers

Although giveaways and contests are great for increasing your traffic, the actual amount of traffic increase that you see at your Web site will depend on what you are giving away and how well you promote the giveaway. Keep in mind that the key to success isn't so much *what* you give away, but *how* you give it away. I call this your gimmick or hook. If your hook is great, your giveaway or contest will attract the masses. To help you promote your giveaway or contest, I guide you to Web sites that specialize in freebies, giveaways, and contests. After all, people need to be able to find your giveaway or contest in order to participate.

What to Watch Out for: The Legalities

Although nothing builds traffic like a good giveaway or contest, there are many things you should consider before you get started. Your primary concern should be the legal ramifications of publishing your giveaway or contest on the Web.

By putting your contest on the Web, you make it available to participants throughout the world, which may make your contest subject to certain laws. Every country has its own laws, and these laws often vary by region within the country as well. For example, each state in the U.S. has its own rules regarding giveaways and contests.

Disclaimers for Age and Residency

Because of the extreme diversity of international laws, most organizations that run contests and giveaways restrict their promotions to specific countries. When you restrict your contest to a specific country or countries, you should post a clear disclaimer along with any contest information. The purpose of the disclaimer is to protect your interests and ensure that you don't accidentally violate the laws of another country.

If you've browsed Web sites that run contests or giveaways, you have probably seen a disclaimer that says "U.S. and Canadian residents only" or "U.S. residents only." By restricting a contest to the U.S. and Canada or the U.S. only, you limit your liability—which is always a good idea.

Another thing to consider is the age of the participants. Because many U.S. states require that participants in contests be at least 18, you should place an age restriction on the contest. You can blend the age restriction right into your original disclaimer, such as "U.S. and Canadian residents 18 and older only" or "U.S. residents 18 and older only." Granted, verifying a person's age over the Internet is difficult; however, clearly marking the age restriction can only serve your best interest.

Other Disclaimers

Generally, within the U.S. and Canada, your sweepstakes or giveaway should be free, meaning that you shouldn't require entrants to purchase something in order to enter and win. In this way, your sweepstakes or giveaway is truly giving something away for nothing. You should post a clear disclaimer at the contest site that notifies readers that no purchase is necessary to enter the contest. An exception is a creative contest, such as an art contest or writing contest that charges an entry fee.

You should also publish a statement to ensure that participants know that local laws apply to the contest and that the contest is void where prohibited. Voiding the contest where prohibited protects you from inadvertently violating the local laws.

Putting the Rules Together

Now that you have made a start on the rules for your contest or giveaway, you should put these rules together in an official form that you can publish on your Web site. In the official rules, you should spell out exactly what you will be giving away and the value of the prizes. If you will be giving away one Sony 19" TV valued at $399, specify this exactly.

After you've decided on the rules for your contest or giveaway, you should publish these for all the world to see. Ideally, you will place a summary of the rules on all the contest pages and make the detailed rules available with a hypertext link.

Listing 5-2 shows an example set of rules for a fictitious contest called the Happy Peacock Sweepstakes. As you read the listing, keep in mind that this is a made-up example that serves only to illustrate some of the points made in this section.

Listing 5-2   An Example Set of Contest Rules

```
Rules for the Happy Peacock Sweepstakes

1. No purchase necessary in order to enter.

2. To enter the sweepstakes, fill out the official entry form
   at the Happy Peacock Web site. We accept only fully com-
   pleted entry forms. Only one entry per person is allowed.

3. Sweepstakes begins January 1, 1998 and ends on December
   31, 1998. Your entry must be received no later than mid-
   night on December 31, 1998. Winners will be selected in a
   random drawing.
```

4. Sweepstakes is open to residents of the United States who are eighteen years of age or older. All submissions become the property of Happy Peacock.

   All federal, state, and local laws and regulations apply. Any taxes due are the responsibility of the winner. Void where prohibited or restricted by law.

5. One first-place prize: Happy Peacock gift set, valued at $299. Ten second-place prizes: Happy Peacock T-shirt, valued at $25. Twenty third- place prizes:

   Happy Peacock coffee mug, valued at $9.

6. A list of prize winners will be published at the Happy Peacock Web site within 15 days after the end of the sweepstakes. Happy Peacock reserves the right to substi tute a prize of equal or greater value.

Before you publish your contest or distribute any information related to your contest, you should check applicable federal, state, and local laws regarding contests and giveaways. The best places to research global law are the Law Library of Congress (`http://lcweb2.loc.gov/glin/lawhome.html`) and the Guide to Law Online (`http://lcweb2.loc.gov/glin/worldlaw.html`).

Boosting Traffic with Giveaways and Sweepstakes

Giveaways and sweepstakes are great for boosting traffic to your Web site. Every day, thousands of people search the Web looking for the latest giveaways and sweepstakes—and why not? They can win hats, T-shirts, books, jewelry, trips, and much more simply by filling out a form. Although there is not much difference between a giveaway and a sweepstakes, the term *sweepstakes* is often used when prizes are donated by sponsors or advertisers.

Creating a Giveaway or Sweepstakes

When you put together a giveaway or sweepstakes, remember the prizes themselves are not what attract readers so much as it is your execution. As a matter of fact, you could give away T-shirts and get more visitors than a site giving away trips to Europe.

Although I'm sure the organization giving away trips to Europe would argue their case heatedly, the reality is that a well-designed and well-promoted giveaway will be successful regardless of the prizes. Well-designed giveaways and sweepstakes have a professional polish that makes them fun, easy to enter, and visually appealing. Well-promoted giveaways and sweepstakes are announced in all the right places, which includes key pages at your Web site and Web guides that promote freebies.

NOTE You learn all about Web guides that promote freebies shortly, under the heading "Sites That Promote Your Freebies."

The best giveaways and sweepstakes have a theme that helps sell people on the idea of the giveaway or sweepstakes. If you are giving away trips, it is not just a "trip," but a "passport to adventure." If you are giving away cruises, it is not just a cruise, but barefoot strolls along windswept beaches, romantic dinners for two, and quiet, moonlit evenings topside.

After you decide on the type of giveaway or sweepstakes to run, consider the prizes that you will award. As stated earlier, the prizes don't have to be extravagant but they should be worth the time and effort that entering the contest takes. Additionally, entering the giveaway or sweepstakes should be as easy as filling out an entry form that asks for contact information, such as name, address, and phone number.

You may also want to add a questionnaire or survey to the entry form. Questionnaires can help you learn more about the type of people who visit your Web site. You can find out whether they use your products and services. You can also learn about reader preferences, such as their favorite area within your Web site, or their interests.

Looking at an Actual Sweepstakes

A good case study for a well-designed and well-promoted sweepstakes is *PC Magazine*'s 15th Anniversary Sweepstakes, which was sponsored by Jeep and ended in June, 1997. On *PC Magazine*'s Web site, the sweepstakes area shows off the prizes in a highly graphical and attention-grabbing manner (see Figure 5-30). The sweepstakes not only builds traffic to *PC Magazine's* Web site but also shows off the products of the sponsor.

PC Magazine enhanced the main sweepstakes page with a trivia quiz that asks you questions about technology (see Figure 5-31). After trying your hand at the trivia quiz, you could check out the answers, which were posted right on the Web site. By combining the trivia quiz with the sweepstakes, *PC Magazine* gave visitors an extra reason to browse the area; meanwhile, the sponsor and the magazine were getting wonderful exposure.

The official sweepstakes entry form required participants to enter key contact information, such as their name, address, and phone number, but also featured an optional reader survey. The survey asked participants a series of questions that helped the magazine put together a fairly comprehensive reader profile.

Figure 5-30

PC Magazine's 15th
Anniversary
Sweepstakes

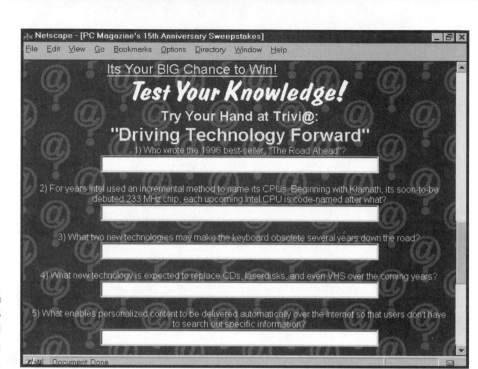

Figure 5-31

The sweepstakes
was enhanced
by adding a fun
trivia quiz.

Gaining Readers with Contests

Contests reward people for their talents or creativity. Because contests often require judging and extensive work on the part of the producer, some contests charge a nominal entry fee, such as $5 to enter a writing contest. Charging an entry fee for a writing contest that offers prestige, publication, and cash awards to the winners makes sense. Charging an entry fee for a contest that is meant more for fun than to be a career builder doesn't make sense.

Running a Contest

Contests can be just as much fun for you as they are for the participants. Your goal should be to use the contest to build traffic to your Web site. Ideally, your contest will tie in to and promote your business, products, and services as well. For example, developers of word processing applications may want to sponsor a write-off for the most creative or bizarre advertising gimmick for their product.

The type of contest that you run will depend largely on your interests. If you are interested in comedy, you may want to have a contest that rewards the funniest submissions. If you are interested in graphic design, you may want to have a design contest. If you love poetry, you may want to have a poetry contest.

To keep your contest as hassle free as possible, you will want to decide on the specific formats that are acceptable for submissions. For a writing or poetry contest, you may want to specify in the rules that all submissions must be saved as standard ASCII text files with the .txt extension. Similarly, for a design or art contest, you may want to specify that all submissions must be saved in either GIF or JPEG format.

Additionally, anytime that you ask for creative submission, you should set limits on the size or length of entries. For a writing contest, you may want to limit entries to 5,000 words. For a design contest, you may want to limit the size of the artwork to 1280 x 1024 with a file size of less than 2MB.

After you decide on the type of contest you want to run, you need to think about how you will judge the contest. Most small contests are judged exclusively by the contest developer. Creative contests, such as writing, art, or design contests, are usually voted on by a panel of judges. You can remove yourself from the judging process entirely by letting visitors to your Web site vote for the best submissions. The bottom line is that your judging process should be fair yet manageable using your current resources.

As with giveaways, you can use an entry form to accept submissions for the contest, and you may want to add a questionnaire to the entry form as well. Keep in mind that if you run a creative contest, many participants will have their entry in separate text or graphic files. Presently, the easiest way to submit files is as an attachment to an e-mail message. For this reason, you may simply want to supply an e-mail address for submissions rather than use an entry form.

With creative works, you must consider one more thing: U.S. and international copyright law. Creative works are the property of the creator unless the rights are granted or sold. Thus, if you plan to publish the winning works at your Web site, you need permission, and you should ask for this permission right in the entry form. The minimum rights that you will want to retain are one-time world electronic rights to the winning entries. Furthermore, you should state that winning entries will be published at your Web site.

Looking at an Actual Contest

An example of a contest that promotes a company's products is the Decorating Disaster Contest from Copper Canyon (see Figure 5-32). The words *decorating disaster* have a wonderful ring that describe the contest's theme. The idea behind the contest is to have participants describe their biggest decorating disaster and then reward the best entry by allowing them to choose any item they want from the company's catalog.

The folks at Copper Canyon kept the submission form simple. As you can see from Figure 5-33, the form has fields for basic contact information and then asks participants to write an essay of 75 words or fewer, describing

Figure 5-32

The Decorating Disaster Contest.

their decorating disaster. The entry form also has a field that lets participants subscribe to the company's mailing list.

When you consider that many people will use search engines or directories to find your contest, trying to build cross-traffic from your contest pages makes sense. As a reminder that the Copper Canyon site has more to offer, the last item on the entry page is a link to the company's home page. This link is also displayed on the page, confirming that the entry has been received.

Using Games, Puzzles, and Teasers to Attract Visitors

Games, puzzles, and teasers can bring in the masses simply because they are entertaining. People of all ages love to play games that are challenging, fun, or stimulating. Still, many game sites take game playing to another level by offering additional incentives such as prizes. In this way, the game sites make a good thing better, by rewarding people for playing. When rewards are involved, you can bet that visitors will come back again and

Figure 5-33

The contest entry form.

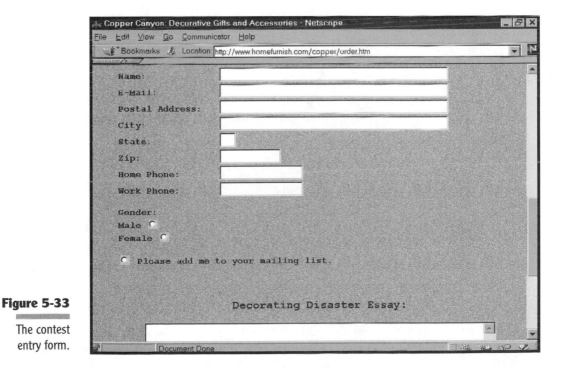

again. Keep in mind that your prize doesn't have to be anything of value. You could simply publish the winner's name prominently on your home page, grant the winner a free home page, or something else that doesn't really cost you anything.

Creating a Game, Puzzle, or Teaser

When you think of games, you probably imagine the zippy video games that you see in the arcades. Although you could certainly spend months programming a truly awesome game for your Web site, some of the best games are those that are simple and compulsively playable. Most card games, such as poker or solitaire, aren't popular because of rip-roaring action; they are popular because they are easy yet challenging to play.

One of the games to consider is a treasure hunt. Treasure hunts are really popular during the holidays, especially at Easter. In a treasure hunt, you hide clues or treasures throughout your Web site and sometimes at participating Web sites. You can display clues or treasures directly on your Web pages using text and graphics. You can also link standardized treasure icons to secret pages at your Web site that describe an item in the treasure hunt.

With a treasure hunt, you need a submission page that lets participants submit a list of all the clues or treasures that they've collected. Usually, prizes in a treasure hunt are awarded to the participants that find all the treasures first. To ensure fair play, you may want to periodically change the clues and treasures during the hunt.

Another game that is a lot of fun and easy to produce is a trivia quiz. Although trivia quizzes can cover any topic, you may want to link the quiz to the theme or topic of your Web site. The best trivia quizzes have at least five challenging questions to which participants can get answers immediately. To keep visitors coming back, you may want to make the trivia quiz a weekly or monthly feature.

If you are giving away prizes based on a trivia quiz, you can post answers with a list of winners at a later date. Because many people may know the answer to your trivia questions, you really don't want to award prizes to everyone who submits the right answers. Instead, you may want to award prizes randomly from the list of participants who submitted the right answers.

Another type of game to consider is a puzzle. The best puzzles are word-based brain teasers, such as a crossword puzzle or a word association game. With a puzzle, you will probably want to reward participants simply for playing and submitting their answers.

A great way to build steady traffic with a puzzle is to change the puzzle often and award prizes randomly to the participants who answer a certain number of puzzles correctly in a given period of time. For example, you can publish a different puzzle every week and award prizes randomly to anyone who gets the answer to four different puzzles in a particular month.

Sites That Promote Your Freebies

You need to promote your giveaway, contest, or sweepstakes to make it successful. Although your promotion efforts should definitely begin at key areas within your Web site, you should also promote the contest through guides and directories that specialize in freebies.

In this section, you will find brief guides to some of the most popular contest directories. When you submit your freebie to a contest directory, be sure to provide the URL to the main contest page and a brief description of the contest. The contest description should specify when the contest ends as well as any age and residency requirements.

Promoting Your Freebie at Playhere

FIND IT ▶
ONLINE

Playhere (http://www.playhere.com) is a terrific guide to fun things on the Web. The site is neatly organized into areas that cover broad, entertainment-related topics (see Figure 5-34). A section called Live Cameras is a directory to the hundreds of live cameras that you can find all over the Web. Celebrity Corner is a guide to Web sites dedicated to famous people. The Arcade covers sites that host online games as well as sites that talk about the latest video games.

One of the main attractions at the site is the games and giveaways section, which has extensive listings for contests, sweepstakes, and other freebies. Because Playhere appeals to a very diverse audience, it is a good place to submit a contest listing. As shown in Figure 5-35, contest listings at Playhere are displayed alphabetically, with brief descriptions.

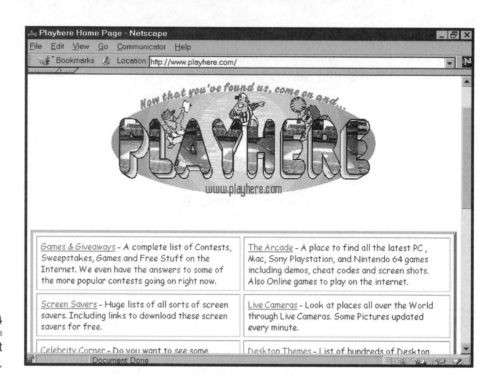

Figure 5-34

Playhere: A contest
directory.

Playhere accepts e-mail submissions for contest listings. You can submit your contest, giveaway, or sweepstakes to `contests@playhere.com`. To make adding your listing easier for the developers, you may want to specify the area at the Web site that best fits your freebie.

Promoting Your Freebie in the Contest Catalogue

The Contest Catalogue (`http://www3.catalogue.com/contests/`) is an extensive guide to contests, sweepstakes, and giveaways on the Web. When I last visited the catalog home page shown in Figure 5-36, the site's developers were in the middle of giving the catalog a complete facelift. Features in the catalog include a What's New? section and areas devoted to specific types of contests, such as treasure hunts and trivia quizzes.

Before you submit a listing to the Contest Catalogue, you should wander through the site to familiarize yourself with the various listing categories.

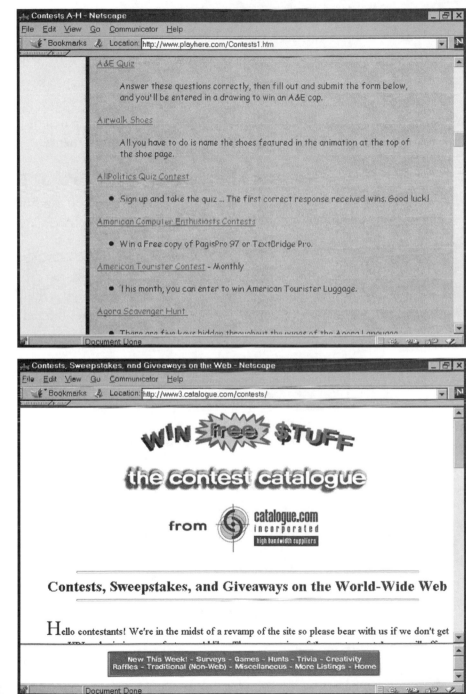

Figure 5-35

Contest listings at
Playhere.

Figure 5-36

The Contest
Catalogue: Another
great contest
directory.

A sample of listings from the Games section is shown in Figure 5-37. As you can see, listings are displayed with a fairly detailed description that includes the requirements and the stop date of the contest, if applicable.

You can submit your contest, giveaway, or sweepstakes to the Contest Catalogue by sending e-mail to `contest-lister@catalogue.com`. Be sure to include the URL to the contest home page, a description for the contest, contest start and stop dates, and any requirements.

Promoting Your Freebie at Virtual Free Stuff

Virtual Free Stuff is a guide to freebies that you can find anywhere, regardless of whether they are available on the Web (see Figure 5-38). You can find the home page for this directory at:

`http://www.dreamscape.com/frankvad/free.html`

Rather than organize the guide by contest type, the developers chose to organize the site based on the type of freebies offered, where they are of-

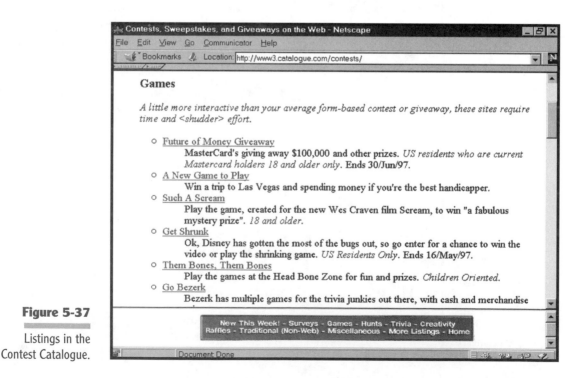

Figure 5-37

Listings in the Contest Catalogue.

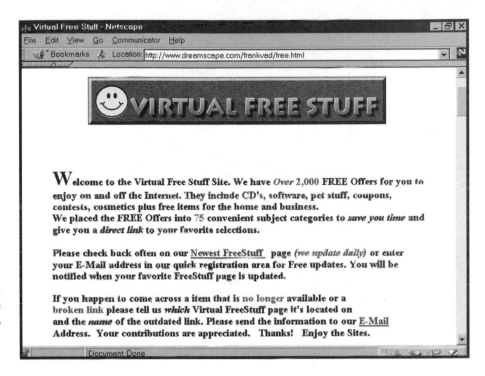

Figure 5-38

Virtual Free Stuff: A
guide to everything
that's free.

fered, and how often they are given away. Because of this unique approach
to showcasing freebies, the directory is divided into nearly a hundred different categories. CD-ROMS alone have a half dozen categories. Categories
exist for daily, weekly, and monthly awards. There is even a category for
"almost free" stuff.

Listings at Virtual Free Stuff are fairly extensive and include requirements
as well as a description (see Figure 5-39). Keep in mind that most of the
listings in Virtual Free Stuff appear in more than one category. For example, your daily contest that gives away T-shirts may be listed in the free
daily contests section and the T-shirts section.

FIND IT
ONLINE

You can submit your listing to Virtual Free Stuff by sending e-mail to
frankvad@dreamscape.com. To ensure that you get the most out of your
listing, take the time to explain the types of prizes that you give away, as
well as how often prizes are awarded.

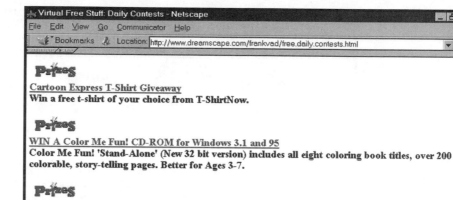

Figure 5-39

Listings at Virtual
Free Stuff.

Other Places to Promote Your Freebies

With thousands of organizations giving away freebies, the existence of dozens of Web guides to free stuff is no surprise. Other freebie guides that you may want to submit a listing to include Free-n-Cool, the ContestGuide, and the ThreadTreader's WWW Contests Guide.

FIND IT ▶
ONLINE

Free-n-Cool (`http://www.free-n-cool.com`) is a guide to everything that is free and that the site's creators consider cool on the Web. The guide is divided into three main sections: free stuff, win stuff, and cool sites (see Figure 5-40). To promote your contest or giveaway, check out the free stuff and win stuff sections. The distinction here is between outright giveaways and contests that award prizes to participants.

Within the free stuff and win stuff areas, you will find pages with extensive cross references based on category, type of offer, method of request, and more. You can submit your freebie to the Free-n-Cool guide using a submission form found at:

`http://www.free-n-cool.com/addurl.html`

Figure 5-40

The Free-n-Cool directory: A place to promote free stuff.

The ContestGuide (http://www.contestguide.com) is a fairly comprehensive guide to contests. This site has a unique focus in that it organizes listings based on how often you can enter a contest (see Figure 5-41). It has listings for contests that let you enter one time only, daily, weekly, and monthly. You can submit a listing to the ContestGuide by sending e-mail to contests@contestguide.com.

Another great contest guide is ThreadTreader's WWW Contests Guide, shown in Figure 5-42. The URL for the contest home page is the following:

http://www.4cyte.com/ThreadTreader/

The goal of this contest directory is to make entering and winning as easy as possible for participants. Toward this end, the site is organized alphabetically, by prize type and by theme. You can also search the directory by keyword. To submit a listing to the directory, use the submission form found at:

http://www.4cyte.com/ThreadTreader/addform.html

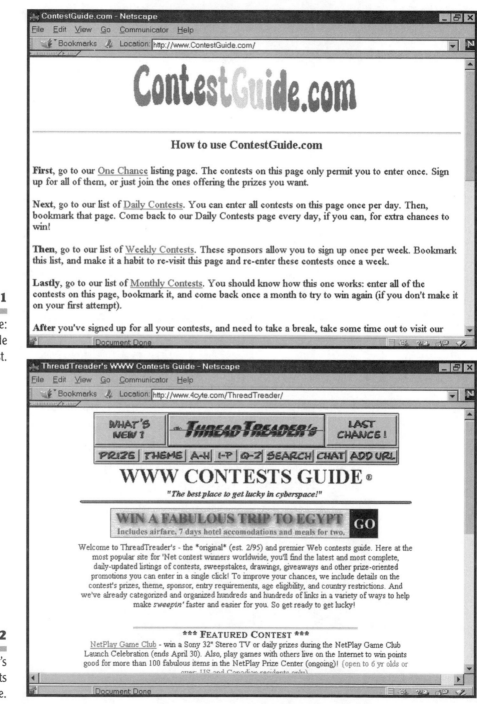

Figure 5-41

The ContestGuide:
A contest guide
with a twist.

Figure 5-42

ThreadTreader's
WWW Contests
Guide.

Wrapping Up and Looking Ahead

Giveaways, contests, and sweepstakes are often used by traditional advertisers to grab the attention of the buying public. You can apply these same concepts to attract an audience for your Web site as well as your products and services. You can also go a step further than traditional freebies and move into the interactive realm of treasure hunts, games, puzzles, and teasers.

After you decide on how to use freebies at your Web site, you need to promote the heck out of your freebie. You do this through promotion at your own Web site and in contest directories. While I'm on the subject of giving something away for nothing, wouldn't it be great if you could get something for nothing? How about getting thousands of dollars worth of advertising for free? Well, cost-free advertising is what the next section is all about.

Cost-Free Banner Advertising: No Joke

If you have browsed the Web, you have probably seen hundreds of banners. The banner is the most frequently used advertising method on the Web. A typical banner ad is placed at the top or bottom of a Web page so that it can catch the viewer's eye and possibly prompt the viewer to click on it. Most advertisers pay thousands of dollars to display a banner ad. Why pay thousands of dollars, though, when you can advertise for free? By becoming a member of a banner exchange, you can advertise at thousands of member Web sites without spending a dime—no joke.

What the Heck Is a Banner Exchange?

FIND IT ▶
ONLINE

Ever since the first banner exchange sprang onto the scene in 1996, banner exchanges have spread like wildfire. Most banner exchanges have a broad focus that allows just about any type of banner advertising. There are also specialty banner exchanges that focus on specific communities of interest, such as travel Web sites.

You can think of a banner exchange as a cooperative advertising program in which participants work together to advertise each other's Web sites, products, or services using banner advertising. I use the word *cooperative* because the amount of cost-free advertising that you receive is directly related to the amount of advertising you give to other participants.

Although cooperative advertising isn't exactly a new concept, it is definitely a breakthrough for anyone who wants to get his or her Web site noticed. Because most banner exchanges have a network of thousands of participants, you can use the exchange to promote your Web site, products, and services to a massive and extremely diverse audience.

How Do Banner Exchanges Work?

The wonderful thing about banner exchanges is that the exchange is responsible for managing the network. To do this, most exchanges have a banner management system that tracks when and where banners are displayed throughout the network. Every time you display the banner of another member, you receive a credit. Based on these credits, the management system ensures that your banner is displayed at other sites in the network.

If you had to manually edit your Web pages to change banners, the banner exchange wouldn't be of much use. Fortunately, the banner management system is also responsible for rotating the banners as well. To enable automatic banner rotation, exchange members are given a section of HTML code that allows the management system to dynamically update banners when the page is loaded. The code snippet also includes an account number that allows the management system to track where a banner is displayed and give credits appropriately.

An added benefit of the banner exchange is the ability to track and view the performance statistics for your banner. Depending on the banner exchange, your performance statistics can range from up-to-the-minute accounting to weekly account summaries. Either way, the stats usually tell you how many times your banner was displayed as well how many times someone clicked on your banner. Generally, you will need to visit the banner exchange to view these stats.

The number of times that your banner is displayed is called *impressions*. The number of times that someone clicked on your banner is called the *click through*. When you divide the total click through by the total impressions, you come up with a *click through ratio*. Some banner exchanges use the click through ratio to determine the effectiveness of your banner advertising.

Exchanging Your Banner

Before you can participate in a banner exchange, you must become a member, which usually involves filling out detailed contact information on yourself, your Web site, and your business. You are also asked questions about the type of material that you publish at your Web site and the types of sites that can be promoted at your site. Although most banner exchanges unanimously prohibit promoting explicit or offensive Web sites, a rating system usually is in place that covers everything from kid-only sites to sites for mature audiences.

The purpose of the rating system is to protect the interests of the exchange members. After all, if your Web site is for kids, you don't want someone to display a banner that is directed at adults. By the same token, you may not want to display advertising for kids at your adult-oriented Web site.

After you complete the membership process, you will be given a section of HTML code that you can add to any pages at your Web site. The purpose of this code is to display the banner advertising of other exchange members. Your unique account number for the exchange is a part of the HTML code. For this reason, you should copy the code that the exchange gives you and paste it into your Web pages.

Because you receive a credit each time that someone views a banner advertising at your Web site, your first instinct may be to add the banner code to every page at your Web site. Instead, I recommend that you place the banner advertisements in well-visited areas of your Web site and primarily on top-level pages. You shouldn't inundate visitors with advertising or make them wait for banners to load on every page.

TIP

Banner exchanges have many checks and balances in place to ensure that the exchange system is fair. For example, exchanges typically prohibit the use of more than one banner from that exchange on a single page. Nothing stops you from putting banners from other exchanges on a single page, however.

After you receive the banner code, the next step is to submit your banner to the exchange. Most exchanges have a form that you can use to submit your banner, but your browser must comply with the latest HTML standards to use this feature. If you don't have the latest and greatest version of your browser, you may have to send your browser to the exchange as an e-mail attachment.

Creating a Banner Advertisement

The banner exchange process starts with you creating a banner to be displayed at other Web sites. Your banner doesn't have to be designed by a professional but should entice people to read it and click on it. Although you will see banners with high-power graphics, it is not the catchy graphics that attract the viewer's eye so much as it is the information.

Information is the key to a successful banner, especially when the file size of your banner is severely limited by the banner exchange. Most banner exchanges restrict your banner to a file size of less than 8K—a tiny amount in the world of high-power graphics. When you develop your banner, the file size limit should be one of your overriding concerns.

Banner exchanges also specify the exact dimensions of the banner. A typical banner size is 400 pixels wide by 50 pixels high. To enforce these dimensions, the HTML code from the exchange usually sets the height and width of the banner to these dimensions. Still, you should create your banner with these dimensions in mind. The reason for this is that Web browsers will use the dimensions to resize the banner, which may distort your image and make it unreadable.

The last restriction most banner exchanges enforce is that your banner must be a noninterlaced GIF image. Further, you usually cannot use transparent or animated GIFs. If you don't know what *noninterlaced, transparent,* or *animated* GIF means, don't worry. Simply save your banner as a standard (noninterlaced) GIF. Most graphics programs will use this standard format unless you specifically change the settings. So, don't change the save options.

TIP If you want to work with multiple banner exchanges, you should note the file and image size limits enforced by each of the exchanges with which you plan to work. Then, you should design the banner with these limits in mind. By resizing your banner to fit the requirements of the exchange, you can use the same banner repeatedly.

Selecting a Banner Exchange

Here I go, looking a gift horse in the mouth again—but the simple truth is that no two banner exchanges are the same. When you select a banner exchange, you need to look past the gilded doorways that say you can promote your Web site for free, and look into the heart of the exchange's management system.

Banner exchanges use what is called an exchange ratio to indicate the display-to-credit ratio offered by the exchange. The most common exchange ratio is 2 to 1. If an exchange has a 2-to-1 exchange ratio, this means that for every two times that someone views a banner on your Web site, your banner will be displayed at a member site one time.

A quick check of the math tells you that, at an exchange ratio of 2 to 1, half of the impressions are going somewhere other than to banner exchange members. Here is where sponsorship comes into the picture. To make up for the costs of running the exchange, most banner exchanges sell the additional space to sponsors. With the average banner exchange racking up millions of impressions every day, a 2-to-1 exchange ratio has a pretty hefty profit margin. I say this to help you make an informed decision, not to dissuade you from using a wonderful service that is free for members.

Beyond the exchange ratio, you should look at the features of the exchange's banner management system. Everything that you do at an exchange should be handled through a password-protected account. Standard features of the account should be to view your current statistics, modify your account profile, and submit a banner. What's more, you should be able to access any of these features directly at the exchange's Web site, and the management system should handle updates automatically.

Some exchanges offer additional features, such as targeting. With *targeting*, you can select the specific categories of Web sites that will display your banner and, often, the categories of banners displayed at your own Web site. In this way, your banner is seen only by audiences that you select, which includes audiences that are interested in products, services, or information similar to what you offer at your Web site.

Finally, you should look at the total membership of the exchange and the throughput of the exchange's Web connection. Together, the number of members and the throughput can suggest an average throughput, which in turn tells you how long visitors to your Web site will have to wait for banner ads to display. For example, a banner exchange with 25,000 member sites and a T1 connection to the Web is probably overloaded. As a result, visitors to your Web site may experience longer-than-normal delays while the banner loads.

Without getting into specific measurement criteria, one way to check the performance of a banner exchange is simply to visit pages of current members and see how long banners take to load. To get a solid assessment, you should check on several different days and at different times of the day. Keep in mind that peak usage times are typically during the week and specifically at midday.

NOTE At the Web site for this book, you will find a banner exchange page that provides summary information about all the exchanges featured in this section. You will find this page at http://www.tvpress.com/promote/bann.htm.

Banner Swapping with LinkExchange

With more than 100,000 members, LinkExchange (http://www.linkexchange.com) may be the largest banner exchange network. At the time of this writing, LinkExchange was offering a 2-to-1 exchange ratio. During the times when other member banners are not displayed, the exchange displays its own banner as well as the banners of paid sponsors.

The LinkExchange home page is shown in Figure 5-43. LinkExchange has many extra features that make it a great choice. These features include:

- ✿ Performance stats updated daily
- ✿ Automatic profile updating
- ✿ The ability to submit and update your banner online

Creating Your LinkExchange Account

To join the LinkExchange network, follow the appropriate links from the home page to the account creation area. The sign-up form helps LinkExchange develop a comprehensive profile of your Web site (see Figure 5-44). Keep in mind that the management system uses this information

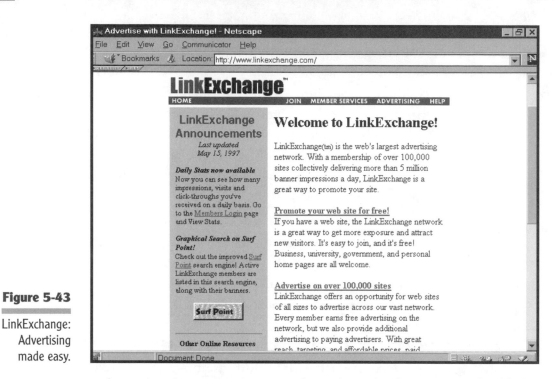

Figure 5-43

LinkExchange:
Advertising
made easy.

to determine the appropriateness of your banner advertisement for display on other sites.

The URL that you supply is the one that users will access when they click on your banner. Before you enter anything in the URL field, you should therefore carefully consider the page or area of your Web site to which you want to direct traffic. Although your banner ad doesn't directly use the rest of the information in the Site Information area, you must fill these fields in. If you use the Surf Point search engine at LinkExchange, you will find that these fields are indexed in the database.

NOTE If you have separate sections with separate topics that you want to promote, you may want to set up different accounts for each section.

LinkExchange also asks you to select categories that best describe your site. These categories are used for targeted advertising. After you select categories for your Web site, you need to specify whether you are running a commer-

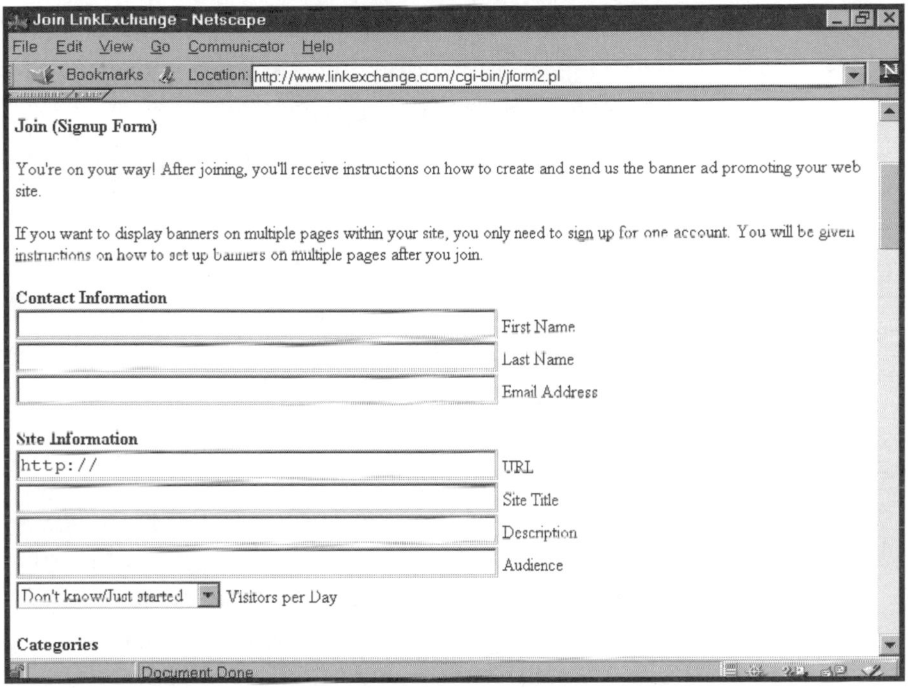

Figure 5-44

Start by creating
your account.

cial or noncommercial Web site. The exchange uses the information on site type primarily to restrict commercial banners from sites that don't want to advertise such sites.

LinkExchange rates the content of all member sites. A level 1 site is for children. A level 2 site is for general audiences. A level 3 site is for mature audiences. To ensure that nobody posts possibly controversial banners on your Web site, you may want to specify that only level 1 and level 2 sites may advertise on your pages.

Adding the Code to Your Web Site

After you complete and submit the registration form, the exchange will ask you to verify the information. After you do so, you will get your account number and the code that you need to add banners to your Web site. Rather than type this code, use your browser's copy feature to select the code. If for some reason you have problems obtaining this code, don't worry; you can view it at any time by going to the member services area and selecting the

View HTML option (see Figure 5-45).

The HTML code for the LinkExchange looks like this:

```
<!- BEGIN LINKEXCHANGE CODE ->
<a href="http://ad.linkexchange.com/X254517/gotoad.map"
target="_top">
<img width=440 height=40 border=1 ismap
alt="LinkExchange"
src="http://ad.linkexchange.com/X254517/logoshowad?free"></a>
<br><font size=1><a href="http://www.linkexchange.com/"
target="_top">
LinkExchange Member</a></font><br>
<!- END LINKEXCHANGE CODE  ->
```

TIP The code displays a banner that is linked to the banner advertiser's Web site, and a text link that is linked to the LinkExchange. At the time of this writing, the LinkExchange FAQ states that you can remove the text link to LinkExchange.

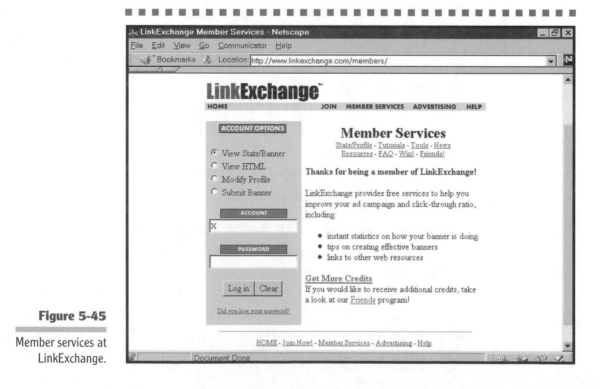

Figure 5-45

Member services at LinkExchange.

In this example, the account number is X254517. When someone views a page containing this code, the account X254517 gets a credit. Because of how LinkExchange is set up, the same banner will be displayed on each page that a user visits within your Web site. Although this behavior is intended to reduce the amount of frustration on the part of the visitor, you don't get any credits for page views beyond the first page view for this individual visit. You can override this feature by assigning a unique designator to each page containing the LinkExchange code.

The unique designator is a number between 1 and 99 that you insert before the account number. Because the account number is specified twice in the code, you must insert the unique designator twice. A slash separates the designator from your account number. An example of using a unique designator follows:

```
<!- BEGIN LINKEXCHANGE CODE ->
<a href="http://ad.linkexchange.com/10/X254517/gotoad.map"
target="_top">
<img width=440 height=40 border=1 ismap
alt="LinkExchange"
src="http://ad.linkexchange.com/10/X254517/
  logoshowad?free"></a>
<br><font size=1><a href="http://www.linkexchange.com/"
target="_top">
LinkExchange Member</a></font><br>
<!- END LINKEXCHANGE CODE  ->
```

Submitting Your Banner to LinkExchange

After you join the LinkExchange, you can visit the member services area to submit your banner. Submitting your banner requires logging in with your account number and password. If you publish your banner on your Web site, you can submit your banner using its URL path (see Figure 5-46). Otherwise, retrieve the banner from your file system using the option provided.

The banner that you submit to LinkExchange must be 400 pixels wide and 40 pixels high. When your banner is displayed, LinkExchange will add its logo to the banner, making the effective size of the banner 440 x 40. The file size of your banner must be 7K or less. The only format that you can use is GIF. Additionally, you cannot use transparent or animated GIFs.

Banner Swapping with SmartClicks

SmartClicks (`http://www.smartclicks.com`) is one of the few banner exchanges that allows everyone to conduct targeted advertising for free. Although targeted advertising is one of the key reasons for the success of SmartClicks, the exchange has many other features that make it a winner. The SmartClicks home page is shown in Figure 5-47.

FIND IT ▶
ONLINE

Like most banner exchanges, SmartClicks offers a 2-to-1 exchange ratio to its members. When other member banners are not displayed, the exchange displays its own banner as well as the banners of paid boosters and sponsors. A *booster* is an organization that pays for a small amount of advertising. A *sponsor* is an organization that pays for a large amount of advertising.

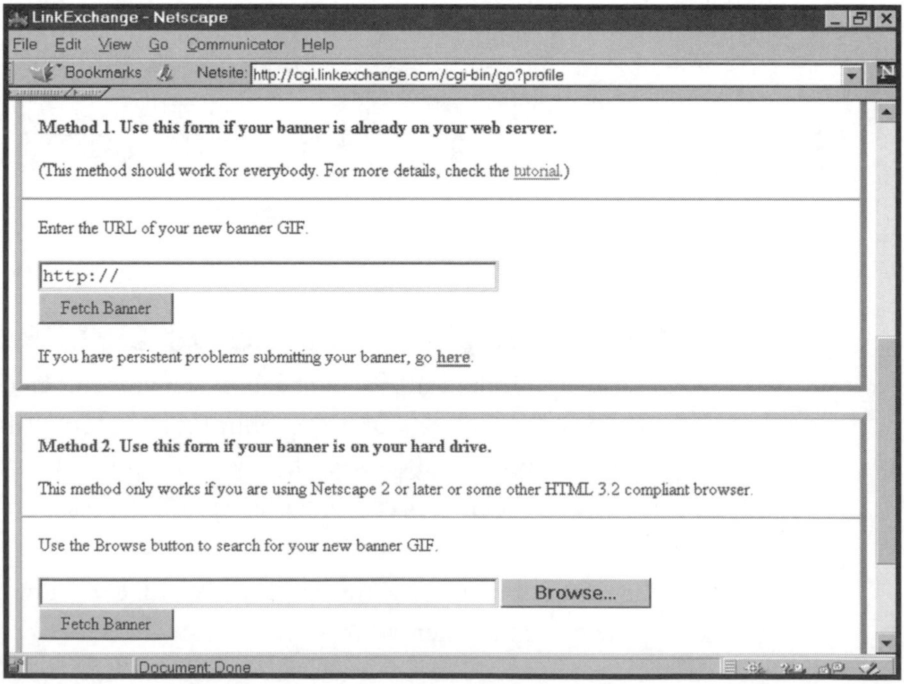

Figure 5-46

Submitting your
banner to
LinkExchange.

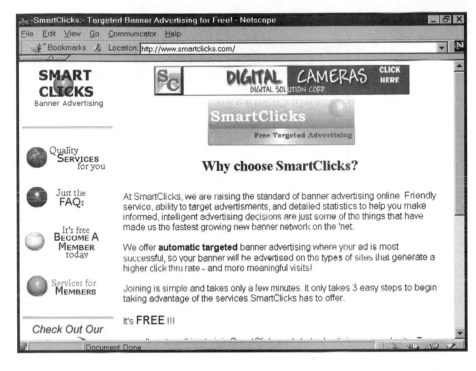

Figure 5-47

Targeted advertising with SmartClicks.

Creating Your SmartClicks Account

To join the SmartClicks network, follow the Become a Member links from the home page to the member application page. Unlike most other banner exchanges, the membership application at SmartClicks is fairly short (see Figure 5-48). After you enter basic contact information, enter the URL that you want users to access when they click on your banner. Next, select the site type that best matches your site. This information will be used to help you select a target audience for your banner advertising.

Be sure to carefully select the categories on which you want to display your site, and the sites on which you allow your banners to be displayed. Smart-Clicks rates the content of all member sites in four categories: kids only, commercial, general audience, and mature audiences. As with most banner exchanges, the mature audiences category is more of a PG-13 than an R rating.

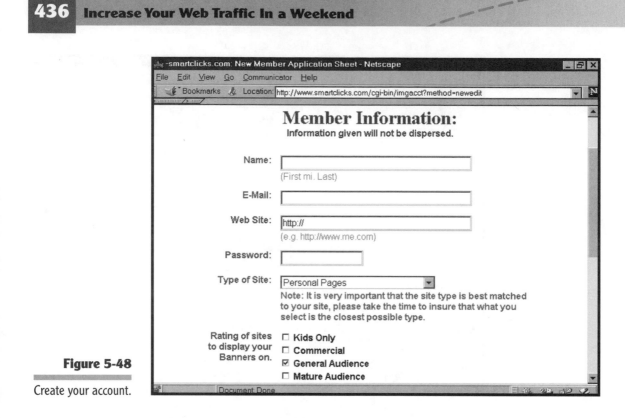

Figure 5-48

Create your account.

Adding the Code to Your Web Site

After you verify your account information, you will get an account number and the code that you need to add banners to your Web site (see Figure 5-49). Use your browser's copy feature to select the code and paste it into your Web pages. Because this code is specific to your account, you can view the code at any time by going to the member services area and selecting the View HTML Example option.

The HTML code that SmartClicks asks you to add to your pages looks like this:

```
<!- Begin SmartClicks Code ——————————>
<a href="http://www.smartclicks.com" target="_top"><img src=
"http://www.smartclicks.com:81/smartlogo" alt="SC: FREE!"
align=bottom border=1 width=50 height=50></a><a href
="http://www.smartclicks.com:81/B020424/smartaddr" target
="_top"><img src="http://www.smartclicks.com:81/B020424/
 smartimg"
```

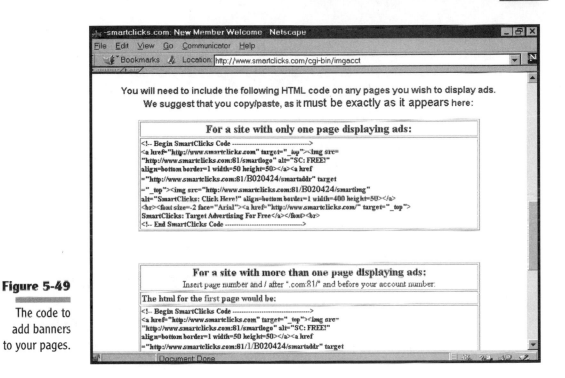

Figure 5-49

The code to add banners to your pages.

```
alt="SmartClicks: Click Here!" align=bottom border=1
  width=400 height=50></a>
<br><font size=-2 face="Arial"><a href="http://
  www.smartclicks.com/" target="_top">
SmartClicks: Target Advertising For Free</a></font><br>
<!- End SmartClicks Code -------------------->
```

Here, the account number hidden in the code is B020424. When someone views a page containing this code, the account B020424 receives a credit. If you want to display banners on more than one page at your Web site, you need to use a unique designator for each page. The unique designator for the first page is 1; the unique designator for the second page is 2, and so on. You must insert the unique designator before each occurrence of the account number. A slash separates the designator from your account number. An example of using a unique designator follows:

```
<!- Begin SmartClicks Code -------------------->
```

```
<a href="http://www.smartclicks.com" target="_top"><img src=
"http://www.smartclicks.com:81/smartlogo" alt="SC: FREE!"
align=bottom border=1 width=50 height=50></a><a href
="http://www.smartclicks.com:81/1/B020424/smartaddr" target
="_top"><img src="http://www.smartclicks.com:81/1/B020424/
   smartimg"
alt="SmartClicks: Click Here!" align=bottom border=1
   width=400 height=50></a>
<br><font size=-2 face="Arial"><a href="http://
   www.smartclicks.com/" target="_top">
SmartClicks: Target Advertising For Free</a></font><br>
<!- End SmartClicks Code ————————————————>
```

Targeting and Submitting Your Banner

Now that you are a member of SmartClicks, you can visit the member services area and log in to your account. As shown in Figure 5-50, you can use the member services area to configure many options in your account. One of the most important options is the targeting control that lets you target specific categories of Web sites for your banner ad.

The whole idea behind targeted advertising is to increase the click through ratio. You do this by focusing on groups of people who might be interested in topics covered at your Web site. For example, targeting allows a sports memorabilia Web site to display banner ads only on sports and entertainment Web sites.

Submitting Your Banner to SmartClicks

Before you can target your banner using the targeting control panel, you need to submit your banner. To do this, select the View Profile/Edit Banner option. If your banner is published on your Web site, you can submit the banner using its URL path (see Figure 5-51). Otherwise, you can send your banner as an e-mail attachment to services@smartclicks.com. Either way, your banner will take about three days to get into the system.

The banner that you submit to SmartClicks must be 400 pixels wide and 50 pixels high. SmartClicks adds a 50 x 50 logo to the banner, making the

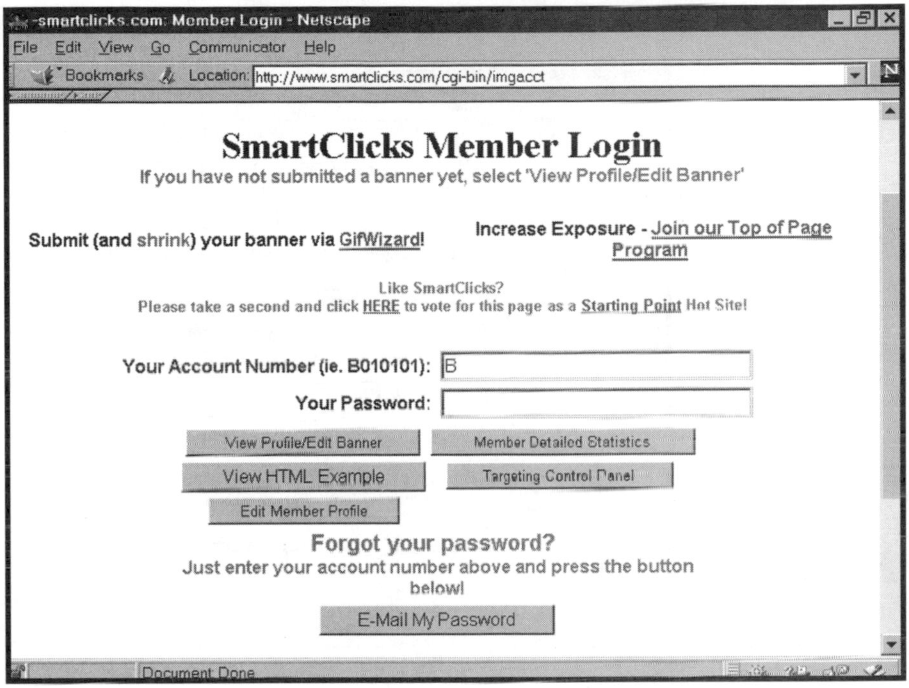

Figure 5-50

Member services at
SmartClicks.

effective size of the banner 450 x 50. Although SmartClicks allows you to use animated GIFs, the file size of your banner must be 10K or less. Additionally, your banner must be in noninterlaced GIF format.

Exchanging Banners with BannerSwap

BannerSwap (http://www.bannerswap.com) isn't afraid to tackle the tough problem of making its members play by the rules. Rather than implement a standard fixed exchange ratio, BannerSwap uses a variable exchange ratio that is based on what the service calls *rating pools* and *site effectiveness ratios*. Basically, the system seeks to reward banner members who place their banner ads in places where they are seen, and punishes sites that place banners in less than optimal places on the page. As a result, the exchange ratio ranges from all-out exclusion to 2 to 1.

Although the rewards system is an effort to maintain the integrity of the network, the whole concept is based on click through ratios. If your site

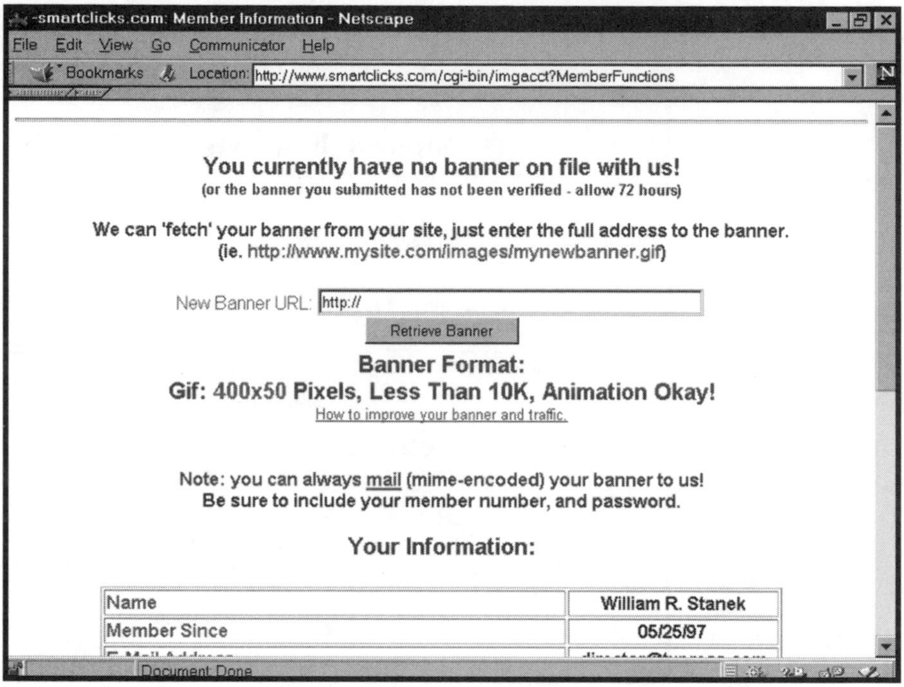
-smartclicks.com: Member Information - Netscape
File Edit View Go Communicator Help
Bookmarks Location: http://www.smartclicks.com/cgi-bin/imgacct?MemberFunctions
You currently have no banner on file with us!
(or the banner you submitted has not been verified - allow 72 hours)
We can 'fetch' your banner from your site, just enter the full address to the banner.
(ie. http://www.mysite.com/images/mynewbanner.gif)
New Banner URL: http://
Retrieve Banner
Banner Format:
Gif: 400x50 Pixels, Less Than 10K, Animation Okay!
How to improve your banner and traffic.
Note: you can always mail (mime-encoded) your banner to us!
Be sure to include your member number, and password.
Your Information:
Name
William R. Stanek
Member Since
05/25/97
Document: Done

Figure 5-51

Submitting your banner to SmartClicks.

has a poor click through ratio, you are punished. If your site has a good click through ratio, you are rewarded. The BannerSwap home page is shown in Figure 5-52.

Creating Your BannerSwap Account

To become a member of BannerSwap, follow the registration links from the home page. BannerSwap breaks down the account registration process into a series of steps. As shown in Figure 5-53, the first step is to specify detailed personal contact information.

In Step 2, you enter detailed site information and ratings (see Figure 5-54). The Business type field is the broad category into which your Web site fits. As with other banner exchanges, the URL that you supply is the one that users will access when they click on your banner.

BannerSwap divides the rating system into three levels: G, PG, and NC-17. Here, a G-rated site is suitable for kids and a PG-rated site is suitable for general audiences. The NC-17 rating is for sites with material suitable only

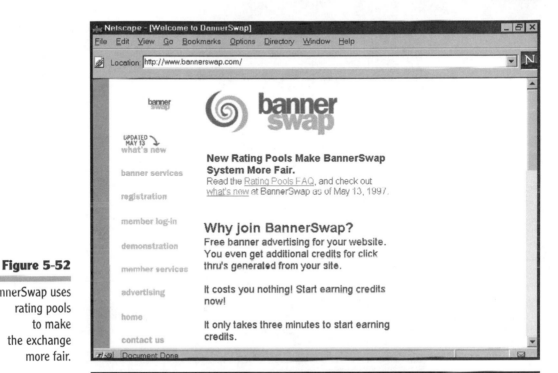

Figure 5-52

BannerSwap uses rating pools to make the exchange more fair.

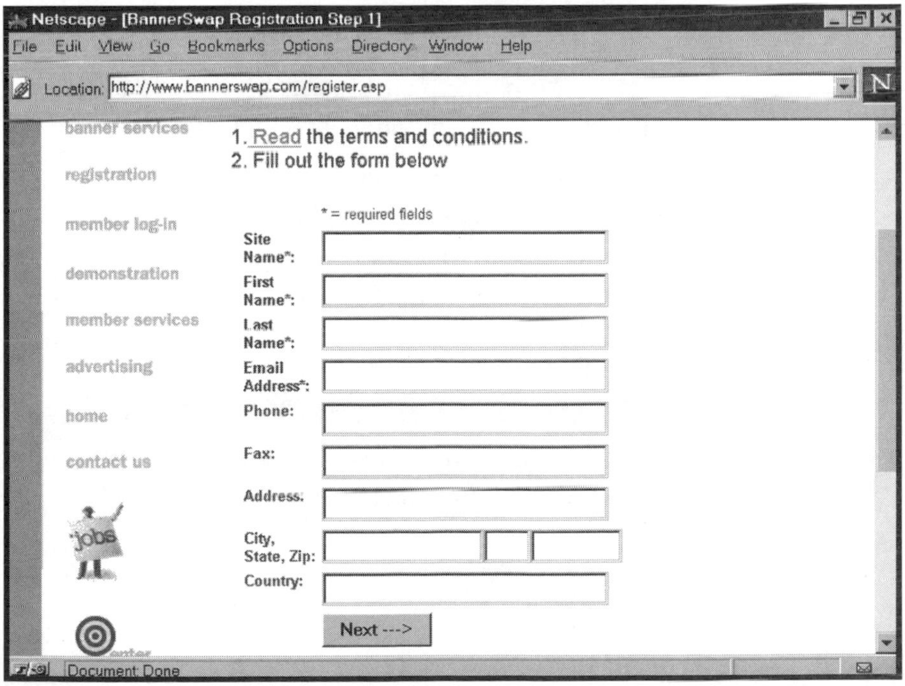

Figure 5-53

Step 1: Enter contact information.

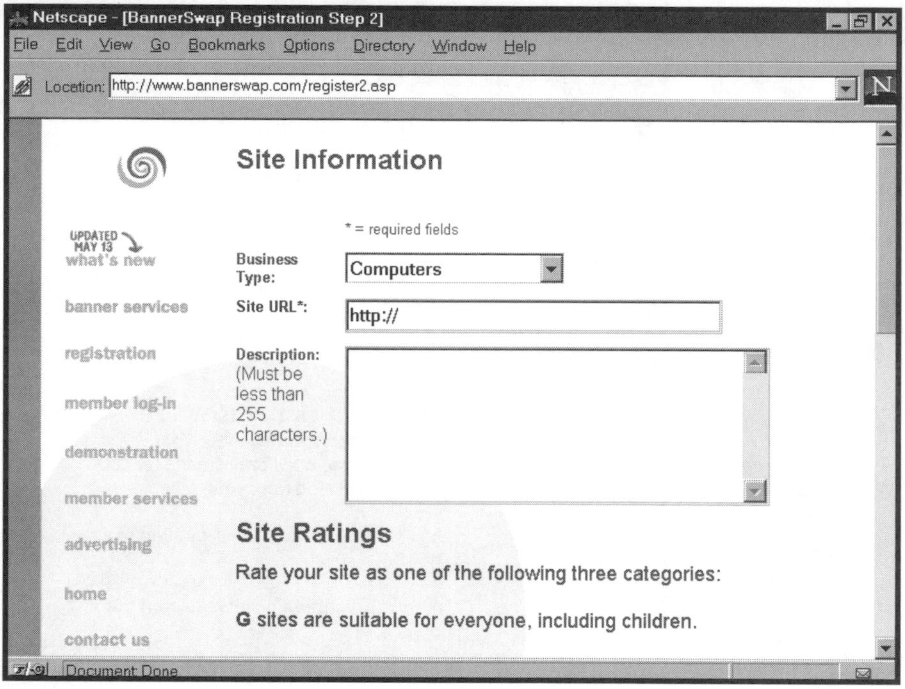

Figure 5-54

Step 2: Enter site information.

for adults over the age of 17. To keep adults-only material that may be offensive to mainstream viewers off your Web site, set the maximum site rating for advertising on your site to PG or G.

The final step is to select a login id and password for your account (see Figure 5-55). To save yourself time and frustration, keep in mind that BannerSwap has thousands of members and most of the common login ids are already taken. For this reason, select a login id that is anything but common.

Adding the Code to Your Web Site

After you complete the registration process, you can move on to the member login area. After you log in, you will see the BannerSwap administration page. To get started, select the View HTML option, which will display the unique code for your account. This code looks like this:

```
!——www.bannerswap.com——>
<center>
```

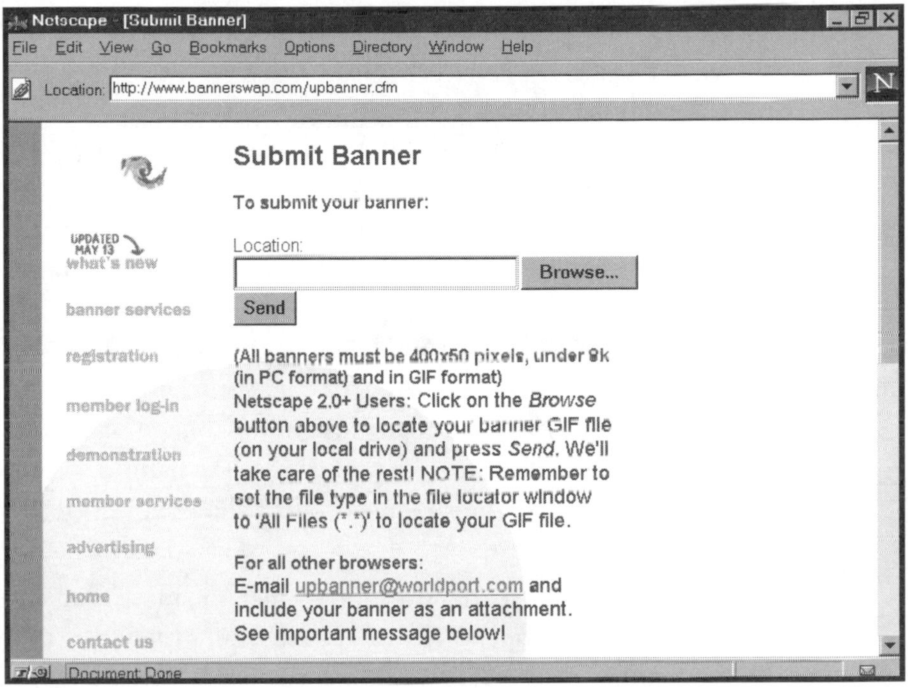

Figure 5-55

Step 3: Select a login id and password.

```
<table border=0 cellspacing=0 cellpadding=0>
<tr><td><a href="http://www.bannerswap.com/">
<img src="http://www.bannerswap.com/images/smbswap.gif"
border=1 width=50 height=50></a></td>
<td><a href="http://www.bannerswap.com/gosite.asp">
<img src="http://www.bannerswap.com/images/prd/
   banner.asp?src=16115&ad=1"
border=1 width=400 height=50 alt="www.bannerswap.com"></A></
   td></tr>
<tr><td colspan=2><center><font size=-2 face="Arial">Proud
   Member of
<a href="http://www.bannerswap.com/">BannerSwap</a></font></
   center>
</td></tr></table>
</center>
<!————End Code————>
```

In this example, the source number associated with the account is 16115. Whenever a page containing this code is viewed, the account associated with this source number receives a credit. Following the source number is a designator for the current ad number. Anytime that you use banners on multiple pages, you need to change the ad number. On the second page that uses a banner, you change the ad number to a 2. On the third page that uses a banner, you change the ad number to a 3.

Submitting Your Banner to BannerSwap

After obtaining the banner code, you can go back to the administration page and select the View, Submit or Change Banner option. If you haven't submitted a banner yet, you will see the banner submission page shown in Figure 5-56. The submission field allows you to retrieve the banner from your file system.

FIND IT ▶ ONLINE If your browser doesn't support file uploading, you can send the banner as an e-mail attachment to upbanner@worldport.com. When you e-mail a banner, you must make the filename the same as your login id.

All banners submitted to BannerSwap must be 400 pixels wide and 50 pixels high. As with most other banner exchanges, BannerSwap adds a logo to your banner, making the effective size of the banner 450 x 50. Additionally, your banner must be in GIF format only and have a file size of 8K or less.

Exchanging Banners with BannerCAST

FIND IT ▶ ONLINE BannerCAST (http://www.BannerCAST.com) is one of the up-and-coming players in the banner exchange business. The BannerCAST home page is shown in Figure 5-57.

At the time of this writing, BannerCAST was offering a 2-to-1 exchange ratio. As with most banner exchanges, BannerCAST fills in the additional banner space using its own banner and the banners of paid sponsors. BannerCAST also offers additional space to members at discounted rates through a premiere membership program.

Figure 5-56

Submitting your
banner to
BannerSwap.

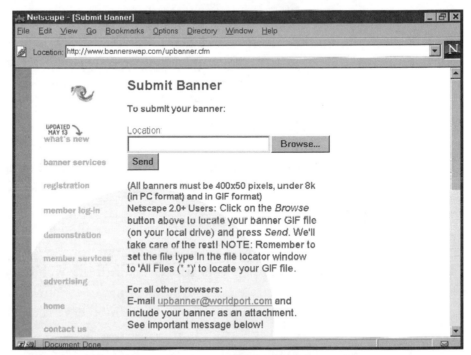

Figure 5-57

The BannerCAST
exchange.

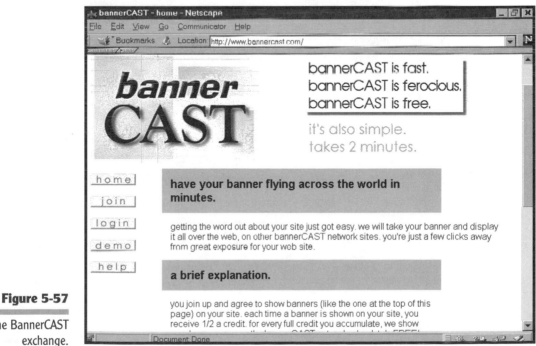

Creating Your BannerCAST Account

To join the BannerCAST network, follow the appropriate links from the home page to the account creation area. The first step in the registration process is to enter your personal contact information, which for some strange reason includes your favorite type of food (see Figure 5-58).

In Step 2, you specify Web site information (see Figure 5-59). BannerCAST asks you to select a category and rating that best describes your site. The categories deal with whether your site is a personal or a commercial site. The rating covers the type of material that you publish at your site. A level 1 rating indicates a site for children. A level 2 rating indicates a site for general audiences. A level 3 site indicates a site for mature audiences.

In Step 3, you set up account information for the types of sites on which you want to display your banner. As with the Web site information, this step focuses on site categories and ratings (see Figure 5-60). This step also asks you to enter a password and your mother's maiden name.

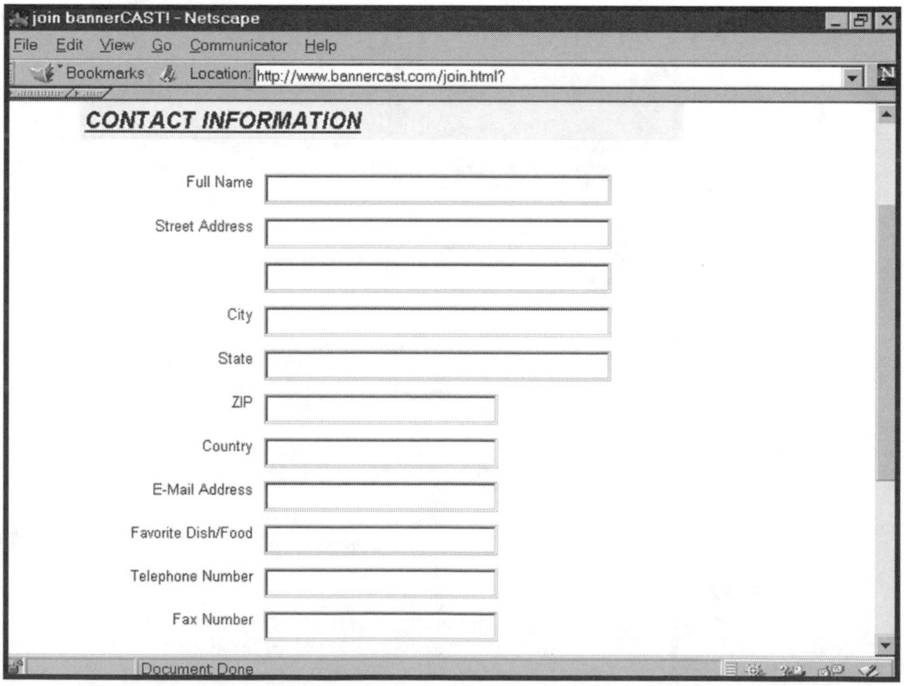

Figure 5-58

Start by creating your account.

Figure 5-59

Step 2: Enter
information on
your Web site.

The figure shows a Netscape browser window titled "WEBSITE INFORMATION - Netscape" at URL http://bannercast.com/join2.html:

WEBSITE INFORMATION

Below you are going to tell us a bit about your site. It is important that we know if you are commercial or non-commercial. It is also important that you RATE your site.

Site Name _____

URL (location) _____

Company/Org. Name _____

Commercial Site? ● YES, it's commercial
○ NO, it's all personal.

Rating for Site? Rating I is for sites that are intended solely for children.

Rating II is the general audience and is what most of bannerCAST consits of.

Rating III is anything that may be considered controversial to other members. This does **not include pornographic sites, sites with links to pornographic sites, sites that promote or encourage illegal activities, racism, or any sites that the administrators of bannerCAST may deem inappropriate. Such sites are not allowed to participate in the bannerCAST program.**

CAUTION

BannerCAST requests your mother's maiden name as a backup to use in case you forget your password. Because I believe that noncreditors should not possess this type of information, I recommend using an alternate name that you will remember.

Adding the Code to Your Web Site

When you click on the Continue button in Step 3, BannerCAST will show you your BannerCAST id. Write down this id and your password. The final registration page also has the code you need to add banners to your Web site. The HTML code looks like this:

```
<!- BEGIN bannerCAST CODE ->
<a href="http://bannerCAST.com/click.cgi?12049"
target="_top">
<img width-440 height=40 border=1 ismap
alt="bannerCAST"
```

```
src="http://bannerCAST.com/show.cgi?12049:00"></a>
<br>
<font size=1><a href="http://bannerCAST.com/"
target="_top">
member of the bannerCAST network</a></font><br>
<!- END bannerCAST CODE ->
```

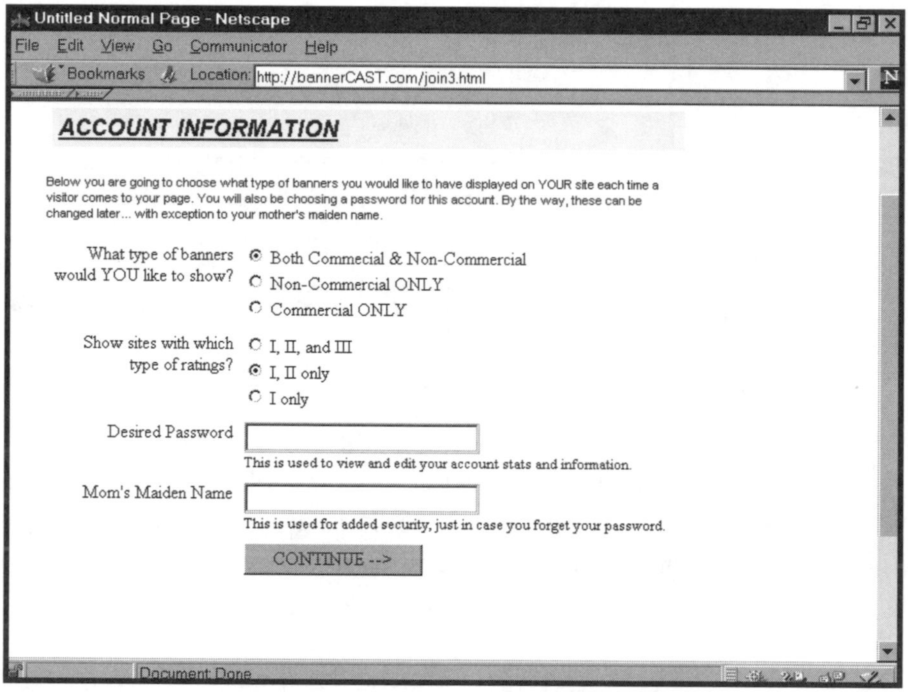

Figure 5-60

Finish setting up
your account.

In this example, the account number is 12049. When someone views a page containing this code, the account 12049 receives a credit. Because of how BannerCAST is set up, each page at your site that displays banners should use a unique page identification number.

The unique designator is a two-digit number between 00 and 99 inserted after the account number that appears on the sixth line of the BannerCAST code. Unlike other banner exchanges, you insert the page designator only one time, and use a colon to separate the designator from your account number.

Submitting Your Banner to BannerCAST

At the bottom of the final registration page, you will find a link that allows you to upload your banner. Another way to find the banner submission page is to access the login area of the BannerCAST Web site. Either way, you need to enter your BannerCAST id and password before you can enter the URL path to your banner (see Figure 5-61). Because BannerCAST doesn't provide an alternative path for obtaining the banner, you must publish the banner at your Web site before you try to submit it.

The banner that you submit to BannerCAST must be 400 pixels wide and 40 pixels high. When your banner is displayed, BannerCAST adds its logo to the banner, making the effective size of the banner 440 x 40. The file size of your banner must be 7K or less. The only format that you can use is noninterlaced GIF. Additionally, you cannot use transparent or animated GIFs.

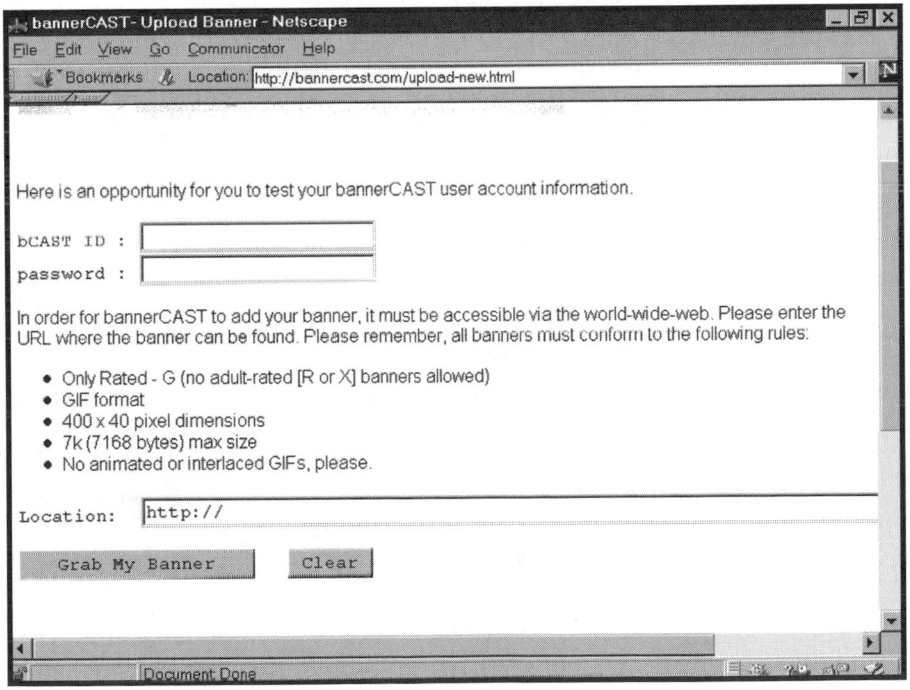

Figure 5-61

Submitting your banner to BannerCAST.

More Banner Exchanges

With dozens of banner exchanges available, you can bet that you have many more choices beyond the top exchanges discussed in this section. Some other banner exchanges that you may want to check out include the 2X Exchange, LinkTrader, Net-On's Banner Exchange, and the Cyberlink Exchange 2000.

The 2X Exchange (`http://www.x-x.com`) is shown in Figure 5-62. This exchange gets its name from the fact that it allows you to display two of its banners on the same page. For example, you can display one banner at the top of the page and a different banner at the bottom of the page.

As with most exchanges, the 2X Exchanges offers a 2-to-1 exchange ratio. To submit your banner to the 2X Exchange, the banner should be in GIF format and not use animation or interlacing. Additionally, the screen size of the banner should be 468 x 60 with a file size of 8K or less.

FIND IT ▶
ONLINE
LinkTrader (`http://www.linktrader.com`) set out to give the best exchange ratio out of all the banner exchanges on the Web. The idea was that by

Figure 5-62

2X Exchange:
A banner
exchange site.

limiting its commercial advertising, the exchange could help its member sites grow and get more hits (see Figure 5-63). Because of its efforts to have the most liberal exchange, LinkTrader offers a terrific exchange ratio of 10 to 7. This exchange ratio changes to 2 to 1, however, if you do not display your banner at or near the top of the page.

Because LinkTrader uses an automated system to check the position of the banner in relation to the text on the page, the system isn't always fair, and you may find that you end up with a 2-to-1 ratio. This inconsistency, combined with the fact that LinkTrader isn't as forthcoming about its bandwidth connection to the Internet and total users as it could be, is the primary reason I did not feature LinkTrader as one of the top banner exchanges.

Your banner for LinkTrader should be a 400 x 50 pixel GIF image. As with most banner exchanges, your banner cannot be animated or interlaced. LinkTrader also restricts the file size of banners to 7K or less. Although this is a relatively small file size, the reduced bandwidth requirements increase the efficiency of the network across the board.

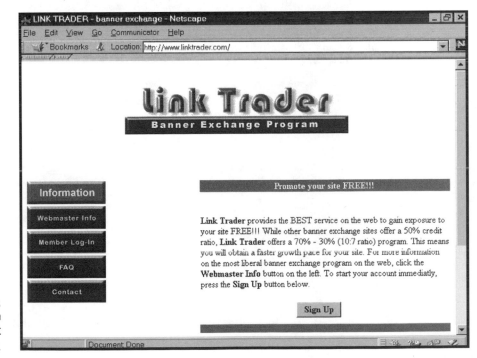

Figure 5-63

Swap banners at
LinkTrader.

FIND IT ▶
ONLINE

The home page for the Net-On Banner Exchange (`http://www.net-on.se:81/banner/`) is shown in Figure 5-64. This banner exchange is one of the few to break most of the rules set by other exchange networks. Net-On offers a variable exchange ratio. Net-On eliminates the maximum file size restriction. Net-On also allows animated GIFs. The only requirements for your banner are that it must be a noninterlaced GIF image with a screen size of 468 x 60.

Another exchange to consider is the Cyberlink Exchange 2000 (`http://cyberlinkexchange.usww.com`). Although this exchange doesn't have the polished appearance of most other exchanges, it offers many extras, including a fairly advanced system for targeting specific audiences (see Figure 5-65). The exchange ratio at the time of this writing was 2 to 1.

To submit your banner to the Cyberlink Exchange 2000, the banner should be a noninterlaced GIF image. Further, the banner should have a screen size of 400 x 40 and a file size of 7K or less.

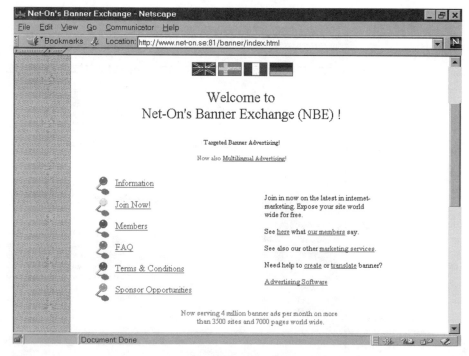

Figure 5-64

Net-On's banner exchange.

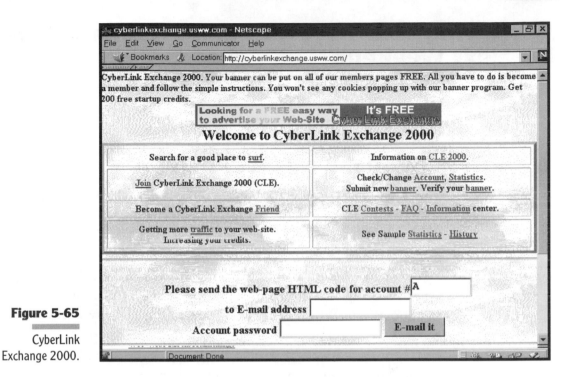

Figure 5-65

CyberLink
Exchange 2000.

Wrapping Up and Looking Ahead

Anyone who becomes a member of a banner exchange network can advertise on the Web for free. Banner advertising with an exchange is not only cost-free but also a highly effective way to drive traffic to your Web site. Most banner exchanges offer their members many additional services, such as banner tracking and banner targeting. These additional services are great for helping you get more out of the exchange network. In the next section, I take a final look at everything that this book has covered.

Reviewing Your Progress and Planning More for Next Weekend

Wow, the weekend is over already! I hope that after reading the sections and following along, you have a great start on the long-term improvement of your Web site's traffic.

What Have You Done This Weekend?

As you learned on the first morning, you really need to understand what is happening at your Web site before you tackle a full-blown promotion campaign. Tracking stats gives you insight into the big picture for your Web site. You can use the big picture to help you improve your Web site and to promote your Web site as well.

One of the biggest reasons to not only promote your Web site but to work to improve your Web site is to get visitors to stay and to come back. After people have found the doorway into your slice of cyberspace, you want to give them every reason to stay. Nothing stops visitors dead in their tracks like an error. Errors are often the result of bad links in your Web pages or bad references to your pages from other Web sites. Using the access log and the error log as your guides, you can fix errors regardless of their source.

After you gather stats for your Web site and know who is visiting your site and why, the next step is to put the stats to work. Not only can you use the stats to make your Web site a better place to visit, you can also use the stats to find your niche in the wonderful world of cyberspace. Enhancing your Web site based on what the stats tell you and using your Web site's niche to your advantage are key ingredients that will help you attract the masses.

Putting the stats to work is only the first step of putting the motion in promotion. The next major step is registering your Web site in all the right places. Because search engines are the primary means of getting your site noticed, I gave you an extensive look at how search engines work and how you can optimize your Web pages for indexing. Although there are hundreds of search engines, it is not practical or worthwhile to submit your Web site to every single one of them. Instead, make the most of your time and resources by registering with the major search engines.

Yet, registering with the major search engines is only the beginning of the promotion process. Next, you need to look at Web directories. Just as there are hundreds of search engines, there are hundreds of Web directories as well. As with search engines, you should focus your efforts on the major Web directories. Afterward, you should look to business search engines and Yellow Pages directories. These business-oriented search and directory sites are great places to tout your products, services, and your commercial Web site.

Because you also want your site to be accessible to people looking for specific types of information, the next step is to register with industry and category-specific directories. Whether your site covers home decorating or famous poets, there are specialty directories that will want your listing. Beyond the traditional and category-specific directories, you'll find White Pages and What's New? directories. As you know, a White Pages directory is a guide to people rather than businesses, and a What's New? directory is a place to announce your Web site.

Awards can make all the difference in the world when it comes to increasing traffic to your Web site. Not just any old award will do, though. The best awards are those that are long-lasting and meaningful. Still, when all is said and done, the popularity of the award site is the most important factor in determining whether the award will help increase the level of traffic at your Web site. The busier the award site, the better the chances that the site's award will increase traffic to your Web site.

One way to spread the word quickly about your Web site is through a registration service that allows you to register with multiple search engines and directories. Although registration services are useful for registering multiple URLs with directories, you get the most out of your site's listing by registering your site with individual search engines and directories.

In the final parts of the book, you saw many additional ways to increase your Web traffic, such as e-mail and freebies. Believe it or not, e-mail is a terrific way to promote your Web site. When you promote your Web site through e-mail, you can use the direct person-to-person method as well as newsgroups and mailing lists. Beyond e-mail, you can steal the thunder of traditional marketers using giveaways, contests, and sweepstakes. Because everyone loves the chance to win something for nothing, freebies can truly bring the masses to your Web site.

To wrap things up, I showed you ways to compete in the big leagues with banner advertising. The banner is the most heavily used advertising method on the Web. Although most advertisers pay thousands of dollars to display a banner ad, you can advertise through a banner exchange network without spending a dime.

Planning More for Next Weekend

Just because you've reached the end of this book doesn't mean that your promotion efforts should end. Next weekend, if you have some time, go back to the sections or topics that you may not have explored as much as you'd like.

After you take another look at the sections, use the main topics in this book to outline a long-term promotion plan. Your plan should focus on the items that you will need to periodically address, such as:

- Tracking Web site stats—weekly or monthly
- Looking for problem areas at your Web site—weekly or monthly
- Updating your listings in directories if you move the furniture around—only as necessary
- Resubmitting your site for awards—wait two or three months between submissions
- Participating in mailing lists and newsgroups—daily or weekly
- Updating your banner—every two or three months

A Final Note

Thanks again for purchasing this book. I truly hope that the discussion has helped you increase traffic to your Web site. By the way, if you see dramatic increases in your traffic, I'd love to hear about it! You can send an e-mail message to director@tvpress.com. And be sure to check out more resources on this book's Web site at www.tvpress.com/promote/.

INDEX